W9-BQM-733

SECOND EDITION

LIVES ACROSS CULTURES

CROSS-CULTURAL HUMAN DEVELOPMENT

Harry W. Gardiner
University of Wisconsin–La Crosse

Corinne Kosmitzki
Southern Methodist University

Allyn and Bacon
Boston   London   Toronto   Sydney   Tokyo   Singapore

Executive Editor: Carolyn O. Merrill
Managing Editor: Tom Pauken
Series Editorial Assistant: Lara Zeises
Senior Marketing Manager: Caroline Croley
Production Editor: Annette Pagliaro
Editorial-Production Service: Nesbitt Graphics, Inc.
Composition Buyer: Linda Cox
Manufacturing Buyer: JoAnne Sweeney
Cover Administrator: Kristina Mose-Libon
Photo Researcher: PoYee Oster (Photoquick Research)
Text Design/Electronic Composition: Denise Hoffman

Library of Congress Cataloging-in-Publication Data

Gardiner, Harry W.
    Lives across cultures : cross-cultural human development / Harry W. Gardiner,
Corinne Kosmitzki.—2nd ed.
        p.   cm.
    Includes bibliographical references and indexes.
    ISBN 0-205-32322-7 (alk. paper)
    1. Ethnopsychology—Cross-cultural studies.   2. Socialization—Cross-cultural
studies.   3. Cognition and culture—Cross-cultural studies.   4. Personality and
culture—Cross-cultural studies.   5. Developmental psychology—Cross-cultural
studies.   I. Kosmitzki, Corinne.   II. Title.

GN502.G37 2002
155.8—dc21
                                                            2001022430

Printed in the United States of America
10   9   8   7   6   5   4   3   2   1   05   04   03   02   01

CONTENTS

◇ **CHAPTER THREE**
CULTURE AND SOCIALIZATION   **49**

◇ **CHAPTER FOUR**
**CULTURAL ASPECTS OF PHYSICAL
GROWTH AND DEVELOPMENT**   **81**

◇ CHAPTER NINE
THE FAMILY IN CULTURAL CONTEXT   209

◇ CHAPTER TEN
CULTURE AND HEALTH   245

◊ CHAPTER ELEVEN
LOOKING TO THE FUTURE   275

FOREWORD

It was a great pleasure for me to write the Foreword to the first edition of *Lives Across Cultures*, and I was delighted when the authors and the publisher invited me to write the Foreword to the second edition. By definition, the revision of any book is a judicious blend of the old and the new, the expendable and retainable, and the measured decisions that go into determining what is to be included in the refreshed version. The same is true with a Foreword. What I wish to retain from the Foreword I wrote for the first edition is a summary of a little story I told. My first full-time academic appointment was at Oregon State University, in 1967. I accepted a one-year NSF-funded assistant professorship in OSU's Science Education department. Fresh from about two years in Germany where I collected data for my doctoral dissertation, the Science Education faculty knew that I wanted to build my career around cross-cultural psychology. Not long after my arrival I was asked to develop a series of seminars around issues pertaining to cognition and learning across cultures. The main participants in the program were to be visiting science educators from several countries, notably India and a few Asian countries. I mentioned to my colleagues that the centerpiece for such a program could be the developmental psychology of Jean Piaget. Piagetian psychology was just beginning to find its way to the North American continent after many years of success in Europe, and especially in Piaget's native Switzerland. I had some superficial exposure to Piaget and his work while attending the University of Minnesota. Moreover, I knew that Piaget hoped that his theory would have universal appeal and universal application. He in fact challenged developmental psychologists and educators alike to put it to a rigorous test in places that were quite different from the French-speaking area of Switzerland that he called home. Equipped with very few references that spoke to cultural considerations, I recall crawling and stumbling my way through a series of presentations, always stretching the limits of my knowledge in this complex domain. I learned much in the process, but it was hard going for a while. In retrospect, that experience early in my professional career would have been vastly simplified if I had been fortunate enough to be able to rely on such an informative book as *Lives Across Cultures* for my presentations. Indeed, the book would have been required reading for all in the seminar.

Of course, no one back then had the advantage of counting on a small and highly readable overview of the various cultural factors that affect human development. It would be some years before such books and review articles began to appear. First a trickle and eventually a small flood of such efforts, there are now several suitable books for use at the college level in this important area of research and scholarship. I believe that *Lives Across Cultures* will continue to hold its own as an excellent source of information regarding child development in other cultures and societies. A distinct advantage of this book is that Harry Gardiner has been dealing with the business of trying to understand other cultures for about 35 years. He has seen trends come and go, and he's been able to keep his pulse on developments in the area. His coauthor, Corinne Kosmitzki, is equally assiduous in covering and summarizing the relevant literature. That's no small task, given the explosion of interest in how culture influences all people, regardless of age, status, gender, or ability level. Indeed, by the time this book reaches college bookstores one can be sure that scores of highly appropriate publications will have been published throughout the world. The age of Information Explosion does not recognize cultural boundaries. Fortunately, Gardiner and Kosmitzki accomplished much by integrating the central publications that appeared since their first edition was published.

Chapter Two, Theories and Methodology, is especially important to understand. A new chapter for this edition, it gives overviews of not only Piaget but also several other well-known methodologists and theoreticians whose careers have been devoted to understanding the interface between culture, ecology, and the developing person. Refreshing new chapters and updated sections of chapters from the previous book carry the reader through the entire life span. The book is relatively small compared with often massive texts in the area of developmental psychology. However, it is densely and authoritatively cultural, never losing sight of the fact that all human behavior occurs in specific, and often quite different, cultural contexts. Quite capable of standing on its own in certain courses, it would also be an excellent "companion" to a more elaborate and comprehensive "mainstream" developmental psychology text.

Like the first edition, this is an engaging book. It reflects the caring and gentle characteristics of Harry Gardiner, and, by virtue of association, Corinne Kosmitzki as well. The students who are fortunate enough to read it will be treated to a tidy and thoughtful overview of a complex area. Instructors who choose this book for their classes will find it delightfully easy to use, and wonderfully suitable as an entry into a fascinating field of inquiry. The authors are to be congratulated and thanked for this revision of a popular book. Like the first edition, it will be highly regarded. Most assuredly, it will make it much easier and significantly less threatening for those who may be asked to conduct seminars on Piagetian developmental psychology and other theoretical perspectives! Where were Gardiner and Kosmitzski nearly 35 years ago when I needed their skillful writing and excellent scholarship in a very bad way?

Walter J. Lonner
Center for Cross-Cultural Research
Western Washington University
Bellingham, Washington

Walter J. Lonner has been involved in cross-cultural psychological research during his entire academic career. He is the founding editor, and currently senior editor, of the bimonthly *Journal of Cross-Cultural Psychology*. A past president and honorary fellow of the International Association for Cross-Cultural Psychology, Lonner is the author or editor of about 15 books having to do with psychology and culture. He is director of the Center for Cross-Cultural Research, and is just inches away from reaching the status of Professor Emeritus. When this happens he will be joining ranks with Harry Gardiner who recently reached that golden plateau.

⬡ PREFACE

In this second edition of *Lives Across Cultures,* our goal is to continue our journey of exploration into the exciting and increasingly influential world of cross-cultural human development begun in the groundbreaking first edition. As before, basic principles are linked to practical everyday events to help readers cultivate a global and multicultural perspective on behavior and gain an improved understanding of, and appreciation for, development as it takes place in diverse cultural settings throughout the world.

The authors are teachers and cross-cultural researchers with extensive experience in small college and large university settings in this country and abroad. As in the previous edition, we focus on connections between these personal experiences and the more formal theories and research that make up this discipline and present it all in a manner that is easy to understand, engaging, and informative to readers.

◇ ORGANIZATION OF THE BOOK

Our presentation of cross-cultural material continues to differ from other books in a number of significant ways. Most notable, perhaps, is our effort to integrate and synthesize viewpoints and perspectives from a variety of disciplines including psychology, anthropology, sociology, and the health sciences.

We look at development from a **cross-cultural perspective**, designed to provide opportunities to expand awareness and sensitivity to global similarities and differences in behavior, while helping to reduce any ethnocentric thinking on the part of readers, whether conscious or unconscious. By allowing readers to experience variations in behavior not normally found in their own societies, this perspective contributes to an understanding of human adaptation. Perhaps most important, this approach encourages readers to look more closely at the interconnections among culture, development, and behavior in their own lives as well as in others.

A major focus is on understanding development within a wide range of cultural contexts using Bronfenbrenner's **ecological systems approach** and Super and Harkness's concept of the **developmental niche**—both of which recognize the bidirectional or reciprocal influence of individuals and their environments.

We also take a **chronological-within-topics approach.** As the table of contents indicates, selected topics, for which a substantial literature of cross-cultural research exists, are discussed chronologically. This approach demonstrates how behavioral processes evolve and change as individuals in a variety of cultures pass from infancy and childhood through adolescence and into adulthood and old age.

In the introductory chapter, we define cross-cultural human development, discuss its connections to other social sciences, provide a historical context for the increasing interest in cross-cultural research and its findings, and present and illustrate the major themes of the book.

Chapter 2, "Theories and Methodology," is new to this edition. Each of the major theories discussed throughout the book is first presented here, followed by a presentation of the methodologies used in conducting cross-cultural studies in human development.

The focus in Chapter 3, "Culture and Socialization," is on ecological systems, the developmental niche, and cultural variations in such important socialized behaviors as sleep, feeding, and crying during infancy; aggression and formal versus informal learning during childhood; adolescent rites of passage; and adult interpersonal relationships.

"Cultural Aspects of Physical Growth and Development" are examined in Chapter 4, with attention given to the role of nutrition and its effects on physical growth and motor development during infancy and early childhood; cross-cultural studies of physical change in adolescence; and cultural reactions to physical changes associated with the transition to adulthood, including menopause and senescence.

In Chapter 5, "Culture, Language, and Cognition," attention is given to the link among these three topics along with language socialization, development of analytical thinking and problem-solving, and communication in the years of later adulthood as well as variations in cognitive and language development across cultures.

Chapter 6, "Culture, Self, and Personality," looks at the development of self and personality, beginning with temperament in infancy and progressing to the emergence of the self-concept in childhood, identity in adolescence, and personality changes during adulthood and aging.

"Culture and Issues of Sex and Gender" are examined in Chapter 7, including a discussion of some universal gender differences and cultural influences on the socialization of women and men. Attention is given to gender relationships in childhood, sexual activity and cultural taboos during adolescence, division of labor in early and middle adulthood, and changes in gender roles and status in old age.

Chapter 8, "Culture and Social Behavior," opens with a focus on ecological contexts and early child–caretaker relationships; moves to influences of family and peer culture during the years of childhood and adolescence, work and leisure activities in middle adulthood; and concludes with a discussion of social support and well-being in the years of later adulthood.

Chapter 9, "The Family in Cultural Context," looks at the birth process and variations in the family life cycle across cultures, including differences in parental belief systems and cultural views of mate selection, parenthood, and grandparenthood.

Issues related to "Culture and Health" are examined in Chapter 10. Topics include difficulties in medical diagnosis across cultures, cultural differences in children's health, adolescent eating disorders and depression, mental health issues during early and middle adulthood, and cultural views on caring for the elderly, many of them victims of dementia and Alzheimer's disease.

Finally, in Chapter 11, "Looking to the Future," the major themes are briefly reviewed and suggestions are made for applying more theoretically and culturally useful approaches to the study of human development. The chapter concludes with some thoughts and suggestions related to directions the study of cross-cultural human development might take in the first two decades of the twenty-first century.

◇ NEW FEATURES

The structure of this second edition is similar to that of the first edition. However, a number of significant changes are reflected in this revision. For example, all chapters have been revised with the addition of new topics and updated with the latest in research findings and references. Each chapter contains additional photographs and boxed material. Some examples include "Parenting Among African Pygmies" (Chapter 3), "Cultural Views and Treatment of the Elderly" (Chapter 9), and "Culture-Bound Syndromes" (Chapter 10). Sections on "Things to Do and Think About" have been dropped from the close of each chapter and incorporated into the *Instructor's Manual*. Each chapter contains new, readable, and easily available suggestions for Further Reading. The introduction (Chapter 1) has been shortened and a new section linking cross-cultural human development to the other social sciences has been added. Presentations of theories have been moved from several chapters, reorganized, and now appear along with fresh material on research methods in a new Chapter 2 titled "Theories and Methodology." Coverage of major models, such as the ecological systems approach and developmental niche, have been significantly expanded. Chapter 5 on culture and cognition has been expanded to include material on language development—a topic not covered in the first edition. Chapter 10, "Culture and Health," has been reorganized and includes a new section on culture-specific illnesses. The final chapter has been revised and updated to reflect some of the latest research efforts in the field and to speculate about new directions that might be taken in cross-cultural human development studies in the first decades of the twenty-first century. Hundreds of new references, most from 1999 and 2000, have been added throughout the book.

◇ SPECIAL FEATURES

Most of the special features appearing in the first edition have been retained, although some have been revised, in this second edition. This includes a number of interesting and readable pedagogical aids to assist readers in learning, remembering, and making practical use of the material covered.

Opening Vignettes. Most chapters open with vignettes of two individuals from different geographical areas of the world who illustrate one or more of the behaviors described in the chapter. Since one of our major goals is to familiarize the reader with as many cultures as possible, we decided to open each chapter with stories of different individuals living in more than fifteen different cultures around the globe. The development of these individuals is integrated into each chapter in which they appear.

Recurring Themes. Throughout each chapter, the principal themes (e.g., ecological and contextual approaches, developmental niche, and developmental and cross-cultural perspectives) are regularly interwoven into the narrative to provide a comprehensive and cohesive understanding of development.

Key Ideas. Efforts have been taken to make concepts easy to understand by placing them in bold type the first time they appear, immediately defining them, and providing numerous examples to illustrate their cultural relevance. For a quick review or preview, each chapter ends with a concise summary of important points.

Cultural Diversity. Unlike some books that claim to focus on culture but only sprinkle a few selected boxes or features in several chapters, this book contains scores of examples of cross-cultural research and findings in every chapter.

Further Readings. Each chapter closes with an annotated listing of recommendations for further reading. The books and articles suggested have been selected for their ability to expand on topics covered in each chapter as well as for their interesting and often amusing writing style.

◇ NOTE TO INSTRUCTORS

Lives Across Cultures can be used as a core text in a course focusing on cultural similarities and differences in human development, whether it is in psychology, anthropology, or sociology. It can also be effectively used as a supplement to basic courses such as General Psychology, Child and Adolescent Development, Lifespan Development, Cross-Cultural Psychology, Social Psychology, Cultural Anthropology, Sociology of the Family, and similar courses in which the instructor might want to provide a cultural focus not represented in standard textbooks. In its first edition, it has been successfully used in international business classes as well.

◇ NOTE TO READERS

You, the reader, will indeed live in the world of tomorrow, where understanding and interacting with people of diverse cultural backgrounds will be a prerequisite for success in the family, school, workplace, and society. It is for you that this book has been written. We hope it will develop an appreciation for and sensitivity to the cultural similarities and differences that characterize those of us who live on this planet Earth today, including your parents and grandparents, and those who will call it home in future generations, including your children and grandchildren. We hope you will find this book enjoyable and informative reading.

◇ SUPPLEMENTS

The *Instructor's Manual,* containing suggestions for teaching, ideas for student projects, guide to films and videos, and test items, is available. Allyn & Bacon's World Wide Web site is: http://www.ablongman.com.

◇ A FINAL COMMENT

We spent more than two exciting and busy years working on the first edition of this book and another year and a half on this second edition. While we have added a number of new topics, there are certainly many more we might have included but the "fun" had to stop some time. It has now passed from our hands to yours. We began the original project because we felt there was a need for a book like this. Wide acceptance of the first edition has (happily) proved us right and now you are able to read about some of the new developments in this second edition. We are proud to have been able to make a contribution to better understanding of development across cultures. Only you, the readers, can tell us if we have succeeded or how we might do better in the future—as many of you did following the appearance of the first edition. Let us know your thoughts by writing or e-mailing us at the addresses listed below. We'd really enjoy hearing from you.

◇ ACKNOWLEDGMENTS

It is impossible to complete a book like this without the generous assistance of a great many people. To those who reviewed this second edition and offered suggestions and revisions for its improvement, we owe a genuine debt of gratitude: Thomas M. Batsis, Loyola Marymount University; Nancy Jago Finley, Seattle Central Community College; Ziarat Hossain, Fort Lewis College; Michael E. Sloane, University of Alabama at Birmingham.

We are also grateful to the editorial, production, and marketing staff at Allyn & Bacon who contributed their time and talent to making this second edition possible.

Finally, we thank our families for their support during the many lonely hours we had to spend in libraries or staring at our computer screens late into the night or early into the morning. Special thanks to Ormsin Gardiner and to our children, Alisa, Alan, Alexina, and Aldric, whose bicultural lives provided many of the examples for this book; and to Gloria Solomon for her support and her many intellectually stimulating discussions about issues represented in this work.

Harry W. Gardiner
Professor Emeritus
Psychology Department
University of Wisconsin–La Crosse
La Crosse, WI 54601
gardiner@vax2.winona.edu

Corinne Kosmitzki
Southern Methodist University
Dallas, TX 75275-0382
ckosmitz@mail.smu.edu

ABOUT THE AUTHORS

Harry Gardiner.   I am Professor Emeritus at the University of Wisconsin–La Crosse, where I designed and taught courses in cross-cultural human development for more than 25 years. It was the inability to find a textbook for this course that led to the writing of this volume. I also offered courses in child development, cross-cultural psychology, the hurried child, and humor in education for teachers. My interest in culture has also led me to continue to teach a course entitled "Orientation to Study Abroad" for students planning extended study and research at foreign universities. I also help orient international students to the university campus and help with their adjustment to life in the American culture. My undergraduate degree is from American International College, in Springfield, Massachusetts. Perhaps that's what started me on my "international" quest so many years ago. My M.A. is from the University of Hawaii, where the real seeds of my interest in cross-cultural psychology were first planted. I completed my Ph.D. at Manchester University in England,

where my personal journey into culture was forever changed when I met a young lady from Thailand, Ormsin Sornmoonpin, who was studying to be an electrical engineer. I followed her to Asia, where we were married in Buddhist and Christian wedding ceremonies. I taught in the graduate program at Chulalongkorn University in Bangkok for two years before we moved to the United States. I live in an Asian American family, consisting of our two sons (Alan and Aldric) and two daughters (Alisa and Alexina), in which I am a minority—"the one with the blond hair and the blue eyes!" I was a charter member of the International Association for Cross-Cultural Psychology and currently serve as president of the Society for Cross-Cultural Research. In addition, I serve as consulting editor for the *Journal of Cross Cultural Psychology* and assistant editor for teaching for the *Cross-Cultural Psychology Bulletin*. In addition to publishing articles in a wide variety of journals and participating in national and international meetings, I have coauthored a chapter with my wife on "Women in Thailand," revised a chapter on "Child and Adolescent Development" for a book on cross-cultural topics in psychology, and prepared a chapter on cross-cultural development for a handbook on culture and psychology. I have engaged in training, teaching, and research in Europe, Asia, and the United States for more years than I will admit. As my children frequently remind me, I have been celebrating my thirty-ninth birthday annually for as long as they can remember. In my "spare time" I enjoy writing for *Cobblestone,* a history magazine for young children, and have contributed interviews with Supreme Court Justice Sandra Day O'Connor and Muppet creator Jim Henson, among others. Another great joy is watching the development of our first grandchild, Macinnes Charoen Lamont, born on March 6, 2000.

Corinne Kosmitzki.   I am originally from Germany, where I completed my first graduate degree in clinical psychology. All of my family still live in Germany, and I would like to visit them more often. I have traveled in almost every Western European country and now want to explore countries in Eastern Europe, which were not accessible before the end of the Cold War. I received my Ph.D. in psychology from the University of California at Berkeley. Berkeley and its surroundings are unique in their cultural and ethnic diversity and provided many challenges as  well as novel experiences. Living and working in this environment and meeting people with a wide range of backgrounds and beliefs taught me what cross-cultural psychology really means. After two years of teaching and research in Virginia, I taught at Drew University in New Jersey, where I also directed the interdisciplinary Behavioral Science Program. For the last several years, I have been at Southern Methodist University, where I am Director of Evening Studies and Adjunct Assistant Professor in Psychology. I have been teaching very successful graduate courses addressing the objectives and utility of cultural training programs. With multiculturalism being a trendy issue, students are eager to learn more about the educational, psychological, political, and social efforts required of those who are trying to make multiculturalism work.

CHAPTER ONE

INTRODUCTION

Many books begin by introducing their readers to the history of the field. This is certainly essential (though sometimes boring) but will come later in this book (you can always skip it if you don't find it very interesting). As one of the authors (Gardiner), I would like to begin this book as I begin most of my classes by relating a few of my humorous cross-cultural experiences.

In About the Authors, I mentioned that my wife, Ormsin, is from Thailand and we have raised our four children in an Asian American family, where I am the minority—the one with the blond hair and blue eyes. I don't like to admit it, but I'm also the shortest, making me a double minority! As you might imagine, raising children in a cross-cultural and bilingual home has resulted in many interesting developmental experiences, some of which may help you to understand the processes involved in cross-cultural human development.

One experience concerns our eldest daughter, Alisa, and the way in which she became bilingual. Our cross-cultural family setting provided a unique opportunity for this to occur. We had been advised that the best approach to helping her become bilingual was to let her hear and speak both languages without emphasizing that they *were* two languages. So, when she was an infant and young child, her mother spent much of the day speaking to her in Thai, while I spoke with her in English. Then, one evening, when she was about three years old, one of my Chinese students came to babysit. Alisa opened the door, saw an Asian face, and began speaking to the student in Thai. The young lady patiently listened to her and then said, "I'm Chinese and I understand English, but I bet you were speaking to me in Thai, weren't you?" I watched as she thought about this and then turned to me and said,

"I speak two languages, don't I? Daddy, I speak two languages!" I told her that indeed she did and asked, "What did you think was happening?" Her reply, based on the experience of her unique developmental niche in a bilingual home, was, "I thought it was all one big language and Mommy understood some words and you understood others and I understood them all!"

Throughout the chapters that follow, we make reference to how important it is to understand another culture and realize that not everyone everywhere has the same understanding of topics and events. Sometimes, when traveling, studying, or working in another culture, our experiences are frustrating, scary, or humorous. I had an opportunity to live in England for three years while completing my doctoral studies at the University of Manchester. During that time, there was one food craving I found nearly impossible to fulfill—*popcorn!* My roommate and I searched everywhere for it. The only place anything resembling it was available was at the cinema. The only problem: it was sticky, caramel-covered goop, not the white, fluffy kernels sprinkled with salt and hot butter with which we were familiar. Eventually, using the skills of Sherlock Holmes and Doctor Watson, we discovered small (tiny, actually) thirty-kernel bags of popping corn at the airport and bought the entire stock! A few days later, we visited a British family that had befriended these two "Yanks from across the pond" and took some with us. When we asked the husband if we could make some popcorn, he replied (much to our surprise), "No, that's impossible." When we asked why, he said, "Popcorn grows on bushes. You pick it and put caramel on it." We told

Harry Gardiner and his British friends making popcorn 30 years later. (Photo courtesy of the authors.)

him he might be confusing this with cotton, which grows on bushes but is not eaten. Nevertheless, he supplied us with a pot, and we put in some oil and threw in some kernels. When it began to make noise, we tried to explain that this was the corn popping. When it was done, we showed him. He took one look and disappeared out the back door! A few minutes later, he returned with his neighbors, looked at us, and said, "Do it again!" When I retire, I think I'll open a popcorn stand on a street corner in London and surprise and amaze the public with the wonders of popcorn! Now, if I could only get it to grow on bushes! The moral of this story: we all grow up in cultures where we understand what happens around us because the experiences are a familiar part of our developmental niche. These experiences are not always easily understood by those living in different ecological settings.

Nearly two decades ago the anthropologist T. Schwartz, writing about the acquisition of culture, declared that "anthropologists had ignored children in culture while developmental psychologists had ignored culture in children" (1981, p. 4). Just two years later, John Berry, a Canadian psychologist and pioneering researcher in cross-cultural psychology, noted that the discipline was "so culture-bound and culture-blind . . . [that] . . . it should not be employed as it is" (1983, p. 449). Shortly thereafter, Gustav Jahoda, a well-known European psychologist and early contributor to the developing discipline, was able to express a more optimistic view and point out that cross-cultural studies of human development had been steadily increasing (1986). Yet, at the same time, he also criticized the field for being "too parochial in its orientation" (p. 418).

These were once serious criticisms of the newly emerging field of cross-cultural psychology. Fortunately, in recent years, great strides have been made in our approaches to, and understanding of, cross-cultural human development. Throughout this book, we hope to show the progress, excitement, and promise of this increasingly important area of study.

In this first chapter we set the stage for the rest of the book by introducing some historical perspectives and expanding on some of the major concepts, themes, and issues briefly presented in the Preface. Let us begin by exploring the origins of cross-cultural human development.

◇ WHAT IS CROSS-CULTURAL HUMAN DEVELOPMENT?

The field of cross-cultural psychology is remarkably diverse, and those who contribute to it bring with them a variety of viewpoints, including different definitions of the field itself. In volume 1 of the revised *Handbook of Cross-Cultural Psychology*, Berry, Poortinga, and Pandey (1997) define **cross-cultural psychology** as *"the systematic study of relationships between the cultural context of* *human development and the behaviors that become established in the repertoire of individuals growing up in a particular culture"* (p. x). This definition clearly states that this is a scientific endeavor that shares with more familiar disciplines the use of theories, scientific methodologies, statistical procedures, and data analysis.

The term human development has also been defined in a variety of ways. For the purpose of this book, we view **human development** as *changes in physical, psychological, and social behavior as experienced by individuals across the lifespan from conception to death.* Although this definition encompasses a wide range of experiences, the intention of this book is not to provide exhaustive and comprehensive coverage of all aspects of human development (aren't you glad to hear that!). Instead, our goal is more limited, focusing on a number of selected topics that provide insight and understanding into how individuals develop and live their lives in different cultural settings. In doing this, we provide examples from literally scores of societies throughout the world. Considering the important dimensions just discussed, and not finding the term **cross-cultural human development** defined elsewhere, we have chosen to view it as *cultural similarities and differences in developmental processes and their outcomes as expressed by behavior in individuals and groups* (Gardiner, 2000).

Since we just mentioned the term **culture,** it should be pointed out that most researchers agree that this is one of the most difficult terms in the social sciences to define. Almost everyone who studies culture has a different way of looking at it. According to Berry, Poortinga, Segall, and Dasen (1992), E. B. Tylor was the first anthropologist to use the term in his two-volume work titled *Primitive Culture* (1871). He defined *culture* as *"that complex whole which includes knowledge, belief, art, morals, laws, customs and any other capabilities and habits acquired by man as a member of society"* (p. 42). More than forty years ago, two other anthropologists, Kroeber and Kluckhohn (1952), compiled a list of 164 definitions of the term. (We have no intention of listing all these definitions here, so if you are disappointed and would like to know what they are, we recommend you look them up yourself.)

When we use the term *culture,* we will be referring to a number of characteristics, including what Herskovits (1948) called *"the man-made part of the environment"* (Segall et al., 1990, p. 5) as well as *"the collective programming of the mind which distinguishes the members of one group from another"* (Hofstede, 1980, p. 21).

As the field of cross-cultural psychology has evolved, concerns in the area of development have undergone a number of significant shifts. Parke, Ornstein, Rieser, and Zahn-Waxler (1994) have succinctly summarized and discussed the changes in developmental focus over the past hundred years by looking at three periods. One hundred years ago, five major areas were of interest: emotional development, the biological basis of behavior, cognitive development, conscious and unconscious processes, and the role of self in development. During the 1950s and 1960s, the focus shifted to learning theory, the rise of experimental child psychology, interest in operant analysis of children's behavior, the emergence of investigations of infant sensory and perceptual development, and the objective measurement of cognitive understanding among preverbal infants. Today, there is a revitalized interest in emotional development and cognitive abilities of children, the biological bases of behavior, and social relationships. According to the authors, the "most unanticipated theme is the continuing discovery of the precocity of infants and young children—not only cognitively but also socially and emotionally" (p. 8). We shall see this point illustrated numerous times throughout this book.

◇ CROSS-CULTURAL HUMAN DEVELOPMENT AND THE OTHER SOCIAL SCIENCES

In commenting on the central role that culture plays in our efforts to better understand behavior, Segall, Lonner, and Berry (1998) posed an interesting and critical question: "Can it still be necessary, as we approach the millennium (as measured on the Western, Christian calendar), to advocate that all social scientists, psychologists especially, take culture seriously into account when attempting to understand human behavior?" (p. 1101). Unfortunately, while the situation has dramatically improved and only continues to get better, the answer remains (a qualified) yes!

When discussing cross-cultural psychology and its sub-discipline of cross-cultural human development, it is obvious they share a long historical connection with general psychology. Although, as the well-known psychologist–anthropologist Otto Klineberg has pointed out, "There is no specific date that can be identified with the onset of interest in cross-cultural comparisons" (1980, p. 34). Jahoda and Krewer have suggested it may be as early as the seventeeth century since the "dominant perspective of enlightenment philosophy was highly compatible with cross-cultural psychology's model of man" (1997, p. 11).

Since the 1960s, "research has focused on phenomena of fundamental importance in general psychology, with particular emphasis on abnormal psychology, cognitive psychology . . . . Topics in social psychology have been studied cross-culturally more than any other domain, followed by developmental psychology" (Segall, Lonner, & Berry, 1998, p. 1105).

In terms of the other social sciences, the closest links are to anthropolgy and sociology with shared interests in specific approaches, methodological procedures, and research interests, including the socialization process and family influences on development. At the same time, this relationship has not always been a smooth one. Some of the difficulties, especially those centering on comparative studies of infant development, were pointed out by Super (1981), when he stated that, for several decades, psychology and anthropology "seem to have withdrawn from the interface . . . to tend to their own theories. Very few studies . . . achieve, or even attempt, an integration of infant care and development, on the one hand, with functional and value characteristics of the larger culture, on the other" (pp. 246–247). At the same time, he noted that "Success in this direction requires both sound ethnographic knowledge of the culture as well as a quantitative baseline of information . . . " (p. 247). As you will discover in reading this book, this is precisely the path that much of present-day cross-cultural human development research has taken (Gardiner, 2000).

In a lively and entertaining book titled *Psychology and Anthropology: A Psychological Perspective*, Gustav Jahoda, a psychologist with a true appreciation and understanding of both psychology and anthropology, noted that "Anthropologists have always been concerned with psychology, even if unwittingly . . . . However, this interest has, in many respects, remained narrowly culture-bound, largely ignoring the wider perspectives provided by anthropology" (1982, back cover).

In bringing this section to a close, it is our sincere hope that cross-cultural psychologists, in particular those interested in human development, will be able to forge a bond with other social scientists, notably anthropologists, and work together as partners in laying a firm foundation for an empirically based understanding of human behavior that places a greater focus on developmental processes within cultural contexts. A welcome step in this direction has been made with a recent volume that focuses on emerging concepts and methods for measuring environment (or context) across the lifespan (Friedman & Wachs, 1999). Efforts such as these greatly enrich our understanding of development and the vital role that culture plays in it.

◇ SOME IMPORTANT THEMES

This book differs in significant ways from most other volumes that focus on cross-cultural aspects of human behavior, most notably in its efforts to integrate a variety of important themes. Let us look at these in some detail and discover how they will weave through subsequent chapters.

A Cross-Cultural Perspective

Over the past two decades, and especially in the last five years, social scientists have become increasingly aware of the contributions that cross-cultural research findings can make to our understanding of human development. A review of recently published developmental books, compared with those of just a few years ago, reveals that references to cross-cultural topics and findings have grown tremendously (Best & Ruther, 1994; Gardiner, 1996).

Any attempt to include all or even most of these findings in a book of this length would be difficult, if not impossible. Therefore, we have decided to be selective and discuss representative areas of interest using a chronological-within-topics approach. For readers desiring a more comprehensive view of cross-cultural human development, or for those wishing to explore particular topics in greater depth, we refer you to the "Further Readings" section at the close of each chapter as well as the references listed at the end of this book. If you are eager to get started, you might consider looking at such classics as *Two Worlds of Childhood: U.S. and U.S.S.R.* (1970) by Urie Bronfenbrenner and a series of volumes on *Six Cultures* by Whiting (1963), Whiting and Whiting (1975), and Whiting and Edwards (1988). There is the recently revised three-volume *Handbook of Cross-Cultural Psychology* (1997), edited by John Berry and others, which contains several chapters relevant to the study of cross-cultural development as well as the role of cross-cultural theory and methodology. Finally, the recently released *Handbook of Culture and Psychology* presents the state of the art of major areas and issues in cross-cultural psychology, including development (Matsumoto, 2001).

Goals for the Field

As to the nature and purpose of the cross-cultural method, Berry, Poortinga, Segall, and Dasen (1992), in a comprehensive overview of cross-cultural psychology, set forth three goals for the field. The first goal involves *testing or extending the generalizability of existing theories and findings*. In earlier writings, Berry and Dasen (1974) referred to this as the "transport and test goal" in which hypotheses and findings from one culture are transported to another so that their validity can be tested in other cultural settings. For example, are parental speech patterns in English-speaking families similar or dissimilar to those in Spanish-speaking families? Are the stages of cognitive development proposed by Jean Piaget specific to certain types of cultures, or are they universal?

The second goal focuses on *exploring other cultures in order to discover variations in behavior that may not be part of one's own cultural experience*. In other words, if findings cannot be generalized, what are the reasons for this, and are these behaviors unique to these other cultures? A good example is a study by Jablensky and colleagues (1992) that successfully demonstrates that a number of symptoms characteristic of schizophrenia (a serious psychological disorder) exist in ten very different cultures but that there is no single factor to explain differences in the formation or outcome of the disorder. At the same time, other psychological conditions appear to be "culture-bound" and occur only among certain groups of people. One example is *pibloktoq*, found only among specific groups of Eskimos, in which individuals, with little or no warning, perform irrational acts (e.g., ripping off clothes, shouting obscenities, throwing objects, and running wildly into snowdrifts, from which they are often rescued by others) lasting a few minutes or as long as an hour (Wallace, 1961).

The third goal, which follows from the first two, is aimed at *integrating findings in such a way as to generate a more universal psychology applicable to a wider range of cultural settings and societies*. Examples of this include efforts by many cross-cultural researchers to refine and expand the usefulness of several theories, including the various ecological approaches cited in this book.

At this point, you might be wondering, "How can a cross-cultural perspective contribute to our understanding of human development?" In answer to this question, Gardiner (1994) has pointed to a number of important benefits. First, looking at behavior from this perspective compels researchers to reflect seriously on the ways in which their cultural beliefs and values affect the development of their theories and research designs. Increased awareness of cross-cultural findings provides an opportunity to extend or restrict the implications of research conducted in a single cultural group, most notably the United States and similar Western societies. Nothing helps to reduce **ethnocentrism,** or *the belief that one's culture is superior to others,* as quickly as looking at behavior as it occurs in another culture.

Second, the number of independent and dependent variables to be investigated can be greatly increased in a cross-cultural design. Examples of studies in which this has been done include investigations of gender differences (Gibbons, Stiles, & Shkodriani, 1991; Morinaga, Frieze, & Ferligoj, 1993), aggression (Scott, 1992), and the effects of parent–child relationships in diverse cultures (Roopnarine & Carter, 1992b). We generally think of an **independent variable (IV)** as *the condition introduced into or systematically manipulated in an experiment by the researcher* and a **dependent variable (DV)** as *the subject's response or the behavior being measured in an experiment.* Without getting too complicated, it should be noted that in the context of cross-cultural research, these are really quasi-IVs and DVs, representing both a strength (more "real worldly") as well as a weakness (some loss of control and/or increased ambiguity). For an excellent discussion of culture as an antecedent, dependent, independent, or intervening variable, the reader is referred to several chapters in volume 1 of the *Handbook of Cross-Cultural Psychology* (Berry, Poortinga, & Pandey, 1997).

Third, cross-cultural studies help us to separate **emics,** or *culture-specific concepts,* from **etics,** or *universal or culture-general concepts.* According to Berry (1969), the emic approach focuses on a single culture, using criteria that are thought to be relative to it, and studies behavior from within the system itself. An example is an anthropological field study in which a researcher lives with a group of people and tries to understand the culture through their eyes and experiences, avoiding the ethnocentrism of his own cultural background. The etic approach, on the other hand, looks at several cultures, comparing and contrasting them using criteria thought to be absolute or universal, and studies behavior from outside the system. An example, which (happily) we don't see as often as we once did in cross-cultural psychology, involves an investigator conducting what has been called "safari research." An example is a professor (not very familiar with the field) who goes on vacation to several countries, taking along a favorite questionnaire concerning _____ (you fill in the blank). She visits several universities, collects data from available students (who may or may not understand many of the colloquial English language terms), returns home, and publishes the findings as "universal" attitudes of those living in cultures X, Y, and Z.

Separating emics from etics is better accomplished by testing theories or principles developed in one cultural context in another. The work of Freud, Piaget, and Kohlberg are examples. In some cases, findings lend support to the universality of behaviors in vastly different cultural settings (e.g., stages in language development and the sequence and timing of such behaviors as smiling, walking, stranger and separation anxiety, and pubertal development). On the other hand, results have sometimes suggested a need for modification of certain culture-bound concepts (e.g., intelligence, medical diagnosis, and, sometimes, gender behavior).

By focusing throughout this book on cross-cultural material, we hope to provide readers with opportunities to expand their awareness and sensitivity to global similarities and differences in human development and to reduce any ethnocentric thinking. The cross-cultural perspective complements and extends the work of earlier researchers who successfully presented the more traditional, but often culture-specific, approach to understanding lifespan development by offering a broader world view. By allowing readers to experience variations in behavior not normally found in their own societies (e.g., accelerated formal operational thought among some Asian populations, decreased susceptibility to visual illusions among certain African groups, and highly developed mathematical skills among Dutch children), this perspective contributes to our understanding of human adaptation. Perhaps most important, it encourages a closer look at the interconnections among culture, development, and behavior—a major theme in contemporary developmental psychology (Parke, Ornstein, Rieser, & Zahn-Waxler, 1994).

While we certainly are not the first to stress the importance of looking at cross-cultural data, we believe we give it greater emphasis because, as Segall so aptly stated more than a decade and a half ago, "It is to . . . theories of ecological, cultural, and socialization forces that we must turn for the most promising insights into why different peoples develop different . . . skills or develop the same skills at different rates" (1979, p. 129).

Can you find the Western anthropologist in this picture? (David
R. Austen/Stock Boston)

*Noted anthropologist Dr. Dawn Chatty, discussing local problems
with Harsous tribal member in Sahmah, Oman, in the Arabian
Peninsula.* (James L. Stanfield/National Geographic Society)

The mention of socialization practices, and the variety of ways in which we are influenced by ecological factors, leads us to another of our major themes.

An Ecological Systems Approach

The importance of viewing behavior within its social setting was first recognized not by psychologists but by sociologists, who stressed the importance of the individual's subjective view. Among the early proponents of this view were C. H. Cooley (1902), W. I. Thomas and F. Znaniecki (1927), and G. H. Mead (1934). When psychologists became interested in the topic, they tended to ignore the social context in favor of the cognitive processes (Koffka, 1935; Kohler, 1938; Piaget, 1954). Such analysis was extended beyond the individual to the study of the environment with the introduction of the concepts of "psychological field" and "life space" by Kurt Lewin (1935). Explicit recognition of the need to study an individual's subjective view of social reality came with the pioneering work of MacLeod (1947).

One of the most important contributions to these evolving ideas, and the one on which much of our presentation is based, is the ecological systems approach presented in the work of Urie Bronfenbrenner (1975, 1977, 1979, 1986a, 1989, 1993), This approach, which divides a child's environment into five nested and interrelated systems or contexts and allows us to clearly see and understand the connection between culture and development, is presented and discussed in detail in Chapter 2.

The Developmental Niche

If Bronfenbrenner is correct in his view that culture and environment make significant contributions to one's development (and we, as well as others— e.g., Brislin, 1993—believe that they do), one might ask, "How does this happen and how can we better understand the processes taking place?"

One possible answer is provided by an exciting and promising idea emerging from the cross-cultural developmental work of Super and Harkness (1986, 1994, 1999). Based on an extensive series of studies among Kipsigis-speaking communities in western Kenya, Super and Harkness, a psychologist–anthropologist research team, have presented a way of bringing together and integrating findings from the two disciplines (Gardiner, 1994). Called the **developmental niche,** it provides *a framework for understanding how various aspects of a culture guide the developmental process by focusing on the child as the unit of analysis within her sociocultural setting or context.* In this regard, it is compatible, in certain respects, with the ideas put forth by Bronfenbrenner and, in combination with it, comprises another major theme of this book. It, too, is presented and discussed in detail in Chapter 2.

A Developmental Orientation

It is well recognized that most of our behavior does not take place at isolated periods in our lives but rather evolves and continually develops throughout the lifespan. Although the body of cross-cultural research literature is significant, it frequently resembles "a confused mosaic of contradictory findings" (Gardiner, 1994). This may explain, in part, why none of the books that currently examine cross-cultural topics systematically presents a developmental perspective as we do here. Not all of the behaviors covered in this book will always fit neatly into this orientation or be easily explained by some of the other themes or approaches. However, many do and, where appropriate, we attempt to demonstrate how these behaviors evolve and change as individuals develop across the lifespan and across cultures.

To illustrate the importance of looking at behavior from a developmental orientation, let us briefly consider the development of memory and attention, or the increased ability to organize information. As children we begin to think, attend, and store away memories. As adolescents and adults we develop the ability to make inferences, understand reversibility, and make use of abstract thought. Information that may have been remembered in childhood as a list can now be recalled in adulthood as a total pattern.

The implications of studying this topic from a lifespan developmental perspective have been nicely summarized by Forman and Sigel (1979), who write that "it is not clear whether the decline in memory and attention that occurs in old age is a function of reduced general cognitive competence or an inadequate problem-solving attitude due to social isolation, fear of failure, and other factors. But it is clear that the error rate of the elderly decreases when tests are not timed and social acceptance is reinforced. We can venture the tentative conclusion that poor performance in the 4-year-old is probably due to lack of a general cognitive competence, while poor performance in the 70-year-old is likely the result of an attitude toward solving problems (provided, of course, that the person shows no pathological signs of neurological deterioration)" (p. 89).

This brings us to another theme that will occur throughout this book—the chronological-within-topics approach.

A Chronological-Within-Topics Approach

In a book of this size, it is impossible to do all things—that is, provide a comprehensive view of development in all the necessary detail and also focus on all the important cross-cultural findings. Recognizing this, we have decided to look at selected topics for which a large literature of cross-cultural research exists and discuss these topics chronologically—from the early beginnings of development through the last years of life.

Using this *chronological-within-topics approach*, we hope to effectively demonstrate how behavioral processes evolve and change as individuals pass from infancy and childhood through adolescence and into adulthood. As a result, it should become clear that our behavior is dynamic and involves change, that it is at times orderly and predictable and at other times chaotic and unreliable, that both individual and cultural similarities and differences exist, and that specific cultural influences become important at different times and in different cultures. This approach includes basic concepts, principles, and theories that describe physical, psychological, cognitive, social, and personality changes that occur across the lifespan in a variety of cultural contexts.

◇ PRACTICAL APPLICATIONS

We believe that a book emphasizing process, content, and skill (at understanding and interpreting cross-cultural behavior), but avoiding unnecessary jargon and seeking a broad perspective, provides a number of benefits to readers. Therefore, part of our focus is on the *everyday experiences* encountered by individuals of differing ethnic backgrounds within their own society as well as between individuals of different cultural settings. We further believe that if readers come to understand the processes involved, they can begin to understand how to apply these principles for a deeper insight into the events and issues that touch their lives beyond the boundaries of their home, neighborhood, classroom, community, and nation. Throughout this book, material is continually related to issues and concerns that are important and relevant to all of us. Efforts are made to encourage critical thinking by using exercises that allow one to examine, question, explore, analyze, and evaluate a variety of everyday situations within diverse cultural contexts.

There is an adage that states "Tell me and I'll forget . . . show me and I'll probably remember . . . involve me and I'll never forget." Simply stated, this is another of our important themes—practical application. Many of today's texts are written for social science majors planning graduate study and frequently emphasize laboratory research—a shortcoming already recognized in our earlier comments on the need for an ecological point of view. While we feel a developmental text should be grounded in carefully researched theory, we also believe that if it is to be maximally useful, it should avoid jargon and focus on readers' "real-life" experiences and ultimately assist them to relate more effectively with other individuals and in diverse environments. This is especially true today as our world, even at the local neighborhood level, becomes increasingly multicultural.

These goals are accomplished in several ways. First, in writing this book we have selected topics that have meaning for one's daily living: socialization (Chapter 3), physical development (Chapter 4), cognition and language (Chapter 5), personality (Chapter 6), issues of sex and gender (Chapter 7), social behavior (Chapter 8), the family (Chapter 9), and health issues (Chapter 10).

We don't expect you to accept what we say without question. We believe in the adage mentioned earlier, and we try to practice what we preach by providing opportunities for you to question, explore, and analyze the topics presented. In doing this, we hope you will arrive at a better understanding of your own behavior, modifying it where necessary and desirable and developing and improving your cross-cultural interactions with others, now and in the future.

◇ DESIGN OF THE BOOK AND SUGGESTIONS FOR ITS USE

Since the transition from theory to practice cannot be accomplished simply by reading about applications, we make an effort to present the material in each chapter in such a way that it explicitly encourages your active involvement.

First, as you notice, each chapter opens with vignettes focusing on issues and behaviors to be addressed by the material presented in a particular chapter. This gives you an idea of what is covered in each chapter, and it allows you to formulate your own ideas as you read the material. For example, "What are the benefits of studying development cross-culturally?" "What are the effects of culture on socialization?" "How does children's play differ from one culture to another?" "In what ways are adolescents similar or different throughout the world?" "How do cultures treat their elders or older adults?"

Second, within the narrative, each new idea is defined, highlighted, and illustrated with cultural examples (many from the authors' own experiences) that, hopefully, you find both relevant and entertaining.

Third, real-life examples are described of cultural variations in childbirth, effects of culture on learning styles, growing old in different cultures, cultural variations in adolescent identity, and other important topics.

Finally, each chapter closes with a section on "Further Readings." Included are materials from a variety of sources that we think are interesting, informative, entertaining, and easy for you to locate.

◇ SOME CROSS-CULTURAL TEASERS

As we bring this chapter to a close, we'd like to leave you with a few "cross-cultural teasers," or questions for which we provide partial answers. Each of these receives further attention in future chapters.

- Is there a unifying concept that might explain reasons for cultural variations in development? The answer lies in the area of adaptation, or the various ways in which peoples of diverse cultures have adapted or adjusted to the events occurring in their lives.

- Are there any universals in human development? If so, what are they? One example of a universal is gender-role assignment. All societies appear to socialize boys and girls into gender roles (e.g., allowing more aggressive behavior among boys and encouraging more caring behavior among girls).

- How can we explain cross-cultural differences in such behaviors as dependence and independence? Part of the answer depends on where infants sleep after they are born. The United States is known as a culture that greatly emphasizes individual achievement; parents generally place babies in their own cribs in their own rooms. Japan, a collectivist culture, encourages dependence; children are allowed to sleep with parents, often for many years. How does this affect development?

- Adolescents in many of the world's cultures confront the problem of identity, or trying to answer the question "Who am I?" For some, living in Nigeria, it is a relatively easy task. For others, growing up bicultural in New York City, it is more difficult.

- Eating disorders such as anorexia and bulimia are common in many Western societies. Do young people throughout the world all strive to attain the ideal body image? You may be surprised by some of the answers found in Japan, Australia, and other countries.

- How do different cultures view their elderly? Is grandparenting the same everywhere? We'll give you some answers to these questions from China, Japan, and the United States.

- How does family life differ from one culture to another? In some societies, the roles of mothers and fathers may surprise you. Did you know children in some cultures become more closely attached to their fathers than to their mothers? Why would this be the case? We'll find out later in this book.

- An increasingly common disorder among older adults today is Alzheimer's disease. Did you know that people suffering from this disease are treated differently by their caregivers if the patient and caregiver are Hispanic, Native American, or Anglo?

- What's important in selecting a marriage partner—money, good looks, security, health? You'll be surprised at some of the views expressed by men and women from cultures around the world. How many chickens or cows do you think you're worth on the marriage market?

Have we gotten your attention? Do you want to know the answers to these and other interesting cross-cultural questions? Would you like to know some of the similarities and differences in human behavior and how people live their "lives across cultures?" Then turn the page and read on.

◇ SUMMARY

This chapter introduced the topic of cross-cultural human development and provided definitions of important terms and concepts. Discussion centered on several themes to be used in organizing developmental topics in a variety of cultural settings. These themes included a cross-cultural perspective, an ecological systems approach, the developmental niche, a developmental orientation, a chronological-within-topics approach, and an emphasis on practical applications. Suggestions were given for using the material in ways to help readers develop a greater understanding of, and sensitivity to, those of a different cultural background than their own and develop and improve any cross-cultural interactions they might experience.

◇ FURTHER READINGS

Dave Barry. (1992). *Dave Barry Does Japan.* New York: Fawcett Columbine.
  An irreverent view of Japanese culture by one of America's premiere humorists. Witty and sometimes insightful. Contains discussion of such topics as "Failing to Learn Japanese in Only Five Minutes (Very much good morning, Sir)," "Lost in Tokyo (Looking for plastic squid)," and "Humor in Japan (Take my tofu! Please!)."

Hubert J. M. Hermans and Harry J. G. Kempen. (1999). Moving Cultures: The Perilous Problems of Cultural Dichotomies in a Globalizing Society." *American Psychologist,* 54, 1111–1120.
  The authors discuss the impact of globalization and compare Western cultural tradition with the rest of the world. They comment on the potential influence of cultural connections and some of the complexities associated with cultural change.

Walter J. Lonner and Roy Malpass. (1994). *Psychology and Culture.* Boston: Allyn & Bacon.
  A collection of forty-three short (five- to six-page), easy-to-read chapters on various aspects of cross-cultural psychology. A sampling of chapter titles includes "Continuing Encounters with Hong Kong," "A Multicultural View of Stereotyping," "Mate Preferences in 37 Cultures," and "Community Health in Ethiopia."

CHAPTER TWO

THEORIES AND METHODOLOGY

Justin Tyme, a graduate student in psychology, has returned from a month in Thailand, where he attempted to collect data for his doctoral dissertation. This was his first visit to a foreign country and it was a memorable, but unsatisfying, experience. Why? Because Justin was not well prepared and made several serious (and avoidable) mistakes. First, he traveled to a culture he knew little about (because it sounded exotic). People spoke a language (Thai) he did not understand and which he found difficult to read, write, or speak in the brief time he was there because of its complexity (forty-four vowels, thirty-two consonants, and five tones, and written in script). He found the weather too hot and humid, the food too spicy, and life in the village where he was doing his research "too slow." He had difficulty finding people to help translate his English-language, Western-designed, marital-role preference scale so that it would have comparable meaning in Thai. He was upset because the few subjects he was able to get often didn't arrive exactly on time (Asians, in general, are not as time conscious as Westerners, especially Americans) and when they did, they usually told him "Mai pen rai" (Don't worry). Finally, representative samples were difficult to obtain in a rural area that would match his samples back in Chicago, Illinois.

Dr. Kitty Litter, an anthropologist from Cornell University, recently spent six months doing an ethnographic field study among a group of Indians in the highlands of Peru. Not only was she fluent in Spanish, the most widely spoken language in the country, but she also had a working knowledge of two native languages—Quechua and Aymara—from two previous trips to the country. She had read extensively about the customs of the tribal groups in this area and was very fond of the food. She especially

enjoyed the tropical climate along the coast and the cooler temperatures in the mountains. She had spent considerable time designing the questions she was going to ask and had even prepared a Quechuan-language version of a psychological instrument she hoped to validate while there.

Theories and methodology—sound exciting, don't they? Perhaps not, but these two topics are central to understanding what happens both in cross-cultural human development and in the chapters that follow. In this regard, we have two goals for this discussion of theories. First, to provide a foundation for those who do not have a background in human development (or could benefit from a review of major concepts) to appreciate their contributions to our efforts to better understand behavior. Second, to provide a framework for identifying complex human behavior and experience as it occurs within different cultural contexts and to explore possible reasons for the similarities and differences that are found in societies around the world. If research (cross-cultural or otherwise) is not carefully designed, conducted, analyzed, and understood, any findings that result are of little value. So, we'll try to make the discussion of these topics as simple, relevant, and interesting as possible.

◇ THEORIES OF DEVELOPMENT

Why do we study human development? There are many reasons, but basically we do it to *understand, explain, predict,* and (in some instances) *control behavior.* To achieve these goals successfully, we need to be familiar and comfortable with theories and their important concepts. As a graduate student in England, I (Gardiner), while trying to select a topic for my doctoral dissertation, was asked by my major adviser if there was an area of psychology with which I felt particularly uncomfortable. Without hesitation, I immediately replied, "Theories." (I shouldn't say this but, as an undergraduate student, I frequently skipped over theories because I found them boring, confusing, and too abstract.) When it was suggested that I devote the next three years to the development of my own theory in order to decrease this discomfort (a form of theoretical desensitization, I guess), I thought this was a "daft idea." Of course, I didn't tell this to my adviser! However, develop my own theory I did (Gardiner, 1966). Not only did I really enjoy doing my original doctoral research (on "newspapers as personalities") but, when it was over, I felt much less threatened by theoretical concepts and gained a greater appreciation for the central role theories play in the social sciences. We hope you feel the same way when you reach the conclusion of this chapter (don't skip over them; they *are* important!).

What Is a Theory?

Simply stated, a **theory** is *a set of hypotheses or assumptions about behavior.* A theory consists of guesses or speculations that allow us to answer such questions as "Why does a particular behavior occur?" For example, why are Chinese children generally calmer, less active, and easier to soothe when distressed than Western children? Why are ethnic customs and values of greater importance to some minority youths than others? What factors most influence the ways in which contemporary cultures treat their elderly?

When we study human development, we can't look at all aspects of an individual's, group's, or culture's behavior. Theories help us organize our ideas and limit what we look at, and serve as a guide (or blueprint) in the collection of data. Sometimes, it seems as if there are as many theories as there are people. In a sense, there are, because each of us has our own informal, unscientific, unverified, and highly idiosyncratic theories. Built up over years of personal observation and experience, these informal theories help us to understand the behavior of those with whom we come into contact. For example, when we meet someone for the first time, our informal theory of personality helps us decide whether we like or dislike this person, if we want to interact with this person again, and so on. However, we must go beyond these informal theories to truly understand and explain the complexity of human development. We need theories that are more formalized and rooted in scientific principles if we are to be able to compare and contrast behavior within and across cultures and draw conclusions about similarities and differences. In the pages that follow, we discuss six theories. While you may (or may not) be familiar with some or all of them, it might be helpful, in terms of our discussion, to think of the theories of Piaget, Kohlberg, and Erikson as traditional or mainstream psychological theories that focus on the individual, with primary attention to internal cognitive processes (e.g., knowing and thinking, moral reasoning, and psychosocial development). On the other hand, the theories of Bronfenbrenner, Super and Harkness, and Vygotsky can be viewed as interactionist theories because they focus on the interactions between the individual and his or her environment in specific psychological domains (e.g., ecology and the interrelationship of the developing individual and his or her changing physical and social environment, links between children's behavior and the developmental niche in which they are raised, and cultural influences on development of language, thinking, and guided participation).

Bronfenbrenner's Ecological Systems Approach

In Chapter 1, we briefly noted that one of the most important contributions to the study of human behavior within cultural contexts, and one on which much of our presentation is based, is the ecological systems approach and model presented in the pioneering work of Urie Bronfenbrenner (1975, 1977, 1979, 1986a, 1989, 1993).

Bronfenbrenner's original model has been "undergoing successively more complex reformulations to attain its present, still-evolving form" (Bronfenbrenner, 1999, p. 4). The most recent versions of this approach (Bronfenbrenner, 1999; Bronfenbrenner & Evans, 2000; Bronfenbrenner & Morris, 1998), now called the *bioecological model,* incorporate earlier concepts, along with new ideas, into a series of propositions that focus more directly on the role of environment and the concept of time in the processes of human development. Those readers who want to know more about this evolving model are directed to the references mentioned earlier.

In this book, we focus primary attention on Bronfenbrenner's earlier approach and model, which we believe continues to offer advantages for viewing and understanding the connection between culture and human development. Where appropriate, we refer to some of his more recent ideas and formulations.

The **ecology of human development,** as defined by Bronfenbrenner, involves *"the scientific study of the progressive, mutual accommodation between an active, growing human being and the changing properties of the immediate settings in which the developing person lives, as this process is affected by relations between these settings, and by the larger contexts in which the settings are embedded"* (1979, p. 21). In short, an individual is seen not as a passive and static entity on which the environment exerts great influence (much like a *tabula rasa,* or blank slate), but as a dynamic and evolving being that interacts with, and thereby restructures, the many environments with which it comes into contact. These interactions between individual and environment are viewed as two-directional, or characterized by reciprocity. For example, while a child's development is being influenced and molded by parents, family, school, and peers, she is, at the same time, influencing and molding the behavior of others.

Building on Bronfenbrenner's definition, the concept of environment is expanded to include increasingly complex interconnections among settings and is a considerably broader and more differentiated view than those previously presented in psychology in general and in developmental psychology in particular.

Bronfenbrenner has suggested that an individual's perception of the environment is often more important than "objective reality" and that this

perception influences one's expectations and activities. A recognition and acceptance of the critical role played by the cultural or environmental context
seem particularly suited to the study of human behavior and development.

In his critique of traditional research carried out on children, Bronfenbrenner has stated, "Much of contemporary developmental psychology is
the science of the strange behaviors of children in strange situations with
strange adults for the briefest possible periods of time" (1977, p. 513). In
other words, while striving to achieve experimental rigor and control, we
have often lost sight of the scientific and practical relevance of our findings
by ignoring how the same phenomena might occur outside such artificial
environments. One of the other major goals of this book is to stress the relevance and practicality of such findings.

The ecological systems approach allows us to go beyond the setting being
immediately experienced—whether in a laboratory, a classroom, or a backyard—and permits the incorporation of indirect, but nevertheless very real, effects from other settings as well as from the culture as a whole. Bronfenbrenner originally divided the ecological environment into four **nested
systems:** microsystem, mesosystem, exosystem, and macrosystem (see Figure
2.1 on page 22). This conceptualization of the ecological environment has
been retained in his more recent bioecological model and is given considerable
attention in our discussions throughout this book. A fifth system, the *chronosys-
tem*, with its focus on time and sociohistorical conditions, has been mentioned
only occasionally in the literature, and seldom by Bronfenbrenner himself.
However, as we soon see, the concept and importance of time has become a
more significant part of the newly reformulated bioecological model.

The Microsystem.   In Figure 2.1, the first level, the microsystem, represents the interactions between the child and her immediate environment
(e.g., family or preschool) and resulting behaviors such as dependence or
independence and cooperation or competition. This is the most basic level,
the one at which individuals engage in face-to-face interactions, and their
behaviors frequently reflect social position. Bronfenbrenner (1993) expanded his original definition of the **microsystem** to include *"a pattern of
activities, roles, and interpersonal relations experienced by the developing person in a
given face-to-face setting with particular physical, social, and symbolic features that
invite, permit, or inhibit engagement in sustained, progressively more complex interaction with, and activity in the immediate environment"* (p. 15). Examples include
home, church, school, hospital, or day-care center. Other factors to consider
include the effects of the physical environment on behavior, including background noise, crowding, and the number and types of toys available to a
child (Wachs, 1987, 1999; Evans, Lepore, Shejwal, & Palsane, 1998; Evans &
Saegert, 2000).

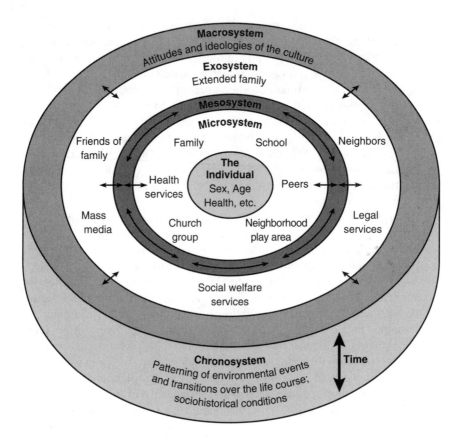

FIGURE 2.1 Bronfenbrenner's Ecological Model of Human Development

Source: From *The Ecology of Human Development* by U. Bronfenbrenner, 1979. Cambridge, MA: Harvard University Press. In *The Child: Development in a Social Context* (p. 648) by C. B. Kopp and J. B. Kaslow, 1982. Reading, MA: Addison-Wesley. Reprinted by permission of Addison-Wesley Longman, Inc.

The Mesosystem. The second level, the mesosystem, recognizes that the individual microsystems in which a child functions are not independent but are closely interrelated and influence each other. According to Bronfenbrenner's newly revised definition, the **mesosystem** *"comprises the linkages and processes taking place between two or more settings containing the developing person"* (1993, p. 22). This is a system made up of two or more microsystems (e.g., home and day care, day care and school, or family and peer group). It is the mesosystem that links or ties together information, knowledge, and attitudes from one setting that help to shape behavior or development in another

BOX 2.1

CHILDHOOD IN SOMALIA: AN EXAMPLE OF THE DEVELOPMENTAL NICHE

In an extremely informative and detailed study, Norwegian psychologist Ragnhild Dybdahl explored childhood within the Somali sociocultural context, using the concept of the developmental niche. As part of her study, she conducted open-ended interviews in Mogadishu, Somalia, with twenty mothers, ranging in age from twenty-two to forty (mean age equals thirty), and twenty-three children (mean age equals ten). Most of the women lived with their husbands, and about one-fourth of them had been raised as nomads. The average number of family members was 7.5 and included various combinations of parents, children, grandparents, parents' siblings, and distant relatives staying as long-term guests. Topics of interest included reasons for having children, normative child care, and the roles played by parents and children in the Somali culture.

According to Dybdahl, the first component of the Somali developmental niche is characterized by the culture's economic and health problems; the nomadic way of life, with its emphasis on the extended family and clan; and the child's social and physical settings organized around school and Quaranic school, play, work, and household chores, especially care of younger siblings. The second component is characterized by socialization practices in which the infant, initially spending all its time with its mother, is gradually "distanced from the mother's back, breast and bed to be cared for by someone else." Although formal schooling plays a role, informal education is far more important and is the means by which children are taught such activities as household chores. Quaranic school serves as a mode of traditional education. The third component, based on interview comments from mothers, is characterized by mothers' focus on "physical health, obedience, resourcefulness, helpfulness and hard work," with expectations differing according to a child's age.

Dybdahl reported on the emergence of several themes associated with Somali childhood: (1) a clear responsibility for family and relatives; (2) the importance of such values as pride, hard work, loyalty, and obedience; (3) a constant struggle for survival and good physical health; and (4) the emotional importance attached to children as sources of short- and long-term security.

As a result of her interviews and observations, Dybdahl argues that Somali society represents a mix of "traditionalism and modernism, and collectivism and individualism." According to Dybdahl, her interviews with chil-

(continued)

BOX 2.1 CONTINUED

dren provided a look at "the niche from the inside." She points out that "in spite of the difficult living conditions at the time . . . [just before "Operation Restore Hope" in 1989] . . . with war breaking out and relatively poor health conditions, beliefs in the future and in the possibility to change and improve one's life were recurring themes." She suggests that this may be due to a combination of factors, including the nomadic tradition of "moving on to another place," stoicism, and the belief that family and relatives will provide help if needed.

Dybdahl concludes that children must be studied in the "context and culture in which they live, and of which they are a part." Since developmental outcomes in Western societies have often come to be the norm for many of the world's children, "to avoid ethnocentrism and develop a global psychology, it is necessary to do cross-cultural research." Dybdahl is further convinced that, in order to make what she calls the "person-setting interaction" the focus of investigation, anthropologists and psychologists need to combine their efforts and that the developmental niche "might be a fruitful concept for this purpose." For a more recent report on this research, see Dybdahl and Hundeide, 1998.

Source: Adapted from "The Child in Context: Exploring Childhood in Somalia," paper presented by Ragnhild Dybdahl at the Twenty-Sixth International Congress of Psychology, Montreal, August 1996. Reprinted by permission.

several circles, while the developing child stands at the center, insulated from the cultural macrosystem by family, neighborhood, school, and other settings and institutions in the microsystem, mesosystem, and exosystem" (p. 281). Super and Harkness go on to suggest, "The anthropological insistence on the immediacy of culture not only better reflects the phenomenological experience of daily life but also brings the cultural environment into reach for the empirical scientist" (p. 282). We agree with this, as you will see in the many examples referred to throughout this book.

The integrating nature of culture is seen in the work of many of the noted anthropologists cited earlier, including Margaret Mead, Ruth Benedict, and John and Beatrice Whiting, and in much of the research being done today. As Super and Harkness (1999) point out, these efforts suggest "a relatively new and promising agenda for interdisciplinary psychologists as they seek a more sophisticated understanding of behavior and development: Look for structures that integrate experience, and look for their immediacy in everyday life" (p. 283). For more on the ways in which culture serves as an integrating force in development and why the authors' expanded cultural perspective on the environment is becoming increasingly important, see Super and Harkness (1999). Some of their suggested research methods and approaches are discussed later in this chapter.

Piaget's Theory of Cognitive Development

Jean Piaget (1896–1980), the Swiss-born psychologist, first developed an interest in cognitive development while working with Alfred Binet on intelligence testing in Paris. Piaget became curious about children's thinking and problem solving and why children of the same age made similar mistakes when trying to solve problems. For years, he carefully recorded the cognitive changes he observed in his three children in their home in Geneva. From these and other observations, he theorized that individuals learn by actively constructing their own cognitive world. To Piaget, development is a dynamic process that results from an individual's ability to adapt thinking to meet the demands of an ever-changing environment and, as a result, to formulate new ideas.

According to Piaget's view, normal cognitive growth passes through four distinct periods: infancy, early childhood, middle childhood, and adolescence (see Table 2.1). Although Piaget provided age ranges for these various developmental periods, he recognized that the exact age at which a particular individual enters a specified period could be significantly affected by that person's physical, cognitive, or cultural experience—what Bronfenbrenner has referred to as the *ecological setting.*

Piaget's term for the first period of cognitive development (birth to two years) is the **sensorimotor period,** characterized by *coordination of sensory abilities and motor skills* when a child understands the world largely through immediate action and sensation. The highlight of this period is the achievement of **object permanence,** *the awareness that objects remain the same or continue to exist even when they cannot be seen* (e.g., a doll not visible because it is covered by a blanket still exists). Piaget's term for the second period of

TABLE 2.1   Piaget's Periods of Cognitive Development

PERIOD	APPROXIMATE AGE	DESCRIPTION
Infancy	Birth to 2 years	Sensorimotor
Early childhood	2 to 6 years	Preoperational
Middle childhood	6 to 12 years	Concrete operations
Adolescence	12 years and older	Formal operations

cognitive development (two to six years) is the **preoperational period,** characterized by *development of language, use of symbols, and egocentric thinking* (e.g., failure to distinguish between one's own point of view and that of another individual). From ages six to approximately twelve, children are in the third period of **concrete operations,** characterized by *performance of tasks involving conservation, in which thinking is governed by fundamental rules of logic.* **Conservation** refers to the *ability to recognize that specific properties of an object, such as amount or number, do not change in spite of rearrangement or superficial modification in their appearance* (e.g., when a child thinks one sandwich cut into four slices is more than another sandwich cut into two slices). Piaget's term for the fourth and final period (age twelve through adulthood) is the **formal operational period,** characterized by the *ability to deal with hypothetical problems and abstract thinking* (e.g., mentally thinking about two different routes that could be taken to the same destination).

It was Piaget's belief that cognitive development occurs as a result of children's attempts to adapt to their environments and to make sense of the many experiences taking place around them. The ability to do this requires the systematic development of progressively more complex mechanisms or structures. At the center of this activity lies the scheme. A **scheme** is *an organized pattern of thought or action applied to persons, objects, or events in an effort to make sense of them.* In short, it is a mental picture of the world and the things in it. For example, infants develop a wide variety of schemes during the first few months, including schemes for mother, breast, bottle, and father's voice. Over the years, increased interactions with the environment result in these schemes becoming more sophisticated and better coordinated, so that by the time an individual reaches formal operations, they are capable of thinking about behaviors and imagining their consequences.

According to Piaget, cognitive development and the ability to adapt to the environment depends on the processes of assimilation and accommodation. **Assimilation** is *the process by which new information and ideas are incorporated or fitted into existing knowledge or schemes.* **Accommodation** is *the process of adjusting or modifying existing schemes to account for new ideas and information.* Anyone who has traveled abroad and attempted to make sense of new surroundings or tried to explain new objects or words to a foreign visitor has engaged in assimilation and accommodation—sometimes with success, sometimes with failure, and sometimes with humor! For example, what happens when Hakon from Norway tries to explain the making of a snowman to Yang, who lives in Malaysia and has never seen or touched snow? In this situation, Yang must make use of accommodation and adjust an existing scheme with which Yang is familiar (perhaps shaved ice) or create a new scheme (snow) to explain this new idea of a snowman. Another illustration of how assimilation and accommodation result in the development of cognitive operations can be seen in Piaget's classic conservation of liquid task.

Children in the preoperational period usually think that a tall, thin glass contains more liquid than a short, fat glass, because the level is higher, although they correctly say the amounts were initially the same. The problem is beyond younger children's capabilities, and they are unable to accommodate their thinking enough to understand that while the shape of the glass may be different, the amount of liquid remains the same. They simply assimilate what they see into their existing scheme, believe it to fit well, and feel no disequilibrium or imbalance in their perception of the situation. With the change in cognitive development that comes with increasing age and experience, children in the concrete operational period are able to consider the differences in the width, as well as the height, of the glasses and are no longer satisfied with their original answer, correctly recognizing that the liquid remains the same. At this point, they have achieved the concept of conservation. It is through active and open interaction with one's environment or surroundings that individuals learn to balance these twin processes of assimilation and accommodation. In terms of Bronfenbrenner's ecological systems approach, these cognitive processes can be said to begin in the family (microsystem); gradually extend to increasingly complex situations that arise in the neighborhood, at day care, or at school (mesosystem); and eventually, as the individual moves into adolescence and adulthood, operate in the workplace (exosystem) and the culture at large (macrosystem).

While there is no doubt that Piaget's theory has had a significant impact on the study and understanding of cognitive development in mainstream Western psychology, his ideas have been challenged on several points. First, some have criticized his emphasis on individual activity occurring apart from social interaction. Such a focus reflects a more individualistic cultural perspective, such as that found in North America and Western Europe, and thereby fails to consider similarities or differences in cognitive development in traditional collectivistic cultures (e.g., China, Japan, and the islands of the South Pacific). Second, some have suggested that Piaget may have overestimated the contribution of motor activity and underestimated the ages at which children are capable of learning and performing a variety of behaviors by themselves. Third, Piaget's claim that once a person moves to a new period of cognitive development, the competencies mastered at that level will be exhibited in other phases of that individual's thinking, does not appear to be fully supported by cross-cultural research findings. While advances may be apparent in some domains of a person's thinking processes, this may not be true in other domains (Wellman & Gelman, 1992).

In the beginning, when Piaget was developing his theory and conducting his early studies, he paid little attention to cultural factors and the effects differences might have on cognitive development. However, as Thomas (1991) has noted, "In later years, Piaget did admit some influence of variations in environments, but still considered genetically controlled maturation to be the primary force behind mental development" (p. 65). Whatever one's position is regarding Piaget's theory, it continues to have considerable influence on contemporary research and practice and, as we see in Chapter 5, has been applied to the study of cognitive development in many cultures throughout the world—with varying success.

Vygotsky's Sociocultural Theory of Development

As we have just noted, Piaget's position was that cognitive development is largely an individual accomplishment, directed and shaped, in part, by the environment (and, in part, by genetics). However, he said little about the importance of the social context in learning. This view was challenged by the Soviet psychologist Lev Semyonovich Vygotsky.

Lev Vygotsky (1896–1934) was one of several children raised in an orthodox Jewish family in Russia. As a young man, he frequently wrote critically about Soviet government policies, with which he did not agree. As a result, his scientific writings were banned, although his highly acclaimed and influential book *Thought and Language* was finally published in 1934, the year he died of tuberculosis. (For an interesting, and generally ignored, view of how Vygotsky's Marxist orientation influenced the development of his psychological principles and also affected his life, see Gielen and Jeshmaridian, 1999.)

Vygotsky suggested that development is the result of interaction between cultural and historical factors. He believed that the key feature of development lies in matching a child's demands with the requirements of her culture. Vygotsky suggested that there were three major components in this process: the role played by culture, the use of language, and the child's zone of proximal development (Kozulin, 1990). Briefly, the **zone of proximal** (nearby) **development (ZPD)** refers to the distance between a child's actual developmental level and the higher-level potential (Vygotsky, 1978). It is *the difference between what children can achieve independently and what their potential level of development might be if given help or guidance.* This concept of the ZPD emphasizes Vygotsky's view that social influences contribute significantly to children's development of cognitive abilities and that mentoring or guidance strengthens their growth (Steward, 1994).

To tie this into several of the major themes already discussed, let us consider the case of twelve-year-old Dabir, a young Saudi adolescent. We might say that the process of learning, which takes place through mentoring in a number of Dabir's diverse ecological settings (home, mosque, school), defines his developmental niche at a particular time in his life. As Vygotsky would view it, Dabir does not have his own ZPD but participates in a shared ZPD with those around him. This is also true with regard to Deratu (introduced in the opening vignette in Chapter 5), who does not go to school but learns the important cultural and practical lessons necessary for living in rural Ethiopia from the daily guidance provided by her mother.

From Vygotsky's point of view, culture is a social construction, and cognition is rooted in language and cultural experience. He describes three sequential stages in the evolution of speech that are considered essential in language and cognitive development. The first is **social speech,** which is *designed primarily to gain the attention of others or to express simple ideas* and lasts until approximately three years of age. **Egocentric speech** is the second; this occurs between the ages of three and seven, *serves to control the child's own behavior, and is usually verbalized.* The third is **inner speech;** this develops around the age of seven, and *consists of self-talk, during which children rehearse what they are going to say before actually saying it* (Vygotsky, 1978). According to Vygotsky, early use of language helps children reflect on their behavior and thus plays a major role in cognitive development.

While much of Vygotsky's work has been praised for its originality and usefulness, like the pioneering ideas of Piaget, it has its critics. For example, some argue that the zone of proximal development is vague and cannot be adequately measured (Paris & Cross, 1988). Others believe that parts of Vygotsky's theory have been lost or misunderstood in translation and therefore are confusing and incomplete (Nicolopoulou, 1993). Nevertheless, the theory still represents an increasingly important contribution to cross-cultural human development, with Vygotsky's zone of proximal development appearing more frequently in educator's teaching methods (Thomas, 1999). As an example, Thomas points out that "Rather than waiting for children to display a particular form of reasoning before attempting to teach skills and knowledge that depend on that form, teachers who follow Vygotsky's lead will attempt to teach the new learnings somewhat before the time children might exhibit their readiness spontaneously" (p. 48).

Erikson's Psychosocial Theory

Erik Erikson, a German-born psychoanalyst and student of Sigmund Freud's daughter, Anna, was the first person to propose a developmental theory encompassing the entire lifespan. Beginning with Freud's stages of psychosexual development, Erikson, a student of anthropology, modified and expanded them to focus greater attention on the social context of development (psychosocial) and less attention on biological and sexual development (psychosexual). Unlike Freud, his emphasis was on the growth of normal or healthy (rather than abnormal or neurotic) personality development, and he was particularly interested in cultural similarities and differences in the socialization of children and the development of identity during adolescence.

Erikson's theory provides a useful framework for attempting to define and unravel some of the major changes in social behavior that take place at various points in the lifespan. As shown in Table 2.2, he proposed a sequence of eight stages ranging from infancy to later adulthood, each accompanied by a psychosocial crisis requiring resolution if one is to move successfully from

TABLE 2.2   Erikson's Stages of Psychosocial Development

STAGE	CRISIS	PSYCHOSOCIAL TASK
Infancy	Trust vs. mistrust	Develop first social relationship with primary caretaker(s); develop a fundamental trust in life and the world
Toddlerhood	Autonomy vs. shame and doubt	Explore the social environment outside the primary relationship; recognize self as an individual being
Early childhood	Initiative vs. guilt	Negotiate one's place within social relationships; learn about the impact of one's social behavior on others; develop a sense of power
Middle childhood	Industry vs. inferiority	Learn the importance of social norms and the personal consequences of conformity and nonconformity; develop a sense of competence
Adolescence	Identity vs. role confusion	Find social roles and social environments that correspond to one's identity and principles; form one's own identity
Young adulthood	Intimacy vs. isolation	Negotiate one's own identity within the context of intimate relationships
Middle adulthood	Generativity vs. stagnation	Make a contribution to the larger society; acquire a sense of accomplishment and a place in the world
Late adulthood	Integrity vs. despair	Become an integral and active part of one's family and community; come to terms with one's life and choices

one stage to the next. These crises or periods of increased vulnerability and heightened potential involve conflicts between newly developing competencies and a desire to maintain the status quo.

When applying Erikson's theory, as we do at different points throughout the book, there are several points to keep in mind. First, although he assigns an age range to each of his eight stages, these should be considered only as a guide, because of differences among individuals . Second, successful resolution of a crisis will depend on how a particular culture views the crisis, the sequence in which a particular stage occurs, and the solution evolving from it. Third, while many of Erikson's original ideas were based on development in Western societies, we attempt to modify some of these to show their increased applicability in other cultural and ecological settings.

Kohlberg's Theory of Moral Development

The study of moral development is closely identified with the work of Lawrence Kohlberg, who completed his first research as part of his doctoral dissertation. Responses to a series of moral dilemmas (hypothetical incidents involving a conflict between an individual's desires or needs and the rules of society) by seventy-two boys ages ten, thirteen, and sixteen years were analyzed to determine how moral reasoning developed. For each dilemma, subjects were asked to evaluate the morality of a specific act mentioned in the dilemma. On the basis of these findings, Kohlberg (1981) identified three levels of moral development with two stages in each level, representing a more sophisticated and complex orientation toward justice and normative moral principles (see Table 2.3 on page 36).

Most children nine years of age or younger are in the preconventional level, but so are many adolescent offenders and adult criminals. Most adolescents and adults are in the conventional level. The postconventional level is not generally reached before the age of twenty, and then generally only by a minority (Kohlberg, 1976).

One of the main assumptions underlying Kohlberg's theory is that these six stages are universal and are present in cultures throughout the world. However, Kohlberg concedes that the stage at which individuals complete their development and the time it takes to be completed may vary from one culture to another.

As we move through the rest of the chapters in this book, we refer back to each of these theories and show how they help to explain various aspects of human development within a wide range of cultural settings and niches. From time to time, we also indicate how these theories might be expanded

TABLE 2.3 Kohlberg's Stages of Moral Development

LEVEL	STAGE	BEHAVIOR
I. Preconventional	1. Punishment and obedience orientation	Obeys rules to avoid punishment
	2. Instrumental orientation	Obeys rules to receive rewards
II. Conventional	3. Good-child orientation	Conforms to rules to avoid disapproval by others
	4. Law and order orientation	Conforms to rules to maintain social order
III. Postconventional	5. Morality of contract, individual rights, and democratically accepted law	Accepts and follows laws for the welfare of the larger community
	6. Morality of individual principles and conscience	Believes in and follows self-chosen universal ethical principles

and modified to better understand and explain cross-cultural similarities and differences in behavior. We now look at some of the methodological issues and approaches related to the study of cross-cultural human development.

◇ METHODOLOGY IN CROSS-CULTURAL HUMAN DEVELOPMENT

As we noted in Chapter 1, there are many different definitions of culture; therefore, it should not be surprising that there are an almost infinite number of ways to approach and measure cultural differences and similarities. For example, psychologists generally tend to focus on individual behaviors, while anthropologists typically tend to look at the behavior of groups. Those doing cross-cultural research in human development frequently make an effort to look at both individual and group behaviors. This is not always easy to do because each culture and those who live within it, including parents, peers, teachers, and others, have their own ideas and beliefs about children and the ways in which they should develop (Harkness & Super, 1996).

Imagine you are a social scientist (e.g., psychologist, anthropologist, or sociologist) interested in studying the effects of childrearing practices on children's personality development. Looking at your own culture, you find the range of behaviors limited. So, it seems like a good idea to seek out other cultures, which may have different practices, such as swaddling (found among the Hopi Indians in the American midwest and many Russian and Chinese families), severe independence training (characteristic of certain African tribal groups), or strict dependence training (often noted in Japanese families). Taking this approach offers several benefits. First, you are able to increase both the range of independent variables (childrearing practices) and their effects on the dependent variable (children's personality development). Second, this approach allows (perhaps) for a clearer distinction between biological and environmental influences. For example, if developmental sequences or processes are found to be similar across a variety of diverse cultures, it might suggest that genetic or biological factors are a significant contributor. If, on the other hand, there are wide differences among the cultures, it is more likely that environmental factors play a larger role. Finally, by conducting cross-cultural research in another culture, one becomes aware of his or her own ethnocentric biases that could influence the design, conduct, and interpretation of the results.

Carrying out a cross-cultural study sounds easy, right? However, here is the heart of the problem: jumping on and off planes in far away and often exotic places can be exciting, rewarding, and great fun, but it's not all beer and curry! Think about the young graduate student, Justin Tyme, in our opening vignette and consider some other possible difficulties—getting required visas to visit certain countries is often difficult, time consuming, and expensive; you may not be allowed to conduct your research once you get there; you and the local food don't always agree; and you can become frustrated and lonely. In short, you have a great many challenges to meet and resolve. But as Dr. Kitty Litter, the anthropologist in our other vignette, demonstrates, with careful preparation and training, an individual can survive the culture experience and return with important research data. As we see in the next section, although there may be problems in doing cross-cultural research, there are also solutions.

Studying Development Cross Culturally: Some Methods, Problems, and Solutions

Our intent is not to cover all possible methods, problems, and solutions in this section—besides being impossible, much of this work has been done very well by others. Our aim is twofold: (1) to familiarize you with some of the important information in this area so that you gain an appreciation for what cross-cultural researchers have to deal with, and (2) to prepare you to understand methods and findings you encounter as you journey through the remainder of this book.

When conducting research in cross-cultural human development, researchers are interested in discovering principles that are universal to all (or most) cultures as well as principles that are unique or specific to certain cultures, such as the emic–etic distinction we made in Chapter 1. At the same time, they are concerned that the methods they employ are (1) **objective** (unbiased and not influenced by a researcher's preconceived notions), (2) **reliable** (findings are observed consistently and accepted by independent observers), (3) **valid** (behaviors and findings are what the researcher claims them to be), and (4) **replicable** (other researchers using the same methods report the same or very similar results).

While cross-cultural psychology shares with its sister social sciences a number of similar needs in designing research (e.g., selecting subjects, defining variables, and choosing appropriate measures and methods), it has to deal with unique issues. For detailed discussions of some of these issues and approaches to their resolution, see Berry, Dasen, and Saraswathi (1997); Berry, Poortinga, and Pandey (1997); Kim, Park, and Park (2000); Matsumoto (2000); and van de Vijver and Leung (2000). For more specific discussions of issues related to measurement in cross-cultural human development, see Friedman and Wachs (1999); Keller and Greenfield (2000); and Super and Harkness (2000).

Matsumoto (2000) discussed some of the critical questions and issues in this area (pp. 130–134), and because many of these also apply to the conduct of cross-cultural human development research, they are summarized here: (1) *theories and hypotheses*—can the theories under investigation be appropriately applied to all cultures in the study and do the hypotheses have the same meaning for all subjects independent of their cultural backgrounds; (2) *methods*—are the subjects representative of their culture and are they equivalent for comparative purposes, and are all measures (e.g., scales, items) reliable and valid in all cultures under investigation and do they have linguistic equivalence (determined through the method of back translation from original language to target language and back to original language until all meanings are equivalent); (3) *data and analyses*—are there any unique cultural responses operating and have they been controlled; and (4) *interpretations and conclusions*—are findings and interpretations of them free of cultural bias and value judgments based on the researcher's own cultural background. These serious and complex questions must be carefully considered and adequately answered if research across cultures is to make significant contributions to our knowledge about similarities and differences in human development.

As for the use of specific methods, there are numerous ways in which these can be categorized. One approach is to consider four possible types of cross-cultural studies: (1) investigation of theories and concepts originally developed in Western countries as they may (or may not) apply in non-Western settings (e.g., Piaget's stages of cognitive development and Kohlberg's levels of moral development); (2) replication in one culture of studies previously conducted in another culture (e.g., children's acquisition of language skills, peer pressure during adolescence, expression of emotion in toddlers); (3) collaborative research in which researchers from two or more cultures participate equally in the design and conduct of a study (e.g., assessment of personality in five cultures, a cross-national study of children's behavior with their friends, and exploration of ethnic identity in Russia, Finland, and South Africa); and (4) administration of test materials designed and standardized in one culture but used in other cultures (e.g., tests of intelligence, personality, and socialization).

Matsumoto (2000) draws attention to two other approaches used with some measure of success by psychologists doing cross-cultural research. The first is the *"bottom-up approach"* in which a psychological phenomenon, observed in one culture, is then studied "across many other cultures to examine and refine theories about it" (p. 11). An example might be the willingness of mothers to seek childrearing advice when raising their first child. The second is the *"top-down approach"* in which investigators "begin with a theory about behavior and incorporate aspects of culture in testing its limitations and broadening its domain" (p. 11). An example might be studying the implications of social cognition theory for understanding behavior in individualistic and collectivist cultures.

A popular approach among psychologists, as well as some sociologists, is **cross-cultural comparisons** in which *individuals from at least two different cultural groups are measured and compared on some aspect of behavior* (e.g., European and Asian attitudes toward the criminal justice system). As for individual methods, a technique widely used by anthropologists in their cultural studies is **ethnography.** Typically, a researcher lives for a time in a culture observing, interviewing, and sometimes testing its members, and produces *a detailed description of a society's way of life, including its attitudes, customs, and behaviors.* The early work of Margaret Mead, Ruth Benedict, and others are examples. More recently, some interesting work has been done in "the ethnography of speaking" in which sociolinguists studied variations in conversational language in different social contexts (Hymes, 1974, 1996, 1999; Nelson, 1992). Information contained in hundreds of these reports has been

*American anthropologist Margaret Mead, who
frequently used ethnographic methods, smiles at
a Balinese infant.* (Ken Heyman/Woodfin Camp
& Associates)

classified and indexed in the **Human Relations Area Files (HRAF)** and is
frequently used in **hologeistic research,** *projects in which hypotheses about
such topics as gender differences in aggression or preference for breast versus bottle
feeding can be tested on a worldwide sample of more than 340 societies.*

Matsumoto points out that "In recent years, there has been an interesting merging of research approaches across disciplines, with an increasing
number of scientists adopting comparative techniques for use in single-culture
immersion research and comparative researchers adopting qualitative ethnographic methods to bolster their traditional quantitative approach" (p. 39). We
see this as a positive sign that these social science disciplines, often at odds, may
be showing signs of understanding and learning from each other.

Keller and Greenfield (2000) look more specifically at some of the
contributions developmentalists and their research make to cross-cultural
psychology—methodologically, theoretically, and empirically. For example,

in terms of methodology, they point to the use of "contextualized procedures, such as naturalistic observation, suitable for studying behavior in its cultural context" (p. 52). Theoretically, "developmentalists point to the fact that the culturally constructed behavior of adults can be viewed as an endpoint along a developmental pathway and that adults provide cultural socialization to the next generation" (p. 52). Finally, empirically, they point out that "a developmental approach leads researchers to investigate the culture-specific shape of developmental stages" (p. 52).

In an impressive work, particularly relevant to this discussion, van de Vijver and Leung (2000) comment on the extent to which methodological tools can be used to correct for the overemphasis on fact finding and, thereby, speed up the slow theoretical progress in cross-cultural psychology. It is their contention that, in the future, there will be two different types of cross-cultural researchers: *"natives* (whose emphasis is on culture and the methodology for the study of culture) and *sojourners* (who make brief, sporadic excursions into cross-cultural research)" (p. 48 [italics added]).

They point out that as a result of clearly different interests, each will take different methodological paths. For example, "Sojourners will be mainly interested in psychological-differences studies and generalization studies . . . [while] . . . Natives will carry out research that is central to our understanding of cultural differences and the influence of culture" (p. 48). The types of studies that will result from these different orientations and the strengths and weaknesses of each are shown in Table 2.4 on page 42. (To learn more about the methodological issues related to these approaches, see van de Vijver and Leung, 2000.)

Van de Vijver and Leung conclude that when greater emphasis is placed on the development and testing of theories and appropriate methodological tools are used in carrying out research, the replicability of cross-cultural findings will improve—a point Gardiner stresses elsewhere in this book. They believe that "impediments to progress in cross-cultural research . . . all derive from what could be called partis pris (preconceived opinions, prejudices) of cross-cultural psychologists" (p. 34). We might add this would apply to any researchers—psychologists, anthropologists, sociologists, or others.

For those who want to know more about cross-cultural research methodology, from a primarily psychological viewpoint, including additional problems and solutions, we recommend the volumes by Segall, Dasen, Berry, and Poortinga (1999), and Berry, Poortinga, and Pandy (1997). Cross-cultural research methodology, as practiced by anthropologists, is discussed in a recent book by Ember and Ember (2000).

Let us now take a closer look at some of these issues and several of the research methodologies used in the cross-cultural study of human development, particularly those associated with our two major theoretical viewpoints—the ecological systems approach and the developmental niche concept.

TABLE 2.4 Types of Cross-Cultural Studies and their Strengths and Weaknesses

TYPE OF STUDY	CONTEXTUAL FACTORS	ORIENTATION	MAIN STRENGTH	MAIN WEAKNESS	EXAMPLE
Generalizability	No	Hypothesis-testing	Attention to equivalence and bias issues	Absence of contextual variables	Schwartz (1992); McCrae & Costa (1997)
Theory-driven	Yes	Hypothesis-testing	Examines relationship of cultural factors and behavior	Focus on single explanation; little attention to alternative interpretations	Berry (1976)
Psychological differences	No	Exploration	Open-mindedness to cross-cultural differences	Ambiguous interpretation of differences	Guida & Ludlow (1989)
External validation	Yes	Exploration	Focus on interpretation of cultural differences	Choice of cultural characteristics to which psychological variables can be related	Williams, Satterwhite, & Saiz (1998); Georgas, van der Vijver, & Berry (1999)

Source: Adapted from "Methodological Issues in Psychological Research on Culture" by F. J. R. van der Vijver and K. Leung, 2000, *Journal of Cross-Cultural Psychology, 31,* 33–51.

Methods for Assessing Components of the Developmental Niche

Super and Harkness (1999) recently presented, in extensive detail, their suggestions for successfully measuring and assessing the components of the developmental niche. In this section, we provide an overview of their methodology, which, as can be seen in Table 2.5, involves a combination of psychological and anthropological research techniques. Anyone with a serious interest in the developmental niche approach is advised to consult this important work that blends theory and methodology in a way seldom done in the study of cross-cultural human development. It stands as a model for

TABLE 2.5   Methods for Studying the Developmental Niche

	COMPONENT	
METHOD	*Identified*	*Measured*
Participant observation and ethnographic interviewing	Settings, customs, and caretaker psychology	—
Spot observations and diaries	Settings, customs, and caretaker psychology	Settings (and customs)
Behavior observations	Customs and caretaker psychology	Customs
Semistructured interviews and focus groups	Customs and caretaker psychology	Customs and caretaker psychology
Structured questioning	—	Caretaker psychology and customs
Passive enumeration	Caretaker psychology and customs	Caretaker psychology and customs
Formal methods: free listings, clustering, multidimensional scaling, and consensus analysis	Customs and caretaker psychology	Caretaker psychology and customs

Source: From "The Environment as Culture in Developmental Research" by C. M. Super and S. Harkness, 1999, in S. L. Friedman & T. D. Wachs (Eds.), *Measuring Environment Across the Life Span.* Washington, D.C.: American Psychological Association.

others in the field and as an example of the effort to bring closer together anthropology and psychology that we hope to see more of in the future.

Looking at Table 2.5, we find several ethnographic, observational, and formal methods (column one), the component to which a particular method contributes qualitative understanding (column two), and, finally, the component for which a method can furnish quantitative information (column three).

According to Super and Harkness, the first group of methods (participant observation and ethnographic interviewing) are "essential methods for identifying and understanding the meaningful elements and organizational structure of the developmental environment . . . [and] . . . they lay the base for knowing what in the environment is worth measuring and for generating hypotheses about how components of the niche relate to one another" (2000, p. 301). The authors point out that **participant observation** (a technique in which an investigator lives for a time with or near a group of people and observes its daily life, activities, and rituals) and **ethnographic interviews** (asking group members to describe their culture's typical behaviors, attitudes, beliefs, and values), if carefully carried out, can help identify elements within each of the three developmental niche components (see Table 3.1). For an example of their use in actual research, see Levy (1996).

Other techniques useful in identifying important aspects of all three components, but settings in particular, include spot observations and diaries. Results from **spot observations** (a series of random unannounced observations of a group, sufficient in number to allow for statistical analysis) and **diaries** (written accounts of changes in daily activities kept by participants over varying periods of time, such as a full 24-hour day) are useful for "describing the physical and social settings of daily life not only in terms of their particular qualities but also in terms of their empirical distributions . . . [and] . . . provide a basis for identifying regularities in settings and activities that may differ between groups, or that one wants to relate thematically to other elements in the niche, or to developmental trends" (Super & Harkness, 1999, p. 304).

Measuring customs (the second component of the developmental niche), according to Super and Harkness (1999), requires (1) a qualitative approach in which behavioral consistencies are identified either through **direct observation** of a cultural group or by means of **ethnographic descriptions** of its everyday attitudes, beliefs, and behaviors, and (2) a quantitative approach producing "measures of individuals' views on the nature and importance of the custom or measures of the frequency of occurrence of the identified practice, or both" (p. 308). They assert that the ideal approach to assessing and measuring the customs component "demonstrates their existence, documents their occurrence, and explains their relationship to the settings of daily life and to the psychological theories that guide them" (p. 308).

Measuring caretaker psychology or parental beliefs and values (the third component of the niche) also requires a combination of qualitative and quantitative approaches. These may include **structured questioning** (frequently based on findings obtained from the methods previously discussed) and **formal methods** originally employed in the cognitive sciences (see Borgatti, 1992 for additional information).

Truly understanding culture and the critical role it plays in human development requires an appreciation of qualitative as well as quantitative findings. In the words of Super and Harkness (1999), "Findings in one domain suggest further exploration or reexamination in another, and replication of patterns suggests salient cultural themes" (p. 312). Their unique approach to theory and methodology provides answers to many questions about culture and development while setting forth even more challenges for the future.

Studying Ecological Systems

Unlike Super and Harkness, who constructed their approach to human development and conducted much of their own research in support of it, Bronfenbrenner has primarily been the developer of ideas and hypotheses while others have carried out research to show the validity of his approach. To illustrate this, let us briefly look at some examples of representative research carried out on each of the four ecological systems.

First, Brown, Lohr, and Trujillo (1990), in an effort to show how the peer microsystem of adolescents becomes increasingly differentiated and influential in one's behavior, reported on the ways in which both positive (acceptance, friendship, status, and popularity) and negative (drinking, smoking, stealing, cheating) behaviors are associated with different adolescent life-style decisions. Second, Muuss (1996) has stated, "A mesosystem analysis examines the quality, the frequency, and the influence of such interactions as family experiences on school adjustment" (p. 325). An interesting example of this is Epstein's study (1983) of the longitudinal effects of family–school–person interactions on student outcomes, which, unexpectedly, reported that the interaction of family and school was of far greater importance and influence than the variables of race and socioeconomic status. Noted among the findings was a continuing influence of the family and school environments far beyond the early childhood years, lending support to the interaction effects among systems proposed by Bronfenbrenner. As an example, the author pointed out that students experiencing the greatest change in independence were those initially scoring low on this behavior (and whose families failed to emphasize decision making) but who attended schools that placed a strong emphasis on student participation.

Third, as you may remember from our original comments, Bronfenbrenner has asserted that decisions made in the exosystem (e.g., in parents' workplaces) can have an extremely important influence on the life of a child or adolescent (even though they are not a part of that setting). Flanagan and Eccles (1993) effectively demonstrated this point in their two-year longitudinal study of changes in parents' work status and their effects on the adjustment of children before and after their transition to junior high school. Results indicated that of four family types identified (based on patterns of change or stability in parental work status), children in deprived and declining families were less competent than their peers in stable or recovery families. Although most of the subjects experienced some difficulty in school adjustment, the transition was shown to be especially difficult for those whose parents were simultaneously dealing with changes in their work status.

Fourth, although the macrosystem, in many ways, is removed from the daily life of an individual, it does consist of extremely important societal influences (political, religious, economic, and other values) that clearly affect human development. Bronfenbrenner (1967) demonstrated the influence of macrosystem values in an early comparison of peer group and adult pressures on children in the United States and the former Soviet Union. At that time, in the Soviet Union, a cohesive core of socially accepted and politically endorsed values left little room for differences in expectations between the adults or peers in one's environment. In the United States, on the other hand, there were frequently unmistakable differences between these significant people, with the result that children and adolescents often found themselves being pulled in different directions. With the breakup of the former Soviet Union, the situation that once existed in the United States (and to a large extent, still appears to) now is much more characteristic of the former Soviet Union as well.

As we close this discussion, it seems only fair to give Bronfenbrenner the last word on the challenge of operationally defining elements of his evolving bioecological model as well as efforts to scientifically measure them. As he states, "Thus far, I have accorded more attention to the conceptual rather than to the operational aspects of this challenge. I did so for a reason; namely, most of the research designs and methods of measurement currently in use in developmental science are not well-suited for what I have referred to elsewhere as 'science in the discovery mode' (Bronfenbrenner & Morris, 1998). To be more specific, these designs and methods are more appropriate for verifying already formulated hypotheses than for the far more critical and more difficult task of developing hypotheses of sufficient explanatory power and precision to warrant being subjected to empirical test. . . . In summary, most of the scientific journey still lies ahead" (Bronfenbrenner, 1999, p. 24). For those interested in reading more about these issues, see any of the several references mentioned in this discussion.

◇ SUMMARY

This chapter focuses on theories and methodologies used in the conduct of cross-cultural research in general and developmental research in particular. We began with reasons for studying human development—to *understand, explain, predict, and* (in some instances) *control behavior.* To successfully achieve these goals, we need to use theories which, simply stated, are *sets of hypotheses or assumptions about behavior.* We discussed, in detail, six theories that will receive significant attention throughout this book—Bronfenbrenner's ecological systems approach, Super and Harkness's developmental niche framework, Piaget's theory of cognitive development, Vygotsky's sociocultural theory of development, Erikson's psychosocial theory, and Kohlberg's theory of moral development. We discussed some of the ways in which cross-cultural methods might be classified, distinguished between different types of cross-cultural researchers (natives and sojourners), and commented on specific techniques including ethnographies, cross-cultural comparisons, "bottom-up" and "bottom-down" approaches, and hologeistic studies.

◇ FURTHER READINGS

Susan Goldstein. (2000). *Cross-Cultural Explorations: Activities in Culture and Psychology.* Boston: Allyn and Bacon.

> This book contains nine chapters with ten activities each revolving around case studies, self-administered scales, mini-experiments, and a collection of content-analytic, observational, and interview data allowing "hands-on" experience. Of particular interest is a chapter on Culture and Psychological Research that explores major issues and techniques in the conduct of cross-cultural research.

Walter J. Lonner & Roy Malpass. (1994). *Psychology and Culture.* Boston: Allyn & Bacon.

> Each of the forty-three short (five- to six-page) easy-to-read chapters on various aspects of cross-cultural psychology provides personal insights into the ways in which the authors carried out their research, often with revealing comments on the mistakes they made.

Theodore Singelis. (Ed.). (1998). *Teaching About Culture, Ethnicity, & Diversity.* Thousand Oaks, CA: Sage.

A book of easy-to-use classroom exercises intended for use in teaching about culture, ethnicity, and diversity. A practical tool for those who want to learn more about these topics and have fun doing it.

CHAPTER THREE

CULTURE AND SOCIALIZATION

Kamuzu Mathebula is fourteen years old and lives in Diepkloof, a section of Soweto, an all-black township outside Johannesburg, South Africa. He lives with his mother, aged grandmother, two brothers, and a sister in a shack made of discarded plastic sheeting and wood with a corrugated iron roof. There is no electricity or running water. Diarrhea and tuberculosis are common here. His mother, a widow, works as a maid for the Martins, an Afrikaner (white South African) family, five miles away. Kamuzu has attended poorly funded segregated schools most of his life. With the end of apartheid (the white-government-enforced system of "separateness") in 1990, his future has been looking better. Rather than working long hours for meager wages in one of the local textile factories, Kamuzu hopes to attend the University of Witwatersrand in Johannesburg and become a doctor and help his people.

Hendrik and Patricia Martin, the Dutch-descended Afrikaner family that Kamuzu's mother works for, have a son named Jeremy who is also fourteen years old. He and his younger sister, Yvonne, live in a wealthy neighborhood of large, well-kept homes. Jeremy's father is president of an import–export company, started by his grandfather, and his mother teaches science at the exclusive private school he and his sister attend. His goal, like Kamuzu's, is to attend the university in Johannesburg and study medicine.

Two young South African boys—the same age, residing just a few miles apart near the tip of the African continent—supposedly live in the same society but have been raised in clearly different environments (developmental niches) by very different families, yet they share a common desire of becoming doctors.

How can we account for the similarities and differences in the development of these two young adolescents? While it is true that Kamuzu and Jeremy share a number of characteristics, in large measure, they are a reflection of two distinct cultures—different social contexts, parental belief systems, societal values, and cultural perspectives. Every one of us, like each of them, is influenced by a unique combination of factors, including the genetic material inherited from our ancestors, the family in which we are raised and the style of parenting to which we are exposed, the friends we make and the schools we attend, the historical period in which we are born, and (of pivotal importance) the culture and ecological context in which we live out our lives. As Sigel and colleagues (1992) noted, "Since it is a culture which serves to define values, beliefs, and actions of families, it is imperative and in fact a virtual necessity for the applied developmental psychologist to develop a knowledge base of cultures" (Roopnarine and Carter, 1992b, p. ix.).

Indeed, while this is essential, a knowledge of cultures is not enough. To genuinely understand and explain cultural differences in development, we first need to look at the way in which a culture defines these values, beliefs, and actions, and this requires an understanding of the crucial process of socialization.

◊ WHAT IS SOCIALIZATION?

Like many concepts in developmental psychology, socialization can be variously defined. For our purposes, we will view **socialization** as *the process by which an individual becomes a member of a particular culture and takes on its values, beliefs, and other behaviors in order to function within it.* According to Elkin and Handel (1989), it is this process that "helps to explain how a person becomes capable of participating in society . . . [as well as] . . . how society is possible at all" (p. 4). It is through the process of socialization that society teaches desirable behavior while inhibiting undesirable behavior, prepares individuals to become successfully functioning members in its principal institutional settings (family, school, community, and workplace), and guarantees that important traditions (although sometimes modified) will be passed to future members of the culture.

It is far from easy to describe or explain cultural socialization. Chamberlain and Patterson (1995) put this dilemma into focus when they state that "in a very real sense . . . socialization . . . is something that emerges from thousands of exchanges between the child and family members spread out over a period of many years. During these exchanges, the child is altering the behavior of the parent at the same time that the parent is presumably 'socializing' the child. It is this mutuality of effects that makes it very difficult to analyze cause and effect relations" (pp. 211–212).

With the steady increase in cross-cultural findings, our understanding of socialization has undergone significant change over the past several decades. According to Maccoby (1992), contemporary theories of socialization place greater stress on the interactive exchanges between parent and child as contributors to behavior. In addition, explanations have become more complex and multidimensional than those offered by earlier approaches.

Edwards (1996) has noted that socialization theories have also undergone substantial revision as theorists and researchers have recognized the cultural limitations of these theories. For far too long, theories and their proponents were ethnocentric (e.g., proposing that explanations of behavior in one society applied equally well in others). As we frequently note throughout this book, such theories relied heavily on research and assumptions based in Western societies, with the result that theories were either nongeneralizable to other cultures or failed to take into account the richness of human diversity. In a sense, theorists were victims of their own socialization and were promoting what Kagitcibasi (1996) has called "an indigenous psychology of the Western world." As evidence, Edwards (1989) cites some of her own earlier work in which Mayan children in Zinacantan, Mexico, learned toilet training and other self-care skills by means of imitation and thereby made a relatively easy transition from infancy to early childhood, compared with other cultures in which these activities are characterized by resistance and great difficulty. There would appear to be an entirely different cultural context operating in this Mayan culture than what we tend to see in North America and some cultures of Western Europe. Values important to the successful functioning of these Mayan children are being transmitted in a way that provides a foundation for the development of infants and toddlers, who closely observe and carefully imitate and respond to their elders and others, rather than expecting others to respond to them (Greenfield, Brazelton, & Childs, 1989).

A researcher who has made significant contributions to our understanding of socialization, particularly in the area of cognition, is Barbara Rogoff. Her book *Apprenticeship in Thinking* (1990) is recommended in Chapter 5 as a source for additional reading in this area. Rogoff's approach to this topic has been greatly influenced by the work of the Soviet psychologist Lev Vygotsky, whose work on culture and cognitive development is discussed in detail in the same chapter. Both Vygotsky and Rogoff use the term *guided participation* to emphasize the bidirectional, or two-way, nature of socialization and the fact that children are active participants in their own socialization. In describing this concept, Brislin (1993) provides an example familiar to those who have lived in or conducted research in many of the countries in South and Southeast Asia—namely, the cultural requirement that children learn that the right (clean) hand is for eating and the left (unclean) hand is to be used for personal hygiene. If children do not learn this behavior through participation in daily home activities, parents, other adults, or even older siblings will guide the children in the appropriate way. For example, while eating, one of these "teachers" might be seen inhibiting use of the left hand while gently guiding the right toward the food. The point, Brislin says, is "that the children's behavior directs the teacher's behavior. If children learn through simple observation, there is no need for the more active intervention of holding down and guiding hands" (p. 130). Contrast this more directive approach with the observational approach of Mayan child training cited above. Let us now consider how the socialization process relates to two of our major themes: the ecological systems approach and the developmental niche.

◇ ECOLOGICAL SYSTEMS AND THE DEVELOPMENTAL NICHE

As we have already noted, socialization is a lifelong process, occurring within a variety of environments or social contexts in which we live, influencing the activities in which we participate, and significantly contributing to our development across the lifespan.

In Chapter 2, we introduced two important themes that are interwoven throughout this book: Bronfenbrenner's (1979) **ecological systems approach** and the concept of the **developmental niche** (Super & Harkness, 1986, 1994, 1999). The ecological systems approach allows us to look at human development as it occurs in its real-world settings or ecology and is composed of four interrelated systems. It is within these interconnected contexts that socialization takes place and in which we begin to see the development of "lives across cultures."

This approach, combined with certain elements of the developmental niche (a theoretical framework for looking at how a child's daily life is culturally shaped), creates a useful structure for better understanding the bidirectional nature of socialization and its effects on human development. According to Harkness and Super (1995), there are three major components of the developmental niche, each of which is directly related to parents (see Table 3.1).

First, there are the **physical and social settings of daily life in which a child lives** (e.g., nuclear family living typically found in many Western cultures versus extended family arrangements found in many Asian or African countries). Aspects of this component include (1) the kind of company a child keeps (e.g., in rural Kenya families frequently consist of eight or more children, who serve as ready-made playmates and caretakers); (2) the size and shape of one's living space (e.g., in a large North American home children have their own rooms, compared with families living in over-

TABLE 3.1   Components of the Developmental Niche

1. PHYSICAL AND SOCIAL SETTINGS OF DAILY LIFE

Size, shape, and location of living space
Objects, toys, reading materials
Ecological setting and climate
Nutritional status of children
Family structure (e.g., nuclear, extended, single parent, blended)
Presence of multiple generations (e.g., parents, grandparents, other relatives)
Presence or absence of mother or father
Presence of multiple caretakers
Role of siblings as caretakers
Presence and influence of peer group members

2. CUSTOMS OF CHILD CARE AND CHILD REARING

Sleeping patterns (e.g., co-sleeping vs. sleeping alone)
Dependence vs. independence training
Feeding and eating schedules
Handling and carrying practices
Play and work patterns
Initiation rites
Formal vs. informal learning

3. PSYCHOLOGY OF THE CARETAKERS

Parenting styles (e.g., authoritarian, authoritative, laissez-faire)
Value systems (e.g., dependence, independence, interdependence)
Parental cultural belief systems or ethnotheories
Developmental expectations

crowded apartments in Tokyo, where small rooms sometimes serve as living, dining, and sleeping areas); and (3) presence or absence of multiple generations living together (e.g., children, parents, grandparents, and other relatives). The differences in these components are clearly observable in the case of Kamuzu and Jeremy described in the opening vignette of this chapter.

The second component of the developmental niche focuses on **culturally regulated customs of child care and childrearing practices.** These include (1) informal versus formal learning (e.g., family teaching of important skills within most rural African tribal groups versus formal in-school learning characteristic of most Western societies); (2) independence versus dependence training (e.g., independence practiced by most Western parents versus dependence or even interdependence found among the majority of Asian parents); and (3) eating and sleeping schedules (e.g., in many North American and European homes there are three meals a day at specified times versus the five to six small meals at unscheduled times customary in many Asian cultures). Again, consider and contrast the educational experiences of Jeremy and Kamuzu. Other examples include the customary use of playpens in Holland to keep infants happy and safe and the care of younger siblings by older ones in Kenya (Super & Harkness, 1994a).

Finally, the third component relates to the **psychology of the caretakers or the psychological characteristics of a child's parents** (e.g., developmental expectations, parental cultural belief systems, and types of parenting styles). According to Super and Harkness (1994a) this component "is an important channel for communicating general cultural belief systems to children, through very specific context-based customs and settings" (p. 98). These authors, like us, see a connection between the developmental niche and Bronfenbrenner's approach when they comment: "Drawing from ecological and systems theory, we suggest that the three components interact with each other as a system . . . to maintain consonance among them. The niche is an 'open system,' however, in that each component interacts independently with elements in the larger culture" (Harkness & Super, 1995, p. 227).

The various aspects of the ecological approach and the developmental niche are illustrated in Box 3.1, which describes some of the ways in which Japanese children become socialized into their culture. To further illustrate this point, we provide three brief examples that will receive detailed attention later. First, if a child is doing poorly in school, this can have an impact on behavior within the family and affect the parent–child relationship in a variety of ways (e.g., neglect or abuse). Baca Zinn and Eitzen (1993) have pointed out that a home situation involving neglect or abuse can have effects on a child's relationships with parents, peers, teachers, and other family members. In addition, a child's temperament within a particular cultural context (e.g., Malaysia or Japan) may affect the way parents interact with that child and, in turn, influence the development of personality and self-concept. Finally, a sick, fussy, or light-sleeping child may keep parents awake at night, making them less effective at work or in their relationship with each other. (Variations in sleep patterns and their relationship to the approaches mentioned above are discussed in the next section.)

With (hopefully) a clear understanding of the ecological systems approach, the developmental niche, and the cross-cultural theme, we are now prepared to look at some cultural variations in socialized behavior.

BOX 3.1

 BECOMING JAPANESE: AN ECOLOGICAL
VIEW OF SOCIALIZATION

In her insightful book on Japanese culture, Joy Hendry (1986) provides a delightful picture of the organization and function of three of the most important microsystems of early childhood development: family, neighborhood, and preschool. Using everyday examples, she shows how these contexts are connected with some of the most important cultural values found in the mesosystem, which, in turn, have significant effects on the surrounding exosystem. In addition, Hendry discusses the strong emphasis the culture places on cooperative behavior; academic achievement; indulgent attitudes toward infants; and the hierarchical nature of parent–child, sibling, and neighbor–child relationships. These fall within the setting of the macrosystem and deepen our understanding of how, accompanied by a traditional respect for age and seniority, these behaviors effectively combine to produce characteristics that are uniquely Japanese.

Hendry describes the family microsystem and the influence of those within it in this way: "The child . . . is in close contact with one set of grandparents and possibly one or two sets of great-grandparents, as well as its parents. . . . Other close relatives are likely to be frequent visitors . . . [and] may well play quite an important part in their early rearing" (p. 36). However, unlike recent developments in Western societies, Japanese fathers tend to play a relatively minor role in early childrearing because "many men [return] . . . home each evening after the children are asleep, and [leave] . . . in the morning before they get up" (p. 38).

According to Hendry, relationships within the neighborhood microsystem are much more institutionalized than in many other countries. For example, "Informal aid is usually given between houses popularly delineated as 'the three opposite and one on either side' (*mukosangen ryodonari*). . . . In this context, mothers of young children meet at the local swings, discuss problems with each other, and occasionally look after each other's children" (pp. 40–41). These neighbors are frequently the first people outside the family with whom the children interact and from which they acquire their first friends. When they enter school, children are organized into a children's group (*kodomogumi*) based on neighborhoods, which arrange "sporting activities, outings and school disciplinary groups [and] . . . gather at a meeting point every morning in order to walk to school together. Thus, the relations established informally at an early age are likely to continue, and even for children whose families move, there are similar groups for them to join in other areas" (p. 42).

(continued)

BOX 3.1 CONTINUED

The third microsystem, that of the kindergarten or day nursery, is also a highly structured setting in which children are separated according to age "so that most of their contact with other children will be with peers, great emphasis being placed on the ideal that all children should be friends (*tomodachi*) and get on well with one another. . . . Conflict and competition is discouraged [and] . . . every child has a turn eventually to serve and to discipline the others" (p. 43). Later, "after-school classes in English and music provide excellent opportunities for kindergarten classmates to maintain their friendships throughout their school lives" (p. 45).

This short excerpt provides only a glimpse into the complex but interrelated ecological world of Japanese children and their families; we highly recommend that the reader look at Hendry's book for a fuller picture.

Source: Adapted from "Becoming Japanese: The Arenas and Agents of Socialization" by J. Hendry (1993) in R. W. Wozniak (Ed.), *Worlds of Childhood Reader* (pp. 34–47), New York: HarperCollins.

◇ SOME CULTURAL VARIATIONS IN THE SOCIALIZATION OF BEHAVIOR

As pointed out in Chapter 1, in a book of this type, with its major focus on cultural similarities and differences, it is impossible to provide as comprehensive a view of human development as do more traditional developmental books. For a general overview of human development principles, we direct the reader to one of these books. Our goal is to consider selected topics for which a large or growing body of cross-cultural research evidence exists and discuss these topics chronologically—from the early beginnings of infancy through the later years of adulthood. Another aspect, unique to this discussion, is the incorporation (and suggested modification) of Erik Erikson's psychosocial theory of development in an effort to place these behaviors within a cross-cultural perspective. (See Chapter 2 for a review of the major aspects of this theory.)

We begin our discussion of selected topics, which are followed in a similar fashion in subsequent chapters, with a consideration of some of the principal behaviors socialized by most parents across cultures. We turn first to socialization during infancy.

Infancy

When a newborn arrives in the world, independent of its particular culture, it has many basic needs that require immediate attention. How these needs are met and the manner in which infants are socialized varies considerably across cultures and often among ethnic groups within a single society. In fact, as we shall see frequently throughout this book, there is often more variability in certain behaviors within cultures than between or among cultures.

It is clear that culture influences patterns of parenting from the first hours of infancy (e.g., when and how parents care for infants, the extent to which they allow them to explore their surroundings, how nurturant or restrictive they might be, and which behaviors they value and socialize). Bornstein (1995) expressed it succinctly: "With the birth of a baby, a parent's life is forever changed. The pattern that those changes assume, in turn, shapes the experiences of infants and, with time, the people they become. Parent and infant chart the course together. Infancy is a starting point of life for both infant and parent" (p. 30).

Sleep

All babies require sleep, but psychological, anthropological, and even pediatric literature reveals considerable variation in cultural sleeping arrangements (Morelli, Rogoff, Oppenheim, & Goldsmith, 1992; Shweder, Jensen, & Goldstein, 1995; Super & Harkness, 1997; Super, Harkness, & Blom, 1997; Wolf, Lozoff, Latz, & Pauladetto, 1996). According to Harkness and Super (1995), the way sleep is organized, including where and with whom, is an intriguing aspect of culture because, although it is a private rather than public behavior, it is highly structured by different societies and tends to be relatively resistant to change. As these researchers point out, "Parents play a primary role in the assignment of settings and routines for sleep, thus perpetuating a cycle of culture transmission within the privileged context of the family" (p. 227). For example, in a 1981 study of Kipsigis farming families in the highlands of rural Kenya in East Africa, Harkness and Super noted that, although the next-to-youngest child continues to sleep with its mother and other siblings after the birth of a younger child, it no longer sleeps at the mother's front but rather at her back. This change, along with the termination of breast-feeding and back-carrying, results in a "fundamental shift in the child's physical and social settings of life" (1995, p. 227).

Characterizing sleep management as one of the earliest culturally determined parent–child interactions, Wolf and his colleagues (1996) suggest that their study may provide a useful framework for interpreting cross-cultural differences in the varying emphases placed on such behaviors as autonomy and dependence. More recently, Shweder and colleagues (1998) have made a similar argument with regard to the development of interdependence and sensitivity to the needs of other people.

While it is common practice among middle-class families in the United States and Canada to put young infants in their own room to sleep (in part, to give them an early start down the road to independence), many Mayan mothers (American Indian peoples of Mexico and Central America) view this custom as "tantamount to child neglect" (Morelli et al., 1992, p. 608). On the other hand, interdependence—a prominent personality and cultural characteristic among Japanese—can be attributable, at least in some measure, to the fact that Japanese children (sometimes due to an overcrowded microsystem) frequently sleep with their parents until the age of six or even, in some cases, to the beginning of puberty, when independent sleeping marks a culturally recognized change in one's developmental niche (Caudill & Plath, 1966, in LeVine, 1988).

According to Erikson's model, which, as we have cautioned, tends to present a predominantly Westernized perspective, social maturation during the first year of infancy is reflected in the development of a feeling of *trust versus mistrust* (e.g., the world is good and comfortable—trust—or threatening and uncomfortable—mistrust). Whichever view develops will depend largely on the parent-infant relationship. For example, many infants learn to trust that if they cry because they are hungry, someone will pick them up and feed them. Parents, on the other hand, learn to trust that their infants will be quieted and comforted when they are fed because the pattern of interaction is consistent.

Similar patterns develop near the end of infancy (during the second and third year) with regard to the second crisis of *autonomy versus shame and doubt*. For example, children will either begin to explore their surroundings on their own (sometimes getting into trouble) and decide for themselves what they want to wear, eat, or do, or they will obediently follow the demands of parents and develop doubts about their abilities and feel incapable of making decisions and governing their own behavior.

If we look at trust and independence, as illustrated in the Kipsigis and Japanese examples mentioned earlier, the Western bias inherent in Erikson's theory becomes obvious. In these cultural contexts, social maturation is not associated with increased independence but rather with increased interdependence within the family. In both cultures, infants first develop trust and attachment as a result of sleeping with parents. Some degree of autonomy in Kipsigi infants is achieved when breast-feeding ends and the older child is moved from the mother's front to her back to accommodate the arrival of a new baby. In the Japanese culture, in which a mother sleeps with the child for an even longer period, interdependence would appear to be even stronger than in Kipsigi society. Consideration of these examples strongly suggests that we may need to make adaptations in Erikson's theory when attempting to apply it in another cultural context.

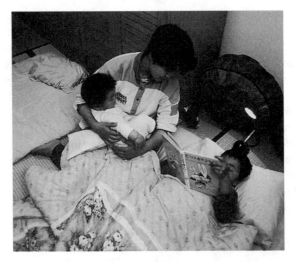

Japanese children often sleep with their parents for the first several years. (Karen Masmauski/Matrix International)

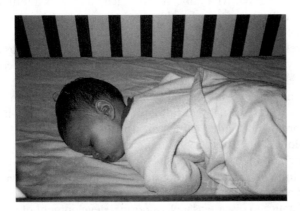

Western infants often begin to develop independence by sleeping alone in their cribs. (Photo courtesy of the authors.)

The practice of co-sleeping (a child sleeping with the parent) is, in fact, routine in most of the world's cultures and was the practice in the United States until shortly after the beginning of the twentieth century. Studies have suggested that the United States and other parts of North America are nearly alone in their expectation that children sleep in their own beds, in their own rooms, apart from their parents (Barry & Paxson, 1971; McKenna, 1993). The well-known pediatrician Benjamin Spock, to whom generations of American parents have turned for advice on raising their children, stated that "it's a sensible rule not to take a child into the parents' bed for any reason" (Spock & Rothenberg, 1992, p. 213). Super and Harkness (1982), on the other hand, have suggested that the expectation that infants will be able to sleep through the night without some contact or involvement with parents may be "pushing the limits of infants' adaptability" (p. 52). Again, we see the importance of cultural as well as individual and familial differences in the determination of a particular behavior such as sleep patterns.

In an examination of sleep practices among parents in Japan, Italy, and the United States, Wolf and others (1996) conclude that "as in other child-rearing practices, it may not be the specific practice itself, but rather the context and values that are the most important factors" (p. 382). This view supports the ecological and developmental niche themes expressed throughout this book and leads us to another basic infant need requiring socialization—feeding.

Feeding

When infants are not sleeping, much of their time is spent eating. Just ask any new parent! How, what, and when to feed a child is another socialized behavior heavily influenced by the developmental niche, social context, parental beliefs, and values of one's culture.

Children need adequate nutrition, before birth as well as during infancy, if they are to grow properly and develop into healthy children and adults. The effects of nutritional deficiencies in infancy can be carried into adulthood and even affect another generation in terms of a mother's poor diet, inability to carry a baby to full term, or delivery of a low-birth-weight infant. According to figures gathered by the United Nations International Children's Emergency Fund (1999) more than 200 million children in developing countries under the age of five are malnourished. This malnutrition contributes to more than half of the nearly 12 million under-five deaths occurring in developing countries each year. It can have an impact on an individual's resistance to disease as well as normal development of intellectual or cognitive abilities. In fact, Pollitt, Gorman, Engle, Martorell, and Rivera (1993), in a study conducted in Guatemala, report finding a link between inadequate nutrition in infancy and cognitive functioning in adolescence, notably among those living in poor socioeconomic circumstances. In a recent study among low-income Nicaraguan mothers, findings revealed a clear relationship between maternal beliefs about infant feeding and a child's nutritional level during the first year (Engle, Zeitlin, Medrano, & Garcia, 1996). The authors conclude their study by stating that "behavioral encouragement to eat as observed here did not reflect the sense of responsibility of the mother about feeding [and that] . . . further work is needed to determine the ways in which mothers translate their belief in helping children to eat into feeding behaviors" (p. 443).

For a long time, mothers around the world have been told that breast-feeding is the ideal method for providing nourishment to babies. The reasons most frequently mentioned include the fact that breast milk is more easily digested than other types of milk (e.g., milk from goats or cows), it protects against disease by providing natural immunization, and it is (obviously) immediately available. In most non-Western cultures, it is the method most preferred by mothers, although one study has suggested a recent decline among mothers in Third World or Majority World (a term suggested by Kagitcibasi, 1996) countries and an accompanying increase, at least on a short-term basis, among mothers in the United States (Ryan, Rush, Krieger, & Lewandowski, 1991). This topic receives additional attention in Chapter 4.

As you might expect, cultural attitudes play a significant role in whether babies are breast-fed or bottle-fed (Rossiter, 1994; Van Esterik, 1989). Some cultures, many of them in the West, tend to make a woman feel embarrassed about engaging in this natural function in public. When mothers return to work shortly after their child's birth, as many tend to do in North American and European countries, they may be unable to continue breast-feeding. On the other hand, if bottle-feeding is the method of choice, more fathers are able to participate in feeding and bonding with their infants.

At this point, we would like to emphasize that research findings have not yet clearly demonstrated that one method has long-term benefits over the other (Van Esterik, 1989). If both options are equally available, we would support the opinion of most experts and recommend breast-feeding for the reasons mentioned above. However, we stress that the method is not as important as what happens during the feeding process. The feeding situation provides an excellent opportunity, through socialization, for parents to establish an emotional connection with their infant (attachment or bonding) that has been shown to have important implications for interpersonal relationships throughout the remainder of the lifespan. (For an excellent overview of this topic, see Virginia Colin's 1996 book.)

As one moves through the lifespan, these early cultural experiences with food strongly influence what, when, and how much an individual will eat. For example, which would you rather eat right now—a hamburger with french fries, a bowl of rice with spicy flavored beef, snake on crackers, octopus, grasshoppers, or (perhaps) nothing? Depending on your cultural training, the mention of any one of these meals might make you hungry or completely suppress your desire to eat. While hunger and the feeding process begin biologically, they are individually socialized by cognitive, learning, and experiential factors deeply rooted in the culture and often within the immediate family. As with other behaviors, eating preferences may show greater variability within families or within cultural subgroups than they do across cultures.

Crying

All babies cry. But what does their crying mean, and is it responded to in the same way in all cultures? Crying is the newborn's earliest form of communication with those in its immediate surroundings—the world of the micro- and mesosystems. Through crying, a baby lets others know that it is hungry, is not feeling well, has a wet diaper, wants attention, would like its older brother to stop annoying it, or conveys other information about its condition. In a sense, when newborns and infants cry, they are bringing their parents and others into their world and socializing them into understanding what their feelings are when they have no other way of expressing them. Although most parents in diverse cultures around the world can clearly differentiate these cries and distinguish one from another, it is almost impossible to teach this skill to others (Gustafson & Harris, 1990); experience seems to be the best teacher.

In addition, numerous studies have shown that infants with various disorders (cystic fibrosis, Down syndrome, and others) cry differently than normal babies and that individuals across cultures can recognize and differentiate among these various cries (Lester, 1984; Molitor & Eckerman, 1992; Zeskind, 1983; Zeskind, Klein, & Marshall, 1992; Zeskind, Sale, Maio, Huntington, & Weiseman, 1985). Recent studies have shown that mothers can discriminate different types of crying in low-birth-weight premature and full-term infants (Worchel & Allen, 1997); that cry analysis can successfully detect effects of prenatal alcohol exposure in newborn infants who do not show clinical signs of abnormality (Zeskind, Platzman, Coles, & Schuetze, 1996); and that crying among hearing-impaired infants differs from those with normal hearing abilities due to the lack of auditory feedback (Moeller & Schoenweiler, 1999). In a new development, Green, Irwin, and Gustafson (2000) have started to synthesize findings from several different approaches into a framework that one day could be used to relate crying to early health and development. Research also shows that fathers and other males respond in as nurturing a way to an infant's crying as do mothers and other women (Rosenblith, 1992).

When and how often should a caregiver respond to a child's crying? If it is responded to frequently, will the child be spoiled? If crying is ignored, will insecurity be the result? These are difficult questions, and not all experts agree on the answers. Bowlby (1989) believes that crying should be responded to frequently, especially during the first year, and will not result in spoiling but rather will greatly assist in promoting secure attachment. In terms of Erikson's theory, frequent responding to crying appears to promote attachment as well as assist in resolving the crisis of trust versus mistrust mentioned earlier.

Childhood

When we use the term **childhood,** we are referring to *the period extending from the end of infancy, about one and a half to two years of age, to just before the beginning of adolescence, typically about the age of eleven or twelve,* depending on the particular culture.

Edwards (1996), in a discussion of the parenting of toddlers, has outlined the developmental tasks she believes children are confronted with during their second and third years. We view each of these as an area of behavior in need of socialization and indicate, in parentheses, the chapters in this book in which they receive extensive discussion. These include, but are not limited to, learning to function independently or interdependently (discussed earlier in this chapter), developing the beginnings of a self-concept (Chapter 6) as well as a moral conscience (Chapter 8), understanding sex roles and establishing gender identity (Chapter 7), becoming a functioning member of a society (this chapter), and taking a place in the larger family grouping (Chapter 9).

Edwards (1996) points out that "although socialization processes in the field of toddler development are by no means fully understood . . . bidirec-

Some children experience difficulties and get "hung up" in the transition between childhood and adolescence. (Joe Oppedisano)

tional, multicausational, and transactional models have become the goal" (p. 59). She goes on to say that "toddler development cannot be adequately described without introducing further theoretical perspectives based on Vygotsky's (1978) writings and using naturalistic observations that clarify the meaning systems and communication processes involved in socialization" (p. 49). Because these topics, in fact, provide the basis for a large part of the discussion on culture and cognition covered in Chapter 5, we will forgo any further mention of it now and direct your attention to that chapter. For the remainder of this section, let us consider some other behaviors that cultures socialize in one way or another during the years of childhood.

Aggression

Most children in most cultures fight, argue, or aggress against one another (peers or siblings) as well as against adults (especially parents) at some time during childhood. Learning the differences between appropriate and inappropriate behavior and how to handle hostility and aggression fall within the realm of socialization.

Let us begin by distinguishing between two often misunderstood terms that are frequently used incorrectly to mean the same thing. **Hostility** is *a motive or desire to cause damage or injury.* If someone calls me a name or insults me, I may feel like I want to strike back by returning the insult or by taking something away from that person. **Aggression,** on the other hand, is *an overt action or behavior intended to cause harm, damage, or injury.* If I follow through on my feeling and actually use an insult, hit the person, or take something away, I am acting aggressively.

The form and extent to which such feelings and actions are exhibited depend on many factors including culture and gender. Research generally shows boys, in most cultures, exhibiting more aggression than do girls. Although there is not a great deal of agreement on why this may be the case, socialization plays a major role, and differences appear to become particularly noticeable between the ages of two and three (Legault & Strayer, 1990; Patterson, Reid, & Dishion, 1998). At least one study (Fagot & Leinbach, 1989) has suggested that an observed increase in aggressive behavior among boys and a corresponding decrease among girls may be related to a greater awareness of one's sex role and a culture's rules regarding the expression of this behavior. (See Chapter 7 for a detailed discussion of the relationship between gender and the development of aggression.)

What causes a particular child to be aggressive? We wish there were a simple answer to this question but none seems readily available. Some say the cause lies in the evolution of the human species; others, in a child's models (siblings, peers, and parents); still others, in the methods by which one's culture rewards or punishes the expression of aggression. We would certainly agree with Cole and Cole (2001) who suggest that social stressors and ecological factors contribute to some of the individual differences observed in aggressive behavior. Rather than attempt to do what others have been unable to do (adequately explain the causes of childhood aggression), we would prefer to view the topic within a cross-cultural context and discuss similarities and differences across cultures with some detailed illustrations.

Bourguignon (1979) gives an example of two children, a girl of seven or eight and a boy of about six, walking along a path in the mountains of Haiti. The girl is hitting the boy and calling him names. He complains loudly but makes no effort to hit back. Why? We learn that the girl's mother has put her in charge of her younger brother and, modeling her mother's behavior, she is punishing him for being disobedient. Bourguignon explains, "We are dealing with an example of child socialization. Children are beaten to enforce obedience toward elders, a central concern in this society. . . . Haitian society is based on a hierarchy of age [and] . . . places less stress on differences in sex" (p. 3). The girl is older and so her brother must obey her and pay her respect. She is permitted to hit him, if necessary, to discipline him, and he is not allowed to hit back. In another example, Bourguignon describes a quarrel between two boys in a village in southern France, who are seen insulting and threatening each other. One boy hits the other, runs away, but is not chased. According to Wylie (1974), who studied the village in which this incident occurred, "If two children start to fight they are immediately separated by any adult who may happen to witness the scene. . . . If it is relatives who separate fighting children, both children are punished. No inquiry is made into the question of which child started the fight or which was in the right. They are both fighting and consequently they are both guilty" (pp. 49–50). Wylie further notes that while French parents discourage physical aggression, they do permit verbal aggression (e.g., insults) as a socially accepted way to deal with anger. According to Bourguignon (1979), adults tend to model this behavior and may themselves "on occasion make a great public show of anger in words and threats, but physical fighting is said to be rare" (p. 2).

As these examples illustrate, there are certainly considerable cross-cultural differences in the amount of aggressiveness various societies tolerate, first among its young people, and later among its adult members. With some effort, it is possible to draw a continuum with the least aggressive cultures on one end and the most aggressive on the other. Among the least aggressive would be the Inuit of the North American Arctic, the Pygmies of Africa, and the characteristically tranquil and polite Amerindian tribes of Zuni and Blackfoot (Moghaddam, Taylor, & Wright, 1993). At the other end would have to be the Yanomamo, living in the Amazon region of Brazil and Venezuela, often described in anthropological literature as the "most fierce and violent people in the world."

According to Chagnon (1983), the first anthropologist to report on Yanomamo society, aggressiveness is the major determinant of status within the group, and learning the aggressive ways of the society begins at an early age. He relates an example involving a four-year-old boy named Ariwari, whose father encourages him to "beat him on the face and head to express his anger and temper, laughing and commenting on his ferocity. . . . He has already learned that the appropriate response to a flash of anger is to strike someone with his hand or with an object, and it is not uncommon for him to give his father a healthy smack in the face whenever something displeases him [and he is] . . . rewarded by gleeful cheers of assent from his mother and from the other adults in the household" (p. 115).

In contrast, Ember and Ember (1993) cite an example from the Semai of central Malaya, a group known for its timidity, who say, "We do not get angry" (Dentan, 1968). The Semai raise their children to be nonviolent and, on the rare occasion that one of them may show anger, do not use physical punishment. As Dentan points out, with this kind of socialization, children are seldom exposed to aggressive models and, as a result, have no aggressive behavior to imitate. Robarchek and Robarchek (1998) have compared the Semai, one of the world's most peaceful cultures, with the Waorani of Amazonian Ecuador, one of the world's most violent societies. The study is worth noting, especially because the two cultures are similar in their ecological contexts, ways of living, level of technology, and social organization, yet their attitudes toward violence and their patterns of behavior are at opposite extremes.

Finally, we would be remiss if we did not mention the findings of the six cultures studies (Whiting, 1963; Whiting & Edwards, 1988; Whiting & Whiting, 1975). These classic studies examined, in great detail, a wide range of behavior in children ranging from three to eleven years of age in India, Japan, Kenya, Mexico, the Philippines, and the United States. In an analysis of this data, Lambert (1971) reported that American parents were fairly tolerant of displays of aggression against other children, whereas Mexican parents were the most punitive. Lambert attributes these differences, in part, to a higher level of interdependence within extended Mexican families, which leads, as we saw earlier, to more adult supervision and greater management of children's behavior. As far as American parents' greater tolerance of peer-directed aggression is concerned, Moghaddam and his colleagues (1993) quote one mother as saying, "If he can't get along with one child, he can always play with someone else. There are plenty of children around to choose from" (p. 126). They conclude with the observation that "this statement clearly reflects the attitude that interpersonal relationships are the product of choice and can be terminated. Given this element of choice and impermanence, it is less consequential to be aggressive against those around you" (p. 126). Once again, we see the intermingling of cultural and individual differences as influences on behavior.

We hope, after reading these examples, you are able to see how early socialization (occurring as part of one's unique developmental niche and place within a culture's ecological system) helps to determine the definition and expression of aggressive behavior. It is only by looking at a topic like this from a cross-cultural and developmental perspective that the richness and diversity of human behavior can be fully observed.

For an especially useful discussion and approach to studying aggression within a cross-cultural framework, see Chapter 12 in the book by Segall, Dasen, Berry, and Poortinga (1990). They end their presentation on a positive note, stating that "because the evidence reviewed in this chapter does not support the view that it is inevitable that male adolescents will aggress, there is hope that the pervasive amount of aggression that presently characterizes the world may be reduced, but only if we become more knowledgeable about the experiential factors, rooted in culture, that presently encourage so many people to aggress" (p. 285). We can only hope that they are right.

How children learn aggressive, as well as other, behaviors is frequently embedded in a variety of environmental settings, including specific types of learning environments. Depending on the culture, these may be formal settings (e.g., a public or private school) or informal settings (e.g., a desert or jungle area). We consider these settings in more detail in the following section.

Formal Versus Informal Learning

Most of the socialization experiences of children in nonindustrialized countries take place in informal settings (e.g., within the family or among peers and siblings) and are a fundamental part of one's daily activities. **Informal learning** is not characterized by a defined curriculum and is *generally picked up by means of observation and imitation.* According to Cushner (1990), "The responsibility for learning falls mainly on the learner, making it rather personal, with extended family members often playing a critical role in the act of instruction. . . . Change, discontinuity, and innovation are highly valued" (p. 100). For example, in certain African and South American tribal groups, young boys learn hunting and fishing skills as well as methods for navigating their way through jungles and rivers by observing and imitating adult males in their culture. Girls learn cooking and child-care techniques, not in school, but by helping their mothers, aunts, and other women in the daily activities of family and village life. Traditions change very little in some cultures; this is the way it has been for centuries and the way it is almost certain to be long into the future.

In other countries, the majority of children learn important cultural skills as part of their society's formal education system. As Cushner (1990) points out, **formal learning** is "set apart from the context of everyday life and is typically carried out in the institution we know as school [and is characterized by] . . . an explicit and highly structured curriculum [in which] . . .

material is learned from a book that may or may not be useful at a later time" (p. 100). For a particularly insightful discussion of the failures of formal schooling, in what Kagitcibasi (1996) calls the Majority World, see Serpell's (1993) work on Zambia.

The issue of formal versus informal schooling gives us another opportunity to look at the two crises Erikson says are characteristic of the stage of childhood. As shown in Table 2.2 in Chapter 2, these are initiative versus guilt and industry versus inferiority. To put these crises into perspective, let us consider the case of Tamiko and Alexina. Tamiko, age ten, lives and goes to school in Akita, Japan. Like most children in her country, her success or failure depends more on her effort and character than on her innate ability. She is learning and working productively and harmoniously in mixed-ability groups similar to what she will encounter when she is an adult. Cooperation is seen as essential to the success of the group as well as the individual, and formal instruction occurs with this in mind. In this case, the developmental niche in which early learning takes place will share certain characteristics with the adult niche in which Tamiko will later live and work. The Japanese believe that parents and teachers must coordinate their efforts so that there is a high level of contact between the school and the home throughout a child's formal schooling. For Tamiko and her parents, academic work comes before everything else and involves long hours of study. There is a Japanese expression—"Pass with four, fail with five"—referring to how many hours of sleep are needed in order to succeed.

Tamiko's education actually began prior to entering formal preschool when her mother taught her to read, write, and perform simple mathematics. She spends more hours in school each year than almost any other children anywhere else in the world. This includes her regular classes, followed by several hours in a "juku" (cram school), and finally studying and doing homework at home until the early morning hours. While the latter is not formal in the strict sense of the word, it is nevertheless very serious and regimented. Alexina, also ten years old, lives in Minnesota in the midwestern part of the United States and is equally serious about her education. However, in her case the focus is more on independence and self-expression. She has learned that autonomy and individual achievement are valued over group collaboration. Getting ahead is a personal goal, as characterized by Alexina's ability to take the initiative to complete assignments on her own. As with Tamiko, there will be a certain consistency between the values and behaviors present in the developmental niches of childhood and adulthood. Unlike the Japanese, Americans believe education is to be provided in the school, not in the home. This again points out the distinction between formal and informal schooling mentioned earlier. If you think about the opening chapter vignettes, Kamuzu's educational experience, while not as rich in opportunities, would be similar in many ways to that of Tamiko (e.g., more cooperative or group learning and more informal home schooling). Jeremy, like Alexina, would be expected to show greater independence, autonomy, and self-expression. Again, in the case of Jeremy and Kamuzu, we observe more variability in their individual educational experiences within the South African culture than we do between the experiences of Jeremy in his culture and Alexina in the United States.

How might we apply Erikson's model and resolution of crises to these four children? In Tamiko's case, *initiative* and *industry* are achieved only after successfully recognizing the need for others to assist in the learning process. The same is somewhat less true in Kamuzu's situation, because his school is underfunded and he had to learn more in the informal settings of his home and community. In Alexina's case, industry is achieved when she is able to take initiative independently and become a "self-starter." Her success in this area is reflected in her school report card, which has a category for "industriousness." In this respect, Jeremy behaves similarly to Alexina. In short, Alexina's culture and Jeremy's subculture view initiative and industry in independent terms, whereas Tamiko's culture and Kamuzu's subculture, to a lesser extent, look at these qualities in interdependent terms. Again, when applying Erikson's theory to non-Western cultures, it is of crucial importance to consider the relevance and cultural definitions of his concepts (e.g., independence and autonomy, initiative and industry). If this is not done, a researcher is liable to make serious misinterpretations of cultural behavior.

Let us now turn our attention to another aspect of formal versus informal learning—the socialization of mathematical skills—and to the current argument that American schoolchildren lag far behind children of other nations, particularly Japan and China, in math achievement (Gardiner, 1994; Ginsberg, Choi, Lopez, Netley, & Chao-Yuan, 2000; Huntsinger, Jose, Liaw, & Ching, 1997; Randhawa & Gupta, 2000). In a study of parents' beliefs, cultural values, and children's math achievement, Chen and Uttal (1988) report that it is more common for Chinese parents to set higher standards for their children and to work more closely with them on homework assignments than for American parents. In a cross-cultural study comparing performance among Thai and American students, Gardiner and Gardiner (1991) reported similar conclusions. A cross-cultural study by White (1987) reinforces our earlier comments (on sleeping and feeding) as to the differential emphasis cultures place on the socialization of such values as cooperation versus competition and dependence versus independence. Specifically, White reported that Japanese "mothers spend many hours in cooperative games and pursuits with their children, such as drawing, reading storybooks, and playing writing and counting games," whereas American mothers give their children materials and games they can enjoy and play with independently (p. 97). On several occasions, the present authors, in their role as teachers, have observed Asian and Asian American adolescents working cooperatively on solving math problems. Such group behavior has sometimes been proffered as a contributing factor in these ethnic groups' superior achievement in math courses (Gardiner, 1994). At the same time, Gardiner, Gardiner, and Gardiner (1994) reported that while such students were more likely to major in science and mathematics than many other ethnic groups, significant numbers did not graduate, had relatively low grade point averages, and were more likely to withdraw for medical reasons or be placed on academic probation. In cases such as these, individual differences in behavior are more important than cultural differences and should be recognized as such.

Summarizing the themes and results of these and several other studies of mathematical achievement, Gardiner (1994) states, "First, there is recognition of the dominant role in this process played by mothers. Second, cross-cultural evidence strongly suggests that an informal learning style, like that found in Asian cultures, focused on building interest, is a more effective way to teach children a variety of skills, including math" (p. 71).

Support for this last statement, particularly with reference to informal math learning, can be found among some of Brazil's more than two hundred thousand *Mennios de Rua* and Colombia's *Gamines* or *Chupagruesos*—street children (Aptekar, 1989). Many of these children survive by selling fruits and vegetables on street corners. Most of them dropped out of school by the time they were ten, before learning good math skills. Although they conduct scores of informal financial transactions each day without making a mistake, the majority of them are unable to complete a formal, written math problem requiring them to calculate change (not unlike what they do every day) without making numerous errors. Their school (ecological setting) is the street, and it is here that they have been socialized and have learned functional math skills that allow them to survive in the street culture of large Latin American cities where they live. For an interesting discussion of these different cultural practices and the advantages and disadvantages of each, see the book titled *Street Mathematics and School Mathematics* by Nunes, Schliemann, and Carraher (1993).

Adolescence

We know that adolescence begins in biology, when hormones that bring about physical changes and prepare the body for sexual reproduction are released into the bloodstream. But adolescent development ends in culture, where one's status is defined by the new role played in society and the transition to adulthood begins. From an ecological or cultural contextual perspective, adolescence is seen as a developmental stage in some, but not all, cultures (Burbank, 1988; Hollos & Leis, 1989; Whiting, Burbank, & Ratner, 1986). According to Cole and Cole (1996), its distinctiveness as a stage depends in large measure on whether "young people reach biological maturity before they have acquired the knowledge and skills needed to ensure cultural reproduction" (p. 629). For example, in the United States and Canada, there sometimes are young adolescents (ages twelve and up) with children of their own who, without a job or educational training, are totally incapable of providing for the welfare of their children or of themselves. Contrast this with the !Kung San living in the Kalahari Desert in Botswana and parts of Namibia and South Africa. Even before reaching the years of adolescence, older children have learned through socialization to hunt animals and gather wild plants as part of their nomadic life. They, like their North American counterparts, are biologically capable of reproduction but already know their developmental niche and have the skills to economically support themselves and a family if necessary (Draper & Cashdan, 1988).

Adolescence provides another opportunity to dramatically illustrate how the major themes of this book can be used to describe and explain how cultures structure and teach the kinds of activities that Cole and Cole (1996) say need to be mastered in order to "carry out the full process of human reproduction [and how these] . . . shape the psychological characteristics that one develops at the end of childhood" (p. 629). It is at this point in the lifespan that we can again clearly observe the development of "lives across cultures." For example, compare two fourteen-year-old girls growing up in cultures separated by both time and space. Mankushai is a member of the Masai tribe and lives on a flat grassy plain in southern Kenya. Her days are spent in her husband's village working side by side with her mother-in-law cooking and taking care of her young daughter, Consolata. Far away, in the United States, in California, Alisa spends her days in school studying chemistry, calculus, and world history so that she will be able to attend college and prepare for a career as an economist. Each lives in a developmental niche within an ecological system, surrounded by family, peers, and teachers, learning her culture's values, and being socialized into an adult role. But how different their lives are and how different they will continue to be as they move through the lifespan. At least part of their development is influenced by the presence or absence of rites of passage.

Rites of Passage

In many cultures, the transition from childhood to adolescence is marked by some sort of public recognition. Called **rites of passage,** these are *ceremonies or rituals that recognize or symbolize an individual's movement from one status to another* (Gander & Gardiner, 1981, p. 498). These "coming-of-age" experiences vary significantly from one culture to another but, according to a study by Schlegal and Barry (1991), are found in most nonindustrialized societies where nearly 80 percent of girls and close to 70 percent of boys go through some form of initiation.

Frequently, these rituals can be harsh and painful. Consider the following passage from Alex Haley's novel *Roots* (1974), which describes the beginning of Kunta Kinte's journey from adolescence into manhood: "Hands knocked him down and feet kicked him. Kunta thought desperately of bolting away somehow, but just as he was about to try, a firm but gentle hand gripped one of his. Breathing hoarsely under his hood, Kunta realized he was no longer being hit and kicked and that the screaming of the crowd was suddenly no longer near by. The people, he guessed, had moved along to another boy's hut, and the guiding hand that held his must be a slave Omoro would have hired, as every father did, to lead his hooded son to *jujuo*" (p. 104). Enduring this painful and abusive four-month journey would teach Kunta the skills he needed to survive and be successful in the Mandinka village of Juffree.

In eastern Africa, ten- to twelve-year-old boys in the Kaguru tribe are led into the bush, stripped of all clothing, and ritually circumcised while being taught the sexual practices of adulthood by male members of the community. Later, they return to their village, are celebrated at a large feast, receive new names, and are expected to become responsible adult members of their society (Beidelman, 1971). Passage for a Kaguru girl is not as complex as for boys and occurs when she experiences first menstruation and is taught

Masai men conduct an initiation ceremony bringing boys into manhood. (Adrian Arbib/Anthro-Photo file)

the ways of womanhood by her grandmother or older women in the tribe. She is fortunate in escaping the very painful and widespread practice of female genital surgery (called "circumcision" by some and "female genital mutilation" by others) already experienced by as many as 114 million women in twenty-eight countries in Africa, India, the Middle East, and Southeast Asia (Armstrong, 1991; Kelso, 1994). The practice is legally outlawed in only three countries—Belgium, Sweden, and the United Kingdom (Nkanginieme & Eke, 1999). For more on the prevalence and effects of these practices, see Obermeyer (1999).

The transition from adolescence to adulthood in North America and many other Western countries is not marked by such clearly defined rituals. In fact, many would say there are no true rites of passage experienced by all members of these societies at this particular stage in the lifespan, and if there ever were, they have disappeared (Elkind, 1984). Among certain ethnic groups within the larger society, there may be some commonly experienced ceremonies, such as the Bar or Bas Mitzvah for Jewish boys and girls, that may come close to being a rite of passage. On the other hand, while not experienced by all adolescents at the same time, or by many at all, the following are frequently mentioned as possible rites of passage in North American society: graduation from high school or college, successfully passing a driver's test, marriage, or the first job.

Age certainly is not a very helpful marker in cultures like the United States, since there are several criteria by which individuals are considered adults (e.g., age sixteen for driving, eighteen for voting, and twenty-one for drinking). American adolescents, and their counterparts in many other countries, often linger in a "cultural limbo" between the ages of twelve to the early twenties when they may (or may not) one day be considered adults.

An exception to the comments made above is the **Vision Quest,** an experience common to many of the more than five hundred culturally diverse Native American tribes in North America. Performed primarily as a rite of passage for adolescent males, it begins with the taking of a boy, age fourteen or fifteen, into a "sweat lodge," where his body and spirit are purified by the heat given off by burning cedar. Sitting with the boy is a medicine man, who advises him and assists him with ritual prayers. Later, he is taken to an isolated location and left alone to fast for four days. He prays, contemplates the words of the medicine man, and waits for a vision that will reveal to him his path in life as a member of his tribal culture (Delaney, 1995). As another example, Navajo girls at the time of menarche take part in a rite of passage that involves morning running and the baking of a ceremonial cake.

It is clear from this discussion that different cultures treat their young people very differently. Some provide a clearly defined niche within the microsystem of the family where the parents, elders, and others initiate and prepare their young people to move into the wider realms of the mesosystem, exosystem, and macrosystem and to deal with the challenges and opportunities available to them as recognized adults. Other cultures, such as many Western societies, could do more to prepare their young people for the often difficult transition to adulthood.

In discussing rites of passage, it is important to keep in mind that each culture uses these as a way of helping their adolescents arrive at an understanding of their **identity,** or s*elf-definition as a separate individual in terms of roles, attitudes, beliefs, and values.* In the case of the Kaguru mentioned earlier, adult male identity is achieved when young boys undergo circumcision, and adult female identity is attained when young girls experience their first menstruation. Identity and adulthood are defined and achieved in terms of tribal customs and beliefs. In North American societies, identity is achieved when adolescents demonstrate some measure of independence, initiative, and industriousness, although these qualities are not always clearly defined.

The differences between these cultures can be considered in terms of Erikson's fifth crisis—*identity versus role confusion.* Failure to achieve identity in these cultures results in what Erikson refers to as role confusion. The difficulty in terms of this crisis lies in how each culture defines identity and marks the onset of adulthood. In many respects, achievement of identity is less ambiguous in traditional, nonindustrialized societies because rites of passage are clearly defined and adolescents know what is expected of them in order to become an adult. Conversely, in many industrialized societies, true rites of passage (which apply to all members of a given society) do not exist; consequently, there is ambiguity in how identity is defined and achieved. The result is that many adolescents do not know who they are or how they are supposed to behave as adults. Erikson refers to this dilemma as role confusion.

Some theorists and researchers imply that Erikson's theory also applies to preindustrial societies. However, when used to explain such behaviors as identity versus role confusion, the theory contains Western biases (e.g., viewing successful identity achievement as rooted in autonomous judgments). (For an extended discussion of identity formation, see Chapter 6.)

Adulthood

Developmentalists have historically devoted most of their attention to the earlier part of the lifespan, particularly the years from birth through adolescence. As a result, there is a great deal of research, many findings, and a host of theories describing, explaining, and predicting the events during the first two decades of life. A similar situation applies to cross-cultural human development: only recently have the last three quarters of the lifespan received serious attention. Even so, treatment of topics has been sparse and inconsistent (Birren & Schaie, 1995; Zarit & Eggebeen, 1995). Cole and Cole (1993) explain it well: "Since psychologists are sharply divided over the relative roles of biology and culture in the process of development, it is only natural that they should be sharply divided on the question of whether development continues into adulthood and old age" (p. 656).

We know from casual observation that the experience of adulthood varies dramatically across and even within cultures and depends on a variety of factors, including age, gender, socioeconomic status, occupation, family structure, and timing of life events (e.g., marriage, parenthood, grandparenthood, and retirement).

Many psychologists (whose research you will become familiar with in subsequent chapters) have paid little attention to developmental changes after adolescence. For example, G. Stanley Hall, who wrote the first book on adolescence in 1904, believed that senescence (old age) began shortly after adolescence ended, generally when one reached the late thirties or early forties (Hall, 1904, 1922). Of course, he based this assumption partly on the fact that life expectancy was much shorter at that time. Jean Piaget, in his theory of cognitive development, proposed that individuals reached the final stage of formal operations during their late adolescence or early adulthood years. Only recently have attempts been made to explain cognitive changes in later adulthood through the establishment of a stage of post-formal operations (see Chapter 5).

Two psychologists who did attribute significant developmental changes to the years of adulthood, and some of whose ideas have been subjected to cross-cultural examination, are Lev Vygotsky and Erik Erikson. Vygotsky, a Russian psychologist and one of the founders of the cultural–historical viewpoint, made some of the earliest contributions to our understanding of cognitive development within social settings, or cultures. (His ideas, many of which are similar to those expressed in our major themes, were introduced in Chapter 2.) Erikson, as we have previously noted, is one of a small number of theorists who emphasize cultural and social development across the entire lifespan, separating the years following adolescence into early, middle, and later adulthood. It is in this area that his views coincide most closely with those of the ecological, or cultural context, approach. Limited findings from anthropological, sociological, and cross-cultural studies, particularly those looking at adolescence, tend to support his theoretical assumptions (Erikson, 1963, 1982; Ferrante, 1992; Ochse & Plug, 1986; Rosenthal, Moore, & Taylor, 1983).

Early and Middle Adulthood

During early adulthood (early twenties to mid-thirties), in cultures throughout the world, a majority of adults are dealing with the crisis of *intimacy versus isolation* (see Table 2.2 in Chapter 2). Decisions are made about establishing a close, intimate relationship with another person, or individuals go their way alone and fail to achieve an intimate relationship. Chapter 7 looks in detail at intimate relationships in a variety of cultures and at the impact of this crisis on one's life.

Lefrancois's earlier comment that age ranges be used only as descriptive guidelines is relevant here in terms of the cultural example we provided in the section on adolescence. Confronting the crisis of intimacy versus isolation usually requires that the individual has achieved a sense of identity, probably is self-supporting, and is involved in a long-term and interdependent relationship. With this in mind, consider fourteen-year-old Mankushai of the Masai tribe in Kenya, East Africa, mentioned earlier. Mankushai lives in her husband's village, cooks his meals, and takes care of her daughter, Consolata. Except for her age, she would appear to be in the stage of early adulthood. What about other cultures, like those parts of India where child marriages are common? In which stage do we put these individuals? Compared with earlier stages of development, there is less cross-cultural research on this stage and the crisis contained within it. This raises additional questions and problems about applying this theory beyond Western societies. We clearly need more critical analysis of ideas and concepts, as well as additional research to extend the cross-cultural usefulness of theories such as these.

For example, consider Catholic nuns and priests, Buddhist monks, or Hindu holy men, all of whom choose a religious life involving vows of chastity and, in some cases, isolation in cloistered settings. Have they failed to resolve the intimacy versus isolation crisis in a positive way? According to Erikson, they have done so only if they have resolved the earlier identity crisis. But we need to look further. Erikson might suggest that these individuals are not necessarily isolated but rather that they have defined intimacy differently. For example, Catholic nuns or priests who have devoted their lives to the service of others in the name of Christ would see themselves as married to and intimate with God. In fact, nuns are considered "brides of Christ." Buddhist monks experience intimacy with nature, Buddha, and the Sangha (membership of monks). In applying Erikson's theory, additional cross-cultural research and modification are recommended.

When one reaches middle adulthood (mid-thirties to mid-sixties), a new crisis appears that involves *generativity versus stagnation* (see Table 2.2 in Chapter 2). Middle-aged adults make work and career decisions, raise children, and show concern by guiding the next generation, or they become stagnant, self-absorbed, and self-centered. Some of our earlier comments regarding the role parents play in socialization would appear to be relevant here. It is through socialization within their ecological settings that individuals have the kinds of experiences that help them as adults find a balance between their self-interests and the interests of others. Unfortunately, as with some other areas, there is a lack of cross-cultural findings related to this stage crisis; the need for additional theorizing and research is clear. For the latest in contemporary thinking and research on the psychological, social, and cultural aspects of generativity in the lives of adults, see McAdams and de St. Aubin, 1998.

Late Adulthood

During the last period in the lifespan (mid-sixties and after), older adults find themselves dealing with the crisis of *integrity versus despair* (see Table 2.2 in Chapter 2). According to Erikson, when individuals reach this stage they tend to reflect on their lives. They find that they are either generally happy and satisfied with their choices, having fulfilled many of their goals and having made their best efforts (integrity), or they find themselves filled with despair over missed opportunities or mistakes made, which leaves them unhappy and dissatisfied.

Considering the example of the nuns, monks, and holy men in the last section, will these individuals look back at their lives from this final crisis and feel unhappy and unsatisfied? Unlike Erikson, who would take this position, we suggest the opposite. In our thinking, most of these individuals will, in fact, feel their lives have been very satisfying and fulfilling and will have feelings of hopefulness and integrity.

In the final analysis, the manner in which this crisis is resolved and the reasons for the outcomes appear to involve a significant cultural component. Consider a nonindustrialized, collectivist, and extended family-based culture in which respect and recognition are given the elderly for their wisdom and accomplishments. For example, most Native American tribes have a hierarchy of elders who are held in high respect for their knowledge of tribal rituals and ceremonies and who pass this heritage on through socialization of the future generation of tribal members.

We hypothesize that a negative outcome to this crisis might be more often found in some Western societies, which place great emphasis on economic and career success and in which nuclear families are the norm. In these cultures, parents or other relatives in their later years are sometimes seen as burdens to be moved from the microsystem of the family to rest homes in the mesosystem or exosystem. In societies in which young people enjoy the greatest status the elderly are more often rejected. Contemporary North American society is currently such a society, but given rapid increases in its older population, the ecological setting will soon undergo dramatic changes. An ecological setting that focuses on youth rather than age places an older person in a developmental niche where either they have few contributions to make or their contributions are not highly valued. In these

Four generations of a Mexican family enjoy an afternoon together in Vera Cruz. (Spencer Grant/Photo Researchers)

In North America, the elderly often feel isolated and lonely living in institutional settings like nursing homes rather than within extended families. (David Spratt/The Image Works)

circumstances, individuals might well feel despair and regret about the past and a real fear of aging. Contrast this with an Asian or African culture in which intergenerational families are the norm and older relatives are looked after by their family or by the village community. These differences are sharply distinguished in the accompanying photographs on page 78.

It is interesting to note that when Erikson reached the eighth decade of his life, he reviewed his theory and suggested that increases in life expectancy might require a rethinking of his ideas, especially those related to development during adulthood (Erikson, Erikson, & Kivnik, 1986). We encourage others to begin this careful rethinking and, in the process, attempt to apply these new ideas to cross-cultural human development.

◇ SUMMARY

It should be clear after reading this chapter that universally accepted generalizations about the complex relationships among family, culture, and socialization are sometimes difficult. Numerous variables contribute to cultural differences, including cultural contexts, societal beliefs and values, individual views of children and their place in society, rural versus urban living, family structure, and parenting styles, to mention only a few. However, cross-cultural research on human development also shows that we are gaining a much better understanding of the significant role culture plays in socialization at all levels, from birth through the last years of the lifespan. Traditional, primarily Western, theoretical explanations of human development are, in large part, obsolete and were never very accurate when transported to other cultures in an effort to describe, explain, and predict behavior for which they were never intended.

You are reading this at a time when many societies are undergoing dramatic change in the way they and their family structures operate. In China, the "one-child policy" is having striking effects on traditional family practices; in the former Soviet Union, political and social changes are affecting parental goals and behavior; in Sweden, children's rights have taken center stage; in the United States, high divorce and remarriage rates and large numbers of working mothers are reshaping family relationships. In countries throughout the world, we have seen major changes in the roles played by children and their parents and yet, as Roopnarine and Carter (1992a) have pointed out, "Perceptions of children and how a culture manages to mesh those perceptions with children's own birthright and value to members of a society, its rituals, functions, and expectations, are not well understood" (p. 251). We have only started the journey toward understanding; much lies ahead of us.

◇ FURTHER READINGS

Robert Coles (Ed.). (2000). *The Erik Erikson Reader.* New York: Norton.
> This new collection of writings, covering Erikson's entire career, clearly shows the influence of his thinking in the areas of child and lifespan development, leadership, and moral growth. A most welcome addition and well worth reading.

John Loughery. (1995). *Into the Widening World: International Coming-of-Age Stories.* New York: Persea Books.
> An edited anthology of twenty-six short stories from twenty-two countries focusing on the adolescent experience and emergence of adulthood. Visit the sun-baked alleys of Cairo, the terrifying forests of wartime Nigeria, a hidden grove in Jamaica, a turkey farm in Canada, a young woman facing an arranged marriage in Malaysia. Fascinating, insightful, and informative reading.

Dana Raphael and Flora Davis. (1985). *Only Mothers Know.* Westport, CT: Greenwood Press.
> A fun book in which the authors describe patterns of infant feeding in seven traditional cultures, including an Egyptian village, a Sardinian shepherd mountain community, a Moslem town in Trinidad, and a Mexican family. An engrossing narrative based on women's stories "about hardships and courage and fun and the wisdom of mothers who know—as their own mothers knew—what keeps babies alive."

CHAPTER FOUR

CULTURAL ASPECTS OF PHYSICAL GROWTH AND DEVELOPMENT

Madam Foo Mei Yin is approaching seventy years of age and lives with her eldest son, Kit Seng, in Petaling Jaya, a suburb of Kuala Lumpur, Malaysia. A widow of twenty-five years, her husband, Boon Seng, died of heart failure at the relatively young age of fifty. Madam Foo, as matriarch of the family, is much respected and well cared for by her four sons and two daughters. She receives frequent visits from her eighteen grandchildren, six great-grandchildren, and other relatives. Since old age is seen as a welcome milestone denoting wisdom, knowledge, and experience, preparations for her birthday celebration have been taking place for months and almost two hundred relatives and friends are invited. A troupe of Lion Dance performers will arrive to the sound of banging drums and firecrackers, bringing prosperity and good luck to the family. Food will be offered to the household gods, and a red cloth will adorn the entryway, symbolizing good health and prosperity and warding off evil spirits. Each member of her extended family will wish her good health and a long life. After a dinner, which includes long-life noodles and sweet bean paste dessert, everyone will toast "Yum seng"—"To your health and success"—to Madam Foo.

On Saturday night, Sarah Lawson will turn seventy in Melbourne, Australia. She is planning her own birthday celebration and hopes her two sons, three grandchildren, and great-granddaughter will be able to come. She lives alone in a three-bedroom house her husband built forty-five years ago. Five years ago, her husband, Patrick, died after a long battle with cancer. Her two sons, who live in the adjoining state of New South Wales, try to visit as often as they can, although distance prevents them from doing so on a regular basis. Mrs. Lawson is very independent and is actively involved in her church and senior citizens' association. She enjoyed good health until a

recent stroke left her in need of a cane. Each Tuesday, she drives thirty miles to get her allergy shots and to volunteer at the regional Red Cross office. She also swims every other morning on the advice of her physical therapist. It's been a tradition in the Law-son household to celebrate birthdays with a barbie (barbecue) in the backyard. A few neighbors and long-time friends will be there to help Sarah usher in the new decade. She has bought the meat; prepared the salads and vegetables; made sure there's plenty of beer, soda, and iced tea; and bought party favors for the guests. Her best friend, Mil-dred, who lives next door, has promised to bake a cake. Sarah is looking forward to seeing her old friends, some of whom she hasn't seen in years. Eventually, the guests will gather around the piano and retell stories of growing up in the outback.

Madam Foo and Sarah are both approaching their seventieth birthdays, but the way in which each has lived her life up until now, and will live the re-mainder of it, differs in many ways. Their developmental niches, family set-tings, relationships, and health concerns illustrate the many ways in which lives are lived across cultures.

◇ CROSS-CULTURAL PERSPECTIVES ON PHYSICAL DEVELOPMENT

When we talk about **physical development** we are referring to *changes in an individual's size and body structure* (e.g., variations in height and weight, in-creases in muscle size, specialization of brain and sense organ functions, im-proved motor skills, and various effects of nutrition and physical health). Changes such as these do not take place in a vacuum separate from one's cognitive experience, social and emotional development, or cultural context. Each realm interconnects with the others and influences one's development throughout the lifespan. For example, when studying child development, we explore the maturation of gross and fine motor skills together with cognitive abilities, social and emotional development, and cultural orientation. While muscle coordination is taking place, a child is also acquiring the language skills necessary for improvements in perceptual and memory processes. At the same time, social and emotional development are laying the foundation for the development of the child's interactions with others in the increasingly complex ecological settings in which we live. While there are many similari-ties in the manner in which these skills and abilities develop, the timing of changes varies across cultures and depends, in part, on the norms prescribed by each society.

In this chapter, we focus on cultural influences on physical development across the lifespan. We begin with the prenatal period following conception.

The Prenatal Period

While we do not discuss prenatal development in great detail (you can find this information in many good developmental books), let us point out that **conception,** or **fertilization,** takes place when a sperm and an egg unite and form a **zygote,** or *fertilized egg.* The zygote then goes through a process of rapid cell division, duplicating the genetic composition provided by the mother and father. This cluster of increasing complex cells moves down the Fallopian tube into the uterus, where it penetrates the uterine wall and becomes implanted. It will progress through the embryonic and fetal stages until birth takes place.

The **prenatal period,** *the time between conception and birth,* generally lasts about 266 days, or thirty-eight weeks. Yet, the physical growth and development at this time can influence individuals' behavior for the remainder of their lives.

Physical development during the prenatal period is critical, and any number of environmental factors can adversely affect this development and increase the odds of giving birth to a child with birth defects (Jacobson, Jacobson, & Humphrey, 1990). Environmental toxins (aluminum, lead, carbon dioxide) or **teratogens** (agents such as chemicals or diseases) can contribute to the development of prenatal abnormalities. For example, recent research suggests that even a small amount of alcohol consumed during a critical period of pregnancy may increase chances of giving birth to a child with physical and cognitive abnormalities (Waterson & Murray-Lyon, 1990). Known as **fetal alcohol syndrome (FAS),** these abnormalities include an unusually small head, low birth weight, facial deformities, neurological impairments, and signs of mental retardation. While it is difficult to know the precise number of cases of FAS throughout the world, Abel and Sokol (1987) report that in comparative studies conducted in Australia, North America, and several European countries, approximately one in every five hundred infants is born with the disorder. The result is that FAS contributes significantly to the number of children suffering from mental retardation. Along these same lines, other studies have shown that if an expectant mother uses **crack cocaine** (*a concentrated form of cocaine*), or another addictive drug such as heroin or methadone, it will have the same effect on her fetus that it has on her (Hutchinson, 1991). The developing fetus is most vulnerable to teratogens during the third to sixth week after conception (the critical period), when the central nervous system, heart, arms, and legs are developing.

As many of the world's cultures move toward increased industrialization, the dangers of pollution to pregnant women and their children can sometimes be carried to horrifying extremes. A particularly graphic example comes from the former Soviet Union, where Tamara Kapanadze, the mother of a child with a birth defect, made a shocking discovery. Acting on her own, she put together a map using data derived from hospital records and a factory producing artificial limbs. She found that over a twenty-year period, at least ninety children in Moscow had been born with the same birth defect as her child—namely, terminal-limb deficiency, which consists most often of a missing forearm. Her figures showed that more than half the children lived in neighborhoods heavily contaminated by industrial emissions. While no definitive link could be made between the incidence of the birth defect and pollution, the number of children with the deformity was higher in these areas than in Russia as a whole (Edwards, 1994).

Turning to another aspect of this topic, two widely studied concepts discussed in cross-cultural psychology are **individualism** and **collectivism** (Hofstede, 1980; Triandis, Brislin, & Hui, 1988; Brislin & Yoshida, 1994; Kim et al., 1994). In the last chapter, we pointed out that in individualistic cultures, the individual frequently pursues autonomy, independence, and personal achievement, often at the expense of the group. On the other hand, in collectivist cultures, emphasis is on group success, and individual ambitions are generally set aside for the attainment of group goals (Hofstede, 1980, 2000).

You might be asking "How are these cultural concepts related to the issue of prenatal care?" In traditional collectivist countries such as Malaysia, Singapore, Indonesia, the Philippines, and Thailand, where childbirth is more family centered, expectant mothers can rely on a large number of individuals to ensure the safe delivery of a healthy child. In a sense, the entire extended family acts as a midwife preparing a woman for childbirth. In fact, in such

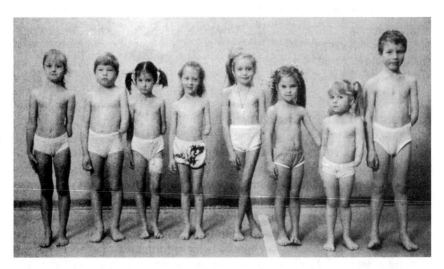

Russian children from two Moscow neighborhoods, born with terminal-limb deficiency, possibly the result of industrial pollutants. (Gerd Ludwig/National Geographic Society)

cultures, it is customary for a young mother to yield to the elders in the family when it comes to decisions regarding diet and other matters. In contrast, in individualistic cultures such as the United States and Canada, childbirth is a more private affair, and precautions taken to avoid environmental hazards are the primary responsibility of the expectant mother.

Interestingly, research shows that more babies die at or soon after birth in the United States than in many western European countries (which, like the United States, are individualistic) and Pacific Rim countries, which have collectivist cultures (Behrman, 1985; Miller, 1987). One possible explanation for reduced infant mortality in these two different cultures may lie in the additional assistance given by extended family members in Pacific Rim countries during the prenatal period and at birth and also in the fact that pre- and postnatal health care is provided without cost in both western Europe and Pacific Rim countries. These cultural and medical practices appear to significantly reduce rates of infant death, low birth weight, and other birth complications (Brown, 1985; Ingram, Makuc, & Kleinman, 1986; Singh, Forrest, & Torres, 1989).

Infancy and Early Childhood

During infancy, enormous changes take place in physical growth and development. In just two years, many infants make the transition from dependent, almost helpless babies to independent, curious children. As their bodies grow and respond to social and cultural cues, their nervous systems mature, and their cognitive experiences are enhanced. They quickly adapt to the world outside the womb, slowly begin to imagine a future involving themselves and others, and discover methods for storing away memories of past and present events.

Physical Growth and Change

The most observable changes during the early years of life are in height and weight. Typically, if well nourished, babies triple their birth weight by the time they are one year old and increase their height by nearly 50 percent in the same period (Wardlaw & Insel, 1993). However, differences do exist. For example, by the time they reach four years of age, some children in Africa and Asia weigh as much as thirteen pounds less than their European and American counterparts and may be as much as seven inches shorter (Hendrick, 1990).

In this regard, the importance of nutrition during infancy cannot be overemphasized (Jones, 1997; United Nations Children's Fund, 2000). Nutrition affects changes in physical stature, brain development, and motor skill mastery as well as other developments. Most of us have seen news reports of chronic malnutrition in many parts of the world. Recent figures indicate that of all deaths throughout the world, one in every three involves the death of a child five years of age or younger (Grant, 1994). More than 250,000 children die each week in developing countries from infection and malnutrition. In fact, the major cause of child mortality is the malnutrition and dehydration caused by diarrhea. Yet, nearly three-quarters of the children who died from diarrhea in 1989, estimated at 40 million, might have survived if their parents had had access to an inexpensive procedure known as **oral rehydration therapy (ORT),** *a treatment that prevents dehydration.* According to Grant (1993), in 1986 the highest mortality rates for children five and younger occurred in Afghanistan (325 per 1,000 births) and Ethiopia (225 per 1,000). During the same year, the countries with the lowest mortality rates were Finland and Sweden (7 per 1,000 births). Although the mortality rate in the United States was lower than in many other countries (13 per 1,000), twenty countries ranked higher. For more recent rankings, see Figure 4.1.

In industrialized countries, bottle-feeding is frequently preferred to breast-feeding, in part, because it allows women to pursue individualistic goals and to engage in professional activities. As developing nations become

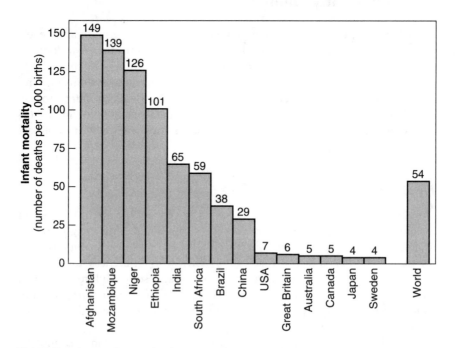

FIGURE 4.1   Incidence of Infant Mortality in Selected Countries

Data Source: CIA World Factbook 2000.

more technologically advanced and increasingly industrialized, there is a reduction in breast-feeding. In some situations this has resulted in many mothers, especially those living at the poverty level, diluting baby formulas and contributing to their infants' already deficient nourishment.

The nutritional status of children and the effects of poverty on physical growth and development have been studied in a number of countries, and the United States ranks fairly high in comparison to other countries (see Figure 4.2).

In the United States, some of the gains in this area have been attributed to federal programs, such as Food Stamps; the Supplemental Food Program for Women, Infants, and Children (WIC); and the National School Breakfast and Lunch programs. Even so, instances of inadequate nutrition are still found among low-income families and children (Human Development Report, 2000; National Center for Children in Poverty, 1990; Wardlaw & Insel, 1993).

On a more positive note, the early effects of malnutrition can, in some cases, be lessened and even turned back. For example, Barrett, Radke-Yarrow, and Klein (1982) conducted a follow-up study on a group of Guatemalan children who had been participants in an earlier investigation carried

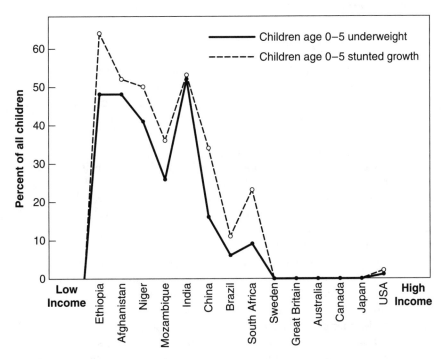

FIGURE 4.2 Impact of Poverty on Physical Growth and Development

Data Source: CIA World Factbook 2000.

out by the Institute of Nutrition of Central America and Panama (INCAP). These children, suffering from the effects of severe malnutrition, were provided with caloric or nutritional supplements during the first several years of their development. As a result, they were significantly more active, physically as well as socially, than children who did not receive such supplements. In a related study involving malnourished Colombian infants, those who received regular food supplements along with home visits were taller and heavier than a comparable group who had not been given such treatment. The former group also demonstrated slightly higher ability in cognitive and social areas (Super, Herrena, & Mora, 1990). The same reversibility of the effects could be observed in children who spent their first years of life in Romanian orphanages, suffering from physical neglect and malnutrition (Rutter & the ERA Study Team, 1998). The children had been adopted by families in Great Britain, where their environmental conditions improved dramatically. Researchers studied the children's physical and cognitive development at age four and found that most Romanian children had caught up physically with their British counterparts. This was especially true for children who had been adopted before the age of six months. During early childhood, young children also show improvements in the development of gross motor skills, especially as a result of their mastery of play (Whitall, 1991).

Motor Skill Development

While parents help their children to develop many of the fundamental motor abilities, individual styles of parenting can vary considerably from one culture to another, and infants raised in these differing ecological settings sometimes show significant variations in physical development. For example, it has been well documented that the motor skills of African infants in such activities as sitting, walking, and running develop several months before they do in Caucasian infants. In Uganda, for example, infants begin to walk at about ten months (earlier than in most countries); in France, fifteen months is more typical; in the United States, the average is around twelve months.

What accounts for these differences? In most cases, it is likely to be the result of a combination of factors, including genetics, activity level, body type, and physical maturation. Genetic factors obviously play a major role in this early motor development. However, cultural and environmental factors (e.g., interactions between the child and others in his micro- and mesosystems and his unique developmental niche) are also extremely influential. For example, in many African and West Indian cultures, parents and extended family members place considerable importance on sitting and walking and actually provide early "formal handling" experiences that stimulate these behaviors. Examples of formal handling practices used by West Indian mothers in Jamaica for helping their infants develop their motor skills are shown in Figure 4.3.

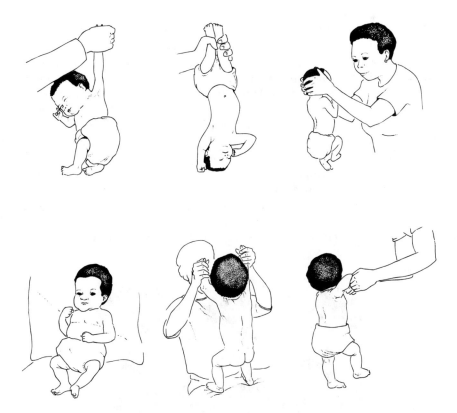

FIGURE 4.3   Handling Practices Used by West Indian Mothers

Source: Adapted from "Maternal Handling and Motor Development: An Intracultural Study" by B. Hopkins and T. Westra, 1988, *Genetic, Social and General Psychology Monographs, 14,* pp. 385, 388, 389. Adapted with permission of the Helen Dwight Reid Educational Foundation. Published by Heldref Publications, 1319 Eighteenth St., N.W., Washington, DC 20036-1802. Copyright © 1988. Reprinted by permission.

Beginning with stretching exercises shortly after birth, parents gradually introduce other activities (e.g., placing infants in a sitting position or playing games that allow them to practice jumping and walking skills) (Hopkins & Westra, 1988; Super, 1981). !Kung infants of the Kalahari Desert also walk earlier than Western infants. In this case, it may be because they spend a great deal of time in slings that keep them upright and give them considerable freedom of movement (Konner, 1976).

Several of these handling practices have been found to be associated with maternal expectations. For example, in a study of Jamaican mothers and their infants, Hopkins and Westra (1990) asked mothers to estimate when they felt their one-month-old infants would be able to sit, crawl, and walk without assistance. Most reported that they planned to provide their infants with a variety of formal handling routines ranging from gentle massage to vigorous bouncing and stepping exercises. Results were compared with those of English mothers, who provided no formal handling for their infants. Findings supported a self-fulfilling prophecy—that is, when handling practices were conducted daily, Jamaican mothers' predictions were accurate as to when these motor skills would develop. English infants, on the other hand, learned to sit and walk somewhat later than did Jamaican infants. Time of crawling did not differ significantly between the two groups.

Dennis and Dennis (1940), in a classic study of infant motor development, disclosed that Hopi Indian children, though traditionally strapped to a cradleboard for much of their first year, still walked at approximately the same time as did children in other countries (e.g., early in their second year). In related research, conducted by Hindley, Filliozat, Klackenberg, Nicolet-Neister, and Sand (1966), infants reared in several European cities generally

Native American children strapped to cradleboards during their first year walk at about the same time as other children. (Lionel Delevingne/Stock Boston)

started walking at about twelve to fifteen months, in spite of any significant differences in the assistance they received for this activity.

On the other hand, African infants do not crawl any sooner than Western infants. There would appear to be at least two possible cultural explanations for this. First, African children are seldom placed on their stomachs and therefore do not receive the practice in crawling that Western infants do (Hopkins, 1991; Super, 1976). Second, African parents do not tend to encourage or value this behavior. In fact, it is generally regarded as dirty and potentially dangerous (Rogoff & Morelli, 1989).

Lack of stimulation or encouragement may also result in a delay in walking. For example, Dennis (1960) observed orphans in two Iranian institutions who spent the majority of their time lying on their backs in their cribs and were never propped upright. The infants rarely interacted with adults and when taken from their cribs were usually placed on the floor and left by themselves. Findings indicated that very few of them ever crawled in the typical hands-and-knees fashion. Instead, they tended to move themselves along the floor in a sitting position. None of the one- and two-year-olds could walk, and among the three- and four-year-olds, only 15 percent were able to walk at all without help.

Play and Physical Development

While play may look like a simple activity to adults, it is a highly complex and intricate achievement for a young child. For example, physical play builds on the relationship among a child's cognitive abilities, social experiences, and cultural context. The simplest, least developed form of play is called **functional play** and consists of a child making *simple, repetitive movements with or without an object.* In **constructive play,** children learn how to *physically manipulate objects in order to construct or create something.* For example, in most cultures, young children are encouraged to play with blocks or similar objects; in addition to being fun, this play also teaches children how to approach and solve problems.

In a study of Kpelle children in Sierra Leone, Lancy (1980) noted that families found a variety of ways to combine constructive play with physical work involving *nee-pele* (make-believe), *sua-kpe-pele* (hunting play), *mana-pele* (dancing and playing musical instruments), and *kppa-kolo-pele* (adult play). As in many other countries, play was used by adults to teach children the importance of play and work, while stimulating coordination, encouraging imagination, and fostering interpersonal relationships.

It is apparent that play is a necessary part of a child's normal physical development and an important expression of cultural heritage. In addition to developing gross motor skills through play and other activities, children also acquire fine motor skills (e.g., tying shoelaces, buttoning shirts, making towers out of blocks, cutting paper, coloring within the lines, and putting together simple jigsaw puzzles). Play is also a critical part of a child's social development and receives extended treatment in Chapter 8.

Handedness

Another topic associated with the development of fine and gross motor skills during infancy and early childhood is hand preference. **Handedness** refers to *the tendency to use one hand in preference to the other in writing and other activities.* Most children tend to show such a preference by about six months, with this tendency becoming stronger in early childhood (Tirosh, Stein, Harel, & Anat, 1999; Shucard & Shucard, 1990; McManus, Sik, Cole, Mellon, Wong, & Kloss, 1988).

Right-handedness appears to be historically dominant in most of the world's cultures (Coren & Halpern, 1991). In fact, ultrasound images and intrauterine photographs have vividly demonstrated that even before culture and parental training can possibly have an effect, more fetuses suck the thumb on their right hand than on the left. In addition, the fact that infants between the ages of five months and two years show a universal preference for the right hand suggests a strong genetic factor (Fischer, 1987; Michel, 1981).

Why might this be the case? When we look at different languages, we find that many meanings for the word *left* involve negative connotations or stereotypes. For example, the French word *gauche* means both "left" and "clumsy" (Coren, 1992).

While more left-handers are reported to suffer from migraine headaches and are diagnosed with reading disabilities, they are also more likely to be musicians, mathematicians, professional baseball and basketball players, architects, and artists than are right-handers (Geschwind & Behan, 1984; Coren & Halpern, 1991).

In a recent review of the handedness literature, Halpern (1996) cited earlier research (Casey, 1996) that supports the link between handedness and genetic predispositions. Halpern reports on a model developed by Annett (1985) that demonstrated that handedness is associated with a single gene believed responsible for both right-handedness and the lateralization, or specialization, of language in the left cerebral hemisphere of the brain. As each society adapts to different ecocultural settings, they develop specific spatial orientations (ways of viewing and understanding dimensions—e.g., horizontal and vertical—within their physical world) and corresponding preferences for right- and left-handedness. Since most people are right-handed (Coren & Halpern, 1991), on the basis of the approach we take in this book, we would suggest that ecocultural systems (including physical settings, family customs, and cultural traditions) tend to establish developmental niches that nurture a genetic predisposition toward left hemispheric dominance, or right-handedness. In this regard, Janssen (2000) recently proposed a functional theory of human handedness based on early childhood experiences and the neural plasticity of the brain that includes consideration of imitation, social learning, personality development, and childrearing styles. This presents an interesting area for future cross-cultural investigation.

Not only is there a universal preference for right-handedness, but moreover children in some countries are deliberately discouraged from using their left hand at all. In Africa, the Middle East, India, and Asia, there is strong social pressure against using the left hand for many activities, because it is used in personal cleansing and other use is viewed as unhygienic. Thus, it would be considered rude to extend one's left hand to a merchant when waiting for change or to pass a drink to a friend or relative with the left hand. Likewise, in some of the areas of the world just mentioned, it would be unwise to use your left hand to pass your driver's license to a police officer about to cite you for a traffic violation. Such insensitivity may cause your fine to increase substantially!

Middle Childhood

Throughout the world, individuals passing through **middle childhood** (*approximately ages four to eleven*) experience changes in physical development that seem slower and less uneventful than in some periods of the lifespan (e.g., early childhood and adolescence). In most societies, school occupies most of children's time and energy, enabling them to build on existing patterns of physical and motor development. However, this does not mean they are any less active. Just watch children between the ages of six and twelve in almost any city or village in the world as they leave school at the end of the day. You will see young people running onto playgrounds, riding bicycles, climbing trees, wrestling, and playing tag and other games. Outside of school, they often take private lessons to learn how to play musical instruments, dance, swim competitively, or participate in group sports like soccer, baseball, and badminton. While possessing a seemingly unlimited supply of energy and excitement, their rapidly growing and changing bodies soon move them from the isolated world of the nursery and day care to the world of the schoolchild.

Physical Growth and Change

During middle childhood, the growth rate begins to slow down a little. Baby fat gradually disappears, and children become slimmer and more muscular. They can run faster, fly a kite higher, and throw a ball farther and with greater accuracy than they once did. As a result of mastering new skills, children are able to compete more effectively against their peers in such board games as chess, backgammon, and mah-jongg.

According to Engels (1993), the average six-year-old child adds about fourteen inches and thirty-five pounds by the age of twelve. For both boys and girls, this results in an average gain of two to three inches in height and seven pounds in weight per year during middle childhood. This pattern continues until the adolescent growth spurt, which typically begins at about age ten or so for girls and twelve for boys.

In addition, in middle childhood growth rates vary with ethnicity and socioeconomic level. For example, in a worldwide sample of eight-year-olds, the mean height of the shortest children included those primarily from Southeast Asia, Oceania, and South America and the tallest were those most notably from Northern and Central Europe, Eastern Australia, and North America (Meredith, 1978). Although genetic differences account for some of this diversity, environmental influences also appear to play a role. While underweight and malnourished children encounter considerable health risks and obstacles to normal physical, social, and cognitive development, overweight children experience unique problems too, particularly as regards childhood obesity.

Childhood Obesity

Over the past three decades, health care professionals in the United States have become alarmed about the growing problem of obesity in middle childhood. This topic has important implications for the consideration of physical growth and development, and more discussion of obesity will follow when we address cultural variations in eating disorders among adolescents and young adults.

Obesity in middle childhood can lead to serious physical and emotional problems later in life. It can cause considerable respiratory and cardiovascular problems and can trigger excessive dieting and consequent complications. In addition, children often reject and ridicule their overweight peers, which negatively affects their self-esteem. **Obesity** is generally considered to be *body weight that is 20 percent or more over the recommended weight for one's age, gender, and body type* (Epstein, 1985). Even with all the attention given to the importance of keeping one's weight under control, research shows that the incidence of obesity among children has increased dramatically within the last several decades (Rossner, 1998; Strauss, 1999). Cole and Cole (2001) point to a 50 percent increase among six- to eleven-year-old children and almost as large an increase among twelve- to seventeen-year-old adolescents. Wolfe and colleagues (1994), reporting on figures for children in the United States, indicate that the greatest increase has been among Mexican American and African American children and for those living in low-income families.

What causes obesity? Many researchers believe it is caused by a combination of genetic and sociocultural factors (Wisniewski & Marcus, 1998). For example, Zhang and others (1994) have reported the results of research with mice that suggests that a specific obesity gene may be linked to obesity. However, this genetic explanation cannot explain obesity entirely; various social factors must also be taken into consideration. For one thing, children often get mixed signals in their culture. In North American society, there is a preoccupation with physical appearance, and being tall and slim are seen as acceptable forms of beauty. Furthermore, children are likely to observe their parents worrying about overeating and gaining weight. This, in turn, can add to children's confusion about how much food they should eat. There is also a tendency in some cultures for parents to overfeed their children in infancy and early childhood. This is often done in an effort to pacify restless children and as a way to cope with parents' busy schedules. Given the amount of food served in many family restaurants—the "all you can eat" specials—it is not surprising that many overweight children exist, particularly in North America.

Another social factor that contributes to obesity is lack of exercise (Epstein, 1992). This may seem paradoxical, since we think of children as running around and being involved in the activities mentioned earlier. But while many children are active, a substantial number of children stay at home spending many hours taking care of younger siblings, playing video games, watching television, or, more recently, "surfing" the Internet. As a result, many school-age children do not get nearly enough exercise. For example, Wolf and colleagues (1993) reported that nearly half of North American boys between six and twelve years of age in their study could do no more than one pull-up and that 25 percent were unable to do even one. Clearly, when children are inactive—spending many hours watching television (with its large number of food-oriented commercials) and snacking the while on junk food—they take in far more calories than they are able to burn off. The result is that obesity becomes a major problem.

Refining Motor Skills

During the school years, children become better coordinated. They are able to master many of the skills they could not manage when they were younger. This is due, in part, to increased levels of myelin in the brain, which is manufactured at a faster rate between the ages of six and eight (Lecours, 1982). Thus, in many Western societies, eight- and nine-year-olds are able to ride a bike, skip rope, draw, write or print, type at a computer keyboard, and play a variety of sports. In other parts of the world, a particular child's eco-cultural system and developmental niche emphasize different skills. For instance, in Malaysia children engage in many of the same activities just mentioned but are also taught how to perform ethnic dances; weave intricate baskets; spin colorful tops; build and fly their own kites; and play soccer, cricket, or *sepak-takrow* with a bamboo ball.

Are physical activities like these dependent on age, experience, and gender—or a combination of all three? Does culture influence the types of motor skills taught to children of one gender or the other? Unfortunately, there is relatively little cross-cultural research focusing on such questions; this suggests the need for future investigation.

Adolescence

Much of the change associated with physical development during adolescence centers on **puberty,** *a period of biological transition between childhood and adulthood lasting approximately one to two years.* While the age at which puberty begins varies from one culture to another, it represents a milestone in most individuals' lives (Rice, 1992).

Cultural Variations in Puberty

In the previous chapter, we introduced the topic of rites of passage and how cultures use these to prepare young people for the responsibilities of adulthood. According to Weisfeld (1997), in many traditional societies, these rites provide insight into how cultures view differences in physical development between boys and girls as well as how cultures mark the beginning of marriage eligibility.

As an example, let us consider how adolescents in eastern Africa make the transition from childhood to adulthood. Ten- to twelve-year-old Kagura boys are taken into the wild and circumcised. They are taught about sexuality and learn ritual songs and riddles that initiate them into adulthood (Beidelman, 1971). After several days in isolation, they are led back to the community by village elders and reintegrated into Kagura society. In contrast, a Kagura girl, when she experiences her first menstruation, is initiated by herself apart from the community. Her clitoris is not surgically removed, as it is in many non-Western cultures, although her genitals are seared with a hot knife to indicate her new status. It is then her responsibility to seek out the advice of parents and grandparents in the selection of a prearranged marriage partner.

One of the most important pubertal changes among girls, regardless of culture, is **menarche,** or *first menstruation.* In a study of ninety-five women from twenty-three countries, Logan (1980) reported that large numbers of Asian women had limited knowledge and understanding about the process of menstruation and that half of these women indicated they were embarrassed by its onset. Fifty percent of Japanese women also stated they were surprised when menstruation began. Furthermore, only about half of the

Asian mothers said they spoke to their daughters prior to menarche, and more than half of the daughters reported feeling surprised when menstruation began. In addition, less than half of these mothers had given their daughters any information about the topic, and over half the daughters said they felt unprepared for their first menstruation. Clearly, each culture views menarche differently and, as a result of the unique interactions between a specific young woman and her developmental niche and ecological setting, has a variety of norms for dealing with it.

The importance of viewing menarche within the cultural context and the ecocultural system is illustrated in a study of young girls living at low and high altitudes in Peru. Gonzales and Villena (1996) compared ten- to nineteen-year-old Peruvian girls living in the mountainous regions of Lima with girls of similar age in Cerro de Pasco. Results indicated that those living at higher elevations, where food sources are more limited, experienced the onset of menarche later than those living at sea level in Cerro de Pasco. The authors concluded that although nutrition is an important factor in determining the age at which menarche occurs, one's physical surroundings and developmental niche also need to be considered. Another example of this close interaction between environment and physical development is a study by Proos, Hofvander, and Tuvemo (1991a, b). They observed that the drastic change in environment experienced by Indian girls adopted in Sweden led to an earlier onset of menarche. This earlier onset may affect the women's overall height by cutting short the period of physical growth.

In recent years, some cross-cultural researchers have focused on the extent to which exposure to modernization alters the menstrual experience of young girls. In one such study, Fitzgerald (1990) examined three Samoan communities as part of an ongoing stress and health project at the University of Hawaii. One community consisted of residents living in remote traditional villages on the island of Savaii in Western Samoa. A second community, experiencing rapid modernization, was made up of seven villages on the southern coast of the island of Tutuila in American Samoa. The third community was composed of individuals living in affluent neighborhoods in Honolulu, Hawaii. Ninety-three young girls reported on their family medical history, menstrual symptoms, menstrual beliefs and practices, and menstrual experiences. According to Fitzgerald, although the literal translation of the Samoan word for "menstruation" (ma'imasina) means "monthly illness," most Samoans view menstruation as a natural part of life—something given to them by God to prepare them for motherhood—over which they have no control. Findings revealed that the more exposed Samoans were to the influences of modernization, the more likely they were to report severe menstrual symptoms. This suggests that as cultures come into greater contact with each other, the values and beliefs of one tend to influence the behaviors of the other. In this case, the values and beliefs characteristic of the more modern society (Honolulu) tended to affect the menstrual experience of the Samoan islanders. Once again, this tends to support the validity of studying behavior from the perspective of the recurring themes of the ecological systems approach and the developmental niche.

Early and Middle Adulthood

Although the process of aging actually begins early in the lifespan, physical growth nears completion by the end of adolescence or the beginning of the early adulthood years. As we have seen in earlier periods, biological processes occur slowly at first but then advance more quickly. For example, around the age of twenty-one, slow, continuous changes begin to affect the functioning of the human body (Spence, 1989). Muscular strength, reaction time, sensory acuity, and heart function approach their peak through the mid-twenties and then, depending on diet and exercise, slowly decline thereafter. By the time people reach their forties, they are well aware of the age-related changes affecting them and their bodies. (Doesn't this discussion make you feel good?)

The Experience of Menopause

A major event for women during these years is the experience of menopause. Since menopause, like menarche, is a universal event, it would be easy to assume that all women experience it in the same way. However, based on our earlier discussions of Bronfenbrenner's ecological systems theory, we would expect that cultural values, expectations, and context would contribute strongly to shaping the experience—and they do. For example, in previous decades, Europeans and North Americans, among others, frequently described menopause as a "change of life." Many early television programs stereotyped elderly and middle-aged women as moody, unpredictable, and depressed. The picture of menopause as presented in contemporary print media does not seem to have significantly improved. According to Gannon and Stevens (1998), while the frequency of articles on menopause has increased over a fifteen-year period, the information was minimal and insufficient, treated it as a negative experience or disease needing medical treatment, contained considerable contradictions and inconsistencies, and ignored or gave little attention to such factors as race and ethnicity, lifestyle differences, stress, or aging.

Today, most North Americans and, in fact, people in many other countries view menopause very differently. Women's own expectations have changed, and for some, menopause is seen as a liberating experience (Matthews, 1992). Part of this new view can be attributed to changing cultural views of aging. For recent research that views menopause from a contextual analysis, see Anderson (1999) and Punyahotra and Dennerstein (1997).

In Israel, interviews conducted among five groups of Israeli women reveal different reactions to menopause (Datan, Antonovsky, & Moaz, 1984). These researchers interviewed four groups of middle-aged Israeli women from central Europe, Turkey, Persia, and North Africa and a fifth group of Moslem Arab women. The women from European and Arab cultures reported experiencing the fewest problems, viewing menopause as simply one more event in their lives. By comparison, women raised in the three remaining cultures reported greater stress related to menopause.

In a cross-sectional study of Japanese women between forty-four and fifty-five years of age, Lock (1991) indicated that only about 12 percent reported experiencing hot flashes, compared with 47 percent of Canadian women. Less than one fifth of Japanese women had experienced a hot flash, compared with nearly three quarters of Canadian women. In fact, there is no specific word or phrase in the Japanese language for "hot flash." However, Japanese subjects reported more physical discomforts (e.g., headaches, ringing in the ears, dizziness, and other complaints not usually associated with menopause).

In an interesting cultural interpretation, some Japanese government officials have suggested that such complaints occur more often among women with little to occupy their time (e.g., no children or work) and even went as far as proposing that caring for elderly parents would fill this idle time and thereby minimize such complaints (Lock, 1991). This topic would certainly make an interesting cross-cultural study.

Later Adulthood

The term **senescence** is used to describe *the process of biological change associated with normal aging.* While the rate of senescence varies individually, socially, and culturally, few people (if they live long enough) can escape the aging process.

A better understanding of lifespan development, along with advances in medical technology, has helped to expand the life expectancy of the world's people. For example, in the United States, nearly 14 percent of the population is sixty-five or older. When the so-called "baby-boom generation" (those born between 1946 and 1960) turns sixty-five, this figure is expected to climb to nearly 20 percent.

Cultural Images of Aging

What images do we have of people when they grow old? What role does culture play in shaping the way we think about aging? Certainly in many Western cultures, notably North America, stereotypes have portrayed the elderly as frail individuals, usually in poor health and unable to take care of themselves. We now know that these stereotypes do not fit the current population of elderly, many of whom remain active, independent, and in good health well into their eighties and nineties and beyond.

It is interesting to note how North American stereotypes of the elderly have influenced societal views of the aging process, especially when we consider how the elderly are perceived and treated in other countries. For example, in Brazil, Colombia, Japan, China, and many other collectivist societies, elderly people are revered and given high social status. Family members look to them as wise and knowledgeable members of the society with much to offer. Rather than attempting to push back the aging process and appear young, many look forward to aging. In traditional Native American culture, old age represents an important time of life when a number of milestones have been attained. Old age is given prominence; elders teach tribal customs to children through the use of campfire stories, songs, games, and dances.

Aging—A Positive View

People are living longer than ever before, many over the age of one hundred, and this number is expected to rise dramatically in the twenty-first century. In fact, several remote areas of the world have become known for having large numbers of people who live unusually long lives. In parts of China and the former Soviet Union, senescence is postponed well into late adulthood, and a disciplined, highly active lifestyle is routine. Why do these people live to such advanced ages? Some commonly cited reasons for longevity include diet (lots of fresh vegetables, little meat and fat), mutual interdependence, family and neighborhood cohesiveness, and regular exercise. Whether it be regular morning tai chi exercises, meditation, walks, or hobbies, maintaining an active lifestyle is a way of life for most of these elderly persons (Pitskhelauri, 1982).

Tse and Bailey (1992) designed a study to investigate the value of tai chi in promoting postural control (balance) among elderly, but healthy, adults. Tai chi is a Chinese method of exercise and self-defense emphasizing balance, coordination, and effortlessness. Their subjects consisted of six men and three women (aged sixty-five to eighty-four years) who practiced tai chi and a similar group of six men and three women (aged sixty-six to eighty-six years) who did not practice the Chinese method. Each participant completed a series of balance tests and a questionnaire concerning wellness issues and was measured for posture control. The tests included being able to maintain one's balance while standing on a single right and then left leg with eyes open, standing on a single right and then left leg with eyes closed, and doing a heel-to-toe walking exercise with both eyes open. Findings supported the researchers' hypothesis that those who practiced tai chi would perform better on the tests than those who did not practice such exercises. The better performance was attributed to a long-established connection between tai chi,

Tai chi, the popular Chinese method of exercise and self-defense, emphasizes coordination, balance, and effortlessness. (Fritz Hoffman/ The Image Works)

improved balance, and self-control. It was suggested that tai chi practice might have therapeutic value in helping to fight disease, lethargy, and listlessness.

It is easy to see how a preferred type of exercise is shaped by cultural practices and traditions. The previous example describes tai chi as a method of exercise that is deeply rooted in the tradition of Eastern martial arts. Similarly, the bicycle is a common and practical form of transportation for people of all ages in the Netherlands. At the same time, it provides daily exercise. Aside from providing the opportunity for exercise in older age, the cultural environment may also provide the motivation for participation in physical activity. A study of older Australian-born and overseas-born Australians found a surprising difference between the groups in their motivation to participate in exercise. Overall, overseas-born adults were more motivated to participate in a community exercise program. Specific motivators for this group were factors such as the opportunity to socialize with peers and the feeling of accomplishment (Kirkby, Kolt, & Habel, 1998), whereas these factors were of little or no importance to Australian-born participants. The authors do not speculate about the cultural factors that may account for differences in exercise motivation in older adults. Nonetheless, at the very least, these results imply that not having been born in Australia is related to greater motivation to exercise in older age.

Studies like these and others suggest that contrary to many myths, aging is not synonymous with disease. We should not assume that illness is a necessary outcome of living longer. What is important to remember is that each culture has its own prescription for growing old and that although it may be different from our own, no one particular approach is necessarily right or wrong, it's simply different. If we look closely at other cultures and the way in which their societies function, we may learn many lessons that could be positively applied to our own lives.

◇ SUMMARY

This chapter discussed cultural similarities and differences in physical development at various stages of the lifespan. Attention was given to important issues of prenatal care, including exposure to environmental toxins and to alcohol (fetal alcohol syndrome) as potential causes of birth defects. Cultural differences in the role of nutrition and its relationship to health and physical development were also considered. Special emphasis was devoted to the interactions between culture and the development of motor skills, play, and coordination, including hand preference, in early childhood. The physical changes of adolescence, especially puberty and menarche, were viewed from a cross-cultural perspective. Cultural reactions to changes associated with the transition to middle and later adulthood, including menopause and senescence, were also explored. As in previous chapters, our discussion placed these topics within the context of our recurring themes: the cultural-ecological model, developmental niche, and individualism–collectivism.

◇ FURTHER READINGS

Frederick W. Bozett and Shirley M. H. Hanson. (1991). *Fatherhood and Families in Cultural Context.* New York: Springer.
> A collection of articles by scholars of cross-cultural human development examining the interactions among different ecocultural systems; the sociocultural and historical context of fatherhood; and the development of physical, cognitive, and social maturation across the lifespan.

Daniel B. Kessler and Peter Dawson. (Eds.). (1998). *Failure to Thrive and Pediatric Undernutrition: A Transdisciplinary Approach.* Baltimore, MD: Paul H. Brookes.
> A variety of contributions from different disciplines address issues related to infants and children who fail to grow according to age and gender standards. Chapters discuss underlying issues such as nutrition, medical aspects, developmental issues, community services, and social policies. The interdisciplinary structure of this book nicely demonstrates the interrelation of levels within the ecological system.

Jaipaul L. Roopnarine, James E. Johnson, and Frank H. Hooper. (Eds.). (1994). *Children's Play in Diverse Cultures.* Albany: State University of New York.
> An extremely interesting and engaging illustration of children's play around the world. An added feature is the way the authors relate play to the cultural–ecological concepts in Bronfenbrenner's model.

CHAPTER FIVE

 CULTURE, LANGUAGE, AND COGNITION

Deratu lives in one of the oldest nations in Africa—Ethiopia, a Greek word meaning "sunburned faces." Like almost 80 percent of the people in this nation in northeastern Africa, she lives in a rural village where her family grows sugarcane and raises goats and chickens. Deratu, like more than half the children in the country, does not attend school nor does she have many toys. What she needs to know, she learns in an informal manner from the work she has been assigned according to her age and gender, since this is the way new members of each generation learn what is expected of them. At five years of age, she helped her mother fetch water and gather wood for the fire. Now, at the age of eleven, she helps with the cooking and cares for her younger brothers and sisters. In just a few years, at about fifteen, she will start a family of her own. Deratu's learning is very much a social activity guided by her mother, who teaches her the important cultural and practical lessons she will need in order to survive in her rural Ethiopian village.

Maria, two weeks away from her twelfth birthday, lives in Brazil, in São Paulo, the seventh most populated city in the world. Brazil is the largest country in South America, occupying almost half the continent. She has attended the country's free public schools since she was six years old. Maria's parents and teachers have always described her as a naturally curious and inquisitive child. Learning how to read and write came easily to her. As a newly emerging adolescent, she is beginning to look more abstractly at the world and is using more logical problem-solving skills than she would have been able to use just two years ago. Now, Maria spends much time with her elderly

grandmother. Although the girl sometimes gets impatient with the grandmother's deliberate speech, she enjoys the stories of the "old days" and admires her grandmother's excellent memory of even small details.

Deratu and Maria live worlds apart physically as well as psychologically. In this chapter, we look at culture, cognition, language and their effects on development. We consider two opposing theoretical viewpoints and some of the cross-cultural evidence that supports or refutes these views. As you progress through this chapter, you will be better able to understand and explain the cognitive and linguistic behavior of these two young women using key concepts from these theories.

First, let us explain what we mean when we use the terms *language* and *cognition*. **Cognition** can be thought of as *the act or process of obtaining knowledge, including perceiving, recognizing, reasoning, and judging* (Gander & Gardiner, 1981). Cognition involves thinking, knowing, remembering, categorizing, and problem solving. **Language** refers to a *system of symbols that is used to communicate information and knowledge*. How does thinking affect language? How does language affect thinking? How do they influence each other? Later in this chapter, we discuss the links between cognition and language as they occur throughout life. Two of the major theoretical frameworks discussed in Chapter 2 will guide us in this discussion: Piaget's cognitive developmental theory, and Vygotsky's concept of the "zone of proximal development."

◇ THE LANGUAGE–COGNITION– CULTURE LINK

One of the early debates linking culture, language, and cognition surrounds the question "Do people who speak different languages think about and experience the world differently?" And if so, are these differences in thinking due to the structural and lexical (language or vocabulary) differences in the languages spoken? Linguists Benjamin Whorf and Edward Sapir are the original proponents of this line of thought, which is known as the "linguistic relativity hypothesis." Elgin (2000) provides an example by comparing the sentence "I was riding a horse" in English and Navajo. She asserts that the most likely translation in Navajo would result in "The horse and I were moving about." It is easy to see that these two sentences describe the relationship between horse and rider rather differently. The English version portrays the rider as the active subject of the action and the horse as the object that endures being ridden. In Navajo, the act of riding is a joint endeavor without expressed subject–object relation. A Whorfian would conclude that Navajo speakers perceive and experience relationship with animals (horses, in this case) differently than English speakers. If people's thinking really is relative to their language, perhaps we could explain cultural differences in cognition by looking at the differences in the languages spoken in different cultures. Unfortunately, research results on the linguistic relativity hypothesis are not that clear-cut. A few supporting findings exist, but there are seemingly just as many findings that contradict Sapir's and Whorf's ideas.

Researchers have come to agree on a less absolute version of the linguistic relativity hypothesis. They believe now that thinking is not entirely determined by the language we speak. Rather, *how* we talk about people, objects, or events may make us pay more or less attention to certain aspects of these events, people, or objects (Slobin, 1990). For example, in different languages, we find different linguistic elements that make it easier to communicate about certain events or objects. For example, English has a progressive form that allows English speakers to distinguish between ongoing events and events that have concluded ("I worked all afternoon" versus "I have been working all afternoon"). Some languages (e.g., German and Hebrew) do not have a progressive form. Speakers of these languages are still able to communicate about the temporal sequence and duration of events, but they have to make a greater effort to do so. A Whorfian may argue that distinguishing between the duration of events may not be as important in German- and Hebrew-speaking cultures but is more important in English-speaking cultures. In other words, if something is encoded in a culture's language, it must be important. This milder form of the linguistic relativity hypothesis led many institutions in the United States, in recent years, to establish "politically correct" language. Many view this as a well-intended effort to change cultural meaning by changing language; others disagree.

What is Vygotsky's position on these issues? He claimed that cultural influence, mental processes, and language are dynamic processes that occur simultaneously (Wertsch & Tulviste, 1994). He further believed that the continuous interaction between language and thought, embedded in a particular cultural context, results in dialogue between individuals, especially a mother and her child. It is this social interaction that helps shape the quality of mental abilities at various ages across the lifespan (Philip & Kelly, 1992). With this theoretical perspective in mind, Vygotsky coined the expression, *"Talking to Learn."* By this he meant that as children verbally interact with others, they internalize language and use it to organize their thoughts (Vygotsky, 1978).

Other researchers go even further and suggest that as parents interact with their children, the children learn language and become socialized into a particular set of cultural values and beliefs (Greenfield & Cocking, 1994; Budwig, Wertsch, & Uzgiris, 2000). For example, in her extensive studies of language acquisition in a Samoan village, Ochs (1988) showed the presence of two major ways of speaking the language: "good speech" and "bad speech." The latter contains fewer consonants and is mainly spoken in informal contexts. Good speech is used when speaking to strangers or in formal settings such as schools, church services, and when talking to a person of high status. Along with learning both "good speech" and "bad speech," Samoan children learn about the social contexts in which using each "language" is appropriate.

Consequently, as children pass through Vygotsky's zone of proximal development, they acquire specific cognitive skills at the same time they are becoming enculturated into a way of life. An effective method for achieving this is **scaffolding,** which refers to *the temporary support or guidance provided to a child by parents, older siblings, peers, or other adults in the process of solving a problem.* In construction, scaffolding is placed around a building to provide temporary support. Once completed, the scaffolding is removed, and the building is left to stand on its own. Similarly, the amount of scaffolding, in the form of guidance and support, a child may need depends on his ability to solve a problem alone. When the problem has been solved, the parent or others can remove the temporary scaffold (guidance) until help is again needed. An example of this guidance, or scaffolding, is illustrated in the accompanying photo.

A mother using scaffolding to help her child learn a new skill. (Photo courtesy of the authors.)

Here a mother is shown mentoring her young son as he learns shapes of objects and how to place them in the right arrangement. As with reciprocal socialization, parents carefully observe their children's behavior to determine how much help they may need in completing a task or activity. As the activity continues, parents become increasingly sensitive to their children's needs, with the result that children do better on subsequent tasks (Pratt, Kerig, Cowan, & Cowan, 1988).

In conclusion, the original question "Is cognition dependent on language or vice versa?" has lost some of its relevance. In shifting from studying language(s) to studying language and culture, researchers acknowledge that both language and cognition are cultural phenomena. Consequently, language and culture are both part of a person's ecological system where they contribute jointly to an individual's experience.

◇ INFANCY

Early Cognitive Development in Cultural Contexts

Piaget's and Vygotsky's interest in children's intellectual development as a focus for understanding how ideas change over time has drawn attention to several important issues related to the study of cultural differences. Over a period of thirty years, hundreds of researchers throughout the world have subjected these theories to careful scrutiny, with the result that the cross-cultural literature is immense and cannot be given here anything approaching the full attention it deserves. However, there are a number of excellent reviews that we recommend to those who would like to pursue the topic further. These include the work of Rogoff and Chavajay (1995); Gielen (1994); Dasen (1994); Bronfenbrenner (1993); Segall, Dasen, Berry, and Poortinga (1999); D'Andrade (1990); and Cole (1992a, 1992b).

Of all Piaget's periods, the sensorimotor (occurring during infancy) has been the least studied from a cross-cultural perspective. A major reason is that observation methods and data-collecting techniques based on Piagetian concepts have only recently been standardized (Cole, 1995). According to Dasen, the first cross-cultural study of sensorimotor intelligence, using a scale developed by Corman and Escalona (1969), was conducted in Zambia (Goldberg, 1972). In general, while minor differences in behavior were noted (a slight advance for African infants over American at six months and a slight lag at nine and twelve months), Goldberg's findings tend to support Piaget's observations. A later study, conducted by Dasen and his colleagues (1978) on the Ivory Coast, suggested that African infants are advanced in their development of object permanency and other object-related cognitive behaviors. In yet another African study, this one conducted in Nigeria, Mundy-Castle & Okonji (1976) reported that while early manipulation of objects is similar for English and Igbo infants, important differences emerge in later interactions. What they have to say about these differences lends support to our emphasis on the importance of looking at cognitive behavior from an ecological point of view. Specifically, Mundy-Castle (1974) proposed that, after a certain age, European and American infants develop increased experiences in the handling of objects, with their attention "more often deliberately focused on objective properties of reality," whereas "African babies receive more social stimulation and early emotional support than European babies. The issue here is whether in the long run this divergent stimulation brings about a differential patterning of cognitive development, with Africans acquiring an intelligence that is more socially oriented, while Europeans acquire one that is more technologically oriented" (pp. 19–20). Although not specifically mentioned, since this was not the concern, the microsystem (family) and macrosystem (cultural values) have an important effect on the development of these cognitive behaviors.

In an early review of the cross-cultural literature, Dasen and Heron (1981) recognized that differences in the ages at which the substages of this period are attained do occur. However, they go on to stress that "in emphasizing these cultural differences, we may overlook the amazing commonality reported by all these studies: in fact, the qualitative characteristics of sensorimotor development remain nearly identical in all infants studied so far, despite vast differences in their cultural environments" (p. 305). Werner (1979), however, concluded that "even in the first stage of cognitive development, that of sensorimotor intelligence, culture seems to influence the rate of development to some extent, although admittedly, the similarity of structure and process is more striking than the differences. Content seems to have little relevance to the activation of sensorimotor schemata" (p. 216).

Language Acquisition

Along with these astounding cognitive developments, infancy is also marked by the first attempts to produce speech and language. Prominent linguist Noam Chomsky believes that language ability is "hardwired" into the human brain. When born, infants have the entire range of human language possibilities available to them. Which language(s) they acquire depends on the languages to which they are exposed on a regular basis. Recent research has shown that the babbling sounds of infants show remarkably similar patterns across many languages (MacNeilage & Davis, 2000). That means that all infants produce basic sounds such as "ma," "da," "fa," "ba," and so on. At this point, parents and others in the child's social environment begin to play a crucial role in language development. If the infant produces a sound that is part of the language spoken in her environment, this sound is acknowledged and celebrated as an attempt to communicate (those of you with children or young siblings can remember the excitement surrounding the first utterance of "Dada" or "Mama"). In contrast, any sound that is not part of the language environment is dismissed as babbling. Soon, due to lack of encouragement, the infant stops producing these non-relevant sounds and focuses on combining relevant sounds into meaningful words. This account of language acquisition demonstrates Vygotsky's concept of scaffolding as well as the developmental niche. The caretakers, with their specific language characteristics, gently guide the child in developing the tools for communication within a specific cultural environment. Once the child has learned language to communicate, the basis for facilitating further cognitive and language development through social interaction is set.

An example of Vygotsky's contextualist research during the sensorimotor period is seen in the work carried out by Bornstein and his colleagues (Bornstein, 2000; Bornstein, Toda, Azuma, Tamis-LeMonda, & Ogino, 1990; Bornstein, Tal, & Tamis-LeMonda, 1991; Bornstein & Tamis-LeMonda, 1989). They studied infant cognition by observing patterns of interaction between American and Japanese mothers and their infants. Interestingly, it was noted that American mothers responded more favorably to their babies' requests when the infants were playing with physical objects. Japanese mothers, on the other hand, were more responsive when their babies were engaged in play with them. The researchers also noted how often mothers responded to their infants' vocalizations. Interestingly, maternal responsiveness appeared to be positively related to the IQ scores of Japanese children when they were about two and a half years of age and to scores of American children at the age of four years. At five months of age, infants in both cultures showed early signs of object permanence and were equally likely to engage in goal-directed behavior. Cross-cultural studies of language development show that the acquisition of certain linguistic elements such as nouns, verbs, and grammatical structure may vary (Gelman & Tardif, 1998; Caselli, Casadio, & Bates, 1999). A variety of studies examining the child's understanding and use of these language markers in Mandarin, Italian, and English showed the following general results: an overall bias in infancy to use nouns; no differences among children in these cultures in the time they begin to use nouns; and as the use of verbs varies across languages, so does the complexity of grammar and vocabulary.

These examples clearly demonstrate Vygotsky's claim that culture plays an active role in directing cognitive activity, even in infancy. More recently, Uzgiris and Raeff (1995), in a study of parent–child play interactions, stated that "the cognitive representations, communicative formats, and affective explorations inherent in play ensure that through the matrix of play interactions available to them, children work to become adept members of their

Family playtimes can be fun and rewarding for all involved.
(Photo courtesy of the authors.)

societies" (p. 372). In other words, the variety of activities involved in play (e.g., talking, touching, and interacting) help children to learn skills that will enable them to be active participants in later cultural interactions. You can probably see how these ideas fit into and support our major themes. For example, it is within the family context (mesosystem) that early parent–child interactions take place. It is here that infants are introduced to activities (e.g., play and the use of language) that help prepare them for successful participation in the broader cultural contexts of the workplace (exosystem) and understanding of important values and attitudes (macrosystem).

Along similar lines, Bornstein and his colleagues (1992) looked at the various ways in which young infants in Argentina, France, Japan, and the United States were engaged in conversation by their mothers. In each of these cultures, mothers were more conversant with older children (thirteen-month-olds) than they were with younger children (five-month-olds) and exhibited a variety of cultural differences in speech patterns when talking with them. For example, expressive speech was employed more often by Japanese mothers than it was by French, Argentinean, or American mothers. This behavior on the part of Japanese mothers is compatible with their culture's stress on interdependence as an important value. (You may recall our earlier discussion in Chapter 3 of interdependence and Japanese childrearing practices, the second component of the developmental niche, as they relate to socialization.)

French, American, and Argentinean mothers, on the other hand, gave greater attention to speech that communicated information to their infant or child. This is consistent with other findings in cultures characterized by individualistic behavior, such as the three Western societies represented in this study (Barratt et al., 1993). Still, not all of these mothers communicated the same kind of information to their children. For example, American mothers asked lots of questions, reflecting, in part, the view within American society that children are active participants in the learning process and often (as we saw in our earlier theoretical discussion) construct their own knowledge. In contrast, French mothers provided their infants and children with less stimulation but greater emotional support. Finally, Argentinean mothers appeared to be the most direct in their interactions with their children, which is indicative of a more authoritarian approach to dealing with children (Bornstein et al., 1992).

◇ CHILDHOOD

As we move from the infancy and early childhood periods to the school-age period, the majority of cross-cultural Piagetian studies have focused on the transition from the preoperational period to the concrete operational period and the attainment of conservation (Gardiner, 1994). These studies show great variability in their findings (Dasen, 1994; Rogoff, 1990). Fishbein (1984) points out that the research literature on these topics, published during the 1960s and early 1970s, reports consistently large differences (as much as seven years) in the favor of children in Westernized cultures when compared with children from developing cultures. However, Kamara (1977) has drawn attention to what he feels are three serious faults with the majority of this work. He makes the following criticisms: (1) the study of thinking in both of these periods depends heavily on the use of language, yet most of the researchers who conducted these early studies had little knowledge of either the culture or the language of their subjects; (2) although Piaget favored the use of clinical interviews for gathering information about children's thinking processes, many of these investigators attempted to employ various types of standardized measures that required little use of language; and (3) accurate birth dates of subjects were not always available, and attempts to approximate ages were frequently off by as much as two years. These are serious criticisms still deserving of further attention on the part of cross-cultural researchers.

Stages of Knowing and Learning

In an extremely interesting and creative cross-cultural study, Nyiti (1982) attempted to avoid the pitfalls mentioned by Kamara by varying the languages used and by employing three of Piaget's well-known conservation tasks for substance, weight, and volume. Subjects consisted of ten- to eleven-year-old Micmac Indian children from Cape Breton Island in Canada and white English-speaking European-Canadians. The European Canadian children were interviewed in English by an English-speaking European, while the Indian children were divided into two groups. In the first group, children were initially interviewed in English by an English-speaking European and later in Micmac by a Micmac-speaking Indian. In the second group, the order of interviewing was reversed. When the white European Canadians and Micmac Indian children were tested in their native languages, their performances on conservation tasks were nearly identical and were comparable to those of other European, Canadian, and American children. However, when tested in English, Micmac Indian children performed at a significantly lower level than the other two groups. More important, the results indicated that nearly twice as many children at both age levels, when interviewed in their native language, were more capable of solving each of the three conservation tasks than were the Micmac Indian children interviewed in English. Nyiti concludes his study by stating that "it appears that cognitive structures described by Piaget are universal and represent a necessary condition for any successful acculturation [and] . . . while children in different cultures may have to deal with different realities, they all apply the same operations or processes of thought" (p. 165).

In an important and exhaustive review of cross-cultural findings on conservation task performance, Dasen (1972) sorted results into four types, each supported by several studies. These included (1) cultural groups in which conservation appears at about the same time as it does in American and European children (i.e., Nigerians, Zambians, Hong Kong Chinese, Iranians, and Australian Aborigines), (2) groups in which conservation generally develops earlier (i.e., Asians), (3) cultures in which conservation appears as much as two to six years later (i.e., African and lower-socioeconomic-status Americans and Europeans), and (4) groups in which some individuals fail to engage in concrete operations even when they reach adolescence (i.e., Algerians, Nepalese, Amazon Indians, and Senegalese). What can we conclude from this vast amount of cross-cultural data? First, support for the universality of the structures or operations underlying the preoperational period is highly convincing. Second, whether or not these structures become functional and the rate at which this might take place appear strongly influenced by factors within one's culture—further validation of the importance of looking at cognitive development from the ecological systems approach.

Finally, it appears that although the rate and level of performance at which children move through Piaget's concrete operational period depend on cultural experience, children in diverse societies still proceed in the same sequence he predicted (Dasen, 1977; Mwamwenda, 1992; Segall, Dasen, Berry, & Poortinga, 1999). The work of Price-Williams, Gordon, and Ramirez (1969) supports this view. For example, in one of their studies, conservation tasks

These young Mexican girls take great pleasure in making traditional pottery figures. (D. Donne Bryant)

were administered to two groups of Mexican children—half from pottery-making families and half from non–pottery-making families. Those children who had helped their families by working with clay showed signs of conservation at earlier ages than those without such experience.

Language Skills and Language Socialization

Jean Piaget's theory of cognitive development also provides clues as to how cognition and language might be related, that is, the ability to understand and use symbols requires certain cognitive skills. According to Piaget, a child first demonstrates the cognitive skills necessary for language use in the pre-operational stage of cognitive development. The child needs to understand that different sounds and gestures do not simply stand alone but can serve as symbols for actual objects. Once grasping the concept of "symbols," she has acquired the necessary cognitive tools to use language as a form of communication about actual objects.

Suzuki (1998) gives another specific example of a particular cognitive skill and language competence. According to Piaget, one of the characteristics of preoperational thought is the inability to take another person's perspective. Instead, the child's thinking is guided only by how the world relates to him or her, for example, a child might answer the question "Why should you not hit your brother?" by saying "So that I won't get in trouble" instead of "Because he might get hurt." Suzuki argues that the ability to use passive construction in Japanese is closely related to a child's ability to go beyond preoperational egocentric thought. The results show that children in this study, between 3.4 and 6.9 years of age, interpreted passive sentence construction very differently, depending on their age and on their ability to adopt non-egocentric world views.

Childhood is the age in which socialization through language is most prominent. A good example of language socialization is a linguistic study by Brooks, Jia, Braine, and Da Graca Dias (1998). These researchers examined the ages at which Portuguese-, English-, and Mandarin-speaking children learn to distinguish between quantifiers such as "all" and "each" in their respective languages. The results showed that Portuguese and Mandarin Chinese speakers had learned to distinguish between "all" and "each" conceptually and linguistically by the time they were five years old. English speakers, on the other hand, were much less discriminating in their use of these quantifiers.

Once again, the ecological systems approach lends itself to the interpretation of these findings. For example, cultural differences may be due to differences in cognitive development. One can assume that a child has had to master basic ideas of quantification. Mastery of these skills depends a great deal on daily experience (microsystem), as we discussed in the previous section.

On the other hand, it is important to keep in mind the larger cultural contexts in which languages are embedded. For example, China and Portugal can be considered as cultures with more collectivist belief systems (macrosystem) than the United States. The words "all" and "each" refer to objects or activities that are either collectively shared or not shared. Children in these cultures may learn words and concepts representing a relationship between "individual" and "collective" earlier than children in more individualistic societies. Eventually, through learning language and using language in social interaction, Portuguese and Chinese children also learn about social relationships that are considered important in their collectivist societies. Although certainly a simplified explanation, it may clarify the idea of language as a contributing influence to both cognitive development and socialization.

Another cognitive and linguistic challenge that faces many children between the ages of three and ten is learning how to read and write. If we consider the vast array of languages and how they are expressed in oral and written form, we can guess that the difficulties confronting children in their quest to become literate also vary greatly. For example, many European languages are phonetically based, meaning that a symbol primarily represents a sound rather than a meaningful word. Words are combinations of symbols and, therefore, sounds. Individually, the symbols and sounds d-e-s-e-r-t are not meaningful. However, when combined, they obtain meaning. This specific attribute of language allows the novice reader who knows the symbol and each sound associated with it, to find the meaning of the word by "sounding" out each symbol. This is difficult to do in languages such as Chinese, which uses a combination of phonetic symbols and logographic symbols. Logographs are symbols that primarily represent a meaning; its sound is secondary. Novice readers have to know the meaning of the symbol to understand it. Good examples of logographs in European language use are Roman numerals. The symbol "X" has a specific meaning, namely the number "ten." Sounding out "X," no matter in what language, will not help find the meaning.

A Chinese boy practices calligraphy while writing Chinese characters with a brush. (Michael Ventura/Stone)

Considering all of this, it should not be surprising to learn that many studies of early literacy show that learning how to read and write are affected by the characteristics of the children's language. For example, a comparison between American and Chinese first graders revealed a different pattern of literacy (Stevenson & Stigler, 1992). English students had learned to break down words into sounds. This enabled them to figure out words that they had not yet been taught. Students who did not have this skill often were unable to read even the words they had already been taught. In contrast, Chinese first graders were able to read almost all the words they had been taught, but very few of the words not yet taught.

◇ ADOLESCENCE AND EARLY ADULTHOOD

Formal Operational Thinking

Piaget's stage of formal operations also has been studied cross culturally, and it is the view of some researchers that individuals in many societies never achieve this type of thinking (Byrnes, 1988; Shea, 1985). In fact, a study conducted among Nigerian adolescents by Hollos and Richards (1993), using Piagetian tasks, revealed little use of formal operational thinking.

One of several tasks frequently used to measure cognitive development in the stage of formal operations is the pendulum problem. In the pendulum problem, individuals are shown several pendulums of different weights that are attached to different lengths of string. When the pendulums are swung, individuals are asked to figure out what determines the speed at which the pendulums swing back and forth. For example, is it the weight, the height from which it is dropped, the force with which it is pushed, the string's length, or perhaps a combination of all of these? According to Inhelder and Piaget (1959), children in the stage of formal operations should be able to solve the pendulum problem through the process of elimination. Several cross-cultural studies have utilized this problem to observe cognitive changes in formal operations. For example, in studies carried out among adolescents in New Guinea, no subjects performed at the formal operational level (Philip & Kelly, 1974; Kelly, 1977). Similarly, few adolescents showed formal operational thought when tested in Rwanda (Laurendeau-Bendavid, 1977). On the other hand, among Chinese children exposed to the British education system in Hong Kong, formal operational performance was found to be equal to or better than the performance of American or European children (Goodnow & Bethon, 1966). Some formal operational thinking was also found among schoolchildren in Central Java and New South Wales (Philip & Kelly, 1974). Based on these and similar findings, Piaget (1972) proposed that development of formal operational thinking is influenced by experience as well as by culture (Rogoff & Chavajay, 1995). As we have seen before, events taking place within one's ecological niche frequently determine how one will perceive and behave in a particular ecological setting.

These examples provide added impetus for considering the ecological setting in understanding why behavior, including cognitive activity, is expressed as it is. For example, Cole and Cole (1996) point out that "a lawyer might think in a formal manner about law cases but not when sorting the laundry . . . a baseball manager might employ formal operational thinking to choose his batting lineup but [not when doing] . . . the combination-of-chemicals task" (p. 674). As evidence, they cite a study by Retschitzki (1989) showing that when African men and older boys play a popular board game involving the capture of seeds from opponents, they make use of complex rules, complicated offensive and defensive moves, and skilled calculations. Interviews with skilled Baoule players from Cote d'Ivoire revealed that their strategies in playing this game used the types of logical thinking we usually attribute to formal operations.

The inability to show evidence for the universality of formal operational thinking among adolescents and adults is not confined to non-Western areas. In fact, earlier studies (Modgil & Modgil, 1976) demonstrated that not all adolescents or adults living in Western technological cultures achieve this type of thinking and that they frequently show low levels of success on formal operational tasks (Modgil & Modgil, 1976). Even earlier studies conducted by Kohlberg & Gilligan (1971) with subjects in late adolescence reported that only between 30 and 50 percent of such individuals perform successfully on formal operational tasks. Werner (1979) sums this up by stating, "Formal-operational thinking might not appear at all or might appear in less-generalized form among cultures and individuals whose experience is limited to one or a few specialized or technical occupations. In other words, survival in a particular culture may not call for, nor be influenced by, formal logical thinking. Thus formal thought processes are probably cultural alternatives that can be learned. Humans have the capacity for it, but may not have realized it in order to 'get by' in their particular society" (p. 224). Shea (1985) has suggested that formal operational thinking (i.e., scientific reasoning) may not be valued in all cultures. For a review of fifty years of formal operational research, see Bond (1998).

Finally, in a discussion of the socialization of cognition, Goodnow (1990) concludes that Piagetian theory can be effectively applied to the conservation of weight, amount, and volume. However, she goes on to say that "if one's goal is to go beyond these domains—to construct an account of cognitive development that cuts across many domains or that takes place in everyday life—then classical Piagetian theory will certainly need some additions" (pp. 277–278). This, of course, is a position with which we certainly agree and which we encourage other researchers to take into account when conducting future cross-cultural studies of cognition.

Analytic Thinking and Problem-Solving

Most of the research in cross-cultural human development has emphasized cognitive growth in childhood and adolescence. By comparison, few cross-cultural studies have examined cognitive development in adulthood. Piaget believed that formal operational thinking represented the highest level of cognitive development and proposed no additional stages in adulthood. He believed that an adolescent and an adult would think in the same way. However, some developmental psychologists have challenged this belief, arguing for a post-formal stage of cognitive development in adulthood. For example, Labouvie-Vief (1986) has suggested that in early adulthood, a change in thinking occurs in which individuals begin to recognize cognitive limitations and may adapt their thinking to the demands of their environment. This process is called **adaptive logic** and involves *balancing critical analyses of objective observations with one's subjective reactions to these observations.* For example, when performing a memory task, older subjects may make a conscious decision to exclude much of the detailed information they remember, believing it may be uninteresting to the researcher or to other listeners. If this is the case, Salthouse (1987) suggests that when measuring cognitive abilities of middle-aged adults, we need to employ strategies different than those used with young adults (e.g., experience and expertise). This represents one more challenge for researchers interested in the study of cognitive development.

According to some theorists (Basseches, 1984, 1989; Riegel, 1975), the highest level of post-formal cognition is what is called dialectical thinking. **Dialectical thinking** *suggests that for every viewpoint there is an opposing viewpoint and these two can be considered simultaneously.* The ability to synthesize and deal with such opposing ideas represents a new level of cognitive flexibility and a deepening of thought, which, in turn, facilitates developmental growth.

The developmental psychologist K. Warner Schaie (1977–1978) has proposed that near the end of adolescence or during the early twenties, individuals advance from the **acquisition stage,** in which emphasis is placed on *attaining concepts for solving problems,* to the **achievement stage,** which involves *goal-directed behavior.* In middle adulthood, Schaie has proposed that individuals enter a third stage, the **responsible stage,** in which *long-term goals and family responsibility take precedence over the goal-directed behavior of young adulthood.* This attention to family responsibilities lays the foundation for the **executive stage,** in which emphasis is placed on *larger social systems and civic involvement* (e.g., serving on a school board or running for local political office). Finally, in late adulthood, there is the **reintegrative stage,** when individuals begin *a review of accomplishments and failures* and put their lives in perspective. While you may see some similarities between Schaie's description of adult cognition and Bronfenbrenner's ecological systems approach, the ideas of Schaie are more general and therefore may not account for much of the diversity found among adults in non-Western or non-industrialized societies. However, these proposed stages do provide a useful framework for describing changes in adult cognition and are worthy of cross-cultural investigation, especially since little is known about adult cognition from this perspective.

◇ MIDDLE AND LATER ADULTHOOD

As one gets older, one supposedly gets wiser. At middle age and late adulthood, one has greater experience, becomes more sensitive to inconsistencies, and responds differently to social, political, and economic changes. These are generally the years of greatest productivity and self-satisfaction in career, avocation, or family.

Studying and understanding cognition during the middle and late adult years presents unique challenges, in part due to a confounding or intermingling of age and experience. Since the majority of research efforts have been conducted in Western cultures, which are youth oriented, the focus has tended to be on cognitive development among children and adolescents, not on the later years of adulthood. As a result, we know very little about changes in cognitive abilities among adults and even less from a cross-cultural perspective.

Intelligence

In their efforts to investigate changes in cognitive development during middle and late adulthood, Cattell (1965) and Horn (1967, 1968, 1970) proposed a distinction between fluid and crystallized intelligence.

Fluid intelligence involves *the ability to form concepts, reason abstractly, and apply material to new situations.* It is thought to be biological or intuitive and to be uninfluenced by culture. It is reflected in an individual's ability to make inferences, draw analogies, solve problems, and understand relationships among concepts. **Crystallized intelligence** refers to *an individual's accumulated knowledge and experience in a particular culture* (e.g., ability to react to social situations or respond to classroom tests).

Previous research in developmental psychology indicates that these two types of intelligence unfold in different directions. While fluid intelligence stays the same or declines somewhat throughout adulthood, crystallized intelligence may actually improve (Horn & Donaldson, 1980; Horn & Hofer, 1992; Lerner, 1990). Over the years, this view has been disputed on the basis of research conceptualization and methodology (Baltes, 1987; Schaie, 1984).

How might the ideas of fluid and crystallized intelligence apply across different cultures? To apply this view would require an understanding of how different cultures value speed, experience, youth, and age. For instance, it has been shown that the speed of cognitive functioning tends to slow down in late adulthood (Salthouse & Coon, 1993; Sternberg & McGrane, 1993), but it is important to consider other factors when addressing this issue cross culturally. For example, it is not clear how the cultural environment will react to or even notice an individual's cognitive slowdown. In some cases, a lack of speed might be compensated for by experience. Individuals who are admired for their experience (or wisdom) are often expected to be more reflective in matters requiring wise decisions. For example, Yang Tsu, an eighty-four-year-old master of martial arts in China, exhibits great discipline and patience (which took many years to cultivate), when teaching his young, impulsive apprentice, Low Chi Tho, who wants to learn everything very quickly. After some time, Low Chi has come to admire Yang Tsu and to realize the need to develop a more reflective approach to learning. In short, what might be negatively viewed by some cultures as a slowdown or decline in cognitive response is positively viewed in this case as a necessary quality for achieving success. Our familiarity with cross-cultural research suggests that there are many instances in which a behavior in one culture is viewed quite differently in another. This richness of differences (as well as similarities) provides many opportunities for those interested in pursuing the study of behavior from a cross-cultural, ecological, or sociocultural perspective.

In Western societies, speed is often more highly valued, and the ability to think quickly and make rapid decisions is seen as an indicator of high intelligence. In many non-Western societies, time and speed are less valued, since individuals are encouraged to first view themselves as part of a group and to concentrate their efforts on the well-being of the family. In these societies, experience is more valuable than quick action. For example, when asked what advice he would give incoming American managers, a Japanese executive who had worked in Tokyo for fifteen years replied, "I'd tell him not to do anything for the first six months." He continued, "I've seen a lot more problems caused by Americans trying to do things too quickly than waiting too long to act." In America, it is often said, "Don't just stand there, do something." In Japan, they say, "Don't just do something, stand there" (Condon, 1984, p. 62).

In Western societies, youth is idolized, and displays of fluid intelligence are often synonymous with quick-mindedness. This attribute is often preferred over experience, or crystallized intelligence. Today, many corporations in the United States actively look for young employees who possess a fresh perspective and demonstrate the characteristics associated with fluid intelligence. At the same time, many senior employees, who have devoted several decades to their employers and have years of accumulated experience, find themselves confronted by the loss of their jobs or by offers of early retirement.

A martial arts instructor patiently teaches his young Chinese apprentice. (Michael K. Nichols/National Geographic Society)

The issue of accumulated experience over time has been associated with wisdom (Smith & Baltes, 1990). But does age alone make an individual wiser? Not necessarily. Smith and Baltes investigated sixty German professionals and divided them into three age groups of twenty-five to thirty-five, forty to fifty, and sixty to eighty-one. Each group was presented with four made-up examples of demanding situations and was asked to prepare solutions for these problems. Their approaches and solutions were rated by a panel of human services professionals. Of the 240 respondents, eleven scored in the "wise" category but were not necessarily older. In fact, they were found in almost equal numbers in each of the three groups. Wisdom, then, would not appear to be characteristic of any particular age group. In short, individuals do not become wiser simply because they get older. Wisdom takes many forms and varies according to each culture's orientation. In this study the criterion for determining what constituted wisdom was set by the researchers, who represent a specific cultural orientation that may or may not apply to all cultures. Replication of this study in a variety of other cultures might produce some interesting findings.

More recent research on this topic has led Baltes and his colleagues to propose several general characteristics associated with wisdom, including the ability to focus on important issues and to exercise good judgment, the development of a broad base of experiences, and recognition of one's wisdom by others (Baltes, 1993).

In the final analysis, it is important to realize that although some aspects of cognitive functioning decline with age, how this change is viewed and evaluated depends largely on one's culture, ecological surroundings, and developmental niche.

Communicating in Later Life

Similar conclusions can be drawn with regard to language use and comprehension in later life. Undoubtedly, some actual changes occur in language with advancing age, particularly when there is a decline of cognitive functions such as memory. For example, Coupland, Coupland, and Giles (1991) point out that older speakers are a little slower and use different strategies in comprehending sentences, and they use less complex sentence structure. On the other hand, grammar, vocabulary, and speech production are relatively consistent across the lifespan. Despite these findings, there is the pervasive stereotype that older people are impaired in their communication. Ryan, Giles, Bartolucci, and Henwood (1986) suggest that the ability of older people to communicate is influenced by several interacting factors. In a society in which aging is associated with negative expectations, older adults are faced with a "communication predicament": physical changes of aging (e.g., hearing loss, voice quality, slowness of movement) are interpreted by others as loss of competence. As a consequence, caregivers and others communicate with the older person in a simplistic and patronizing way. This in turn leads to diminished self-esteem, social withdrawal, and, ultimately, to a decline in communicative competence. Here, negative cultural expectations actually lead to a self-fulfilling prophecy. Consider, once again, the ecological systems approach. Although scientific evidence is lacking, it is conceivable that older adults in cultures that hold their elders in higher esteem will not experience the communication predicament described above.

Just as cultural expectations differ in important ways, so do languages. Perhaps aging affects speakers of different languages in different ways. Although research on cross-language differences and aging is sparse to date, Kemper (1992) shares a few interesting observations. Some languages are very strict in their structure. For example, English has a fixed word order of subject–verb–object. Other languages, such as Russian and informally spoken Japanese, rely heavily on contextual cues and word order may vary. Kemper points out that the more "contextual" languages may make it easier for older people to comprehend and speak because they do not have to follow complex, strict language rules. This means that older adults who may have problems processing complex sentence structure can still understand and convey the meaning of a spoken sentence by interpreting the larger context.

◇ SUMMARY

Cognition is a general term referring to thinking, reasoning, decision making, remembering, categorizing, and problem-solving. Cultural factors and beliefs found in the interaction among Bronfenbrenner's ecological systems, the developmental niche, and the sociocultural orientation contribute in a variety of ways to cognitive development across the lifespan.

The theories of Piaget, Vygotsky, and others provide a useful framework for conceptualizing cognitive growth and development and its relationship to language and culture. The linguistic relativity hypothesis states that different languages provide us with different frameworks within which we understand and communicate our experiences.

Vygotsky's sociocultural theory emphasizes the strong influence of social and cultural factors on both cognitive and language development. He introduced the zone of proximal development, which refers to what a child is presently capable of doing and what she could potentially do if guided by adults or capable peers. Vygotsky argued that cognitive development is enhanced when instruction is focused on an individual's potential rather than on the level of actual development. According to Vygotsky, the development of egocentric speech, inner speech, and external speech are grounded in one's social and cultural orientation. Vygotsky also emphasized the need for guided instruction (scaffolding) in which adults provide assistance (scaffolds) for children as they attempt to solve difficult problems.

According to Piaget, children's thinking differs significantly from that of adults, which is acquired only after successfully passing through a series of discrete stages. These stages have been studied from a cross-cultural perspective, and research evidence suggests that some aspects may be universal (the sequence of stages) while others (the stage of formal operations) may not.

Cross-cultural investigations of human development have tended to focus primarily on children and adolescents and devote less attention to middle and late adulthood. At the same time, research in adult cognition has revealed that a fifth stage of cognitive development (post-formal thought) may emerge after formal operations. This new thinking allows an individual to move beyond abstract conceptualization and to integrate diverse reasoning abilities with pragmatic problem-solving strategies. The work of several researchers suggests that adult cognition is characterized by adaptive logic and dialectical thinking. The ability to synthesize new ideas and to realize that there are at least two sides to every point of view provides adults with more flexibility, effective problem-solving skills, and a broadening of thought.

The developmental psychologist K. Warner Schaie has proposed that adult cognition passes through five stages, beginning with a period of acquisition in childhood and adolescence. In adulthood, an individual advances to the achievement, responsible, executive, and reintegrative stages. While these stages may provide a reasonably accurate description of adult cognitive development in Europe and North America, there has been little effort to examine these stages from a cross-cultural perspective to learn if they apply equally well to other, non-Western societies.

Cognitive development in middle and late adulthood follows a different pattern than in childhood and adolescence. Cattell and Horn have suggested that a distinction be made between fluid and crystallized intelligence. Fluid intelligence is a person's ability to solve problems, think abstractly, and to apply new material in creative ways. Crystallized intelligence is learning that is based on experience. Early cross-cultural research indicates that as we get older, fluid intelligence declines, whereas crystallized intelligence increases. More recent research by Baltes and Schaie disputes this claim and suggests the need to consider cultural and contextual factors when attempting to explain individual differences in cognitive decline during late adulthood.

While some cognitive decline may influence communication in older age, other factors also influence language competence. Negative views of the elderly embedded in culture leading to perceived incompetence may be much more influential than actual loss of language competence. Moreover, changes in language competence in older age may be more or less relevant, depending on the characteristics of the language spoken.

◇ FURTHER READINGS

S. H. Elgin. (2000). *The Language Imperative.* Cambridge, MA: Perseus Books.
    In a conversational style, this book addresses many issues of culture and language. It discusses the linguistic relativity hypothesis, debates about multilingualism, and the power of language in different social and cultural contexts (business, family, medicine, religion).

John Naisbitt. (1996). *Megatrends Asia: Eight Asian Megatrends That Are Reshaping Our World.* New York: Simon & Schuster.
    One of the world's leading trend forecasters describes the significant political, social, business, and cultural values and beliefs that will change the world as we know it. A "new Asian way" of thinking is emerging that reflects increased individualism and urbanization and a more modern role for women.

Barbara Rogoff. (1990). *Apprenticeship in Thinking.* New York: Oxford University Press.
    This book overflows with examples of parents leading their children through rough and calm cognitive seas to new levels of thinking. Illustrations of daily activities performed in scores of cultures fill almost every page of this book, which was written by one of the most prominent proponents of the cultural context perspective.

CHAPTER SIX

CULTURE, SELF, AND PERSONALITY

Sergej was happy, agreeable, and easy to care for as a child. He grew up on a kolkhozy (collective farm) in the Ukraine, one of the fifteen republics in the former Soviet Union. Sergej was quiet, and even his adolescent years were not characterized by the confusion and psychological turmoil experienced by so many young people. Sergej did well in school, completed an apprenticeship, and, following the breakup of the Soviet Union, now works on his family's small farm. He has been married for several years, and his wife Tamara describes him as a "good husband" who works hard, stays at home, and cares for his family.

Yuen, born in Guizhou province in south central China, was what her mother considered a difficult child. Her moods were unpredictable and when upset, she took a long time to calm down. Yuen never developed a regular sleeping and feeding schedule, making it difficult for her mother to coordinate her work and child care. Her adolescent years were equally challenging. Yuen had few friends and struggled with discipline problems at school. Now in her mid-thirties, she has assumed a leadership position in her work. Occasionally, she has to be reprimanded for her creative and sometimes radical ideas.

Sergej and Yuen clearly are very different people and showed very distinct character traits as children and as adults. Were they born with different personalities? Are these differences due to innate cultural patterns of personality? How much do cultural expectations about the course of one's life influence adult personality? We address these and other questions in this chapter by examining issues of personality, self, and individual differences and their embeddedness in a cultural context.

◇ INFANCY AND TEMPERAMENT

Many of the childhood behaviors exhibited by Sergej and Yuen can be explained according to differences in **temperament**, or *a person's characteristic behavioral style or typical pattern of responding to events in the environment*. Individual differences in temperament can be observed in the earliest hours following birth. For example, while some newborns and infants are irritable and cry frequently, others appear to be good-natured and calm. During the first few months of life, some infants are extremely expressive and react to people and events by making sounds and waving their arms; others are less active, may hardly respond to their environment, and appear withdrawn and uninvolved. Frequently, the differences we see in temperament among infants tend to be characteristically consistent throughout individual lives. In fact, some researchers maintain that infant temperament reliably predicts adult personality (Buss & Plomin, 1984). The infant who is shy and anxious around strangers is more likely to be a shy adult than is an infant who curiously approaches strangers (Cheek, 1989). The potentially powerful relationship between infant temperament and adult personality has led many researchers to the conclusion that traits of temperament are, to a significant extent, inherited. They argue that environment and socialization can influence temperament only within the limits initially defined by heredity.

The concept of heritability of temperament has received support from careful studies of twins (identical and fraternal) reared together and apart (DiLalla & Jones, 2000; Plomin, DeFries, & McClearn, 1980; Rushton, Fulker, Neale, Nias, & Eysenck, 1986). These studies are based on the hypothesis that identical twins share 100 percent of their genes and therefore should be identical in their temperamental dispositions at birth. In contrast, fraternal twins, like other siblings, share only 50 percent of their genetic makeup and therefore should be less similar in their temperament. Studies such as these should be able to provide answers to such questions as the following: (1) Are identical twins more similar in their temperament than fraternal twins? (2) Are identical twins raised in different environments more similar in temperament than are fraternal twins reared together? and (3) Are fraternal twins (who share half of their genes) more similar to each other than are adopted siblings (who do not share any genes)?

If the answer to all of these questions is "yes," we can conclude that genetic disposition, rather than environment, is responsible for the differences in temperament observed among people. However, to accurately assess the results of twin studies, it is important to understand the way heritability is measured. In general, the degree of heritability is expressed by the **heritability quotient,** which is *an estimate of the percentage of the variability in a given trait that can be attributed to genetic differences.* For example, a heritability quotient of 50 percent for trait X means that approximately half of the variation, or individual difference, found in a sample is due to genetic differences among those subjects in the sample. The remaining half of the variation is assumed to be the result of complex environmental factors or, possibly, unexplained errors in measurement. With this in mind, let us consider some twin research and what it tells us about the inheritability of temperament.

In general, twin studies have produced moderately high heritability quotients. For example, a study of 13,000 sets of Swedish twins showed a heritability quotient of about 50 percent for the traits of extraversion and neuroticism (Floderus-Myrhed, Pedersen, & Rasmuson, 1980). Similarly, a study of 350 twins in Minnesota revealed that approximately 40 percent of variability among subjects in such traits as stress reaction (related to neuroticism and general anxiousness) and aggression could be attributed to genetics (Bouchard, Lykken, McGue, Segal, & Tellegen, 1990).

While results like these suggest that certain temperamental traits are genetically transmitted, they also suggest that in specific instances other traits are heavily influenced by socialization within the family environment. In fact, most recent explorations in the field suggest that individual temperament is influenced by nutrition (Wachs, 2000). After all, a heritability quotient of 40 to 50 percent also means that 50 to 60 percent of variation is due to environmental rather than genetic factors. The issue of environmental and genetic influences on temperament continues to be controversial, and researchers are not yet able to provide a definitive answer as to which plays the most significant role in determining differences in temperament. Most researchers recognize the existence of an intricate relationship between individual temperament and the larger sociocultural environment. In the next section we will discuss some theoretical perspectives that attempt to explain that relationship.

Temperament, Ecological Systems, and the Developmental Niche

As we pointed out in Chapter 2, a child's developmental environment consists of four subsystems: (1) the microsystem, consisting of interactions between the child and her immediate environment (e.g., home or day-care center); (2) the mesosystem, made up of individual microsystems (e.g., family and preschool); (3) the exosystem, consisting of influential social settings (e.g., parents' place of work); and (4) the macrosystem, consisting of customs, values, and laws important to the child's culture. Together, these subsystems provide the individual child with her developmental niche, or unique combination of socialization experiences. Each of these subsystems is influenced by, and in turn influences, a child's individual temperament. A child's behavior will initiate a specific response from a caretaker in a particular setting (home or preschool). However, these responses differ from one environmental setting to another. For example, a mother's reaction to a child who exhibits irregular sleep and eating patterns differs from North America to East Africa. A North American mother typically pays more attention to an infant who is unpredictable in eating and sleeping patterns, and she arranges her schedule to take care of the child's needs. In contrast, Super and Harkness (1994) report that mothers in Kokwet, a small farming town in Kenya, interact more with children who operate on a regular daily schedule. Knowing when her baby will be awake and alert, the mother can more easily arrange her many other duties and activities. Kokwet infants who are less predictable in their daily patterns are more often left to the care of an older sister or another caretaker.

This example illustrates how a child's temperament influences the environment. At the same time, however, specific patterns of response exhibited by others in the child's environment may facilitate or inhibit particular behavioral styles on the part of the child, thus making the child–environment relationship a two-way interaction. A fussy child receives more attention from the primary caretaker in most Western cultures, thus potentially rewarding and facilitating the child's dependency on the caretaker. In non-Western cultures, dependency and emotional attachment to the mother are often less pronounced because mothers may not be available to respond with immediate emotional attention to fussy children.

Temperament and "Goodness of Fit"

Another theoretical explanation that contributes considerably to the understanding of how temperament, development, and culture relate to one another is that of **goodness of fit**—*the quality of the adaptation, or "match," between a child's temperament and the demands of his immediate environment.* This concept was introduced by Thomas and Chess (1977) in an elaborate longitudinal study of children's temperament that eventually included a wide range of environmental factors. The researchers began by interviewing and observing middle-class families of European background living in New York. They were able to identify clusters of traits that characterized three different temperament types among infants: (1) the "easy" child, (2) the "difficult" child, and (3) the "slow-to-warm-up" child.

An **easy child** was *characterized by a good mood, regular sleeping and eating cycles, and general calmness.* Mothers considered these babies unproblematic and easy to raise. On the other hand, temperament traits of a **difficult child** included a *negative mood, slow adaptation to and withdrawal from new experiences and people, irregular sleep and feeding patterns, and high emotional intensity.* More-over, these "difficult" infants were found in later childhood to be less well adjusted and prone to more behavioral problems. A **slow-to-warm-up child** generally *shows few intense reactions, positive or negative, and tends to be mild and low in activity level.* Thomas and Chess assert that it is not the individual child's temperament itself that is related to future maladjustment but rather the match or mismatch of the child's temperament with the environment that predicts problematic behavior. If "difficult" temperament disrupts family routine and leads to negative parental reactions, negative developmental outcome is likely.

A follow-up study by Korn and Gannon (1983) with Puerto Rican families in New York provided additional support for the goodness-of-fit concept but sounded a note of caution as well. For example, early "difficult" temperament did not predict poor adjustment and behavioral difficulties in later childhood. The researchers point out that in these families characteristics that were originally classified as "difficult" were not perceived as necessarily problematic and therefore did not disrupt family life or evoke negative parental reactions toward the child. These studies and others provide convincing evidence that culture is a critical determinant of the "goodness of fit" between an individual child (temperament) and her environment.

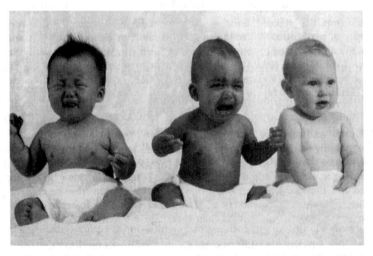

Differences in infant temperament can often be observed side-by-side within the same cultural context. (Gary Buss/FPG International)

DeVries (1994) and DeVries and Sameroff (1984) further illustrate this concept by describing two individual cases encountered in the study of infants from different parts of Kenya. The case of Hamadi, a Digo boy, demonstrates how an "easy" temperament can lead to poor adjustment due to a mismatch between the boy's temperament and his environment. For example, as an infant, Hamadi was energetic and active and exhibited healthy approach tendencies. He was described as one of the most advanced infants in the entire study. However, after starting school, Hamadi began to withdraw, became shy, and showed clear signs of distress through acting-out behavior.

What caused this transition? The researchers interviewed Hamadi's parents and teachers and were told that Hamadi's temperament did not fit with the cultural expectations of how a Digo boy his age should behave. The efforts of teachers and parents to control his energetic temperament and discourage his curiosity, instead of rewarding his enthusiasm and challenging his intellect, led Hamadi to withdraw and become angry and fearful.

The second case reported by DeVries introduces Enkeri, a Masai boy born in the same year as Hamadi. According to traditional temperament measures, Enkeri scored as "difficult." He was the classic "fussy" child—very intense, persistent, overactive, irregular in his daily behavior patterns and not easily distracted or consolable. In a Western culture, these temperament traits would place Enkeri at risk for future adjustment problems. However, the behaviors that Western mothers dislike and describe as undesirable and difficult are valued highly in Masai society.

The Masai are an agricultural society and often have to struggle for survival in an extremely hostile environment. In times of drought, when herds of cattle and goats are destroyed, infant mortality is high because families cannot rely on the usual supply of milk. Under these kinds of conditions, infants who show "difficult" behavior tend to survive at a higher rate than infants who are quiet and undemanding. Why? Because infants who cry are fed and attended to, whereas those who don't are assumed to be content. Consequently, infants who cry a lot are fed more and are in better physical condition, which contributes to their survival.

Finally, Meijer, Super, and Harkness (1997) have recently attempted to further clarify the nature of "goodness of fit" and find a systematic relationship between maternal judgments of "difficult" and specific dimensions of child behavior. In a comparative study of mothers in Bloemenheim, Holland, and towns near Cambridge, Massachusetts, the researchers reported that parents in the two different cultural settings systematically interpreted the causes of difficult behavior differently. For example, while more American parents viewed difficulty as inherent in a child, more Dutch parents viewed it as a result of environmental factors. Clearly, the interaction of culture and individuality are different in these two ecological settings, and the resulting behavior and the interpretation of it are strongly influenced by the presence of different developmental niches.

◇ CHILDHOOD AND THE EMERGENCE OF THE SELF-CONCEPT

If you were asked to draw a picture of your mother, what would your picture look like? Would it show a single figure in the middle of the page? Would you attempt to portray the most typical features of your mother (e.g., her hairstyle, her clothes, her facial features)? Or would you show your mother at work, at home, with her friends, or with her family? The way we think about persons, as individual entities or in a social context, is influenced by the cultural understanding of what a person is and what characterizes her.

◇ CULTURAL VIEWS OF THE INDIVIDUAL

After decades of research, anthropologists, psychologists, and sociologists have determined that cultural views of the person frequently fall into one of two main categories: cultures with either a collectivist view or cultures with an individualistic view of the person. Not surprisingly, the collectivist/individualist distinction coincides with the distinction between Asian and Western cultures. How does the Asian/collectivist concept of the person differ from the Western/individualistic view? Perhaps this distinction can be best understood by using several of our themes (cross-cultural perspective, ecological systems approach, and the developmental niche) as a way of looking at life within a number of culturally diverse environments.

Individualism and Collectivism in a Balinese Village

Anthropologist Clifford Geertz (1973) spent years studying the lives of people in a small Balinese village. Among his many observations were those involving cultural customs related to the manner in which individuals describe and address another person. He found that the Balinese use six distinct labels to address another person and to identify him as a unique individual: (1) personal names, (2) birth-order names (first child, second child), (3) kinship terms (sister, aunt), (4) tekonyms, (5) status titles or cast names, and (6) public titles or occupational titles.

Personal names are rarely used among the Balinese. These and birth-order names are principally applied to children or adolescents. Kinship names are also used sparingly. Balinese most frequently use tekonyms when referring to or addressing each other. **Tekonyms** describe the relationship between two people, typically *the relationship between older and younger family members*. Geertz points out that as soon as the first child is born and named, the parents are referred to as "mother-of" and "father-of" that particular child. These terms then take on the function of personal names. Only after the first grandchild is born are the parents addressed as "grandmother-of" and "grandfather-of" a child. This approach to identifying individuals is quite different from practices found in Western cultures and denotes a very different understanding of the person, emphasizing the connectedness of the individual with the family—what Bronfenbrenner would view as part of the microsystem. On the other hand, individuals in Western cultures are designated by personal names, and their personhood is not usually derived from their relationship to others. The only comparable practice in Western culture may be the custom of the bride giving up her personal name and taking on her husband's family name. She may then be referred to as "Mrs. John Smith," creating a new identity that reflects her relationship to her husband. However, this practice is not as common as it once was, and married women are finding new ways of both retaining their premarriage identity and denoting their new relationship. Some women continue to be known by their maiden name, some place a hyphen between their maiden name and their husband's last name, and many find other ways to express their individuality.

Personhood in China, Japan, and the United States

Hsu (1985) has presented an interesting description and analysis of the concepts of personality and self in three very different cultures—China, Japan, and the United States. We chose this exemplary study to illustrate some of the existing cultural differences in conceiving of what defines a "person." We should note, however, that Hsu's study is not exhaustive, and thus we cannot draw conclusions about many other cultural concepts that exist. Hsu emphasizes the similarities between the two Asian cultures and their dissimilarity with North American culture. For example, the Asian concept of *jen* (Chinese for "*man*," used also in the Japanese language) is defined by a person's place within her system of relationships (again reminiscent of the microsystem in the ecological systems approach). According to Hsu, personal wishes, motives, and feelings are only important to the individual in relation to their consequences for interpersonal relationships.

In China, the immediate family provides a place for the person and a framework for his sense of personhood. Similarly, in Japan an individual's personhood is also tied to one's relationship with others and not to oneself as an individual. However, in Japanese culture it is not exclusively kin members that provide a consistent system of social relationships. Japanese families are more willing to accept unrelated individuals into their family circle. Hsu concludes that in general, Japanese tend to form larger social networks than do Chinese because they have fewer ties to their kin and need to seek their social network outside the immediate kinship group.

In contrast, American culture subscribes to the belief that a person is defined by her innermost feelings, thoughts, and motives. The individual's behavior as it relates to others is only an expression of these personal attributes. Personal boundaries are generally defined by the physical body (i.e., a person ends and the environment begins at the outer layer of one's skin). Personhood, therefore, is not directly tied to relationships with others. People in the environment are not considered a consistent feature of the person and thus seem readily exchangeable. For example, Hsu points out that the parent–child relationship in Western cultures is more voluntary than it is in Asian cultures, particularly after an individual is recognized as an adult. An individual can decide whether or not she wants to continue a relationship.

This brief discussion of personhood raises an interesting question: "What impact do these different conceptions have on individuals' perceptions of themselves?" After all, when I speak about myself, I am speaking about a person. My understanding of what it means to be a person must also apply to the special case of myself as a person.

◇ CULTURAL VIEWS OF THE SELF AS A PERSON

Before discussing culture-specific aspects of the self, we should point out that there are considerable similarities among humans in terms of the development of their sense of self. For example, psychologists generally agree that in many cultures individuals develop an understanding of themselves as distinct and separate from others. In addition, some developmental researchers argue that the sense of oneself as distinct from others develops within the first year of life (Mahler & Pine, 1975).

These processes help to lay the foundation for development of the **self-concept**—*the perception of oneself as a person with desires, preferences, attributes, and abilities.* The unique structure and content of the self-concept, as well as some of the psychological processes related to it, are largely influenced by one's developmental niche and the level of the ecological system (microsystem, mesosystem, exosystem, or macrosystem) in which one finds oneself at a particular time in the lifespan.

Culture-Specific Aspects of Self

As with the concept of the person, the concept of self differs, depending on the cultural context. Since the self can be seen as a special case of the concept "person," it is not surprising that cultural differences in self-concept parallel differences in the person concept. Those who write most frequently about the topic of self-concept tend to discuss cultural variations in relation to the dimension of individualism–collectivism.

Triandis (1989), who has written extensively about individualism–collectivism, suggests that culture-specific views of the self result from early exposure to differing values and beliefs about the person in general. For example, childrearing patterns in collectivist cultures tend to introduce and reinforce the welfare of the collective over the welfare of the individual. In contrast, parents in individualistic cultures teach their children that the individual's primary goal is independence and the establishment of a unique self. Based on these fundamentally different approaches it seems logical that collectivist and individualistic cultures should vary in how they view themselves. Some authors make a distinction between interdependent and independent selves (Markus & Kitayama, 1991; Gardiner & Mutter, 1994), whereas others look at Asian and Western conceptions of self (Page & Berkow, 1991; Spiro, 1993).

Figure 6.1 shows both the collectivist and the individualist conceptions of the person. The collectivistic/interdependent conception of self is defined by the individual's relationships with members of groups significant in that person's life. The larger circle of self touches each group, illustrating the situational flexibility of the self-concept: the self must change if relationships change. In contrast, the individualistic/independent self-concept remains relatively stable and consistent, because interrelations with others are not defining elements of one's identity. This is represented in the figure as a smaller circle that does not contact the groups that surround the person.

The Self in Buddhism

The Singhalese monk Walpola Rahula (1959), explaining the role of self in Theravada Buddhism, has written: "Buddhism stands unique in the history of human thought in denying the existence of such a Soul, Self, or Atman. According to the teaching of Buddha, the idea of the self is an imaginary, false belief which has no corresponding reality. . . . To this false view can be traced all the evil in the world" (p. 51).

The self in Buddhism, which is more a psychological system than a religion, is thought of as an imaginary construct that limits the experience of total reality. Page and Berkow (1991) compare the sense of self to a "powerful belief" that results from the "desire to achieve an [illusory] sense of permanence within the ongoing flux of reality" (p. 89). The focus on "self" clouds a person's perception and experience of reality because one organizes experiences according to this limited belief (self) and is unaware of the reality beyond. Once this belief is abandoned and the self "ends," the perception

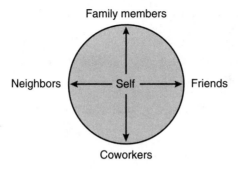

a. Collectivist/interdependent

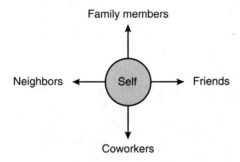

b. Individualistic/independent

FIGURE 6.1 Collectivistic and Individualistic Conceptions of the Person

and experience of reality are thought to be more comprehensive and unified. The loss of self, according to Buddhist teachings, is not the loss of identity. In fact, individuals continue to refer to themselves by name and are aware of themselves as individuals. Rather, the loss of self provides a new way of perceiving the world characterized by empathy, awareness, and deepened experience of reality (Beck, 1995).

These ideas are quite unlike what we find in Western thought, in which the self is viewed as a distinct and functional construct that psychologists have even succeeded in "assessing" and "measuring." Individuals are taught from an early age to become aware of, express, and satisfy their own wishes and needs. In fact, in Western societies, any significant or unusual change in the typically consistent and unitary entity called the self is considered pathological. When a person is "just not himself" or is "beside himself," he is frequently thought to suffer from disturbed perceptions, thinking, and behavior. Moreover, a person with multiple individual selves (or personalities) is considered severely mentally ill and highly dysfunctional.

Buddhist thinking exerts a very strong influence in many Asian cultures (Gardiner, 1995). How do Buddhist ideas regarding the self translate into the beliefs of the people in these cultures? Are conceptions of self the same in all Asian societies? Do individuals really deny the existence of self and strive to dissolve it in order to achieve a more complete understanding of reality?

Spiro (1993), while conducting field work in Burma, discovered that the cultural norm or ideal represents only one aspect of a culture's concept of self. Interviewing Burmese villagers, Spiro determined that the cultural ideal of the selfless person is not generally reflected in the personal beliefs of many people nor does this ideal fit the personal understanding of their spiritual aspirations. In short, at least in Burmese Buddhist society, the ideal of the selfless person does not make sense to many people. For example, the idea of a selfless person appears to conflict with other strongly held beliefs, such as those related to reincarnation or rebirth in a different physical body. According to Buddhist thinking, the form rebirth takes depends on an accumulation

Phra Bhavana Visutthikhun, Abbot of Wat Luang Phor Sodh Dhammakayaram, Damnoen Saduak, Thailand, finds peacefulness and wisdom in meditation. (Photo courtesy of the authors.)

of actions and behaviors performed in previous lives. Several of Spiro's subjects expressed the following reservations: If there is no self and it is not me who is reborn, then why should I be concerned about my actions in my present life? After all, it is not me who would benefit from my virtues or suffer from my misdeeds in the next life. The inference, from these statements, is that contrary to this particular society's cultural ideal, a very strong sense of self exists among individuals. Yet the selfless being remains an ideal and a norm in this culture. The occasional conflict of cultural ideal with personal beliefs is integrated into the person's identity without causing overt emotional distress or other psychological discomfort. Those familiar with Asian thinking do not find this unusual. In fact, Asians have generally been much more pragmatic in their thinking than Westerners and quite capable of resolving what for others would appear to be serious contradictions in beliefs or behavior. For example, in Japan, couples are married according to Shinto traditions (which celebrate life) but perform their funerals according to Buddhist practices (which celebrate death). In contrast, Western families often are seriously divided by issues centering on religious differences.

◇ CONTENT AND CONTEXT OF THE SELF-CONCEPT

Numerous comparative studies have revealed distinct cultural patterns in the way individuals conceptualize the self as well as in the content of the self-concept. In a cross-cultural study of self-concept in Japan and the United States, Cousins (1989) reported that subjects differed in the way they described themselves as individuals. Cousins used the Twenty Statements Test, which asks individuals to write twenty responses to the question "Who am I?" Results indicated that Americans used more psychological attributes, such as traits or dispositions, to describe themselves. In contrast, Japanese subjects frequently included the larger context when describing who they were. For example, Japanese subjects used more preferences and wishes, social categories, and activities in their self-descriptions.

Interestingly, the results from this study support several of the major themes we discussed in Chapter 1. For example, in terms of Bronfenbrenner's ecological systems approach, Americans can be said to view the self as part of the microsystem. The individual selects characteristics derived from early interactions between the child and the immediate environment, most notably the family. This conception reflects the individualistic nature of the American culture. The Japanese, on the other hand, select characteristics that emerge from interactions in social settings or institutions—that is, in the exosystem or even the macrosystem—where they have come into contact with the customs, values, and laws of their culture. Such behavior reflects a collectivist society. This contrast can be seen in the examples of Sergej and Yuen in the opening vignettes of this chapter.

In another study using the same methodology (the Twenty Statement Test), Bochner (1994) reported similar results when comparing adults from Malaysia (a collectivist culture) with adults from Australia and Britain (individualist cultures). Interestingly, unlike Cousins's study cited earlier, Malaysians gave more responses referring to personal traits and dispositions than responses associated with social groups, and members of the two other cultures (Australia and Britain) gave more socially oriented responses. However, overall Bochner's cross-cultural comparison showed significantly fewer personal responses and significantly more group-related responses among Malaysians than in either the Australian or British samples.

In yet another study, Miller (1984) found similar differences in perceptions between Americans and Hindus in India. When adults in these two cultures were compared, Indians attributed their actions more to contextual factors, whereas Americans explained actions in terms of personal dispositions. Miller suggests that these differences are developmental in nature (another theme weaving through our topical discussions). For example, self-descriptions among young American and Hindu children (eight to eleven years of age) did not differ in any significant way; both groups referred more to context than to personal characteristics. This suggests that Americans, with age, may learn to focus more on the person than on the context when perceiving and evaluating behavior. This also casts some doubt on the definition of the individualism–collectivism dichotomy and its effect on actual behavior (in this case, self-description). After all, it would be naïve to assume that cultural effects on self-concept and behavior could be reduced to two distinct categories of cultural values (Killen & Wainryb, 2000). This might be an interesting area for future research.

Additional evidence for the early influence of culture comes from a study conducted in the Netherlands (Van den Heuvel, Tellegen, & Koomen, 1992). Moroccan, Turkish, and Dutch children in grades six through eight were asked to describe five things about themselves, about one classmate who is like them, and about one classmate who is different from them. As hypothesized by the researchers, children from the two more collectivist cultures (Morocco and Turkey) used more social statements indicating group memberships, social activities, or clearly interpersonal traits (e.g., friendly toward others) when describing themselves or a similar classmate. Dutch children used significantly more psychological attributes, such as traits and personal preferences, in their description of themselves or a similar classmate. The authors conclude that the significant psychological differences found between individuals with an individualistic cultural background and those with a collectivistic background emerge at an early age and continue to develop across the lifespan.

Development of self-concept is greatly aided by language development and the words we use to describe ourselves. Pronouns such as *me, mine, you, us,* and *them* distinguish between self and others. Through the use of such words we learn to understand ourselves as unique and different from others (Sheriff & Cantril, 1947). In an early study, Mead (1934) suggested that personal names were at the center of self-concept development. Personal names help identify the self and distinguish oneself from others who are not referred to by that name. In many cultures in which names are carefully selected for their meaning, the person is thought to adopt characteristics associated with that name. These attributes become part of their self-concept (Olowu, 1990). How often have we met someone with the same name as someone else we know and compared the characteristics of the two individuals?

Self-Esteem

A recurring question in the study of self-concept is whether we can and should separate how we *think* about ourselves from how we *feel* about ourselves. Some contend that the content of the self-concept and its evaluation, which results in self-esteem, are virtually inseparable (Shavelson & Bolus, 1982). However, recent developments in self-concept research increasingly demonstrate that self-esteem may indeed be a distinct aspect of self-concept (Markus & Wurf, 1987). From a developmental perspective, Harter (1982) has shown that a global sense of self-esteem (perceived competence), distinguishable from the descriptive aspects of self, emerges around the age of eight.

Watkins and Dhawan (1989) argue that the distinction or lack of distinction between self-esteem and self-concept may be a cultural phenomenon. In several studies, these investigators examined aspects of the self-concept and self-esteem of children and adults from diverse cultural groups. As before, they found distinct differences between members of Western and Asian cultures. For example, in one study, Dhawan and Roseman (1988) reported that 62 percent of responses of American young adults were classified as self-evaluations, compared with 35 percent of responses among Indians of the same age group. In addition, most of the self-evaluations made by Western subjects were positive rather than negative.

These results, along with others, suggest that the distinction between self-concept and self-evaluation is more pronounced in Asian cultures, whereas both aspects of self are intertwined in Western cultures. As before, the explanation seems to lie in the individualistic or collectivistic orientation of the cultures involved. If an individual is independent and responsible for her success or failure, a focus on specific positive aspects of the self is an efficient protection against low self-esteem (Gardiner & Mutter, 1994). In contrast, in cultures in which individual success and enhancement are less important, personal attributes and accomplishments are not an immediate source of self-esteem and their value need not be emphasized.

As we noted previously, particularly in our discussion of the developmental niche and the ecological systems approach, childrearing practices and family environment are major contributors to cultural differences. These factors are also believed to be very influential in the development of personality and self-esteem, especially during the first years of life (Maccoby, 1980). Therefore, the fact that cultural differences in self-esteem are related to cultural differences in childrearing should not be surprising. Childrearing that emphasizes warmth and acceptance, together with consistent rules and achievement expectations, is clearly related to high self-esteem. For example, Olowu (1990) argues that many African children have higher self-esteem than children in Western countries because they enjoy the warmth and acceptance of an extended family. Such parental warmth can be provided by aunts and uncles as well as grandparents (Jegede & Bamgboye, 1981). Western children, on the other hand, frequently rely on one or two caretakers for their self-esteem needs.

In Burkina Faso, a senior Lobi man shows warmth and affection towards a young friend. (Bertrand Rieger/Stone)

Another example of the direct influence of the family atmosphere on self-esteem can be found in Jamaica. Phillips (1973) notes that it is common for Jamaican parents to separate and remarry several times. Children from previous marriages are expected to adapt to new environments and form relationships with new family members. While the family structures are very loose, children experience strict and authoritarian discipline from both parents and teachers. According to several researchers, this combination of unstable family dynamics and overly strict discipline results in a lack of self-esteem and self-worth in Jamaican children (Phillips, 1973; Smith & Reynolds, 1992).

◇ ADOLESCENCE: THRESHOLD TO THE ADULT WORLD

Adolescence is a particularly interesting period of transition in the lifespan. It begins with biological maturation and ends with society's acceptance of the young person as an adult. In many cultures a young person is considered an adult when she becomes sexually mature. A girl's first menstrual period is a celebrated event that signifies her transition to womanhood. She is now physically able to conceive and bear children and fulfill adult roles. In Western cultures, adolescents may be sexually mature but not considered emotionally mature enough to take on full adult status. Most Western societies have clear social markers that define when a young person is considered mature enough to assume adult responsibilities (voting in elections) and adult privileges (driving a car or consuming alcohol). In contrast to many nonindustrialized cultures, adolescence generally lasts several years in most modern Western cultures. According to Kett (1977), adolescents in non-Western societies assume adult responsibilities much earlier because these societies cannot afford to let their young people be "nonproductive" and engage in idle "self-discovery" for an extended time.

Identity Formation

During the adolescent years, young people encounter one of the most important developmental tasks of their lives—the establishment of an individual identity. **Identity** is *a person's self-definition as a separate and distinct individual including behaviors, beliefs, and attitudes.* Simply stated, the individual is trying to answer the question "Who am I?" Finding the answer isn't always easy and involves many of those within one's various ecological systems, including family and friends, members of peer groups, and teachers. Some adolescents find the journey particularly difficult and have to deal with serious issues, including antisocial or delinquent behavior. These topics receive attention in the section that follows.

Psychologist Erik Erikson is generally credited with the first complete analysis of identity development (Erikson's stage theory is discussed in detail in Chapter 2; see Table 2.1). Furthermore, he proposed the integration of identity, social roles, and the broader cultural context (Erikson, 1963). In his cross-cultural research he collected evidence for the universal existence of identity development, yet the exact process by which individuals achieve an adult identity is influenced by specific contextual factors. The basic premise of identity development across cultures is that it is rooted in the physical and psychological developmental changes an individual experiences during the adolescent period. Achievement of physical and sexual maturity is regarded as a prerequisite for fulfilling adult tasks and roles (Marcia, 1980).

According to Erikson, finding one's identity depends to a large degree on the manner in which four earlier childhood issues or crises have been resolved. These issues center on developing *trust,* establishing *autonomy,* taking *initiative,* and developing a sense of *competency.* However, as the individual matures and develops socially and cognitively, these issues take on a different meaning, and previous solutions may no longer fit the adolescent's view of himself. For example, while autonomy for a three-year-old may mean exploring the neighborhood or village without telling parents, autonomy for an adolescent takes on larger meaning (e.g., making one's own decisions or choosing one's own lifestyle). If the four issues of trust, autonomy, initiative, and competence are successfully revised and integrated, the young person will be able to resolve the identity crisis and achieve a healthy adult identity (Erikson, 1968).

What makes this task of **identity formation** even more challenging is the fact that individuals must take into account not only their own view of themselves but also the views of others and of society (Erikson, 1968, p. 22). In other words, *identity is achieved through a complex process of judging oneself (1) as an individual, (2) in comparison with others' judgments, and (3) in comparison to social and cultural norms.* It is this last sociocultural aspect that is primarily responsible for cultural differences in identity formation among adolescents.

Empirical evidence of cross-cultural differences or similarities in identity formation is surprisingly scarce. Only a few studies have explicitly addressed adolescents' identity development in relation to their sociocultural environment (e.g., Stiles, de Silva, & Gibbons, 1996). Two studies serve as examples of this type of research. The first discusses the implications of living in a collective context on identity formation. Wiseman and Lieblich (1992) learned, through in-depth interviews in an Israeli kibbutz, that these Israeli adolescents were concerned with issues of autonomy. In particular, they were struggling to integrate their own individual identity with the norms of the collective, which emphasized conformity, communal rules and control,

Personal identity is expressed in interesting ways throughout the world. (PhotoDisc, Inc.)

and close relationships. Asserting their own individuality and still fitting into the adult world of the collective were challenges for these adolescents not shared in exactly the same way by their counterparts growing up in more urban areas (Sharabany & Wiseman, 1993).

A second study examines identity conflict in two cultural groups within the same nation—Israeli Jews and Israeli Arabs. Tzuriel (1992) was interested in knowing whether adolescents exposed to multiple (and sometimes conflicting) sets of norms and expectations experience more identity conflict than adolescents with a less ambiguous environment. Israeli Arabs, who represent a relatively small minority in Israel, grow up experiencing elements of both their traditional culture and the Jewish majority culture. Would they have a more negative view of themselves or express more confusion regarding their identity? Among the six factors of identity examined in this study, Arabs scored higher on three and lower on the other three, showing no difference between the two groups in the total identity score. In particular, Arab youths expressed more self-confidence, a stronger sense of ideological and vocational commitment, and more genuineness. In contrast, Jewish adolescents reported more feelings of alienation and discontent with their appearance and behavior. However, they also recognized that others valued them and their abilities.

These findings suggest that Jewish adolescents experienced a greater struggle in their identity formation than did Arabs. Tzuriel speculates that the ambiguous environment, especially among Israeli Arabs, may actually facilitate identity exploration and self-awareness in relation to identity issues. Thus, a seemingly ambiguous environment may have a more positive influence on identity formation than common sense would suggest. With the resolution of the identity conflict, most adolescents achieve an identity with which they are comfortable and adjust their behavior accordingly.

It has long been assumed, particularly in Western societies and most notably in the United States, that the transition to adulthood is a rather painful and psychologically challenging event (Hall, 1904). However, research shows that the experience of stress during adolescence varies cross-culturally (Offer, Ostrov, Howard, & Atkinson, 1988). Some writers suggest that adolescence is more stressful when individuals are confronted by a large number of choices, as they frequently are in Western cultures. In non-Western societies, in which roles are frequently more clearly defined and choices are more limited, the transition to adulthood appears to be much smoother. For example, if the firstborn child is expected to take over the family business and assume care of the aging parents, it is not necessary for him to explore a variety of social roles to find a suitable adult identity. The important decisions have already been made for him. In contrast, those societies that value independence offer adolescents numerous opportunities to explore different social roles, making the search for identity more difficult and of longer duration.

◇ ADULTHOOD AND AGING: A TIME OF STABILITY AND CHANGE

Given a secure identity by the early to mid-twenties, along with a set of relatively stable personality dispositions, one might assume that personality would not change much after that time. Indeed, some psychologists argue that most aspects of personality are set by the age of thirty (McCrae & Costa, 1984). This appears consistent with traits that are related to temperament, such as extroversion/introversion, proneness to anxiety, energy level, or risk taking. However, during the transition from adolescence to distinct patterns of personality, development related to temperament traits continues to take place. In particular, young adults become more emotionally stable, socially independent, conventional, prosocial, and goal directed (Costa et al., 2000). Studies in several cultures, such as Germany, Italy, Croatia, Portugal, and South Korea, showed this pattern to be consistent, suggesting a universal

BOX 6.1

 CULTURAL VARIATIONS IN BODY IMAGE
AND SELF-CONCEPT

Body image refers to *one's concept of one's physical appearance*. Initially, the self-concept is characterized by such clearly noticeable physical characteristics as skin color, primary sex attributes, and body size and shape. Later, significant individuals in one's exosystem or macrosystem, such as parents, peers, or teachers, respond to physical appearance in particular ways. To a large extent, this social feedback influences how individuals see and feel about themselves. For example, many individuals with physical disabilities are sometimes considered weak and helpless and are even ridiculed. It is easy to understand how potentially harmful this could be to one's self-concept.

One's body image and the satisfaction with it result from comparisons with an implicit cultural ideal or standard. This ideal may vary considerably from one culture to another. For example, females in Western cultures frequently compare themselves with the "tall and thin" ideal considered desirable in these cultures. Such an ideal appears to be associated with high socioeconomic status, youth, health, and success (Anderson, Crawford, Nadeau, & Lindberg, 1989). In these cultures, young women are constantly exposed to images of slender (and often severely underweight) models (e.g., models used in advertising "Virginia Slims" cigarettes or Calvin Klein products to young women) and female cast members of popular television shows (e.g., Ally McBeal, Friends, etc.) who frequently appear almost abnormally thin. Through these means, women are encouraged to attain a thin body shape to appear young and healthy. Only after accomplishing this image will they receive the admiration and praise that positively influences their view of themselves as desirable and attractive. Attitudes toward overweight women in Western cultures are generally negative, and obesity is associated with a negative self-concept.

This cultural ideal of thinness leads to distortions in body perception in young women in several Western countries. The underweight "ideal" is mistakenly perceived as a "normal" standard, with the result that women who fail to attain the norm tend to perceive themselves as "abnormally" overweight (Stroz & Greene, 1983).

Are these distortions in body image less pronounced in cultures with a more "realistic" body ideal? Jamaican culture promotes the image of the "curvy and plump" female as desirable and attractive (Smith & Cogswell, 1994). At the same time, Jamaica is a popular destination for tourists from Europe and North America, who bring with them their cultural values and beauty ideals. Smith and Cogswell (1994) wondered if the Jamaican body

(continued)

BOX 6.1 CONTINUED ▬▬▬▬▬▬▬▬▬▬▬▬▬▬▬▬▬▬▬▬▬▬▬▬▬

image ideal would be strong enough to counteract the Western body image ideal. In their study of young Jamaican women, they reported that only 13 percent of all adolescents within normal weight range considered themselves overweight, compared with 30 percent of Australian and 43 percent of American female adolescents (Desmond, Price, Gray, & O'Connell, 1986; Paxton et al., 1991). This finding suggests that for Jamaican young women, the Jamaican ideal of the heavier woman dominates as a standard for young women's physical identity, at least as far as body shape and weight are concerned. Nonetheless, earlier studies of other aspects of physical appearance (Miller, 1975) suggest that Jamaican adolescents prefer Caucasian features and express dissatisfaction with their own skin tone, eye color, and hair texture, thus demonstrating that contact with Western culture has affected the Jamaican cultural definition of beauty. Although it was not explicitly examined in these studies, it is likely that young women who were dissatisfied with their body image also had a more negative overall attitude toward themselves.

In contrast to girls' ideal of thinness, boys in Western cultures strive for a large, muscular body (Jourard & Secord, 1955; MacKinnon, 1987). Austin, Champion, and Tzeng (1989) found strong evidence for the relation between perceived strength and activity and positive self-concept among adolescent boys from thirty different cultures.

In his study of Nigerian and British adolescents of both genders, Olowu (1983) noted that a heavier, well-built body was traditionally associated with wealth and prosperity among Yoruba adolescents in Nigeria. However, he also found that overall, Nigerian adolescents paid less attention to the enhancement of physical appearance than did British adolescents.

---

maturational change that is powered by genetic predisposition inherent in temperament. Before considering these findings positive proof that the majority of individual personality is tied to temperament, and therefore is genetically rather than culturally determined, let us consider the following arguments and explanations. First, culture affects the rate of adult personality change. For example, personality changes in North American young adults progresses rapidly at first and then slows, whereas the same changes in Chinese young people progress in a steady, more linear fashion (Costa et al., 2000). Second, the seemingly universal pattern in personality development in early adulthood may be tied to universally similar role expectations. At some point every culture expects their young adults to participate as productive members in society, become responsible, and conform to social norms. Many of these universal role expectations could account for the similarities in personality development across cultures. Finally, other aspects of personality are strongly influenced by changes that occur over the lifespan. Among these are self-concept, self-esteem, intellectual abilities, caring, and competence.

Social Clocks

Every individual experiences unique changes in life such as moving to a different location or having an illness, but some life transitions are culturally defined. All cultures have defined times when certain life events are supposed to take place. For example, at some point in their lives individuals in most cultures are expected to find a partner, start a family, produce offspring, and retire. These age-related milestones and the times at which various cultures expect them to occur are referred to as the **social clock**—*the schedule by which individuals are presumed to complete the major tasks within the lifespan* (Neugarten, 1979).

It has been suggested that these markers affect the adult personality in several ways. First, people adjust more easily to transitions that occur according to the social clock than to transitions that are "not on time." The unexpected death of a child represents an "off-time" event, because parents are supposed to be survived by their children. However, the same event, while unexpected, is not considered off-time in societies with high infant mortality rates. Second, a new stage of life requires changes in behavior that frequently result in personality changes. For example, new parents develop their nurturing skills, become less independent, and take fewer risks than they once did. Similarly, on entering the work force, an individual's competence in a particular area tends to improve and is accompanied by a change in self-concept related to that competence. Finally, certain personality traits appear to be associated with adherence or nonadherence to the normative social clock. Helson and her colleagues (1984) examined 141 women over a period of several decades and found that those whose lives followed the cultural expectations of women at that time (e.g., prescribed role of wife and mother) displayed an increase in tolerance, responsibility, nurturance, and self-control but also a decrease in self-confidence and feelings of competence. Those women who chose a career path and departed from their prescribed roles as mothers and wives and who adhered to the "masculine occupational clock" adapted to this role by developing high levels of confidence, initiative, and intellectual independence. Finally, those who did not adhere to any normative social clock (feminine social clock or masculine occupational clock) appropriate for their cohort suffered from self-doubt and low self-esteem. These findings demonstrate that the women in Helson and others' study have defined a developmental niche for themselves. Women responded to the feminine social clock by developing attributes that would benefit them in their roles as wives and mothers. In contrast, women who chose a different niche, namely the masculine occupational clock, developed skills and abilities that would help them succeed in that environment. Social clocks are the result of cultural expectations, and thus social clocks in different cultures vary.

The Female Normative Social Clock in Samoa

Margaret Mead (1928), in her well-known book *Coming of Age in Samoa,* presents a description of important normative transitions in a Samoan woman's life and the changes that follow. Mead's work focused mainly on girls and young women but she also discusses the lives of adult women. Although her work has been criticized for its potential biases, it is still a rich source of information about the lives of women in Samoa (Freeman, 1983). Before puberty, girls are assigned light household chores, and their primary role consists of caring for younger children. With the onset of adolescence, around the age of twelve or thirteen, girls are expected to assume more demanding tasks and responsibilities almost equal to those of adult women. Adolescence also is the time of first sexual explorations and experiences. A young Samoan woman is expected to be married by the time she is twenty-two years old. Although marriage is an important event, not much changes in a woman's life. She may move into the house of her husband's family, but her status and her tasks do not differ markedly from those of unmarried women her age.

A much more important transition is the first pregnancy and the birth of the first child. During pregnancy, a woman's life is limited by a number of rules. For health reasons, she is discouraged from doing work that is too physical or from exposing herself to the cold or the heat. At the same time, there are many social taboos for pregnant women. For example, they are prohibited from doing anything alone. This is based on the belief that most activities that are considered "wrong" are committed when one is alone. Any wrongdoing by the mother may hurt the unborn child; therefore, the mother is expected to be around others at all times. With the birth of a child the woman and her family gain status in the community, and the birth is a celebrated event. The arrival of other children is taken for granted and does not represent a significant life event. After this, women settle into their lives without having to fulfill any other specific social expectation. Some may become more influential in the political and social organizations of their village by virtue of the rank of their family, but their participation is a voluntary choice rather than a normative expectation.

Women who do not adhere to this social clock, who are not married, or who do not have children later in life are looked down on. Nevertheless,

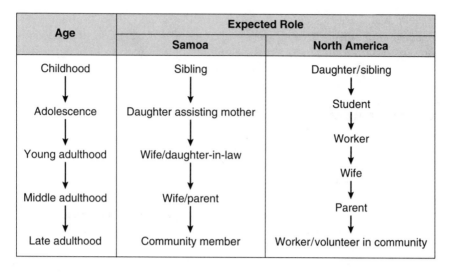

Age	Expected Role	
	Samoa	**North America**
Childhood ↓ Adolescence ↓ Young adulthood ↓ Middle adulthood ↓ Late adulthood	Sibling ↓ Daughter assisting mother ↓ Wife/daughter-in-law ↓ Wife/parent ↓ Community member	Daughter/sibling ↓ Student ↓ Worker ↓ Wife ↓ Parent ↓ Worker/volunteer in community

FIGURE 6.2   Normative Social Clocks of Samoan Women and
North American Women

Source: Adapted from *Coming of Age in Samoa* by M. Mead, 1973 [1928], New York: American Museum of Natural History; and "Personality Patterns of Adherence and Nonadherence to the Social Clock" by R. Helson, V. Mitchell, and G. Moane, 1984, *Journal of Personality and Social Psychology, 46,* pp. 1079–1096.

they usually enjoy some status in the community because they have developed valuable skills and knowledge that compensate for their lack of children. Figure 6.2 directly compares the normative expectations of Samoan women in the earlier part of the twentieth century and North American women in the latter part of the twentieth century.

◇ SUMMARY

This chapter discussed the development of individual, self, and personality across cultures and in specific cultural contexts. It was pointed out that some aspects of personality and behavior are clearly influenced by innate temperamental dispositions. The ways in which individual temperament is expressed and what is considered acceptable were shown to be largely dependent on cultural values and practices. Discussion also focused on cultural variations in the concept of person and self and their relationship to the early development of self-concept. While adolescents in most cultures experience the need to establish an identity, the manner in which they accomplish this and the specific issues and behaviors related to it show great cultural variation. Finally, examples from a variety of environmental settings illustrated how cultural expectations influence the development of life themes and patterns that continue to affect development in adulthood and beyond.

◇ FURTHER READINGS

B. Blauner. (1989). *Black Lives, White Lives.* Berkeley: University of California Press. An interesting study of cultural and ethnic differences within the American culture.

Sigmund Freud. (1961). *Civilization and Its Discontents* (Vol. 21). London: Hogarth. One of the most important writings on the interaction between personality and culture by one of the most creative and influential contributors to the field of psychology.

L. E. Harrison and S. P. Huntington (Eds.) (2000). *Culture Matters. How Values Shape Human Progress.* New York: Basic Books. A collection of essays that addresses the controversial question: Are some cultures better than others in creating conditions that offer a better quality of life to its people? This book provides an excellent starting point for a discussion about "cultural character."

Margaret Mead. (1973). *Coming of Age in Samoa.* New York: American Museum of Natural History. The author's best-known book; compares the lives of Samoan adolescents with adolescents in Western cultures. The comparisons have been seriously challenged, causing anthropologists to give greater attention to multiple interpretation of findings gathered by field research. Nevertheless, a classic and worth reading.

CHAPTER SEVEN

 CULTURE AND
ISSUES OF SEX
AND GENDER

Jessica and Jarrat are middle-aged adult siblings who grew up in a small town in the midwestern United States. As young children, they lived in a single-parent home with their mother, who worked as a secretary. Growing up, they experienced typical gender socialization for that time. Jessica, dressed in her favorite frilly pink party dress, enjoyed playing with her dolls and stuffed animals in her room, while Jarrat, in his sturdy jeans and T-shirt, played rough-and-tumble games outside. During their school years, Jarrat was encouraged to study science and went on to become an engineer. Jessica, who did well in school, hoped to have a career too but was raised to see her future role as a wife and mother. Both Jessica and Jarrat married and had children. One of Jessica's daughters is an astronaut in the American space program and another is a surgeon. Now divorced, Jessica takes care of her elderly mother since Jarrat lives and works in Germany.

Harin and Tippa, also in their middle adult years, grew up in rural Thailand with their parents, two brothers, two sisters, and various aunts, uncles, and cousins. As children, they played the same games, took care of their younger siblings, and worked in the rice fields. They both went to the same schools and enjoyed studying together. After graduation from high school, they went to Chulalongkorn University in Bangkok, where Harin studied to be an elementary school teacher and Tippa became an electrical engineer. Both are married today with families of their own.

These two pairs of mixed-sex siblings experienced childhood in very different ways. Harin and Tippa shared most of their activities and interests; Jessica and Jarrat grew up in two different worlds. Did Jessica and Jarrat deliberately "choose" different interests or were they "assigned" those interests? Was Harin and Tippa's experience really that similar? Did the upbringing experienced by these children influence the choices and preferences all four made in later life? How did culture contribute to these differences in upbringing?

Many introductory textbooks in psychology carefully differentiate the concepts "sex" and "gender." **Sex** is usually defined as *biological aspects of femaleness and maleness;* **gender,** as *acquired behavioral and psychological aspects of being a woman or a man* (Ashmore, 1990). This nature–nurture distinction provides the illusion of two nearly independent sources of behavior. However, on further review, it becomes clear that the two are not as independent as these definitions might suggest. Rather, it is essential to understand that the relationship between biological sex characteristics and gendered social behavior is much more complex.

West and Zimmerman (1987) argue that a person's sex is initially determined by applying culturally agreed upon biological criteria, such as external genitalia at birth. Depending on the evaluation of these criteria, the person is placed in one of two sex categories: female or male. This sex category represents the person's biological sex, even though the biological characteristics greatly vary from person to person and sometimes the classification as male or female is ambiguous at best.

A person's sex is determined by four different criteria: chromosomes, hormones, gonads, and external genitalia. In most cases, all variables correspond with each other and with the designation of female or male. Yet, there are exceptions. For example, one female may carry the XY chromosomes usually occurring in males yet show all "female" physical characteristics. In contrast, a female with the "normal" XX chromosomes may have a naturally occurring hormonal imbalance (e.g., adrenal hyperplasia) that causes her to develop muscle patterns and genitals similar to those of males (Nelson, 1994). In short, culture creates an artificial dichotomy of two mutually exclusive groups, "female" and "male," while disregarding the wide range and variety of biological variables. Once the nurse or doctor announces "It's a girl" or "It's a boy," the first major decision in a child's life has been made for her or him.

A great deal of social behavior is determined by one's assigned membership in one or another such exclusive category. For example, there are distinctly different sets of normative expectations associated with each category that guide the interaction between people in most situations. West and Zimmerman (1987) even suggest that gendered behavior is a necessary social requirement, since it helps identify a person as a member of one or the other gender, even if biological characteristics are ambiguous or lacking. For example, some traditional Islamic societies demand that women not reveal their faces to strange men. In this case, a woman needs to know if a stranger who approaches her is a woman or a man so that she may dress accordingly. Identifying another person as male or female provides us with one of the most basic social clues as to how this person is likely to behave toward us and how we are expected to behave toward that person. In this chapter, we discuss the developmental challenges involved in growing up female or male in different cultures.

Before we reflect on the role gender plays in every stage of a person's life, we introduce some of the issues and theoretical perspectives relevant in gender research today.

◇ DIFFERENCES BETWEEN THE GENDERS

Decades of psychological and anthropological research have produced evidence showing that differences between women and men appear in many known cultures. How many consistent differences exist and to what degree they can be rendered truly "universal" is the subject of much discussion in the field. We selected two aspects of behavior that are likely to vary along gender lines—activity level and aggression—to illustrate the relationship between gender and social behavior. Female children typically engage in limited behavior involving fine-motor movements, whereas male children engage in more exploratory behavior involving gross-motor movements (Rogoff, 1990). At the same time, young boys are encouraged more frequently by adults to engage in high-activity behaviors. Rogoff (1990) further argues that boys' behavior is more often noticed by adults and therefore attracts more attention and encouragement than does the behavior of quietly playing girls. Consider, for example, Brazilian children living near Rio de Janeiro. Girls might huddle together in a small group, stringing seashells to be worn as necklaces, while boys chase an escaped chicken through the village.

Cross-cultural research reports a convincing contrast between male aggressiveness/dominance and female nurturance/submissiveness (Block, 1983; Khan & Cataio, 1984; Maccoby, 1990; for a discussion of female aggression, see Bjorqvist & Niemela, 1992). For example, girls tend to engage more in interactive games involving cooperation and large amounts of verbal interaction, whereas boys tend to take part in more physical activities, often testing their strength or their skills in competitive games. Jessica and Jarrat, in our vignette at the beginning of the chapter, experienced these differences in their childhood play. In this connection, Salamone (1983) has described differences in the games played by girls and boys in Yauri, Nigeria. A popular girls' game is called *sunana bojo ne* (My name is Bojo). Ten to fifteen players,

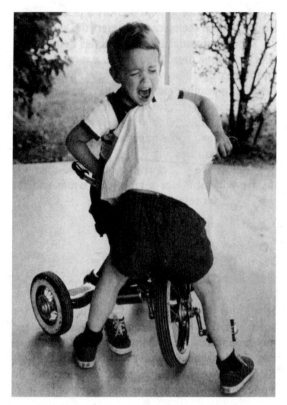

Gender-specific play in childhood is often characterized by competition and aggression among boys. (Suzanne Szasz/Photo Researchers)

holding hands, form a half circle and move clockwise while singing and dancing. They dance around one girl in the middle, who serves as the song leader. Eventually, and without warning, this girl falls backward into the circle, trusting her playmates to catch her. Girls take turns playing the role of the lead singer. In contrast, a popular boys' game is ring toss, where each boy tosses a rubber ring at a bottle or a stick with the goal being to get the ring to land around the neck of the bottle. This game involves a great deal of competition, since none of the players wants to be the last one to score and be teased by his playmates as the loser. These gender-specific games illustrate the interaction of individuals within their specific developmental niche. The traditional games played by girls reinforce behaviors considered desirable for females in that particular culture. By playing *sunana bojo ne* girls practice co-operation and interpersonal skills rather than focusing on their physical and motor skills. The reverse is true for the boys. At the same time, girls would probably not think of playing ring toss, because they would be teased by the boys for their lack of skill.

Nonetheless, not all games are gender segregated, as illustrated by Harin and Tippa, the Thai siblings in the chapter vignette. However, even in mixed-gender groups we find evidence showing gender differences in interpersonal behavior. Based on elaborate observations of same-gender and mixed-gender play groups, Maccoby (1990) observed that girls' groups have a more egalitarian structure and girls are more likely to make polite suggestions to each other. Boys, on the other hand, interact with each other by making demands or issuing direct orders. In mixed-gender groups, the interactional style common to girls was ineffective when dominant boys were involved. As a result, girls dropped out of the game, reinforcing male dominant behavior in the context of this particular game. Unfortunately, there are few cross-cultural studies of this type and therefore little concrete evidence to support the universality of this pattern of behavior. However, Weisfeld, Weisfeld, and Callaghan (1982) did find interaction patterns similar to those observed by Maccoby in their studies of African American children in Chicago and Hopi Indian children in Arizona. In mixed-gender competition (dodgeball), girls in both groups tended to be noncompetitive and passive and ultimately lost interest in the game. Some studies have focused on cross-cultural gender differences in children's pretend play. For example, Haight and colleagues (1999), comparing Irish American families in the United States and Chinese families in Taiwan, suggest that cultural dimensions appear to include the centrality of objects, the participation of specific play partners, and the extent of child initiations of social play with caregivers. Farver and coworkers (2000) compared Korean American and European American preschoolers and found similar patterns, suggesting that individual factors related to pretend play transcend culture and gender.

◇ THEORETICAL PERSPECTIVES ON GENDER DIFFERENCES

Biological Perspectives

It is generally accepted that females and males of any species exhibit distinct biological and physiological differences. These include differences in chromosomes, hormonal production, and reproductive capabilities. It is unclear, however, how directly connected these physiological differences may be to differences in social behavior. For example, there is evidence that testosterone level is related to aggressiveness (Wilson & Herrnstein, 1985). Since men are known to have higher average levels of testosterone than do women, they should be expected to exhibit more aggressive behavior than do women. However, it is entirely possible that in cultures that encourage aggressive behavior in both genders, women will be more aggressive than men in cultures that discourage aggressive behaviors in general. In addition, there is clear evidence that females show more aggressive behavior than males in certain situations, for example protecting their offspring from predators (Björkqvist & Niemelä, 1992). Consequently, we can only assume that physiological makeup may predispose women and men toward different behaviors (Lee & Daly, 1987).

The extent to which these behaviors are actually expressed depends in large part on environmental expectations and restrictions. Viewed from Bronfenbrenner's ecological systems approach, the degree to which a child's behavior becomes gender appropriate in a given society depends heavily on the ecological system surrounding that particular child. The macrosystem (or larger outer ring) provides general customs and values regarding gender. For example, it is customary in most cultures for men and women to wear clothes and hairstyles appropriate for their respective gender. At the microsystem level, girls and boys may be assigned different roles in the family depending on their gender and may be given different rights and responsibilities (e.g., taking care of siblings, helping with household chores, or working in the garden).

Evolutionary Perspectives

Proponents of the evolutionary perspective suggest that many gender differences may be explained by an organism's motivation to pass on genes by producing offspring (Buss, 1994a, b; Low, 1989). The particular way in which this is accomplished appears to differ among men and women. Women, who have the ability to produce a limited number of children over a lifetime, put their energy into creating an environment that ensures the survival of a maximum number of children. Such an environment requires food, drink, shelter, and protection from enemies. To accomplish this, a large number of a woman's activities are directed toward the family and involve food preparation, home maintenance, and creation of a protective network of other people who will assist in larger tasks and also help protect against enemies (a part of the microsystem). At the same time, women need to let suitable mates know that they are interested in having children. In other words, the woman creates a developmental niche (or a microsystem) that will be most favorable for the development of her children.

In contrast, men can produce an almost unlimited number of children, given the availability of women. According to the evolutionary perspective, men strive to produce as many children as possible because the more they have, the more will be likely to survive. To do this, they have to compete with other men. Under these circumstances, much of their energy is devoted to competing with other men for available women and the focus is on physical strength and aggressiveness.

Despite these different reproductive strategies, women and men have a common goal; this ensures that their children have the greatest possible chance of survival. According to Darwin's "survival of the fittest" doctrine, children have a greater chance of survival if both parents have healthy genes. Consequently, men and women can increase the chances of their children's survival if they mate with a healthy partner. Therefore, the goal is for both men and women to enhance those characteristics that are evolutionarily attractive in order to be chosen as mates. According to this perspective, men tend to exhibit behavior that conveys strength and sexual prowess, such as engaging in challenging sports and games or displaying symbols of wealth and status (ranging from a Mercedes Benz in Europe to camels in Egypt) (Buss, 1988). Women, on the other hand, tend to reinforce symbols of youthfulness and health, such as smooth skin, healthy teeth and hair, and a strong body, to communicate that they are young and fit enough to bear many children (Buss, 1988). Women in most cultures draw attention to these characteristics by artificially enhancing these attributes. If one accepts this evolutionary view of reproductive strategies, it may help explain those social behaviors that are considered specific to women and men in most societies. Regardless of the universality of reproductive strategies, culture-specific ecological systems determine the manner in which these behaviors are expressed. For example, women in one society may strengthen their youthful appearance by wearing clothes that reveal the leanness of their bodies and smoothness of their skin. This approach may not be appropriate in cultures in environments with harsher climates; in these cases women may color their hair or wear it in elaborate styles, since long and healthy hair may be viewed as a symbol of youth.

Socialization and Learning Perspectives

Beginning at birth, individuals are socialized into their particular culture and taught the values, beliefs, and behaviors that will permit them to successfully function within it (see Chapter 3). From an early age, as part of the socialization process, children learn to conform to the roles that culture considers consistent with their biological sex. In general, girls are rewarded and praised for exhibiting behavior considered desirable for a woman in that culture and discouraged from showing undesirable, or gender-inappropriate, behavior. In turn, boys are rewarded for male behavior and ridiculed if they exhibit behaviors reserved for girls or women.

By no means are "feminine" and "masculine" behaviors consistent across cultures. Occasionally, gender-specific norms may interact with cultural norms and modify gender roles. For example, while modesty and humility are viewed in China as culturally important values for all individuals, in other cultures these traits are more desirable, and more expected, in women than in men. For example, Chinese women have been found to be more self-effacing, modest, and less likely to take personal credit for accomplishments than are men, even though the cultural norm requires modesty from both genders (Crittenden, 1991). However, other sources suggest that these values, as well as gender socialization, are undergoing significant change in China and in other Asian countries (Ruan, 1991; Smith, 1992; Yi, 1993).

In addition to direct reinforcement and punishment, children in most cultures also observe same-sex adult role models and imitate the gender-appropriate behavior exhibited by these models. These behaviors are further reinforced and become internalized as attributes of gender-appropriate behavior patterns.

As Gibbons, Stiles, and their associates have demonstrated, these cultural "systems" in turn influence the gender socialization of children (Gibbons, Stiles, Perez-Prada, Shkodriani, & Medina, 1996).

In their studies, the researchers obtained drawings of the "ideal" woman and the "ideal" man from children and adolescents in several different countries (see Figure 7.1 a–d). Although they found a common tendency for the children to portray women as caring for children and the men as occupied in work roles outside the home, the researchers also found specific cultural differences. For instance, adolescents were more likely to draw the ideal woman in a nontraditional role as businesswoman in cultures with "masculine" work values, and the ideal man in a nontraditional role as caretaker in "feminine" cultures. The latter was the case in Norway, where adolescents more often expect the "ideal" man to participate in housework (Stiles & Gibbons, 1995). The researchers explain this finding by pointing out that Norwegians hold very egalitarian beliefs about the roles and status of women and men in their society and convey these beliefs to their children. Ideals may not always reflect social reality. Loscocco and Kalleberg (1988) point out that in highly "masculine" cultures such as Japan, positions of power are largely held by men, and women have only limited opportunity to achieve status and power and tend to remain in subordinate positions, both in the workplace and in private life. However, there is evidence that the role of Japanese women is slowly changing, affecting the image of women throughout Asia (Smith, 1992).

In summary, these different perspectives all propose a slightly different explanation for why some behaviors seem to vary with gender. The biological perspective considers gendered behavior a result of underlying biological and physiological processes. The evolutionary perspective describes gendered

a. Drawing by a fourteen-year-old girl from Mexico

c. Drawing by a thirteen-year-old boy from Guatemala

b. Drawing by a fifteen-year-old girl from the Netherlands

d. Drawing by an eleven-year-old boy from Spain

FIGURE 7.1   Drawings of Ideal Women by Children of Various Cultures

Source: From material from J. L. Gibbons and D. A. Stiles. Reprinted by permission.

behavior as the result of evolutionary processes. Gendered behaviors represent behaviors that have evolved as most adaptive, considering both biological attributes and environmental challenges. Finally, socialization and learning theories see gendered behaviors as the result of a person's individual learning history within a specific sociocultural context. None of these perspectives can explain the phenomenon of gender differences and how they originated. Nonetheless, they show clearly that gender, like many other concepts in this book, cannot be viewed just from one perspective. Keep that in mind when we now turn our attention to how issues of sex and gender relate to development in each of the stages of the lifespan.

◇ INFANCY AND CHILDHOOD

As we pointed out in Chapter 3, parents are the primary source of socialization in the lives of young children, and they introduce the important knowledge, values, beliefs, and expected behaviors of the culture. One aspect of this concerns society's expectations regarding appropriate behavior for women and men, or gender-role stereotypes.

Gender Socialization

One of the most exhaustive investigations of gender stereotypes and attitudes was conducted by Williams and Best (1990), who found significant differences between male and female stereotypes in each of the twenty-five countries studied. In general, passivity, submissiveness, affiliation, and nurturance were seen as more typical in descriptions of women, whereas activity, dominance, achievement, and aggressiveness were more typical of men. In this study, Williams and Best also found fascinating evidence related to differences in the socialization of gender stereotypes among children five to eleven years of age. For example, across all age groups, children in most countries were more familiar with the male stereotype than with the female, suggesting that male stereotypes are more dominant in their lives and are learned earlier. Only in Brazil, Portugal, and Germany did five-year-old children clearly identify more items associated with the female stereotype. Overall, Williams and Best suggest that gender stereotypes are well established in children by the time they are eight years old. After that age, they serve as powerful "blueprints" for behaviors that are reinforced throughout life. Gender-role stereotypes not only promote overt behavior and prescribe types of clothing and social rituals but also influence the way in which men and women in a given society view themselves and others. According to these researchers, by the age of nine, children are already applying gender stereotypes in their descriptions of themselves. In the case of the midwestern siblings Jessica and Jarrat, both did well in school and both wanted a career. Yet, Jessica was raised according to the cultural stereotype of women as caretakers. She cared for her husband and two children, and even after her divorce she continues her role as the caretaker of her elderly mother.

Feminist scholars (Chodorow, 1978; Rhode, 1990) argue that these gender blueprints socialize women into lower-status roles and dependency due to the differential positions of power either group holds in society. Since, in most known societies, men tend to hold positions of power and to distribute available resources, they frequently have the opportunity to define social roles for both women and men (Johnson, 1988). They also have the potential to use resources and status as rewards. To preserve male social dominance, younger men are rewarded for conforming to the behavior that later enables them to achieve positions of power in society. Among these desirable behaviors are competitiveness, aggressiveness, and dominance. If men conform successfully and "play by the rules," they will gain power, status, and access to resources.

Women, on the other hand, are usually discouraged from exhibiting behaviors that are reserved for men. Instead, an entirely different set of normative behaviors is defined for them. In many cultures, they are expected to be submissive, nurturing, and weak. This feminine ideal is defined by men in

Being a "homemaker" takes on a new meaning in today's society. (CoCo/Rainbow)

More fathers are staying at home to care for their children while mothers enter the workforce. (Ronald Mackechnie/Stone)

order to preserve male privilege. The idea is that weak and submissive individuals are not likely to compete for resources and power (Johnson, 1988). By conforming to this feminine ideal, women become attractive and gain the recognition of powerful men. In turn, they may be rewarded by receiving indirect access to power and resources. Women who refuse to conform to the female gender role will be denied these resources and status. In this case, the differing social status and power of women and men represent an important part of the ecological system in which children grow up. Power differences between women and men are related to their differential treatment by society as well as gender differences in behavior.

Low (1989) examined the training of children in relation to different reproductive strategies prevalent in several cultures. In polygynous societies, in which it is customary for men to have multiple reproductive partners, the competition among men for women is very strong. In polygynous societies like those of sub-Saharan Africa, young boys are taught to be aggressive and competitive. In societies in which monogamy or even polyandry prevails, the number of reproductive partners is restricted, and men are not engaged in competition to the same extent. For example, the role and socialization of boys in Nyinba, Tibet, are quite different. They are taught cooperation and sharing rather than competition and aggressiveness, since they will one day share a common wife and children with one or more men (Levine, 1980). In addition, polyandrous societies grant women more control over resources and more independence from one particular man. Consequently, socialization of girls focuses more on independence and assertiveness and less on obedience and submissiveness.

Cultural Influences on Female and Male Socialization

In spite of the widespread similarities in gender-role expectations across cultures, there are distinct differences in how gender-related behaviors are transmitted to young girls and boys (Davenport & Yurich, 1991; Maccoby, 1998). Depending on availability of role models, displays of expected role behavior, or influence of socialization agents, children in different cultures experience their socialization differently. Examples from Russia and New Guinea illustrates this point.

Socialization in Russia

Kerig, Alyoshina, and Volovich (1993) present a revealing description of male and female socialization and the conflicts that sometimes result from socialization practices running contrary to gender-role expectations. In Russian society, children are surrounded by female caretakers (mothers, teachers, doctors, day-care workers), whereas men are relatively little involved in family and household matters. This situation provides a young girl with many female role models in different familial and professional roles. She is presented with an image of women that is versatile and active, and she has the opportunity to practice behavior appropriate for her gender, following that of her mother or other female role models. As a consequence, she is socialized into a very active and dominant role. This socialization pattern is continued in adolescence and adulthood.

Russian society expects women to be as involved in the workforce as are men and to take over most of the housework. This dual identity reinforces the image of the woman as active and dominant. However, the Russian stereotype expects women to be passive and obedient; active, masculine behaviors are viewed as highly undesirable. This apparent contradiction between stereotype and social norm provides a dilemma for Russian women unless they are very flexible in their behavior and adjust to the demands of different situations. At home and at work, they need to be active and energetic, but in their social interactions with men they need to be feminine (i.e., passive and weak). In this way, Russian society has created an ecological system for women in which the values and norms representative of the microsystem (interactions with men in the immediate environment) are at odds with the values and norms of the exosystem (expected economic contribution and role as the head of household).

Russian boys, on the other hand, have few opportunities to practice active, dominant behavior. They are surrounded by female authority figures and caretakers involved in female activities. At the same time, Russian culture strongly disapproves of aggressiveness and emphasizes cooperation and caring. As a result of these social constraints, a young boy frequently withdraws and responds with passivity, which represents highly unmasculine behavior. Understandably, a young boy experiences a certain amount of confusion trying to define his gender identity in a context in which he is not able to observe or practice masculine behavior. Only later in adolescence do many young men compensate for their lack of practice of masculine behavior by becoming involved in motorcycle gangs or even engaging in antisocial activities such as vandalism, substance abuse, and physical and sexual abuse of women. (See Box 7.1 for more on violence against women.)

Socialization in New Guinea

In Sambia culture in Papua New Guinea, male aggression plays a salient role in the development of men and women over the lifespan (Herdt, 1986). For example, during childhood boys often are treated in aggressive ways by older men to teach them obedience and to serve as punishment for "unmanly" behavior. Young boys direct their aggression toward peers, younger siblings, and women in their families. At the same time, women and girls are discouraged from showing any aggressive behavior. Instead, they are expected to show the qualities of passivity and subordination.

After their first initiation ritual, which customarily consists of physical thrashing and ritualized nose bleeding, boys are separated from their families and go to live in the "men's house," where they are under the constant supervision of elders who also serve as powerful role models. Boys are encouraged to act aggressively toward their peers in competition to attain status; occasionally, aggressive behavior is even directed toward an elder for this same purpose. However, at this stage, boys are still the main target of aggressive treatment by their elders. Separation from boys also represents a change in the lives of girls. They are introduced to a more active role, namely taking responsibility for many household tasks. During this time, they are frequently victims of aggressive attacks by younger brothers or older boys who are attempting to establish their warrior status.

By the time of puberty, young men have learned to express their aggression toward women in their tribe as well as women of other tribes as

BOX 7.1

 VIOLENCE
AGAINST WOMEN

Physical and sexual abuse of women exists and has existed in all societies. Cultures differ in the degree to which intergender violence falls within culturally accepted behavior. Physical violence toward women is accepted in Sambian culture and condoned as a part of male socialization. While generally viewed negatively in China, it is justified in certain instances (e.g., when resulting from alcohol use or as "punishment" of one's wife). In Russia, aggression against women is socially unacceptable but does occur frequently when men "act out" their masculinity as a reaction to their "demasculinizing" socialization.

In a cross-cultural examination of variations in the occurrence and meaning of rape, Rozee (1993) randomly selected thirty-five world societies and analyzed available data. She found that rape, defined as sexual contact against a woman's will, occurred in all of these societies. In 97 percent of these cultures, some form of rape existed that fell within social norms for acceptable behavior. These types of rape included marital rape, ceremonial rape, exchange rape (in which guests or friends are granted access to one's wife as a friendly gesture), or punitive rape (done to reprimand a woman). Not unlike other aspects of gender relations, violence against women, and rape in particular, is also directly related to social stratification. Rozee argues that "in every known society, women and men have different status, with males having authority over females. Rape legitimizes male authority, assures the right of sexual access to females, confirms entitlement, and demonstrates male dominance. Rape is prevalent precisely because it is so intimately tied to the meaning of gender in all societies, including our own" (p. 512).

evidence of their dominance as warriors and for the sake of aggression itself. Yet, elders still use nose bleeding and other aggressive rituals to instill a strong sense of obedience and discipline in young men, because the ultimate goal of male socialization is controlled aggressiveness. Impulsiveness and self-indulgent aggression are undesirable in warriors and tribal leaders and are occasionally punished with death. The only socially recognized expression of aggression by Sambia women lies in their acknowledged powers of sorcery. Since sorcery is greatly feared by men, female shamans are used in rituals to keep male aggressiveness in balance and provide peace within the village.

In conclusion, one cannot view the socialization of certain behaviors independently from the cultural context. Cultures define the basic values and ideals as well as the agents who teach the values and the settings in which they are taught. In turn, individuals growing up in this developmental niche will shape their environment by adding individual characteristics to that setting. As a consequence, the socialization experiences of youngsters in Russia and Papua New Guinea take very different paths.

Gender Relationships in Childhood

Apart from parents and caretakers, the role of peers in childhood socialization cannot be underestimated. In fact, Hartup (1983) points out that "in most cultures, the significance of peer relations as a socialization context is rivaled only by the family" (p. 103). Consequently, same-sex and mixed-sex peer groups provide an effective context for the observation and practice of gender-role behaviors. For example, it could be argued that early gender segregation indicates very large differences in normative expectations for women and men in that society; these differences need to be reinforced early. On the other hand, mixed-sex peer groups throughout childhood and the relative lack of differential treatment of the two genders may indicate greater equality between the genders in adulthood. The examples of our two pairs of siblings in the chapter vignettes may suggest that this is indeed the case. Harin and Tippa shared many of their childhood activities and did not experience much gender segregation. As adults, they have chosen professions that appear to contradict the stereotype associated with many occupations, suggesting greater flexibility of gender roles. However, a look at different cultures shows that the relationship between gender relations in childhood and adult gender-role behavior is not always as linear.

Overall, there is a large range of cultural variation in the extent to which children's playmates are of both genders or predominantly of the same gender (Whiting & Whiting, 1975). Gender relations in play groups range from completely segregated, to segregated for part of the time, to inter-gender relations. The makeup of play groups can be more or less dictated by cultural conventions that include the gender constellation of the groups (Leaper, 1994).

As an example, there seems to be clear evidence that even though most activities are not gender segregated by definition in early childhood, children in North America prefer to interact with peers of their own gender (Maccoby, 1990; 1998). On the other hand, Harkness and Super (1985) report that rural Kenyan children are segregated by gender starting at about six years due to gender-specific duties expected from boys and girls. However, regardless of this culturally imposed segregation, the authors argue that there is evidence that children do not interact more with same-sex peers than with opposite-sex peers, even when more of them are present. According to an early description of Truk society in Oceania, children there associate with playmates of both sexes without distinction until the age of about six, when groups tend to become more structured according to gender (Gladwin & Sarason, 1953). Similarly, Sambia culture in Papua New Guinea (mentioned in the previous section) does not formally segregate girls and boys until they are six or seven years old. However, expectations for girls differ greatly in this mixed-gender setting. While boys are expected to assert their dominance toward younger siblings and female peers, girls are expected to be passive and endure the often hostile behavior expressed by boys without complaining. Beginning in middle childhood, girls and boys are strictly segregated and are taught gender-appropriate tasks and behaviors by their peers and their elders. (This mentoring or teaching of gender roles is a good example of children passing through Vygotsky's zone of proximal development, being guided by adults and capable peers; see the discussion in Chapter 2.) Gender relations are nearly taboo until marriage, when submissive women and aggressive men practice their now well-socialized behavior patterns in their relationships with each other (Herdt, 1986).

Another example of gender segregation in childhood and its consequences for gender relations later on is reported in an early study from Taiwan (Wolf, 1972). In childhood, relationships between girls and boys are characterized by competition, especially in schools that are coed but separate girls and boys in the classroom and during other activities. Interactions between girls and boys are characterized by heated exchanges in which it is the goal to insult the other group. Wolf reports that this hostile attitude is often carried into adulthood, when women and men are expected to cooperate in usually mixed-gender work settings. These examples demonstrate the different arrangements for gender interactions during childhood (and beyond) in various cultures. However, even when culturally determined arrangements are seemingly similar, there are variations in how gender relations develop. For example, even lacking cultural demands for gender segregation, younger children nonetheless may prefer to interact more with same-sex peers (Farver & Howes, 1988; Maccoby, 1990; Maccoby, 1998; Super & Harkness, 1994).

Harkness and Super (1985) explain these differences in terms of the developmental niche, in which children actively explore and define gender relations within the parameters set by cultural expectations. For example, the girls in Yauri (discussed in an earlier section) may enjoy the playful and musical interaction with other girls while playing "My name is Bojo" more than the teasing, competitive atmosphere boys thrive on during their ring toss game. Yet, there may be "androgynous" children who feel comfortable with either gender role and create their own developmental niche within the confines of their culture. These children may engage in activities with both genders or create suitable variations of existing gender-specific activities. For example, playing baseball may not be appropriate for a girl in the United States, but playing a variation of the game, such as softball, is entirely acceptable.

◇ ADOLESCENCE

Markers of Sexual Maturation

In addition to clear biological markers of sexual maturity, such as menarche and development of breasts in girls and growth of facial hair and change of voice in boys, there are distinct cultural markers that indicate a readiness among women and men to find a sexual partner. Biological and cultural markers may or may not coincide, depending on cultural norms. For example, Hindus consider a girl sexually mature with the onset of menstruation. However, a sexually mature unmarried woman living in her father's house is considered unfortunate for all involved, and it is the duty of the father to marry off his daughter as soon as she reaches puberty or even before (Kumari, 1988).

The transition from adolescence to adulthood is often considered a highly spiritual event that is celebrated with elaborate initiation ceremonies. These ceremonies often involve a ritual change of hairstyle, clothing, tattoos, or even circumcision in order to make the newly gained status as adult visible to all. However, transition to adulthood is not always marked by one single event. Mayan culture, for example, considers young women and men sexually mature and allows them to find a mate when they begin to feel sexual desire (Bertrand, Ward, & Pauc, 1992). Parents or other members of the community do not get involved in the young person's decisions about who or when to marry. Bertrand and others (1992) report that this generally does not happen until the ages of sixteen to eighteen for women and twenty for men.

Sexual Activity and Cultural Taboos

Once young women and young men are considered sexually mature, they are prepared to experience their first initial sexual encounter. Across cultures, these experiences vary greatly in terms of how strictly they are guided by cultural norms and which forms they take. The expectation of chastity until marriage (particularly for women) is a norm among many cultures. Patriarchal societies and those based on traditional Catholic or Islamic values generally have very strict chastity norms. Consequently, young women have little or no sexual experience or instruction until they marry. In societies in which girls are allowed to explore their sexuality more or less freely, such as the Masai of Kenya or the Hopi Indians of North America, there are some legal or normative rules about the age at which a girl may become sexually active. Usually, the minimum age is no younger than thirteen or fourteen. Chastity norms rarely apply in the same way to young men. Instead, boys are frequently encouraged to engage in various types of activity in order to practice sexual behavior, satisfy their sexual desires, or express their virility and dominance. Young men's sexual experience is seen as preparation for a long-term relationship or marriage. It is the practice in some cultures for older women, frequently prostitutes or unmarried women in the community, to instruct adolescent boys in sexual matters (Ruan, 1991).

In some cultures, such as the indigenous societies of North and South America, communication about sexual matters is largely taboo and surrounded by myths, so that adolescents are left to explore their sexuality on their own. In their study of Mayan culture in Guatemala, Bertrand, Ward, and Pauc (1992) report that adolescents receive little education or information about sex. Young girls do not learn about menstruation until they experience menarche and also have few sources from which to learn about sexual matters. In contrast, boys learn about physical development in school, from friends, or even from television or movies. While these are informal sources of information, culturally sanctioned information about marriage is conveyed during a traditional religious ceremony. However, according to Bertrand, Ward, and Pauc's findings, this ceremony is considered primarily a ritual and does not provide practical advice and instruction regarding sexual relations.

In addition to prohibiting sexual intercourse before marriage, some societies have strict taboos about sexual activities. In China "the only sexual behavior which is acknowledged to be legally and morally permissive is heterosexual intercourse within a monogamous marriage. Every imaginable variation is explicitly proscribed. Thus, prostitution, polygamy, premarital and extramarital intercourse (including cohabitation), homosexuality, and variant sexual behaviors are illegal" (Ruan, 1991, p. 159). Traditional Hinduism prescribes a very specific definition of sexuality, and following that definition is absolutely essential. Any unnatural sexual activity, including extramarital relations or homosexuality, results in losing one's caste, mutilation, or even death (Kumari, 1988). It should be noted that these norms refer to the most strict followers of traditional Hindu teachings. In modern India, as in many other cultures, the norms themselves, as well as the consequences for breaking them, vary greatly.

Young adolescents in many other cultures are permitted to explore and express their sexuality in a variety of ways. For example, among the Maya in Guatemala, it is common to freely choose one's sexual partner. Parents do not have much to say regarding the selection of a mate or the age of marriage. Nonetheless, Mayan adolescents respect cultural traditions and generally abstain from sexual contact before marriage. Their interactions are typically limited to talking, holding hands, kissing, and embracing.

In cultures in which premarital relations between women and men are not prohibited by cultural norms, they are considered an expression of love and affection. Yet, how love and affection are perceived and expressed is, again, subject to wide cultural variations. In a comparison of college students of four different ethnic backgrounds, Dion and Dion (1993) found that Asian subjects of both genders view love relationships more in terms of friendship and caring than do women and men of European or Anglo–Celtic backgrounds. The authors argue that this view of love is consistent with the notion of self and others in cultures that emphasize collectivism (see also Ting-Toomey, 1991).

◇ EARLY AND MIDDLE ADULTHOOD

The life tasks individuals encounter in early and middle adulthood can be considered universal. In any culture, adults are faced with responsibilities related to childrearing and providing for themselves and their families. In short, they have to "make a living." How these responsibilities are distributed and what the settings in which people "make a living" look like depends, in large part, on the individual's ecological system. Cultural values, socioeconomic status, and family size are just some examples of ecological influences, as well as characteristics of the developmental niche. In this section, we look at the specific ways in which gender influences the lives of adults in different cultural environments.

Status and the Division of Labor Within the Family

Based on universal gender-role stereotypes and gender-role socialization, the adult roles of women and men are very different. Throughout history, and in almost all known societies, women take primary responsibility for childrearing and housework, while men are responsible for work outside the home. Industrialization and increasing economic pressures have brought about drastic changes that have affected the exclusive nature of this arrangement. Today, agricultural communities can no longer sustain all their families, and many men have to leave their villages and towns to find work in larger cities. As a result, traditional family structure is disrupted and along with it traditional gender roles. Women then find it necessary to seek work outside the home to fulfill some of the tasks the departed men leave behind. Also, in highly industrialized countries, technology has made housework much easier and less time-consuming, but sometimes more expensive. In many cases, these additional financial needs can only be met by an additional income provided by the woman.

Surprisingly (or maybe not so surprising to some), increased participation of women in the workforce has not led to a significant change in gender roles at home. Numerous studies show that men tend to participate more in housework when their spouse works outside the home (Coverman, 1985). However, even if both spouses are employed full time, childrearing and housework are still the main responsibility of the woman. Similar patterns are found in families in the United States, Switzerland, Indonesia, the Philippines, Taiwan, and South Korea (Charles & Hoepflinger, 1992; Sanchez, 1993).

Kerig, Alyoshina, and Volovich (1993) describe some psychological and social consequences of these changing demands and unchanging gender roles within some Russian families. Russian policies strongly emphasize equality of men and women in the workforce, and the large majority of families are two-income families. However, traditional gender-role socialization puts the burden of household chores and child care exclusively on women while men actively focus on their work and career. Women may request that their husbands take more responsibility for the family, but husbands are reluctant to become involved in gender-inappropriate activities and often respond by distancing themselves even further from the family. As a result, wives become more demanding and husbands withdraw more, causing great distress for all involved. The authors point out that "rates of divorce are higher in Russia than in any other industrialized nation except the United States, and that births among ethnic Russians have been rapidly declining" (p. 402).

Division of Labor in the Workforce

In addition to the gendered division of labor in the family, women and men are frequently segregated into different occupations in the labor force. Many occupational fields are either female dominated or male dominated. One possible explanation is that those occupations requiring female stereotyped attributes (e.g., nurturance) are female dominated because women have better skills for that work or simply prefer it. For many women and men, these gender-stereotyped occupations represent an important aspect of their developmental niche. Not surprisingly, in many cultures women tend to be teachers, nurses, or caregivers. Similarly, occupations requiring physical endurance, strength, or assertiveness (e.g., laborer jobs or executive positions) tend to be dominated by males. However, stereotypic gender roles are only one possible explanation for occupational gender segregation.

As his daughter plays with a baby goat, this Tibetan man grinds roasted barley into a flour called tsamba *that can be eaten dry, stirred into tea, or mixed with tea and butter to form patties.* (Dr. Melvyn C. Goldstein/National Geographic Society)

Occupational fields are also frequently segregated by status. For example, female-dominated occupations generally have a lower status than male-dominated occupations, regardless of the work involved. For example, activities that involve interpersonal communication and interaction are often associated with women because they tend to have stronger verbal and interpersonal skills. This helps to explain why more women than men become teachers, therapists, and social workers. Yet, few women are involved at the highest levels in international politics, business, or academia, all of which require a great deal of interpersonal and verbal skills (Blau & Ferber, 1986; Dexter, 1985; Reskin, 1988). Harin, mentioned in our opening vignette, who prepared to be an elementary school teacher in Thailand, probably has many more female colleagues than male colleagues, unless this occupation is highly regarded in his culture.

High-status occupations typically are better paid and are associated with access to greater resources, resulting in frequent wage and status gaps between some women and men (Blau & Ferber, 1986; Reskin, 1988). As a consequence, women are often economically disadvantaged and dependent on their husbands or other men as financial providers. Tang (1996) revealed that men in the United States with high money ethic endorsement (MEE) allocated significantly more money to the highest position and less money to the lowest positions (creating a large pay differential) than did those with low MEE. Women's allocation of money was not affected by their MEE. In a subsequent study, Tang and his colleagues (2000) conducted a cross-cultural comparison of pay differentials (in the United States, Taiwan, and the United Kingdom) as a function of the rater's sex and MEE. Findings showed that Taiwanese allocated more money to different positions than did their British and American counterparts. Men tended to have a significantly higher top/bottom pay differential than women. In another study focusing on the devaluation of women's work, England, Herman, and Cotter (2000) found that there is a "wage penalty" for working in occupations that have a higher percentage of women. The following section discusses how this societal stratification may, as part of the ecological system, affect interpersonal relationships in some contemporary societies.

Gender Relations in Social Status, Religion, and Public Policy

Social and economic stratification is deeply rooted in culture (Lee & Daly, 1987), contributes to gender inequality, and is reflected in relationships within the family. Assuming that economic power equals social power, the family member with the greatest social power will be most dominant within the family and thus be a powerful influence within the microsystem. Asserting this power can mean making financial and social decisions, asserting one's needs, assigning tasks to other family members, and yielding or denying access to resources. Since men generally have more economic and social power than women, they are likely to control and shape interpersonal relationships with a spouse and within the family. While women may manage everyday financial or social affairs, the ultimate power of approval or disapproval for decisions often lies with men, who may choose or not choose to exercise this power. Since these status differences are so pervasive, they are often reinforced by the religious and political institutions present within a culture's various ecological settings. Traditional Christian and Islamic religious teachings present arguments for the "destructiveness" of women as justification for the superiority and dominance of men.

Similarly, traditional Hindu religious texts assert that women represent an inherently dangerous spiritual force that needs to be controlled and restrained through all stages of her life (Kumari, 1988). Thus, first the father and then the husband are assigned the religiously sanctioned task of subordinating and subduing the woman. In interpreting this philosophy, Kumari (1988) writes, "Thus, the ideal Hindu woman is one who sees her highest good in her husband, is devoted to him with a religious zeal and is good and chaste. In other words, she is under the control of her husband, and the wifely role is one of subordination and devotion whatever may be the circumstances.

The woman's place is primarily confined to the home, her role limited to procreation and the bringing up of children and catering to the needs of her husband. Chastity and control of sexuality are the most important aspects of the role of a wife. The maintenance of chastity requires control of sexuality and a woman's sexuality should always be under the control of a man. Before marriage it is the father who controls her, and after marriage the husband" (p. 11).

Following these religious prescriptions is beneficial for women. Religious texts further command that the woman who meets this ideal is to be worshipped and held in the highest regard. Thus, her subordinate role to man is to be seen as an honorable subordination that contributes to spiritual salvation of both herself and the husband who successfully fulfills his task of controlling her "evil" powers. Demonstrating a certain ambivalence about "femaleness" in Indian culture, Bhogle (1999) points out the following: (1) the Indian constitution gives women and men equal rights, (2) India has had powerful women leaders (most notably Indira Ghandi, the former Prime Minister), and (3) an Indian temple contains as many goddesses as gods (wealth, learning, and power have been associated with goddesses rather than gods). Faced with this seemingly contradictory image of the ideal woman, when the modern Hindu woman, "due to economic reasons or from a psychological need for self-fulfillment . . . broadens the boundaries of her traditional sphere to include matters outside 'home and hearth,' she comes into conflict with her gender roles" (p. 282).

In cultures where there is an absence of support for working mothers, policies that prevent women from managing their own financial affairs, and neglect of health issues, women frequently find themselves in a position of dependency. Making changes in such policies would reverse these situations and contribute to greater gender equality and a reduction in gender-role stereotypes. For example, in contemporary China, the government's practice of assigning some individuals to selected work sites separates many married couples, who are only allowed to see each other for about two weeks in a given year (Ruan, 1991). As a result, husbands and wives have little opportunity to develop and practice traditional gender-role behavior in the home. In addition, China's one-child policy gives women the opportunity to make nontraditional career choices and increase their financial independence (Hong, 1987).

Furthermore, China has seen a dramatic change in sexual attitudes. Even though public policy explicitly prohibits any sexual relations between women and men outside of marriage, premarital and extramarital sexual activity has increased sharply (Ruan, 1991). While all of these factors may contribute to high divorce rates and marital dissatisfaction among Chinese couples, they also promote more egalitarian relationships between men and women.

Similarly, children's views of men and women have begun to change in countries where public policies have addressed gender equity. For example, in one study, when asked to draw their image of the ideal woman and the ideal man, adolescents in North America depicted women as working at a job and men as caring for children (Stiles, Gibbons, & de la Garza-Schnellman, 1990). Williams and Best (1990) found the same trend in Norway, a country in which the government has promoted gender equity for many years.

◇ LATER ADULTHOOD AND OLD AGE

In Chapter 9, we shall discuss cultural views on marriage. At this point, it may be sufficient to point out that men and women in later adulthood, in most cultures and religions, consider marriage to be one of the highest sacraments. However, in any society there will be a number of individuals who do not have a spouse, either because they never married or because they lost their mate through divorce or death.

Divorce and Widowhood

According to traditional Hindu beliefs, divorce is unacceptable. If men are not content in their marriage, they are allowed to take a second wife. After their wife's death, men are also permitted to remarry immediately. Widowhood for women, on the other hand, carries a strong social stigma. Without her husband, she is considered incomplete and even sinful. She is not allowed to remarry, becomes a social outcast, and simply awaits her own death. As a result, some women choose to burn themselves at their husband's funeral to attain spiritual salvation. **Sati,** or *widow immolation,* is a sacred practice (Kumari, 1988). Although the current Indian government strongly discourages this practice, a widow's memory is still held in high regard if she dies within a reasonable time after her husband's death.

Among the Hausa of Northern Nigeria, marriage also plays an important spiritual role. Adults who die while still married are expected to move on to **Lahira,** or *paradise* (Smith, 1965). While divorced and widowed adults are stigmatized, they are not met with nearly as much resentment as adults who never marry. Previously married women can still acquire some status by becoming prostitutes and remarrying later, an option denied to women who were never married. Similarly, Wolf (1964) reports a surprisingly high number of divorced women who work as prostitutes in Hokkien society in Taiwan.

In many Native American societies, a widow secures her livelihood by marrying one of her husband's brothers or another close relative

(Niethammer, 1977). Divorced women may return to their parents or marry another man. Divorce proceedings are relatively uncomplicated unless wife and husband share a great deal of property or the wife's relatives want to negotiate the return of the bride price paid to the husband. These examples of women in different societies show that even in adulthood, individuals create their own developmental niche in response to cultural norms and expectations associated with, in this case, divorce and widowhood.

Gender Roles and Status in Old Age

In traditional societies, age is frequently associated with a gain in community status. Older adults are respected and accepted as leaders who bring with them a wealth of life experience. Furthermore, they are frequently thought to have supernatural powers, and they hold important spiritual and religious responsibilities. Finally, both female and male elders are considered important to the socialization process because they pass on the group's cultural heritage to the next generation. In societies in which status is based on age and role as much as gender, older women may actually gain considerable power, both within their families and in society, once they have broken through the "seniority" barrier. Lebra (1999) suggests that this may be the case in Asian societies more so than in Western cultures.

Sangree (1992) examined two societies, with a particular focus on older men and women. The Tiriki of Kenya and the Irigwe of Nigeria are two societies that view their elders with great respect and appreciate the wisdom they bring to the society. On closer examination, Sangree discovered it is not seniority alone that leads to status and influence among these elders. A necessary condition for being recognized as an elder is grandparenthood. In order to achieve the highest respect as an older person, one has to have at least three living children. Being accepted as an elder represents a gain in status, particularly for Tiriki women. According to cultural norms, Tiriki women cannot be initiated as adults and are denied important positions in the clan or the village. Moreover, their activities are limited to domestic work and farming. As elders, women achieve considerable power and influence by being involved in community affairs, although their contributions are not publicly recognized.

Among the Irigwe, elder status derives from the cultural belief surrounding a mystical relation between death and birth. The Irigwe believe that the soul of a deceased person will eventually be reincarnated as a newborn. The departure of one soul is essential for the creation of a new life. Elders who are approaching death are held in high esteem because their death ensures the continuation of life.

Although Irigwe women are not granted formal leadership in the form of a public office, they nevertheless play a critically important role in community life. In contrast to Tiriki society, women have more opportunities to excel in certain areas and gain public recognition (e.g., as healers or craftswomen). As grandmothers, they achieve even more status and are held in high regard.

With changes brought about by modernization, the gender roles and status of older adults, as well as of younger adults, have changed, particularly in Irigwe society. Sangree (1992) describes how young educated men are taking over community activities formerly conducted by the male and female elders. Such changes are not characteristic of younger women. They are often too busy with their family responsibilities or limited by their lack of education to compete with men for jobs and status.

Among the Tiriki, male elders retain their influence in some local affairs. The culture has preserved the elder males' role as an essential agent in the socialization and initiation of younger males. They are also more involved in their sons' lives, since they manage their sons' property while they are away from home working. The influence and status of female elders are gradually disappearing, and there are fewer opportunities for them to be involved within the community. Overall, the status of Tiriki individuals in late adulthood and how they are viewed increasingly resemble the view held by other modern cultures.

◊ SUMMARY

This chapter discussed the development of women and men across the lifespan. Whereas some gender differences can be viewed from a biological perspective (see Chapter 4), the emphasis here was on social and cultural forces that contribute to the psychological development of men and women in different societies. In early childhood, prevailing gender stereotypes already influence the socialization of gendered behavior. Cultural customs and arrangements determine the structure and content of social interaction between boys and girls. These interactions become increasingly important during adolescence, when young people are preparing for their roles as adults. Aside from biological maturity, cultural norms determine when a youth may engage in sexual activity. In addition, cultural rules may dictate mate selection as well as acceptable or unacceptable sexual activities. The years of adulthood are characterized by clearly stipulated roles and obligations, many of which are defined by gender. Although many of these roles show great similarities across cultures, the status of men and women and their relationships may differ depending on their cultural environment and their unique developmental niche.

◇ FURTHER READINGS

John Colapinto. (2000). *As Nature Made Him: The Boy Who Was Raised as a Girl.* New York: HarperCollins.
   The story of a couple who arranged for one of their twin sons to undergo sex reassignment. The case, initially proclaimed a success, was considered a landmark in explaining the shaping of human sexual identity. However, thirty years later, the subject tells of his participation in an experiment in psychosexual engineering gone wrong. When informed of his medical history, at age fourteen, the subject decided to live as a male and shares his eventual triumph in asserting his sense of self against his medically and surgically imposed identity. Fascinating reading.

Leslie Feinberg. (1995). *Transgender Warriors: Making History from Joan of Arc to RuPaul.* Boston: Beacon Press.
   A historical look at the social and cultural constructions of gender. The author's discussion of gender issues, ranging from pink and blue to bathroom taboos to transexuality/transgenderism, opens readers' eyes to the ways in which gender shapes everyday experience.

Annette Lynch (1999). *Dress, Gender and Cultural Change. Asian-American and African-American Rites of Passage.* Oxford, UK: Berg.
   The author tries to show how dress is used to negotiate gender and ethnic identity in American society. The book explores important social events and the traditions of dress in the lives of young women and men in African American and Hmong communities.

Deborah L. Rhode. (Ed.). (1990). *Theoretical Perspectives on Sexual Difference.* New Haven, CT: Yale University Press.
   A unique study of the nature, origins, and consequences of sexual differences by experts in a variety of disciplines including history, law, philosophy, biology, sociology, psychology, political science, and anthropology. The focus is on male–female differences as well as those among women and the ways in which these differences mediate gender relations and social change.

CHAPTER EIGHT

CULTURE AND
SOCIAL BEHAVIOR

Shula grew up in a kibbutz not far from Haifa, Israel, where she lived with her parents and two siblings. Shortly after she was born, her mother returned to her job on the farm, leaving Shula in the care of the kibbutz day care. At day care, Shula built close relationships with the three or four women who were assigned to take care of her. When she was older, Shula spent her mornings in school and her afternoons at the communal area, where she and the other children played and worked under the supervision of adult kibbutz members. Even though her family expected her to stay in the kibbutz, she could not wait to leave to be on her own. She now attends Ben Gurion University in Beer-Sheva, where she dedicates most of her time to her studies and her political activities.

Manami and her parents live in a small apartment on the outskirts of Sapporo, Japan. Even though her father is an engineer, his salary alone barely supports the family. Manami's mother, Midori, gave up her job as an architect when her daughter was born. As a woman who was raised in a traditional Japanese family, Midori decided it was best to stay at home and raise the child herself rather than leaving Manami in the care of someone else. Manami has no siblings, and the first year in school was very difficult for her. She missed the undivided attention of her mother and did not get along well with the other children. After a while she built a circle of friends with whom she stayed close all through college. Now in her early thirties, Manami is an independent woman with a career in the competitive business of real estate.

Manami's and Shula's social and cultural environments were very different from the day they were born. How did these aspects influence their development as social beings? Did the emphasis on collectivism in the kibbutz instill values such as sharing and cooperation in Shula? How do single children like Manami fare in a collectivist culture? In this chapter we examine psychological and cultural factors that influence how people relate to their social environment and develop as social beings.

◇ INFANCY

During the first year of life, children actively begin to explore their environment; their curiosity seems almost limitless. To ensure continued learning and growth, the caretaker must encourage this exploration. At the same time, the child must trust that the caretaker is nearby and provides a safe haven when needed. The emotional bond between child and caretakers that allows children to feel secure and to know to whom they can turn in threatening situations is known as **attachment** (Maccoby, 1980). Early studies with baby monkeys (Harlow & Zimmermann, 1959; Harlow & Harlow, 1962) showed that infant–caretaker attachment goes beyond the fulfillment of physical and security needs. In fact, Harlow and others argue that the social interaction that takes place within a secure infant–caretaker relationship is necessary for the development of healthy social behavior.

Child–Caretaker Relationships and Attachment Patterns

The process of attachment over the first two years appears to be similar across different cultures. It is assumed that children have developed an attachment with their caretaker if they show distress when separated from the caretaker. As illustrated by Figure 8.1, most children in the four cultures studied by Kagan and his colleagues (1978) did not show behavior indicating attachment until about their seventh month of life. This does not necessarily mean that they were not attached to their caretaker earlier. Rather, they may not have had the psychological and social abilities to interpret the departure of the caretaker as threatening and to translate their attachment into social behavior. Toward the end of the first year, social development interacts with development in other areas and accounts for a dramatic change in the child's social behavior. At about seven to nine months, children first acquire **object permanence,** *recognition that objects and/or persons continue to exist even when they cannot be seen.* At the same time, infants begin to communicate and respond more by means of language rather than facial expressions

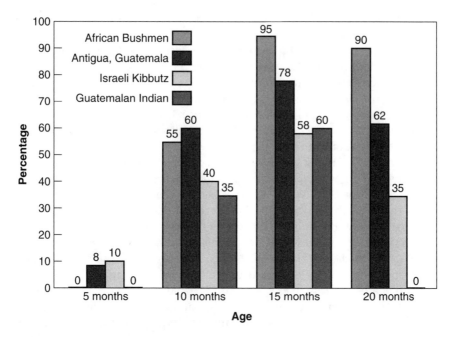

FIGURE 8.1 Cross-Cultural Comparison of Children Showing Distress in the Strange Situation

Source: Adapted from *Infancy: Its Place in Human Development* by J. Kagan, R. B. Kearsley, and P. Zealazo, 1978, Cambridge: Harvard University Press.

(Bates, 1976), and they actively check for their caretaker's responses to their behavior (Campos & Stenberg, 1981).

In addition to the similarities of attachment across cultures, there are also differences. Caretaker–child interactions and relationships are influenced by the environment in which they take place. From the two examples at the beginning of this chapter, one may conclude that Manami and Shula had very different relationships with their mothers during their first years of life.

Ainsworth and her colleagues (Ainsworth & Wittig, 1969) are credited with developing a standardized event (the **strange situation**) that makes it possible to observe the type of bond a child has with her primary caretaker. In the strange situation, a mother and child are placed together in a room equipped with toys. A stranger enters the room and sits quietly in a chair. The stranger begins a conversation with the caretaker, and after a while slowly approaches the child. The mother leaves the room while the stranger keeps interacting with the child. After a few minutes, the mother returns, reunites with the child, and the stranger leaves the room. Another few minutes pass and the mother leaves the room again. Shortly thereafter, the stranger reenters and tries to distract the child. Finally, the mother returns and reunites with the child.

The child's responses are recorded at specific times during the situation. How close does the child stay to the mother during the initial period? How does she react when approached by a stranger in the presence of the mother? How distressed is the child when the mother leaves the room? How does she react when alone with the stranger? Is the child happy when reunited with the mother? Specific responses indicate the type of attachment the child has with the primary caretaker.

Ainsworth and her colleagues observed that children could be classified according to three categories of behavior patterns when faced with the strange situation (Ainsworth, 1982). Children classified as *anxious/avoidant* will not pay much attention to whether the primary caretaker is absent or not. If they experience distress, they may turn to a stranger for comfort. On the mother's return, these children do not actively strive to reunite and be close. Children classified as *anxious/resistant* tend to stay close to their caretaker and become very distressed when she leaves the room. Even when comforted after the caretaker's return, these children will take a long time to settle down and remain anxious about the caretaker's whereabouts. Finally, *securely attached* children will be calm and not threatened by strangers in the presence of the caretaker. When the caretaker departs, the distressed child is unlikely to be comforted by a stranger. When the caretaker returns, the child is eager to reunite and will settle down and relax very quickly. Main and Solomon (1990) proposed an additional category—disorganized—to account for those children who appeared to have no specific pattern for coping with the discomfort created by the strange situation.

This approach to the study of attachment remains popular among researchers, with a significant number of recent studies (Lewis, Feiring, & Rosenthal, 2000; Waters, Hamilton, & Weinfield, 2000; Waters, Merrick, Treboux, Crowell, & Albersheim, 2000; Waters & Valenzuela, 1999). Although cross-cultural comparability of the strange situation has been questioned (LeVine & Miller, 1990; Takahashi, 1990), findings from numerous studies in Europe, Asia, Africa, the Middle East, and North America demonstrate that these attachment patterns occur in a wide variety of cultures (Lamb et al., 1985; Grossman, Grossman, Huber, & Wartner, 1981; Miyake, Chen, & Campos, 1985). In recent years, the strange situation has been extended to the Indonesian caregiving context (Zevalkink, Riksen-Walraven, & Van Lieshout, 1999) and to East German and Russian family settings (Ahnert, Meischner, & Schmidt, 2000). However, societies differ in the percentage of children falling into each of these categories. Table 8.1 shows the distribution of the three attachment styles in eight different cultures, according to Van Ijzendoorn and Kroonenberg (1988). Their findings reveal that the anxious/avoidant classification is relatively higher in West European countries and the anxious/

TABLE 8.1   Cross-Cultural Comparison of Children's
Attachment Classifications

	ANXIOUS/ AVOIDANT	ANXIOUS/ RESISTANT	SECURELY ATTACHED
Germany (3 studies; N = 136)	35.3%	8.6%	56.6%
Great Britain (1 study; N = 72)	22.2	2.7	75.0
Netherlands (4 studies; N = 251)	26.3	6.4	67.3
Sweden (1 study; N = 51)	21.5	4.0	74.5
Israel (2 studies; N = 118)	6.8	28.8	64.4
Japan (2 studies; N = 96)	5.2	27.1	67.7
China (1 study; N = 36)	25.0	25.0	50.0
United States (18 studies; N = 1,230)	21.1	14.1	64.8

Source: Complied from data from "Cross-Cultural Patterns of Attachment" by M. H. Van Ijzendoorn and P. M. Kroonenberg, 1988, *Child Development, 59*, 147–156.

resistant classification is relatively more prevalent in Japan and Israel. They also point out that the intracultural variation in classification is 1.5 times greater than the intercultural variation, indicating that the attachment patterns in various cultures are, in fact, more similar than different. It is important to keep in mind that similar behaviors in the strange situation may have very different meanings in different cultures. For example, while Westerners may interpret anxious/resistant behavior as "clingy," Chinese parents may interpret it as "bonded."

Cultural Explanations for Variations in Attachment Patterns

The contexts in which early social interactions take place are characterized by different parameters that define the developmental niche, such as characteristics of the caretaker, general conditions of infant development, and the child–caretaker relationship itself. As these parameters vary from culture to culture, so does the developmental niche, providing unique developmental challenges and opportunities for each child in his first months of life.

Caretaker Characteristics

Both the infant and the caretaker bring certain characteristics to the caretaker–infant relationship that become a crucial part of the ecological system in which the child grows up. This happens when some of the behaviors and characteristics of the mother interact with the characteristics of her child to create a unique developmental niche. For example, Richman, Miller, and Levine (1992) studied the behaviors Mexican mothers showed in response to their infant's distress signals such as crying and worried facial expressions. One factor that influenced mothers' responsiveness was their level of education. Mothers with more schooling tended to respond with more talking and facial expressions than mothers with less schooling, who tended to hold their infants more. In explaining these findings, the researchers pointed to earlier research suggesting that mothers with more education generally tend to initiate more verbal interaction with the children.

Caretakers also bring their unique cultural beliefs about parenting to the relationship (Harkness & Super, 1996). These beliefs may be culturally influenced, but they are also based on the caretaker's unique experiences. For example, Grossman and colleagues (1985) noticed that mothers in their German sample appeared quite unresponsive to their children's crying. Closer observations revealed that this behavior resulted from a shared cultural belief that infants should become independent at an early age and learn that they cannot rely on the mother's comfort at all times. In contrast, traditional Japanese mothers instill a strong sense of dependence in their young children by being available at all times (Miyake et al., 1985).

General Conditions of Infant Development

The conditions under which a child experiences her first year are often determined by the specific cultural setting. These conditions may influence the relationship between caretaker and child considerably. Two of these conditions involve availability of the primary caretaker and the number of other individuals involved in child care. For example, parents' economic circumstances or the structure of the community may require them to work outside of the home, leaving the care of the children to family members or others in the community.

Sagi (1990) speculates that the high rate of insecurely attached children in the Israeli kibbutz may be a result of the specific childrearing arrangements. For example, caregivers in the kibbutz (metaplot) are often assigned to work with three or more infants during the day, while all of the infants are watched by a single caretaker at night (in kibbutzim with communal sleeping arrangements). Sagi argues that this "multiple mothering" leads to inconsistencies in maternal behavior and may result in different (possibly less secure) attachment patterns.

Tronick, Morelli, and Ivey (1992) describe the childrearing arrangement among the Efe in Zaire. Here, children also enjoy multiple social relationships with other children and adults. However, particularly during the first year, the mother is involved in more than half of the child's social activities. This also means that children spend half of their time with individuals other than their mothers. For example, during the time the mother works away from the camp, her child is left in the exclusive care of other adults or older children. Even when the mother is present, other family members, the children's peers, or other adults are continually engaged in social interactions with the child. In fact, the authors point out that at a given time about ten people are within sight or close hearing range of the child. Unfortunately, there are no data available from this culture describing specific attachment patterns resulting either from these continuous multiple relationships with others or from the close relationship with the mother. However, the authors suggest that the children benefit from this setting in that they develop a multitude of social skills early in life; this leads to better adjustment in social situations later on.

Similarly, Indonesian children not only enjoy much attention from their mother but also from their older siblings. For example, Farver and Wibarti (1995) found that mothers and older siblings engage in different types of playing behavior with young children. In particular, older siblings were more active playing partners and facilitated pretend play more often than mothers, thus adding an important dimension of social interaction to the young child's microsystem.

In other settings, mothers keep their infants with them during work. Women in Madura, Indonesia, for example, systematically adjust their work patterns to accommodate their children (Launer, 1993). Several North American Indian societies utilize the cradleboard. Niethammer (1977) has written that "all [cradle boards] provide a firm, protective frame on which babies felt snug and secure (see photo on page 90). A baby in a cradle board could be propped up or even hung in a tree so it could see what was going on and feel part of family activities. After spending much time in their cradle board, Indian children became very attached to them. One Apache mother related that whenever her toddler son was tired or upset he would go and get his cradle board and walk around with it on his back" (p. 15).

Similarly, the Quechua use a **manta pouch** to carry their infants. This is a backpacklike device that protects the infant from the harsh elements in the Peruvian mountains and provides a secure environment close to the

A Peruvian mother uses a manta pouch to keep her infant near her. (Craig Duncan/DDB Stock)

mother (Tronick, Thomas, & Daltabuit, 1994). These and similar devices allow parents to keep their infants near them and to provide the necessary restraint so that children's physical activity does not interfere with the mother's work.

According to Bronfenbrenner, these general child-care arrangements could be classified as part of the macro- or mesosystems in the child's ecological environment. In setting the stage for the microlevel aspects of parent–child interactions, these general settings are crucial in the development of social relationships and behavior in early childhood.

Specific Settings of Parent–Child Social Relationships

As pointed out in earlier chapters, infants spend most of their time sleeping and eating. Thus, feeding practices and sleeping arrangements provide an important context for social interaction and bonding with caretakers during the first year of life. Consequently, these represent a central aspect of each child's developmental niche and attachment with caretakers.

Although the sucking reflex represents a universal neonatal ability, mothers in different cultural settings respond with a variety of nursing behaviors (Cole, 1989). Depending on the mother's obligations, both within and outside of the family, she may nurse the infant herself, employ a wet nurse, or bottle-feed the child. It is easy to see how feeding practice may shape the early relationship of mother and child. For example, the child may develop a different relationship with the mother if a wet nurse is present during the first year. On the other hand, babies who are bottle-fed may have a similar social relationship with their mother as children who are nursed, simply because the social interaction between mother and child is regular and continuous, regardless of the mode of feeding.

The mode of nursing for infants is also guided by cultural norms or taboos. For example, while the use of a wet nurse is common in many cultures, Cosminsky, Mhlovi, and Ewbank (1993) report that wet nursing is generally not accepted among members of communities in rural Zimbabwe. They believe that a baby nursed by another woman would "make the child sick, or the child might die from it" because "the blood does not go hand in hand or the other person might be dirty" (p. 943). However, concessions are made if the woman is in any way related to the mother such as her sister, mother, sister-in-law, or the husband's cowife. The duration of nursing is also determined by several individual and cultural factors, such as the health of the mother and the child, availability of suitable nutritional supplements for the child, and cultural beliefs about the developmental adequacy of nursing (Cosminsky et al., 1993).

Even after the child is weaned, the context of eating continues to play a crucial role in the development of social relationships. Dettwyler (1989) argues that "who controls what and how much the child eats, how this control is achieved, and the basis for these decisions" shapes long-term power dynamics between child and parents (p. 696). For example, force feeding is a routine practice among Ibadan mothers in Nigeria. The mother pours liquid into the baby's mouth while simultaneously holding its nose (Meldrum, 1984). While force feeding is not a common practice, parents in England, Sweden, the United States, and Newfoundland routinely use techniques to coerce their children into eating (Dettwyler, 1989). These techniques include feeding games (e.g., the spoon represents an airplane transporting each bite into the mouth), rewards for finishing a meal (e.g., dessert), punishment for not finishing a meal (e.g., withholding privileges), and passive restraint (e.g., high chair).

In contrast, Raphael and Davis (1985) found that mothers in the Philippines, northern India, and Sardinia, Italy, allow their children much more control in deciding how much they want to eat and when they want to eat.

Filipino mothers accept the child's refusal, Indian mothers may try to distract their children and offer them food again after a period of time, and Sardinian mothers use merely gentle coaxing to get their children to eat more.

Similar to feeding practices, sleeping arrangements influence early parent–child relationships and reflect cultural beliefs about infants' social development. Morelli and her colleagues (1992) observed that Mayan infants usually slept with their mothers, fathers, or siblings until the birth of a new sibling. In contrast, cosleeping is not very common among middle-class U.S. American families. In this culture, the newborn may sleep in the same room as the mother but not in the same bed. In such cases, an infant would eventually move into a different room when about three to six months old. The differences in these practices appear to be firmly rooted in parental beliefs and cultural values. According to Morelli and her coresearchers (1992), mothers in the United States believe that cosleeping interferes with their efforts to train their children early to become self-reliant and independent. In contrast, Mayan parents believe that the closeness that occurs as a result of cosleeping arrangements fosters the baby's social awareness and social learning. Japanese parents express similar views and consider cosleeping as a way to develop the child's interdependence with others (Caudill & Weinstein, 1969). Abbott (1992) observed a similar practice in a non–middle-class Eastern Kentucky community and, in a report (1997), indicated that 90 percent of children in her Appalachian samples either slept in the same bed with their parents or in the same room with them.

Sleeping arrangements and their implications for social development—the interaction between the child and the environment—represent a good example of the developmental niche. The presence or absence of the caretaker during the night may even facilitate and reward a certain attachment style (e.g., anxious/resistant). This attachment style involves social behavior patterns that are adaptive and desirable in certain cultures, since they tend to emphasize interdependence with others in a collectivist or group-oriented culture.

Consistency and Inconsistency of Attachment over Time

Much of attachment research over the years has shown that attachment patterns can be stable over long periods of time. This means that a child who is securely attached in infancy is likely to show secure attachment patterns through adolescence and early adulthood (Waters, Merrick, Treboux, Crowell, & Albersheim, 2000). On the other hand, developmental researchers are also quick to point out that significant negative life events may disrupt the stability of attachment. For example, a securely attached child who experiences the loss of a parent, parental divorce, psychiatric parental disorder, or physical abuse may change to an insecure attachment pattern in adolescence (Weinfield, Sroufe, & Egeland, 2000; Hamilton, 2000). As we discussed in the previous sections, the developmental niche plays a crucial role in initial infant attachment. These recent research findings further illustrate the importance of the developmental niche in the stability or instability of attachment later in life. Changes in caretaker characteristics (e.g., illness of parent), specific setting of child–parent relationship (e.g., parental divorce), or general childcare conditions (e.g., lack of social support for single parents) all are related to changes in attachment.

What about Harlow's assertion (at the beginning of this chapter) that secure attachment in infancy is necessary for the development of healthy social behavior? While this claim makes intuitive sense, a recent long-term study finds no evidence between infant insecure attachment and adolescent maladjustment (Lewis, Feiring, & Rosenthal, 2000). This suggests that even infants with secure attachments may be at risk for maladjustment later in life if at some point they experience negative life events and a transition to insecure attachment.

Research examining stability and instability over time, and adjustment in different cultures, is not readily available. Therefore, it is difficult to assess if we would find attachment patterns mediated by negative life events and changes in the developmental niche. A review of several studies of children (ages five to eighteen) in India raises some doubts (Sharma & Sharma, 1999). These studies included street and working children, school drop-outs, children of disabled parents, children in single-parent families, and children with disabilities, low birth weights, or chronic disease. All of these children in "difficult circumstances" were deemed at risk for psychological and social maladjustment. However, the researchers conclude that "at-risk" children who were "nestled or vicariously encircled in their family network, seemed to be coping and getting ahead" (p. 412). Although "at risk" from the outside, these children seemed to experience a resilience within their developmental niche that allowed them to develop and maintain a secure attachment, fostering healthy social and psychological development over time.

◇ CHILDHOOD

When children pass the stage of infancy, they begin to develop social relationships that extend beyond caretakers and the family. These relationships include children in the immediate neighborhood or at school and frequently become quite complex and multifaceted. Corsaro and Eder (1990) refer to these expanding relationships as children's "peer culture."

Peer Culture and
Social Relationships

In their review of relevant research, Corsaro and Eder identify three central themes that characterize peer culture from early childhood to adolescence. These include (1) dealing with confusion, concerns, fears, and conflicts; (2) resisting and challenging adult rules and authority; and (3) sharing and social participation.

Dealing with Confusion, Concerns, Fears, and Conflicts

In the company of their peers, children learn to cope with everyday conflicts and fears through fantasy play (e.g., role-playing the defeat of a monster). Children also engage in fantasy play to deal with anxiety and violence. For example, children in several South African communities, where daily life was often interrupted by riots or police raids, played out the violence and aggression they saw around them (Dawes, 1990; Liddell, Kvalsvig, Qotyana, & Shabalala, 1994). In a related study, Kostelny and Garbarino (1994) explored the drawings of Palestinian children living in Israeli-occupied territories. The drawings of the five- to eight-year-olds frequently showed themes of victimization (e.g., large soldiers with guns threatening small children).

Resisting and Challenging Adult Rules and Authority

Corsaro and Eder (1990) maintain that challenging adult rules serves to establish a sense of independence from parents. At the same time, children strengthen their peer group identity by developing rituals and routines that make fun of adult authority or challenge adult rules. Corsaro (1988) observed frequent violations of Italian and American nursery school rules prohibiting children from bringing toys from home to school. Children attempted to break this rule by bringing in concealed toys or candy, which were then shared with other children who gladly became coconspirators in the violation. Similarly, Marshall (1976) describes a game called "frogs" played by !Kung children. In this game one participant poses as the "mother," and the others are the "children." While the "mother" pretends to prepare "frogs" as food, the "children" openly refuse to perform tasks, disobey the orders of the "mother," steal the frogs and hide them, and so on. The game ends by the mother chasing the children, who run away in all directions in an effort to avoid being caught.

Aside from challenging rules and authority, it is through games and play that children come to understand concepts of creating and enforcing rules as well as cheating and breaking rules. Schwartzman (1983) provides a thoughtful analysis of the socializing function of children's play and includes examples of children in the kibbutz, Australian Aborigine children, Kpelle children in Liberia, and several more.

Sharing and Social Participation

As they get older, children begin to seek the company of other children and enjoy social activities. In interaction with other children and without the presence of adults, they acquire a sense of **cooperation** and sharing. One of the most important settings in which social interaction takes place is that of play and games, which represent a crucial element of the ecological system during childhood. Games like tag, hopscotch, and jacks as well as soccer and baseball are played in similar forms in many cultures (Avedon & Sutton-Smith, 1971; Duda & Allison, 1990; Reynolds, 1989). All these games facilitate taking turns, cooperation, and negotiation, yet the rules or content may vary with different contexts. Children in the United States may play soccer (what most of the world refers to as football) in an organized league governed by adults and consisting of set teams, coaches, scheduled match play, and so on. Soccer may also be played without adult participation and with makeshift goals and changing teams in a back alley of São Paulo, Brazil, or in a farmer's field in Nigeria. The social interactions taking place in each of these settings may be quite different. For example, organized sports and games tend to focus on competition, achievement, rules, and success, whereas free play activities tend to focus on participation, equality of players, and adapting or creating rules in order to ensure everyone's enjoyment of the game (Figler & Whitaker, 1995).

Games and play also introduce children to concepts of competition and differential status. Observers of children's peer culture have noted the cultural variation in competitiveness and cooperation in children's play. For example, children in North America generally appear to be more competitive than children in many other societies (Madsen, 1971). On the other hand, Domino (1992) found Chinese children to be more concerned than American children about group accomplishment. In this study, children were asked to complete a task in which tokens could be exchanged for various prizes. Depending on the task, tokens could be obtained by working alone or collaboratively. Most of the American children preferred to work individually, trying to accumulate as many tokens as possible for themselves. Chinese children tended to adopt strategies that emphasized collaboration with others rather than individual success.

In another example, Sparkes (1991) used a dyadic (two-person) marble game in which children had the choice to play cooperatively or to compete with each other. Findings showed that Chinese children were more competitive in this situation than American children in the comparison group. Starkes points out that these differences may be due to the different teaching styles practiced in these cultures. She suggests that the Chinese emphasis on teacher-directed large-group activities leaves little room for dyadic interactions. As a result, Chinese youngsters may have less experience in negotiating roles and taking turns with a partner. These selected examples demonstrate that cultural differences or similarities in competitive and cooperative behavior may depend on the definition of these concepts and the specific context in which the behavior takes place.

Studies in Africa provide additional cues for environmental factors that may influence cooperative and competitive behavior. Friedman, Todd, and Kariuki (1995) studied 120 Kenyan children from different backgrounds (a middle-class Westernized suburb of Nairobi, poor semiurban Kikuyu, and a poor rural mission village). Results showed that middle-class children behaved competitively, even when cooperation was the most adaptive strategy. Surprisingly, rural children also engaged in competitive behavior. Poor semiurban children from Kikuyu were the most cooperative of all groups. One could speculate that the degree of Westernization corresponds to the degree of individualism found in these settings (i.e., the more individualistic the environment, the greater the emphasis on competition).

Marshall (1976) reported a complete absence of competitive games among !Kung children living in tribal communities in Southwest Africa (tug-of-war being the exception because of its special historical meaning). The author suggests that the collectivist nature of !Kung society emphasizes group performance rather than individual achievement and success. Taken as a group, these studies suggest that the degree of collectivism–individualism may play a role in the social behavior of children since it is part of the ecological system in which social behavior develops.

Kagitcibasi (1990) has recently criticized the use of the collectivism–individualism dimension as a simplistic explanation of cultural differences in competitiveness and the health concern it may pose for children. As an alternative, Searle-White (1996) proposes a Vygotskian approach. As you may recall from our earlier discussion, this framework emphasizes socialization and language as "psychological tools" for mental growth and development. Depending on how these tools are used, children and adults view themselves as being at a point along a continuum of interdependence, where cooperation reflects, in part, the inclination to stay socially connected to others.

This approach fits in with our themes of the developmental niche and the ecological systems approach. When children cooperate with others, they work within their developmental niche and recognize that they are interconnected with others. Likewise, in terms of Bronfenbrenner's model, the child interacts with other people within her microsystem. At first, this system may be small, involving just a few caregivers. However, as children get older, they do more things with others, expanding their social world. As they become socialized within the mesosystem of the school and the neighborhood, they recognize the benefits of working together to accomplish their academic and personal goals. They learn the rules of cooperative play and practice social behaviors. Later, as children express the cultural values of cooperation and interdependence through language and social behavior, they begin operating within the cultural context of the macrosystem.

Moral Development and Prosocial Orientation

With increased social participation in early childhood, children begin to understand how to relate to others in socially desirable ways. As they acquire the foundations of moral reasoning and behavior, they begin to understand concepts such as "right" and "wrong." Developmental psychologists have proposed that moral development progresses in stages, each stage representing more mature reasoning about moral thought and conduct (Kohlberg, 1981; Gilligan, 1982; for a detailed overview, see Shields & Bredemeier, 1995). Kohlberg's theory of moral development was introduced in Chapter 2.

Cultural Influences on Caring and Justice Orientation

Kohlberg's definition and assessment of moral reasoning is not accepted by everyone and has been challenged by several researchers (Eckensberger, 1994; Snarey, 1985; Shweder, Mahapatra, & Miller, 1987). In fact, a number of studies suggest that individuals in many non-European cultures, as well as women, exhibit moral reasoning equivalent to that of an adolescent in Kohlbergian terms. Critics argue that an Anglo male bias is built into the model because the highest level of moral development is based on interviews with a 1960s sample of Harvard male undergraduates. In addition, the hypothetical moral dilemmas Kohlberg created to elicit moral reasoning responses and the scoring of the responses may also be culturally biased. Carol Gilligan (1982) specifically pointed to the gender bias in Kohlberg's theory. In her own research, she learned that women's moral thought is *guided by caring and maintaining the welfare of others*, whereas men emphasize *more abstract principles of justice*. Gilligan concludes that women develop a different kind of morality altogether, due to their different socialization. Stack (1974) found a similar **caring orientation** (as opposed to a **justice orientation**) described as "what goes around comes around" in a midwestern African American community.

Different socialization, parental beliefs, and customs of child care—that is, different aspects of the developmental niche—may explain many research findings in the cultural domain. For example, studies of Buddhist monks showed that young adolescent monks reasoned at stage 2 and even mature adults barely reached stage 4 in Kohlberg's schema (Huebner & Garrod, 1993). Can we conclude that the monks' moral reasoning is less highly developed compared with Western adolescent males? Huebner and Garrod (1993) argue that Kohlberg's model is only partially applicable in this context because the Buddhist conception of morality is different than the Western, Christian, liberal democratic view inherent in Kohlberg's theory.

According to the authors, the ideal moral person from a Western perspective is an autonomous individual with strong convictions who stands up for her own, as well as others', rights. She is an influential individual who uses her power to influence others in a "good" way. In contrast, among Buddhists, ideal moral individuals are those who are ultimately connected (to others, the environment, the cosmos) through their compassion and detachment from their own individuality. Buddhist morality is characterized by an understanding of interconnectedness and interdependence and is more reminiscent of Gilligan's caring orientation than Kohlberg's justice orientation. Similarly, Bersoff and Miller (1993) found that people from India were more likely to forgive moral violations if there were extenuating circumstances or emotional hardship.

In a comparative study of adolescents from China, Hong Kong, and England (Ma, 1989), both Chinese samples showed a stronger orientation toward abiding by the law as well as being altruistic or affective toward others. Ma concludes that this cultural difference may result from the Chinese practice of rearing their children in a more authoritative manner than the English, encouraging them to obey authority and follow norms. At the same time, Chinese cultural values are inherently collectivist, emphasizing human relationships and interdependence.

This discussion of various cultural influences on aspects of moral reasoning demonstrates that moral development may not strictly follow a universal psychological script, as suggested by Kohlberg. Instead, the ecological system in which early social participation takes place shapes individual development of moral thought and behavior.

Cultural Influences on Distributive Justice

Based on Kohlberg's broad model of moral reasoning, Damon (1975) focused specifically on children's understanding of one aspect of moral reasoning that has important implications for the development of social judgment and social behaviors, namely **distributive justice**—*the judgment of what constitutes crite-*

ria for the fair distribution of goods and resources in society. Damon's six levels of distributive justice reasoning, which occur from early to middle childhood, are presented in Box 8.1 on pages 196–197.

In order to assess children's distributive justice capabilities, Enright, Franklin, and Manheim (1980) created the **Distributive Justice Scale (DJS),** which is *a pictorial instrument used as a tool in one-on-one interviews.* Researchers have since adapted the DJS for use in a variety of contexts. For example, Box 8.1 shows Solomon's (1997) Adapted Distributive Justice Scale, which is used to assess the thinking of children from different ethnic backgrounds within a sports context.

Cross-cultural studies have suggested that cultures may differ in their normative beliefs of what constitutes a "fair" distribution of resources. For example, Sweden is considered more of a need-based society (i.e., everyone receives according to his needs), whereas the Protestant work ethic (i.e., everyone receives according to his effort) still prevails in the United States (Enright et al., 1984). Similarly, the concept of reciprocity , a central concept in Damon's model, is conceptualized differently depending on cultural context. In Damon's model, mature reasoning about the just distribution of goods and resources in society is guided by two principles: equality and reciprocity. Equality refers to the judgment that people are equally deserving of receiving resources and goods. Reciprocity refers to the reception of resources, either in exchange for a behavior (e.g., work) or to meet a need. At the most mature level of reasoning, children are able to take both equality and reciprocity into account when making judgments about the fair distribution of resources. Miller and Bersoff (1994) point out that in India, exchanging helping behavior for money is considered a personal choice but exchanging helping behavior for previous helping behavior is a social obligation. In contrast, either type of reciprocity is considered a personal choice in the United States. Based on these differences in ecological systems, it would be easy to assume that developmental patterns of distributive justice reasoning may also vary for children in different cultures. Surprisingly, studies in Japan, Sweden, Germany, and the United States indicate that children show similar patterns of distributive justice reasoning corresponding to Damon's developmental model (Eisenberg, Boehnke, Schuhler, & Silbereisen, 1985; Enright et al., 1984; Watanabe, 1986). Other researchers found distinct patterns of distributive justice reasoning in India and Japan, both considered more collectivistic cultures. They found that distributive justice reasoning was guided by equality and need (Krishnan, 1997; Naito 1994). Even though the results are mixed, differences in ecological systems deserve consideration as a possible explanation for differences in moral reasoning development. For example, Krishnan (1999) proposes an adapted model for distributive justice development, a model that explicitly includes the influence of cultural factors through socialization. (See Figure 8.2 on page 198.)

BOX 8.1

THE ADAPTED DISTRIBUTIVE JUSTICE SCALE

The following example is from Solomon's (1997) Adapted Distributive Justice Scale:

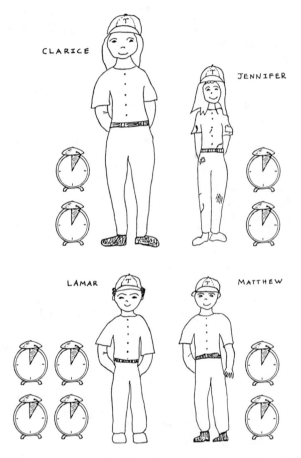

   All of these boys and girls are on the same baseball team. There is Clarice, the oldest one on the team; Jennifer, whose family is poor and does not have much money; Lamar, who is a hard-working ball player; and Matthew. One afternoon they thought it would be a good idea if they helped the younger children learn how to play baseball. When they were done, Clarice had helped for two hours, Jennifer had helped for two hours, Lamar had helped for four hours, and Matthew had helped for two hours. After

BOX 8.1 CONTINUED

they did this, the coach decided that the children were so nice to help the younger children that she gave them eight quarters. The children have to decide how to divide up the quarters. What is the best way to do this?

Answer options in the ADJS and Damon's corresponding levels of reasoning:

Answer Option	Level of Reasoning	Judgements about fair distribution of goods are guided by
Matthew gets the most quarters because he wanted the quarter more than anything.	O-A	The mere expression of a wish: "Whoever wants it most, gets it."
Clarice gets the most because she is the oldest.	O-B	External characteristics such as size or age: "Whoever is older or bigger gets the most."
All children get the same amount so there won't be any fights about who gets more.	1-A	Strict equality, regardless of other attributes or actions: "Everyone gets the same."
Lamar gets the most quarters because he helped more than the other children.	1-B	Reciprocity for behavior or actions: "Whoever works hardest gets the most in return."
Jennifer gets the most quarters because she is poor and needs them more than the other children.	2-A	Psychological or material need: "Whoever needs it most gets the most."
Both Lamar who helped most and Jennifer who needs the quarters get the most.	2-B	Compromise between need and equality: "Everyone should get what she or he deserves, which may differ by person and situation."

Source: G. B. Solomon, Fair play in the gymnasium: Improving social skills among elementary school children, 1997, *Journal of Physical Education, Recreation, and Dance, 68,* 22–25. Reprinted by permission.

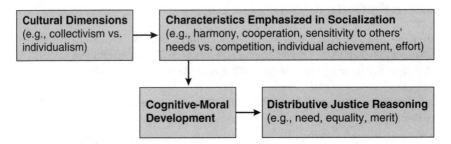

FIGURE 8.2 Proposed Model for the Study of Cultural, Socialization, and Developmental Influences on Distributive Justice Reasoning.

Adapted from Krishnan, L. (1999). Socialization and cognitive–moral influences on justice rule preferences: The case of Indian culture. In T. S. Saraswathi (Ed.), *Culture, socialization, and human development: Theory, research, and applications in India.* Thousand Oaks, CA: Sage Publications.

◇ ADOLESCENCE

Social Identity Formation

We tend to think of identity as something that is unique and represents the individual's personal history, experiences, and personality. However, our lives are inextricably connected with those around us, whether our family, our peers, or our coworkers. From an ecological systems view, the groups of people in a given context show a great degree of overlap. Therefore, it is not surprising that part of what we like to think of as our self results from what we share with others. Psychologists call these shared aspects of self social identities. French psychologist H. Tajfel (1981) defines **social identity** as *"that part of an individual's self-concept which derives from his knowledge of his membership of a social group (or groups) together with the value and emotional significance attached to that membership"* (p. 255).

We tend to belong to multiple groups; some are assigned to us (e.g., gender, nationality), some we choose (e.g., political affiliation). Among these, ethnic or cultural identity has been singled out as particularly important to self-concept and psychological functioning of ethnic group members. Phinney (1990) and other researchers suggest that the formation of ethnic/cultural identity is very similar to the formation of ego-identity outlined by Erikson (Atkinson, Morten, & Sue, 1983; Cross, 1978).

In particular, ethnic/cultural identity formation progresses in three stages: the first stage, usually occuring in adolescence, is characterized by the lack of exploration of ethnic identity. The second stage involves becoming aware of and actively exploring one's ethnicity. At this stage, the person may engage in ethnic group activities, including reading and talking to people about the culture and participating in cultural events. The completion of this stage results in the final stage: ethnic identity achievement. This stage is characterized by a deeper understanding of one's ethnicity and the internalization of ethnic identity into the self. Since this understanding of ethnic identity varies from person to person according to personal history, the implications for the self-concept and, ultimately, social behavior may also vary. For example, one person may become deeply involved in the activities of her ethnic group by maintaining the language, wearing traditional garb, and practicing ethnic rituals and customs. For another person, ethnic identity achievement may result in an intrinsic confidence in his ethnicity and not necessarily require strong ethnic involvement.

Cultural Influences on Social Identity

Just as the larger cultural context influences the specific content of adolescents' self-concepts and personal identity (see Chapter 5), culture also plays an important role in the progression of social identity formation and its psychological consequences such as self-esteem. The position an ethnic group holds in the larger society (minority or majority status) and the relationships between ethnic groups are the most influential of these cultural factors (Phinney, Lochner, & Murphy, 1990).

Research in the West Indies (Gopaul-McNichol, 1995) shows how general cultural conditions and beliefs (i.e., macrosystem) shape the basis from which young people begin their ethnic identity formation. Gopaul-McNichol (1995) presented black and white preschool children with black dolls and white dolls. The investigator asked the children questions such as "Which doll would you like to play with?" "Which doll do you want to be?" "Which doll is rich, ugly, pretty?" Similar to research in the United States almost five decades earlier (Clark & Clark, 1947), most of the children chose the white doll in response to the positive questions. The author concludes that colonialism, along with the representation of blacks and whites in the media, has made a marked impact on attitudes toward and perceptions of ethnic groups in the West Indies. It is not far-fetched to assume that these attitudes and perceptions will later play an important role in the ethnic identity formation of the black children and white children who participated in the study.

The research examining the relationship between ethnic identification and self-esteem is inconclusive. Some studies indicate that stronger identification with one's ethnic group is related to higher self-esteem among adolescents (Grossman, Wirt, & Davids, 1985; Paul & Fisher, 1980). Other studies have failed to find a definitive link between these two concepts (Houston, 1984; White & Burke, 1987). On the other hand, Phinney (1990) points out that the role of ethnic identity and self-esteem becomes clearer when looking at stages of identity development. In fact, she and her colleagues have reported in several studies of African American, Asian American, Mexican American, and European American adolescents that lower self-esteem was associated with lower stages of identity development. When individuals reached the stage of "achieved identity" and had a clear sense of who they were, their self-esteem was higher than that of individuals who were in the identity fore-closure or moratorium stages of identity development. This finding was true for all ethnic groups, although the relationship was stronger for members of minority groups (see Phinney, 1990, for a review of this research).

Cultural Influences on Adolescent Social Behavior

Arnett (1992) suggests a theoretical framework that is helpful in understanding why adolescent behavior is judged so differently in different cultures. He suggests that the socialization of adolescents is largely influenced by factors other than family and peers within the microsystem. The larger cultural influences include school, community, legal system, cultural beliefs, and the media (meso-, exo-, and macrosystems). According to Arnett, some cultures are characterized by **broad socialization** in which *independence and free self-expression are more highly valued than conformity.* Cultures such as these have no commonly accepted belief systems that judge right and wrong behavior, and deviations from cultural expectations are not severely punished. In these cultures, the range of behavior that falls within the norm is much greater than in so-called **narrow socialization** cultures. The latter clearly *prescribe an ideology that strictly sets forth the basis for right and wrong behavior.* These cultures value conformity and adherence to the standards of the community rather than autonomy and severely punish deviations from community norms.

Arnett's framework is useful in explaining why behaviors considered delinquent in one society are merely frowned on or even acceptable in others. For example, drinking is unacceptable for adolescents in many kibbutzim in Israel, with the exception of some Jewish festivities, during which moderate alcohol consumption is allowed (Kaffman, 1993). In contrast, the attitude toward alcohol consumption by adolescents in Jamaica is casual, and few legal restrictions apply. In Jamaica, adolescent drinking is not a sign of delinquent behavior (Smith & Blinn Pike, 1994). Similarly, compared to the United States, adolescents in Spain are able to consume more alcohol per week before they are categorized as "drinkers" (Recio Adrados, 1995). Among European countries, the prevalence of weekly drinking varies considerably. For example, adolescents in Greece and Italy drink about twice as much alcohol per week as their counterparts in Ireland (van Reek, Adriaanse, & Knibbe, 1994). Possible explanations for these variations probably can be found in the cultural differences in beliefs related to alcohol consumption and adult drinking patterns.

An additional factor that needs to be taken into account when defining adolescent social behavior is the status of a given group within the larger culture and this group's attitude toward the majority culture. Gotowiec and

Beiser (1993) found a much higher rate of school failure, substance abuse, and suicidal behavior among aboriginal Canadian adolescents than among majority culture adolescents. Similarly, drug consumption patterns of Australian aboriginal peoples differ significantly from that of urban Australians, who represent the majority culture (Fleming, Watson, McDonald, & Alexander, 1991).

Calabrese and Noboa (1995) closely examined Mexican American gang culture. They report that Mexican American adolescents may decide to join a gang as a way of retaining their culture of origin and of resisting the majority values found in American public schools. In this case, violence must be interpreted from the standpoint of the minority culture, since majority views are rejected (Harris, 1994). Another example of differential perception of delinquent behavior is the street-fighting code of a minority youth culture in Mexico (*cholo*). The mass media in Mexico choose to portray *cholo* youth as uncontrolled, violent, and destructive. In contrast, Cummings (1994) describes a complex system of *cholo* street-fighting rules based on fairness and honor. This social structure contains rules about who can fight with whom about which matters and under which circumstances. For example, fights only take place when the groups involved are perceived as equal in strength or number; women may intervene on men's behalf, but men never interfere with women's fights.

Regardless of the specific parameters of their ecological systems, young people are faced with the difficult developmental task of identifying and establishing their place in the adult world. For some, this process may progress more smoothly; for others, it may be characterized by inner conflict and turmoil. Nonetheless, young people across cultures share general concerns about the world, their lives, and their future, as described in Box 8.2 on page 202.

◇ ADULTHOOD AND AGING

While achieving a healthy adult identity is one of the most challenging life tasks, Erikson asserts that psychosocial development does not end with this task. The next challenge (or crisis) faced by adults involves finding intimacy and requires the individual to integrate his own identity with the identity of a long-term intimate partner. (The cultural aspects of this particular stage of development are discussed in detail in Chapter 9.)

Developmental Tasks in Middle and Later Adulthood

The two remaining psychosocial crises or challenges occur in middle and late adulthood and focus on *generativity versus stagnation* and *integrity versus despair* (see Table 3.1 in Chapter 3). The former refers to the *generation of something*

BOX 8.2

 WHAT ARE ADOLESCENTS
CONCERNED ABOUT?

The difficult psychological task of defining one's identity is frequently accompanied by many concerns and problems. Studies reveal that there are many concerns that are shared by adolescents and adults around the world. Some of these include questions such as "What will my life look like in five years?" "What kind of person will I be then?" "Will I ever get along again with my parents?"

Gibson and others (1991) examined seventeen nations in Europe, North America, and Asia and found adolescents' primary areas of concern were family, education, and self-concept. Young people in Singapore reported that their worries revolve around succeeding in school, getting a high-status job, and general concern about the future (Isralowitz et al., 1990). Turkish adolescents are concerned about their personal future, relations with others, and their identity. However, they also think about local and universal issues and drug use (Sahin & Sahin, 1995).

Nurmi (1991) provides an extensive review of studies on adolescents' future concerns. This review includes thirty studies conducted between 1959 and 1989 in fourteen different countries. He concludes that there are three main domains of concern shared by adolescents in different cultures: (1) major normative life tasks (e.g., having a career and establishing a family), (2) nonnormative life events related to parents (e.g., death or divorce of parents), and (3) global events (e.g., nuclear war). In spite of these similarities, Nurmi also points out that adolescents from traditional cultures seemed to be more concerned about issues relating to family, whereas those in urban cultures worried more about future education and career.

---

lasting that represents oneself. A successful resolution of this developmental issue leads to a sense of accomplishment and achievement. Such accomplishments can be expressed in material wealth, artistic or intellectual creations, raising children, or having achieved status in the community. This developmental phase clearly influences individuals' attitudes and behavior in social and work-related situations.

Integrity versus despair reflects older adults' attempts to *integrate previous identity resolutions and make sense of life as a whole.* Successful resolution of this final stage is characterized by an acceptance of oneself and one's accomplishments and failures. Unsuccessful resolution, on the other hand, leads to bitterness, resentment, and in extreme cases, may be accompanied by withdrawal from the social environment.

Work and Leisure in
Middle Adulthood

Cultural beliefs and values influence how individuals come to judge their efforts and accomplishments. Hofstede's (1980) initial examination of more than forty countries revealed significant differences in how people in these countries viewed and interpreted work and approached their social relationships at work. In particular, cultures differed on the following four work-related values: power distance, uncertainty avoidance, individualism/collectivism, and masculinity/femininity.

Cultures low on **power distance** put *less emphasis on organizational hierarchy and status between people.* In some cultures, it may be acceptable for a president of a company and a warehouse worker to socialize outside of work. Examples of countries low in power distance are Denmark, Israel, and Austria. Countries high in power distance are Mexico, Venezuela, and India.

The workplace in cultures low in **uncertainty avoidance** tend to *have few rules, policies, and codes that guide workers' communication and interpersonal relations.* In these cultures, a worker's complaints may be handled by different people in a relatively informal way, rather than by an appointed person according to specific procedures. Cultures low in uncertainty avoidance are Singapore, Denmark, and Sweden. Countries with the highest uncertainty avoidance are Greece, Portugal, Belgium, and Japan.

Collectivism, according to Hofstede, refers to the *degree to which a culture facilitates conformity, compliance, and the striving for harmony in the workplace.* Peru, Pakistan, Colombia, and Venezuela score high on collectivism, whereas the United States, Australia, Great Britain, and Canada tend to foster individualistic work values.

Finally, work environments in **"feminine cultures"** *promote gender equality, interpersonal contact, and group decision making.* This dimension can best be described as "working to live" versus "living to work." Scandinavian countries rate the highest in "femininity," whereas Japan, Austria, Italy, and Switzerland tend to promote "masculine" values.

More recently, Furnham, Kirkcaldy, and Lynn (1994) studied forty-one nations with regard to seven work-related beliefs. Their results showed that people in North and South America scored highest on work ethic (commitment to work), mastery (need to master problems), savings (importance of saving money), and conformity (identification with the organization and its success). Asian and Eastern countries scored highest on competitiveness (motive to be better than others) and money beliefs (importance of money). In addition, European countries scored lower than non-European countries on all seven dimensions, including achievement (need for excellence).

These beliefs about the work environment are also related to the nonwork environment. Studies of leisure activities show that these are both similar and different across cultures. Beatty, Jeon, Albaum, and Murphy (1994) questioned adults in the United States, France, Denmark, and New Zealand about their participation in recreational activities. Findings revealed three consistent clusters: *aesthetic-intellectual* (e.g., reading for pleasure, attending the opera, ballet, or dancing), *sports-action* (e.g., attending sports events or individual sports participation), and *social-entertainment* (e.g., going to the movies, having drinks, and enjoying entertainment). Two additional dimensions that were also examined did not replicate across cultures: *outdoor-nature* (e.g., walking for pleasure or bicycling) and *passive-in-home* (e.g., watching TV and playing sedentary games). The United States and New Zealand were most similar in their leisure activity preferences, with both scoring higher than their European counterparts on the sports-action and social-entertainment dimensions.

Among Chinese adults (Hu, 1990) the first choice for a hobby is reading, followed by social and intellectual activities. Physical exercise is third, tied with other productive activities such as knitting or crafts. One could speculate that leisure activities, defined as the antithesis of work (see Beatty et al., 1994), provide an environment or context that fulfills needs not met in the workplace. Therefore, one could possibly draw conclusions from predominant work values about the preferences for leisure activities. For example, individuals in cultures that emphasize collectivist work environments may choose to spend their leisure time in solitary activities, as is the case in China. On the other hand, people in individualistic societies such as New Zealand, Canada, and the United States, where people work independently and often autonomously, may prefer leisure activities that are social and cooperative.

Sport as a Social Phenomenon

As we have seen earlier in this chapter, play serves multiple important functions in the lives of children. In the following section, we outline how play and games are a central part in the ecological systems of adults in many societies. Games and sport can consist of spontaneous activity or highly organized sport and participation may range from passive spectator to participating spectator (e.g., referee, coach) to player. Anthropologists and sport historians have identified multiple functions of sport in society. We shall summarize these findings and illustrate how cultural settings shape sporting activities and, at the same time, are shaped by them (for an overview, see Calhoun, 1987). Two of the main historical functions are the practice of economic skills necessary to make a living and military training. The former is expressed in kayaking contests among Eskimos and rodeos among North American cowboys. Boxing, fencing, martial arts, and tug-of-war are classic examples of sports used for building strength, endurance, and skills in the interest of warfare preparation. However, sport and games also serve important social functions.

In many cultures, games or sport can have a ritual or ceremonial function. As such, the game or contest is dedicated to requesting help from, or expressing gratitude toward, a supernatural being. The Native American game of lacrosse or Japanese sumo wrestling are representative of this function. The origins of sumo were religious in nature. The first sumo matches were rituals dedicated to the gods. Along with dances and prayers, sumo matches expressed gratefulness for a bountiful harvest. This ancient sport dates back about 1,500 years and its ritualized character has survived to this day. As Hall (1997) describes, the ceremony preceding sumo matches is marked by strict traditional etiquette. The *rikishi* (participating sumo wrestlers) enter the ring in their colorful ceremonial aprons (*kesho-mawashi*) and perform a short sumo ritual. After they depart, the wrestlers scheduled to fight enter the ring. Over their *kesho-mawashi* they wear a large braided hemp rope tied in the back and decorated with patterned paper strips in the front. This kind of decorated rope is a religious symbol that can be found in many Japanese homes and in temples. Each sumo wrestler then performs the prefight ceremony with great dignity. He claps his hands to attract the attention of the gods. Then he extends his arms to the side, palms up to show that he does not carry any weapons. Finally, he lifts first one leg high in the air and brings it down with a thundering stomp on the ground. This move is repeated with the other leg. This maneuver is meant to symbolically drive the evil spirits from the ring. After this, the match begins. Throughout Japan today, sumo wrestlers are not only honored as successful athletes but also as representatives of a small group of individuals who preserve and celebrate religious and cultural traditions. In a culture that is characterized as a tight

Sumo grand champion Taiho performs the annual ritual of Dohyoiri at Tokyo's Meiji Shinto Shrine. (Hulton Getty/Liaison Agency, Inc.)

culture, high in uncertainty avoidance and high in power distance, the sport of sumo emphasizes these cultural values.

At the microsystem level, games and sport serve as recreational and communal activities. They also are an acceptable way of expressing rivalry and settling disputes. On the more distant level of the ecological system, sport expresses social identity and strengthens the sense of unity among members of a culture. Archetti (1999) provides a thorough account of the cultural meaning of sport in Argentina. He discusses football (soccer) as a cultural institution that permeates history, politics, and social and national identity. Archetti describes the evolution of the distinctive style of Argentinian soccer as a result of two main social forces: British imperialism and the ecological settings in which young Argentinian boys learn to play soccer. As opposed to the highly organized system of sport in Britain, most young Argentinian boys learn to play the game in the streets, in confined spaces with uneven surfaces. This setting lets them develop strong dribbling and ball-control skills, but little strategy. This led to a style of soccer much the opposite of the British style, which is very linear and strategic. Hence, soccer may be interpreted as a form of expression of independence from the British, and as such it has become part of Argentinian national identity and pride (macrosystem).

The Argentinian soccer player has also become an idealized role model for male social identity and behavior. The *pibe criollo* (ball-playing boy) represents one of the male ideals in this culture: he is spontaneous, free spirited, and positive; feels responsibility toward family and society; and seeks to achieve. He remains imperfect, but imperfections are forgiven because he is, after all, only a boy (Archetti, 1997, p. 182). Young boys strive toward this ideal and are reinforced by family and peers (microsystem). In Argentina, as in many countries, spectators rally behind their national team in international competition. The unity of spectators is expressed by uniform colors, national anthems, the display of flags and other symbols of national pride (exosystem). Victory of the national sports team equals victory of the nation and fills the members of that nation with pride, reinforcing the loyalty and unity of the country at large. This phenomenon of social identification through sports is nowhere more clearly observable than during the Olympic games, which bring many nations together in competition.

These cultural examples of sport show that this social activity is an important element in the ecological systems of adults who participate (actively or passively). In that capacity, students of human development have to consider sport and games as central to adult social development. For example, as an individual ages and makes a transition from active to passive participation, his or her ecological system changes, which, in turn, influences the individual.

Social Support and Well-Being in Later Adulthood

The relationship between well-being and social support in later adulthood appears to be largely universal. Comparisons of diverse cultures show a remarkable similarity in patterns of social support from spouses, relatives, adult children, and friends and their influence on well-being (Lennartsson, 1999). At the same time, cultural differences can be found in the expectations or norms regarding social relationships maintained by elderly persons.

Normative expectations that children care for their elderly parents in Thailand result in the common arrangement that at least one adult child lives in the same household or very close by, thereby providing a minimum level of social support (Knodel et al., 1995). Even if the caregiving is perceived as demanding, a deep sense of family obligation and emotional bond maintains this system of social connection in old age (Caffrey, 1992).

However, cultural change may affect the social support system of some elderly. For example, shifts in familial positions in Taiwan have recently produced situations in which the daughter-in-law gains more importance in some families than the formerly powerful mother-in-law. With decreased responsibilities, older women have begun to experience feelings of uselessness and reduced social support. This change in social relationships has been related to an increase in suicide risk among the elderly in Taiwan (Hu, 1995).

It is not merely the presence of a social support system that is relevant to well-being. Reciprocal relationships, in which individuals both receive and provide support, are related to greater life satisfaction. Such relationships seem to be more prevalent in France than in North America (Antonucci, 1990). For example, the elderly in France perceive their social relationships as more reciprocal than do both Caucasians and African Americans in the United States.

◇ SUMMARY

While virtually all social relationships and roles change over the lifespan, some aspects are more salient at different ages. The types of relationships children develop with their primary caretakers early in life set the stage for many social relationships to come. Yet, the attachment patterns of infants are seemingly influenced by caretaking practices and general conditions under which children grow up. As children learn to communicate, they begin to form more social relationships; these are initially built and later maintained through play. Social relationships require basic skills, such as conflict resolution and cooperation, which involve a general understanding of moral principles. Kohlberg's theory of moral development addresses some important aspects of morality, namely the understanding of normative principles of justice. However, Gilligan has demonstrated that individuals may also base their moral decisions on nurturance and caring. Though they represent interdependent elements of moral reasoning, the salience of either of these moral orientations may vary from culture to culture.

Adolescents face the difficult task of defining an adult identity for themselves. This process, which Erikson calls identity formation, has many implications for social relationships, roles, and behavior. In exploring their identities, adolescents redefine relationships with parents and peers and negotiate their role in their community and the larger society.

Middle adulthood is dominated by concerns of productivity, which manifest differently depending on values and expectations. As in childhood, the social functions of games and play continue to shape social development in middle and later adulthood. Active and passive participation in sport are part of the ecological system. Finally, social support and satisfying social relationships facilitate well-being and peace of mind in older adulthood.

◇ FURTHER READINGS

Cheryl Bentsen. (1989). *Masai Days*. New York: Anchor Books.
> The author provides a close-up look at this traditional African culture. This book is not so much a scholarly account but an informative and lively view of Masai everyday life. Among other things, the reader learns about the concerns of two young boys torn between traditional and modern ways, young adult women and their social network, and young men who take great pride in their role as warriors.

Robert Kaminski and Judy Sierra. (1995). *Children's Traditional Games: Games from 137 Countries and Cultures*. Phoenix, AZ: Oryx Press.
> The authors provide practical educational activities based on folk games from more than 130 countries and cultures. Although the book is designed mainly as a practical reference book for teachers, it also discusses the function of games in childhood development, their cultural importance, the types of games found around the world, and the rationale for using folk games in the classroom.

Robert R. Sands. (1999). *Anthropology, Sport, and Culture*. Westport, CT: Bergin and Garvey.
> This unique collection of current research on culture and sport discusses issues including ethnicity, identity, ritual, and culture change as well as the effect of environment and genes. The book illustrates the importance of studying sport as a universal phenomenon that both shapes and is shaped by its cultural context.

CHAPTER NINE

THE FAMILY IN CULTURAL CONTEXT

The sun is just beginning to rise in Boslanti, along the Saramacca River in central Suriname, the smallest country in South America. Sindy Sowidagkijm, twenty-four, and her husband, David, twenty-six, surrounded by a midwife, and several female relatives, including two grandmothers, are nearing the birth of their third child. The two older children, on the other side of the small wooden house, are lulled to sleep by the rhythmic sound of light rain on the corrugated-iron roof. Suddenly, a baby's cry fills the room, and little Jacob makes his arrival known to all. Sindy, exhausted but happy, will breast-feed her newborn and take a deserved rest. David will dream of the day when his new son will join him and his uncles on the family fishing boat. The others will proudly spread the word about the newest citizen in Boslanti.

At Mt. Sinai Hospital, in downtown New York City, Walter and Patricia Mezzanotti have just entered the brightly lit delivery room on the eighth floor. At thirty-eight, this is Patricia's first pregnancy and it has been unusually difficult. She is lightly sedated with an intravenous needle pumping a labor-inducing drug into her arm. Two hours later, following an emergency Cesarean section performed by two doctors and two nurses, she is sleeping quietly in the recovery room awaiting the time she will see her new son for the first time. Just down the hall, relaxing in a rocking chair in a birthing room and talking with her husband, five-year-old daughter, other family members, and two close friends is Anne Kane. In a half hour, she will give birth to a daughter in a quiet homelike atmosphere and begin the bonding process by immediately holding and feeding her newborn.

◇ CULTURAL VARIATIONS
IN THE FAMILY LIFE CYCLE

In the words of William Kenkel (1985), *"Families have a beginning, they grow in numbers, their membership next declines, and eventually the original family exists no longer.* The individual is born, grows, enters a period of decline, and inevitably passes from the scene. The striking parallel between the life pattern of a normal individual and the history of a typical family gave rise to the concept **family life cycle"** (p. 375). Although not a literal analogy, this concept provides a framework that allows us to consider the shifting attributes that affect individual behaviors and interactions within the family, community, and cultural context. As we make our way through this chapter, we shall be looking at the family life cycle in terms of the developmental stages used in previous chapters and relating these to real-life examples of families living in a wide variety of ecological settings throughout the world. We begin with the selection of a mate and the process of marriage.

Mate Selection

Buss (1994b) begins his study of mate preferences in thirty-seven cultures with a statement that cannot be disputed: "Every person is alive because of a successful mating. People in the past who failed to mate are not our ancestors" (p. 197). One of my students (Gardiner) found an even more interesting way to make the same point when she said, "If people did not reproduce, there would be no people and without people, it would be rather difficult to study different people's cultures." I certainly can't argue with that. The important questions are "How do we select a marriage partner?" "What characteristics do we consider important?" and "Are there cultural differences in selecting a mate?"

In an effort to answer these questions, Buss (with the help of fifty other researchers) conducted an extensive study of more than ten thousand individuals living in thirty-seven cultures. The approach involved asking subjects to indicate how important each of eighteen characteristics was in selecting a mate and then to rank thirteen of these in terms of their desirability. Findings revealed that, across cultures, men and women looked for mates who were kind and understanding, intelligent, had an exciting personality, and were healthy.

Buss indicated that he and his team of researchers were surprised by some of the results, particularly cultural variations concerning the most variable characteristic—chastity or the lack of previous sexual experience. For example, they expected that men throughout the world would highly value this quality more than would women. It would be surprising if cultures did not vary in the value placed on chastity, since other sources on sexuality usually note cross-cultural variation in practices, values, and expectations (Hatfield & Ropson, 1996; Hatfield & Specher, 1996; Lindisfarne, 1998). Such variation was indeed shown in Buss's study. While chastity was considered irrelevant or unimportant in a prospective mate by both men and women in the Netherlands, Sweden, and Norway, it was viewed as indispensable in China and scored very highly by those from India, Taiwan, and Iran. Among those who viewed chastity as only moderately desirable were those living in Colombia, Estonia, Japan, Nigeria, Poland, South Africa, and Zambia. Yet, in an overwhelming majority of countries (two thirds), chastity was desired in a marriage partner more by men than by women. (See Figure 9.1.)

Other categories showing large cultural differences in response were: "*good housekeeper* (highly valued in Estonia and China, little valued in Western Europe and North America); *refinement/neatness* (highly valued in Nigeria and Iran, less valued in Great Britain, Ireland, and Australia); and *religious* (highly valued in Iran, moderately valued in India, little valued in Western Europe and North America)" (Buss, 1994, p. 199). The author cautions that although these differences are important, there is undoubtedly much variability across individuals within these cultures. This once again reinforces our point that there are often greater differences within cultures than between or among cultures.

Looking more specifically at what each of the genders wanted in a mate, Buss (1994) found some interesting differences. As for women: "From

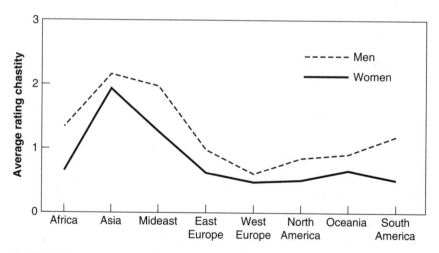

FIGURE 9.1 Cross-Cultural Differences in the Importance of Chastity

Source: From *Love and Sex* (p. 124) by E. Hatfield and R. L. Rapson, 1996, Boston: Allyn & Bacon, p. 124. Copyright © 1996 by Allyn & Bacon Publishing Co. Reprinted by permission.

the Zulu tribe in South Africa to coastal dwelling Australians to city-dwelling Brazilians, women place a premium on good earning capacity, financial prospects, ambition, industriousness, and social status more than men—characteristics that all provide resources" (p. 199). Men were found to prefer women who are younger than they are—how much younger depends on the culture. For example, "In cultures that permit men to acquire multiple wives, such as Zambia and Nigeria, men prefer brides who are much younger than they are—by as many as 7 or 8 years" (p. 200). In cultures where only one wife is permitted (e.g., Germany, Spain, and France), the preference was for brides only slightly younger. In all cultures, women had a preference for older men, "because men mature somewhat later than women and because older men often have access to more resources than younger men" (p. 200). Finally, "in *all* known cultures worldwide, from the inner-continental tribal societies of Africa and South America to the big cities of Madrid, London, and Paris, men place a premium on the physical appearance of a potential mate" (p. 200). According to Buss, there is a good reason for men to favor youthfulness and physical appearance, even though they may not be fully aware that "these qualities provide the best signals . . . that the woman is fertile and has good reproductive capacity" (p. 200).

Do men and women actually act on these preferences? Perhaps we'll get some answers when we look at the next topic—marriage.

Marriage and Other Long-Term Relationships

Children generally benefit from a stable system of primary caretakers, commonly including, but not limited to, the biological parents. Thus, heterosexual long-term relationships are facilitated, sanctioned, and protected in most societies. The motivation for marriage is to provide a stable environment for children. In fact, the cultural definition of "family" influences the ecological system on many levels. For example, it shapes the microsystem by ensuring (in many cases) that two parents are present, and regulates the macrosystem because it views this form of "family" as an important element of societal structure. It also affects all three components of the developmental niche in a variety of ways such as determining family structure, presence or absence of parents and other relatives, customs of child care, parenting styles, values, belief systems, and developmental expectations.

In addition to providing a good environment for children, individuals commit themselves to long-term relationships for other reasons. For example, Hindu religion considers marriage to be sacred and a symbol of the marriage between the sun goddess Surya and the moon god Soma. Without a wife, a man is considered spiritually incomplete (Kumari, 1988). The motivation for marriage is the striving for spiritual growth. Chinese cultural philosophy proposes that all objects and events are the outcome of two interacting principles: Yin, the *negative, passive, weak,* and *female,* and Yang, the *positive, active, strong,* and *male.* Harmonious interaction of the female and male principle, ensures the continuation of reality as we know it. Thus, in Chinese culture long-term relationships between women and men are a spiritual necessity for the survival of humankind (Ruan, 1991).

Marriage may also be a means to gain or maintain status in one's society. In most cultures, simply the fact of being married gives married men and women a higher status than their unmarried counterparts (Kumari, 1988; Sonko, 1994). Unmarried adults may be stigmatized and denied full adult status. In addition to social status, marriage may result in higher economic status. The pooling of resources of two families or a dowry paid by the family of the bride can mean considerable financial gain for both spouses. Finally, individuals may be motivated to share their lives out of a desire for love and companionship.

Anthropologists have demonstrated that marriage takes many forms in cultures around the world. These include **monogamy** in which *one man is married to one woman,* **polygyny** in which *one man is married to several women,* **polyandry** in which *one woman is married to several men,* and **group marriage** in which *several women are married to several men.* Polygyny is found on every continent. It is common in many Islamic countries, African societies, and parts of Asia, but is also found in North America (Levine 1980; Sonko, 1994). An abundance of wives of different ages not only represents wealth and power, but also ensures the reproductive success of the man. Polyandry is much less common. In some regions of Tibet and Nepal, brothers may share the same wife. However, in most cultures in which polyandry is accepted, husbands do not share blood relations. In general, polyandry is associated with greater economic power of women. Men in polyandrous societies have to be more considerate of women's needs to prevent them from switching their attention to more generous and caring husbands. Thus, wives can rely on generous shares of their husbands' wealth or income and may acquire considerable wealth themselves (Sangree, 1992). Only a few societies allow both women and men to be married to multiple spouses. Sangree (1992) points out that these polyandrous–polygynous societies have been found only in some regions in Western Africa.

You may be surprised to learn that the most "favored" form of marriage across societies is polygyny. However, Kenkel (1985) points out that "if we were to judge solely on the basis of a preponderance of a given marriage form, then few, if any, societies could be classified as polygynous. . . . No society . . . could arrange for all its males to have plural wives unless . . . the sex ratio could somehow be upset" (Kenkel, p. 22). In other words, for each man married to two women, there would have to be a man who was not married at all. Therefore, only those cultures in which more than one wife is pre-ferred are typically considered to be polygynous. Using this criterion, G. P. Murdock (1967), the pioneering anthropologist, in a study of a large sample of the world's societies, classified 721 as polygynous, 137 as monogamous, and only four as polyandrous. Kenkel (1985) states that while "monogamy is actually the preferred form in a relatively small number of societies . . . it [is] . . . the only form of marriage that is permitted and recognized in every soci-ety throughout the world, although it is not always the form of marriage that receives highest approval. . . . The great bulk of the world's married popula-tion, by lot or by intent, is monogamously wed" (p. 23).

A number of cultures permit sexual relations of some sort between in-dividuals of the same sex (Cabaj & Purcell, 1998). The very few studies that address the subject in a cultural context mainly focus on homosexual rela-tionships between men. In reviewing research conducted in many different cultures, Carpo (1995) distinguishes two main forms of socially recognized long-term homosexual relationships: mentorship and pathecism. Mentorship *refers to relationships between partners of different ages and social status.* Sexual relations by no means occur in all mentorships, and when they do take place are only one aspect of the relationship. More importantly, the older man frequently serves as a socializing agent for the younger man and introduces him to the fundamentals of warfare, politics, and religion. Pathic (not to be confused with pathetic) relationships *involve partners of similar age and status who commit themselves to a long-term partnership* comparable to heterosexual marriage.

Because cross-cultural studies of homosexual relationships are limited in number, it is difficult to know with certainty what percentage of societies accept, tolerate, or even support same-sex relationships. Nonetheless, Bolton (1994) concludes from a review of anthropological studies that male homo-sexual relations are common in 41 to 64 percent of societies studied. By com-parison, data on lesbian relationships are not as readily available, but Bolton argues that "societies which are tolerant of homosexuality are consistent in expressing that tolerance across age and gender categories" (p. 162).

The presence or absence of homosexual relationships in a given society once again illustrates the concept of the developmental niche, namely how certain behaviors may develop or be inhibited in response to cultural condi-tions. In societies that tolerate or even support relationships between people of the same sex, there will be a greater number of gay and lesbian relation-ships. In contrast, societies that strictly prohibit homosexual relations report fewer instances of homosexuality. These differences do not occur as a result of a higher or lower percentage of gays and lesbians in the population, but as a result of differential opportunities to develop a certain preference and be-havior within one's ecological surroundings and to express it as part of one's developmental niche.

How and why individuals are attracted to each other varies significantly across cultures. Another distinction might be referred to as the "Eastern versus Western ideal." In many Western cultures, perhaps best represented by the United States, marriage is often viewed as the culmination of romantic love. The belief is that each of us has an "ideal" mate that we are destined to meet, fall in love with, marry, and live with "happily ever after." One of the authors (Gardiner) recalls a student telling him how her parents, living in Yugoslavia, met and married. One day, her father climbed a hill next to his village and watched a young woman washing clothes in the river below. He returned the next day and watched her again. On the third day, he walked down to the river, told her he had been watching her for three days and had fallen in love with her and wanted to marry her. She said "yes." They were now celebrating their twenty-fifth wedding anniversary! However, there are other people who find "true love" several times and have the marriage certificates to prove it.

The "Eastern ideal" continues to characterize many of the arranged marriages in Asia, Africa, and some other parts of the world. This ideal is based on the premise that each person has several possible mates with whom they could develop a successful marriage. Frequently, India being one example, families will discuss a possible future liaison between their infant children. Sometimes, the children are aware of this arrangement; sometimes, they are not. They are expected to marry (or bring shame and embarrassment to their families); if they are lucky, they may one day fall in love with each other. A female Indian graduate student, speaking in one of the author's (Gardiner) cross-cultural courses, related that she was returning home to Bombay to get married. When asked what her future husband did, she replied, "I don't know because I've never met him." The liberated young American women in class told her that she shouldn't marry someone she didn't know. Her reply, which makes an interesting point, was that she trusted her parents to make a wise decision regarding a future husband because they knew her and him and his family. In the meantime, she could concentrate on her studies while they (the American women) would have to search for their own husbands, go through the trials and errors of dating, and hope that in the end it would all work out.

Many of those who live in collectivist cultures view marriage as the coming together or blending of two families. For example, in northern Kenya, the creation of a new house is a significant part of the marriage ceremony. Once the wedding date is established, based on lunar calculations, the groom's family literally disassembles the new house, moves it to the bride's village, and rebuilds it. Prior to the wedding ceremony, the bride is taken through a rite of passage during which she is initiated into womanhood by the village's female elders and is taught what to expect from married life. Among the Mande, another African group, girls between ages twelve and eighteen attend clitoridectomy schools, where they have their clitorides removed and are formally taught how to be wives. They learn secret languages and codes that allow them to communicate with other married women. In today's Africa, wedding customs are undergoing change and reflect a mixture of the traditional as well as the modern (Hudgins & Williams-Snyder, 1995).

The same might be said of contemporary Japan, where love marriages have increasingly replaced the earlier practice of arranged marriages. Whichever practice is followed, certain traditional customs remain. For example, according to Fukada (1991), a *yuinou,* or ceremonial betrothal gift (often in the form of money), is first presented by the bridegroom-to-be, through a go-between, to the bride-to-be's household. In anthropological terms this represents the bride's price. The bride's parents are then expected to spend several times the value of the *yuinou* on a new home for the couple. Most wedding ceremonies in Japan are performed according to Shinto customs, followed by the drinking of sake (rice wine) as confirmation of the marriage and later by a celebration party.

In Thailand, couples tend to marry at later ages (late twenties to early thirties) as they continue their education and establish careers. According to Gardiner and Gardiner (1991), "While young people frequently reject arranged marriages in favor of making their own choices, they still observe the traditional ceremonies associated with marriage, including the morning blessing and chanting by monks, the pouring of lustral water, and a large evening reception for friends and relatives" (p. 180).

Harry and Ormsin Gardiners' Thai wedding ceremony.
(Photo courtesy of the authors.)

◇ THE BIRTH PROCESS ACROSS CULTURES

As the vignettes that opened this chapter illustrate, although newborns arrive every day in cultures around the world, the birth experience depends very much on cultural traditions and is deeply embedded in an ecological setting influenced by family, community, and culture.

In some societies, having a baby is just another normal event in one's life and takes little preparation. This is illustrated in the following example taken from the !Kung in the Kalahari Desert of Africa: "The first labor pains came at night and stayed . . . until dawn. That morning, everyone went gathering. Mother and I stayed behind. We sat together for a while, then I went and played with the other children. Later, I came back and ate the nuts she had cracked for me. She got up and started to get ready. . . . We walked a short way, then she sat down by the base of a large nehn tree, leaned back against it, and little Kumsa was born" (Shostak, 1981, pp. 53–54). Similarly, in rural Thailand, pregnancy does not significantly change a woman's behavior, and she "generally carries on with her household chores until the time of birth—even, in some cases, up to the last few minutes before delivery. Rural children are usually born at home with the mother resting on a mat or mattress on the floor assisted by a non-medically trained midwife and older relatives or neighbors" (Gardiner and Gardiner, 1991, p. 183). A few hours later, the new mother is often up and participating in family activities.

In many parts of North America, including the United States, fathers-to-be are typically present during labor and encouraged to actively participate in the delivery of their child, whether it is at home or in a hospital. Not so in some parts of the former Soviet Union or in East Africa, where an expectant Ngoni mother is assisted by other women while husbands and other men are completely excluded.

Clearly, not every culture approaches childbirth in the same way. In the next section, we look at the birth process in more detail and consider its variations across cultures.

The Ecology of Birth

For a long time, what we knew about childbirth practices came from a Western, largely American, perspective that viewed the procedure as a medical event. Interestingly, this was not always the case. In fact, according to Wertz and Wertz (1979), childbirth in Canada and the United States, like most other countries, was handled exclusively by women until the middle of the nineteenth century, when physicians, almost all of whom were men, began delivering babies and made it a medical rather than a social event.

In the original edition of her now classic cross-cultural investigation of childbirth in four cultures, Brigitte Jordan (1978) anticipated the approach we take here when she noted that "we have paid little attention to the social-interactional and socio-ecological aspects of birth [which address] . . . what is biological and what is social and cultural in the process of childbirth" (Preface). In the Preface to the fourth edition of this book, Jordan (1993) states that "an anthropology of birth must focus on the study of birthing *systems* and not the comparison of individual and isolated practices. We know that birth is everywhere a socially marked crisis event that is consensually shaped and socially patterned [consisting of] . . . practices that make sense from the inside out, though not necessarily from the outside in" (pp. xi–xii).

In a section of her book titled "The Ecology of Birth," Jordan discusses the particular locations in which babies are born and how these reflect culture-specific patterns (or ecological settings, as we would view them) within which individuals' lives are forever entwined. She also comments on the cultural implications of these specific arrangements.

Yucatan

Of the four cultures studied by Jordan (1993), the Yucatan imposes the least changes in the expectant mother's surroundings, maintaining its familiar and reassuring qualities by encouraging the Mayan woman to lie in the same

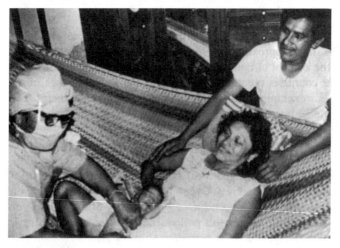

A Mayan woman, lying in her hammock, surrounded by her husband and a midwife, gives birth. (From *Birth in Four Cultures*, 4th ed., by B. Jordan, 1993, Prospect Heights, IL: Waveland Press, Inc. Reprinted by permission of Waveland Press, Inc.)

hammock in which she sleeps each night "whose strengths and tautness she knows to exploit for maximum support and comfort [thereby providing] . . . the kind of security that marks the event as a normal part of family life" (p. 68).

In Yucatan, there is a clear expectation that the father-to-be will be present during labor and birth, not only to take an active role, but also in order to observe "how a woman suffers." Frequently, if a child is stillborn, it is blamed on an absent father. In addition, the pregnant woman's mother should be present, often in the company of others from the family micro-system, including sisters, sisters-in-law, mothers-in-law, godmothers, and sometimes neighbors and close friends. According to Jordan (1978), all of these people make a contribution to a successful birth, and the intensity of their emotional and physical involvement is "mirrored in the strain on their faces and in the signs of fatigue that become evident in them as well as in the mother" (p. 38).

Immediately following birth, it is believed that the mother and her child are susceptible to the influence of evil spirits from the bush and must remain inside the house for one week before returning to normal activity. An infant girl will have her ears pierced within the first hour after birth and sometime within the next three days will receive her first earrings, often a family heirloom. Nearly all newborns are breast-fed, with nursing beginning a few minutes after birth and continuing whenever the infant appears hungry or anxious.

Holland and Sweden

In Holland, like Yucatan, women generally give birth at home, assisted by a midwife or physician, and the country continues to maintain one of the lowest infant mortality rates in the world (U.S. Bureau of the Census, 1992). In Sweden, often cited as the country with the lowest infant mortality, almost all babies are delivered in hospitals with the help of highly trained midwives. According to Jordan, what these two countries have in common is a program of government-sponsored prenatal care for every woman as well as availability of abortion on demand, with the result that "for all practical purposes, all pregnancies are wanted pregnancies and all babies are wanted babies" (p. 46).

In both Holland and Sweden, the mother-to-be is usually assisted by a midwife and her assistant and sometimes by a husband, male or female friend, or relative, who is there to provide help and emotional support. According to Jordan (1978), Dutch and Swedish midwives do not view the woman as a patient to be delivered but as an individual capable of giving birth on her own. Their role is to give encouragement, be prepared for complications, and take care of cutting the umbilical cord.

United States

In the United States, ranking twenty-first in the world in infant mortality, the majority of births (approximately 98 percent) continue to be in hospital settings under the control of medical specialists (Declercq, 1993). However, unlike the three countries mentioned above, there is a wider range of options available. For example, while some families prefer to have their babies delivered at home with the assistance of a midwife, increasing numbers, like the Kane family in our opening vignette, are taking advantage of birthing rooms located in hospitals, where technology is available but a home atmosphere is provided.

In this regard, an experimental project cited by Jordan is of historical (and perhaps contemporary) interest. Over a period of three years during the early 1970s, two nurse-midwives conducted the majority of normal deliveries in a California hospital. During this period, there was a dramatic drop in the number of stillbirths, fetal deaths, premature births, and neonatal deaths. When physicians once again took charge, all of these types of incidents increased, with the prematurity rate going up nearly 50 percent and neonatal mortality more than tripling (Levy et al., 1971). Jordan concludes that not only is the birth experience significantly influenced by who is allowed to be present during birth but so is the outcome of the birth process itself.

Discussing the consequences of a culture's choice of birth setting (home, hospital, bush, or elsewhere), Jordan (1993) makes an intriguing comment when she notes that when babies are delivered in hospitals, "responsibility and credit are clearly the physician's . . . visible in the handshake and 'thank you' [exchanged] . . . after the birth. . . . Typically, nobody thanks the woman [who] . . . has delivered rather than given birth" (p. 71). However, when babies are delivered at home, birth arrangements are the choice of the expectant mother and her family—"Their choice, their problem, their task, and . . . finally . . . their achievement" (p. 71). These may be subtle differences in language but they represent significant differences in cultural views and belief systems that form a crucial part of one's experiences within different developmental niches and ecological surroundings.

Writing more than twenty years ago, Jordan (1978) concluded her original birth study with the following statement: "What we need to keep in mind here is that birthing systems themselves are part of a larger cultural system . . . within an economic and political structure, via the socialization of birth participants" (p. 73). This point is even more relevant today, especially in light of our recurring themes, which focus on the cultural context in which development takes place.

In a sense, if you know a society's approach to childbirth, you will understand a great deal about the values and beliefs that are at the heart of its ecocultural system, how it socializes its members, and how it conducts its interpersonal relationships.

◇ THE TRANSITION TO PARENTHOOD

Kenkel (1985) puts the transition to parenthood in perspective when he states that "one of the significant features with regard to the parent role is a general lack of preparation for it. . . . Related to [this] . . . is the fact that the transition . . . is abrupt [and] . . . is largely irrevocable" (pp. 455–456).

Becoming a parent results in major life changes that affect not only the parents and their infant but also many others within the ecological setting where this event occurs. For example, Heinicke (1995) writes that within a family system "the personality characteristics of the parents as well as their relationship support systems (partner and extended family) to a significant extent define future parenting transactions with their child" (p. 277). We might ask "What about other niche influences such as the social and physical environment and customs of child care?" These surely play an equally important role and are worthy of future research on the part of those interested in cross-cultural human development.

In this regard, Belsky (1985) hypothesizes that "supportive developmental experiences give rise to a mature healthy personality, that is then capable of providing sensitive parental care which fosters optimal child development" (p. 86). This again points to the importance of the ecological setting and the transmission from one generation to another of successful parental belief systems learned within a healthy family environment. In fact, Vondra and Belsky (1993), in a study of the developmental origins of parenting, state that "by assuming an ecological perspective . . . and by adopting a longitudinal design, research has begun to provide a more adequate test of developmental and clinical theory on the origins of parenting" (p. 25).

◇ INFANCY AND CHILDHOOD

According to the National Center for Health Statistics (1994), each day throughout the world, approximately 750,000 individuals become new parents. Contrary to what many of these parents may think, a newborn is not always the pretty, smiling, curly-haired cherub they have imagined or seen in pictures or television commercials. Rather, a newborn is frequently an unattractive little creature—sometimes very small (or very big), often bald, toothless, hungry, and complaining—that has come to live with the new family for many years. During the first few days and weeks, most new couples wonder if they are capable of nurturing this new person and attending to its needs. Fortunately, the majority of parents are capable and, with later additions to the family, often get even better at it.

On arrival, most **newborns** (the *term applied to babies from birth through the first two weeks,* after which the term *infant* is used) are well equipped to deal with their new environment. For the most part, their senses work well, and they have a large repertoire of reflexes to help them adjust to the world beyond the womb. So effective are these reflexes, and so resilient are newborns, that following the devastating earthquake in Mexico City in September of 1985, babies were found alive in the ruins of one hospital nursery six days later.

In the initial days and months following birth, parents devote much attention and concern to satisfying their child's basic needs for sleep, hunger, and elimination (see Chapter 3). As Bornstein (1995) aptly observes, "Infants forever alter the sleeping, eating, and working habits of their parents; they change who parents are and how parents define themselves. . . . Parenting an infant is a 168-hour-a-week job" (p. 3). As children get older and move into the years of early, middle, and later childhood, development keeps pace. At the center of all this activity, largely determining the nature of the parent–child relationship, are parental belief systems.

Parental Belief Systems

In every culture, parents tend to develop shared ideas about the nature of children, their developmental processes, and the meaning of their behaviors. Strongly influenced by the cultural context, these ideas are entwined with other aspects of life, including time and place, meaning of self, family, and parenthood.

As Harkness and Super (1996) point out in an important contribution to the literature of culture and human development, these cultural understandings are organized into categories referred to as **parents' cultural belief systems** and "relate in *systematic ways to action—including . . . styles of talking to children, methods of discipline, or seeking advice from experts.* Ultimately [these belief systems] . . . exert a powerful influence on the health and development of children, and they are a key component in the development of parents themselves" (pp. 2–3). Parental beliefs represent one component of the developmental niche—the psychology of the caretaker.

Developing a philosophy of childrearing is one of the major tasks faced by new parents (Francis-Connally, 2000; Kenkel, 1985). In a particularly interesting application of this idea, Richman and others (1988) observed mother–child interactions in five cultures (three industrial and two agrarian) and reported several prominent differences. Among the more interesting was the finding that Gusii mothers of Kenya hold their nine- to ten-month-old infants and engage in soothing physical contact more than do middle-class mothers in Boston, Massachusetts, but, at the same time, look at and talk to them less often. Why? According to Richman and her colleagues there are several reasons for this behavior, all of which make perfect sense once you understand the ecology of the cultures involved. For example, among the

Gusii (1) infant mortality rates are high, and holding and soothing provide a greater chance of survival; (2) there is a belief that language is not understood by children until about the age of two; and (3) the culture teaches that one should avoid making direct eye contact with others. On the other hand, in the American culture there is a belief that (1) language learning should begin early, and (2) placing infants in playpens where they can play by themselves begins the process of independence so highly valued in American society.

Ever since Sigel (1985) edited one of the first volumes discussing this concept, interest in parental belief systems as an approach to understanding cultural similarities and differences has grown rapidly (Goodnow & Collins, 1990; Sigel, McGillicuddy-DeLisi, & Goodnow, 1992). This concept has also been fostered by the emergence of parallel trends in social anthropology, psychology, and new interdisciplinary approaches to culture and human development (Harkness & Super, 1996, 2000).

Also contributing to this unifying new concept are some of the approaches serving as major themes for this book. For example, the ecological systems approach of Bronfenbrenner (1989, 1993) provides a dynamic, interactive paradigm of parent–child interactions as they occur within a continually expanding cultural context that shapes the development of effective parental beliefs and practices. The developmental niche framework proposed by Super and Harkness (1986) assists in "conceptualizing relationships among parental belief systems, customs, and practices of childrearing and the organization of physical and social settings for children's daily lives" (Harkness & Super, 1996, p. 5). The concept of an "ecocultural niche" integrates ideas from these approaches and connects parental belief systems and parental behavior with these beliefs and family and community ecology (Gallimore, Weisner, Kaufman, & Bernheimer, 1989). Parents in the ecocultural niche of the family and in the developmental niche of individual children play a crucial mediating role between children's experiences and the larger culture in which they live. In the words of Harkness and Super: "The conceptualization of parents in the child or family's niche leads naturally, in turn, to an interest in the cultural construction of experience from the point of view of parents themselves, in particular their cultural belief systems or 'parental ethnotheories' regarding children, families, and parenthood" (1995, p. 228). Finally, the developmental models emerging from the Vygotskian perspective (discussed in detail in Chapter 2) focus on the relationship between individual development and cultural meaning systems as well as between parenting behaviors and symbolic systems (Harkness & Super, 1996; Holland & Valsiner, 1988; Lave & Wenger, 1991; Rogoff, 1990).

After reviewing these and numerous similar studies, we find that the following questions have not been adequately answered by the research literature: "In general, are there relationships between specific parenting beliefs

BOX 9.1

PARENTING AMONG
AFRICAN PYGMIES

There are about 150,000 Pygmies living in parts of several African countries including Rwanda, Cameroon, Gabon, Congo, Burundi, and Zaire. The majority range in height from 4 feet to 4 feet 8 inches (1.2 to 1.42 meters). While no one is sure why they are so small, research studies suggest it may be a combination of factors including a growth hormone deficit and an evolutionary adaptation to their ecological setting that allows them to move quickly and silently through the forest.

One group, the Efe (who prefer to be known by their tribal name rather than the derogatory term emphasizing short stature), are hunters and gatherers living in the Northeastern region of the Ituri forest in the Congo, formerly Zaire. They are believed to be the oldest pure ethnic group in the world with a culture, language, and tradition at least ten thousand years old. They live in small, extended family groups (about twenty to thirty people) consisting of brothers and their wives, children, unmarried sisters, and perhaps parents. They live in temporary camps composed of leaf huts used for sleeping, food storage, and protection from the weather. These huts, moved when the food supply runs low, are arranged in a semicircle creating a shared communal space where most day-to-day activities take place.

Sharing and cooperation among the Efe, in terms of food, work, and child care, are essential to their survival. The work load is high and many

An Efe mother braids the hair of a child in the Ituri forest in Zaire. (Anthro-Photo File)

BOX 9.1 CONTINUED

activities, such as foraging, are engaged in by both men and women, although only men hunt.

There is a strong belief among Efe that mothers *should not* be the first person to hold a newborn baby. This belief not only prevents an Efe woman from going off to give birth on her own, but it also introduces a child to multiple caregivers early. In fact, infants are frequently nursed by women other than their own mothers.

Fathers have an early presence in the child's life. For example, it is common practice for them to view the birth from the doorway of the hut. When not hunting, they and other men are often present in camp and often watch and hold the children (theirs and others), although most child care is the responsibility of mothers.

The developmental niche of the Efe is intensely social. The continuous presence of others, along with early multiple care, helps prepare Efe children for their social world while protecting them from common dangers in the physical environment.

Source: Adapted from *Infusing culture into parenting issues: A supplement for psychology instructors* by Vicki Ritts, 2000, unpublished manuscript, St. Louis Community College. Reprinted by permission.

and parenting behaviors?" "Are there universals, as well as variations, in what we might call 'good parenting'?" "Do certain kinds of parenting lead to certain kinds of outcomes for children, both cross-culturally as well as within cultures?" "What form do parental cultural belief systems take in cultures where relatives, other than parents (e.g., uncles, aunts, grandparents, and in-laws) play critically important roles?" We offer these questions in the hope that those who might pursue future studies in these areas will help extend our understanding of human development within the context of culture. Throughout the remainder of this chapter, we will learn how parents' cultural belief systems influence the manner in which lives develop across cultures, beginning with mothering and fathering behaviors.

Mothering

In their research on mothering, Barnard and Martell (1995) note that cultures consider this behavior extremely important, especially since mothers are the primary day-to-day teachers of culture. The authors also point out that opportunities to view similarities and differences in the mothering role have been limited because mothering generally takes place in the privacy of the family. Although these researchers do not use Bronfenbrenner's ecological systems terminology, their thinking sounds similar. For example, they state that "the role [of mothering] . . . develops in relation to the family system wherein roles of father, siblings, and other extended family members are enacted as well. . . . Each person's role is connected with all others in the family system and because that is true there are always variations within cultures. [For example] . . . as the position of women changes, aspects of the mothering role will be assumed by others in the family or in the society" (p. 3).

According to Harkness and Super (1995), mothering has historically been associated with women, because in most cultures women have provided primary care for children. In this regard, and in light of our discussion of Japanese families in this chapter, it is interesting to consider Barnard and Martell's (1995) analysis of the Japanese words for *woman, mother, man,* and *father:* "The character for woman is a stick figure with a protuberance, resembling a pregnant abdomen, whereas the character for mother resembles the chest with two breasts. The symbol for man, on the other hand, is the rice field illustrating work. The character for father is a stone axe symbolizing power" (p. 4). More accurately, the symbol for man is a combination of two characters, one representing a rice field and the other representing power which symbolizes hard work (Gardiner, 1996). *Parenting* is represented by three characters literally translated as "to stand," "a tree," and "to watch," which, when combined, can be interpreted as "watching over a growing child" (Gardiner, 1996). For a visual representation of these characters, see Figure 9.2.

Barnard and Martell also point out that these characters came from the original Chinese language and represent ethnic and intergenerational thinking about these roles within both these cultures. These character distinctions raise several intriguing questions: "Are mothering, fathering, and parenting distinct roles?" "Are birthing and nurturing unique characteristics of the

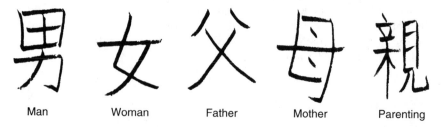

| Man | Woman | Father | Mother | Parenting |

FIGURE 9.2 Japanese Characters Related to Parenting

Source: Drawn by Alan V. Gardiner.

mother's role whereas support and family control are assigned to the father's role?" "Is parenting different than mothering and fathering?" Hopefully, with an increased interest in cross-cultural analysis, these and related issues will be answered in the not too distant future.

Fathering

Research on the role of fathers is of relatively recent origin (Biller, 1993; Parke, 1995; Mackey, 1985), and research on cross-cultural comparisons is still comparatively rare (Aldous, Mulligan, & Bjarnason, 1998; Gardiner, 1994; Lamb, 1987; Lykken, 2000; Yang, 1999). However, it is promising to note that when fathering is studied, it is being increasingly observed from both the ecological systems and contextual approach (Bronfenbrenner, 1989; Repetti, 1993) as well as the lifespan perspective (Elder, Modell, & Parke, 1993; Parke & Stearns, 1993). Of interest is a study by Marsiglio and Cohan (2000) clarifying the basic features of a sociological perspective as it relates to the study of fathers' involvement with, and influence on, their children. The authors focus on the social, organizational, and cultural contexts of fathering with particular emphasis on the interplay between social structures and processes at the macro, meso, and micro levels, along with social psychological issues.

In this regard, Parke (1995) stresses "the importance of examining developmental changes in the adult because parents continue to change and develop during adult years" (pp. 27–28). He points out that the age at which an individual becomes a parent can significantly affect the ways in which men and women carry out their paternal and maternal roles and that education, self-identity, and career tasks are related to the demands of being a parent. For example, the average age of marriage in Egypt and the Sudan is twenty-five to thirty-five years for men and twenty to thirty years for women in urban areas, twenty to twenty-five for men and sixteen to eighteen for women in rural areas (Ahmed, 1991).

In Nigeria, among the Muslim Hausa, a boy usually enters his first marriage around the age of twenty, often to a girl of thirteen or fourteen who has just reached puberty. For a Yoruba male, marriage typically takes place when the man is in his middle to late twenties and the girl is about sixteen to eighteen years of age (Okafor, 1991). Among the Southeast Asian Hmong, large numbers of whom have migrated to the United States, it is common for men in their twenties to thirties to marry young girls in their early to middle adolescent years. While many of these young people may be adequately prepared, as part of their developmental niche, to assume parental responsibilities at these relatively young ages, others are not and, recently being children themselves, will find married life and childrearing difficult.

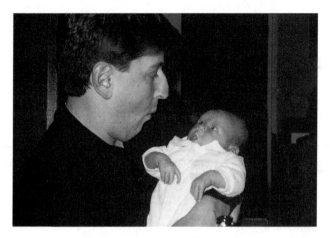

Father and son find mutual enjoyment during caretaking. (Photo courtesy of the authors.)

One of the leading views of fathering or father involvement has been presented by Lamb, Pleck, Charnov, and Levine (1987) who consider three components to be of crucial importance: interaction, availability, and responsibility. They describe these in the following way: "Interaction refers to the father's direct contact with his child through caregiving and shared activities. Availability is a related concept concerning the child's potential availability for interaction . . . whether or not direct interaction is occurring. Responsibility refers to the role the father takes in ascertaining that the child is taken care of and arranging for resources to be available for the child" (p. 125). In addition, Radin (1993) has recommended that a distinction be made between absolute and relative involvement as well as between a father's participation in child-care activities and in leisure, play, and related activities, since these are likely to be independent and have an effect on the way children and adults view the father's role.

In cross-cultural studies focusing on a variety of cultures (United States, Great Britain, France, Belgium, Israel, Sweden, and Australia), in which quantitative assessments were made comparing mother and father involvement with children of a wide age range (one month to sixteen years), on a large number of measures (basic care, holding, reading, verbal interactions), the overall pattern was the same: mothers spent more time and engaged in more activities with their children than did fathers (Collins & Russell, 1991; Coltrane, 1996; Jackson, 1987; Lamb et al., 1982; Russell & Russell, 1987).

In concluding his review of father–child relationships, Parke (1995) points out that studies of this topic are now "a more fully contextualized issue. Fathers in the context of their social relationships both within and beyond the family are increasingly the appropriate point of entry for understanding the issue of both parental roles and their impact on themselves and others" (p. 56).

This approach and the need for meeting the needs of fathers within an ecological perspective has been effectively presented in the work of Meyers (1997). In order to provide maximum benefits for fathers (and mothers), he proposes that parent education programs address issues such as the enhancement of child and marital communication skills, provide social support for parents, increase their involvement in childrearing, and provide authoritative child-care knowledge while acknowledging diversity among parents in terms of their differing social and cultural backgrounds, including parents who are single, adolescent, low-income, or minority.

◇ ADOLESCENCE

According to Holmbeck, Paikoff, and Brooks-Gunn (1995), parenting of adolescents has only recently become a topic of concern in the research literature. In fact, as recently as a decade and a half ago, one author found so little information on family relationships during the adolescent years that it was impossible to write a very lengthy review of the area (Adelson, 1980, 1985). While a significant body of relevant literature, as well as several useful reviews, have since appeared (Collins, 1990; Paikoff & Brooks-Gunn, 1991; Steinberg, 1990), little detailed attention has been given to the study of adolescence in many cultures other than the United States and a few other societies around the world.

The lack of cross-cultural parent–adolescent research from the standpoint of cultural context may be the result of several factors. First, many theories of adolescent development place greater emphasis on biological than on social or cultural factors as primary determinants of psychological characteristics. Second, there is continuing disagreement within the field as to whether adolescence represents a universal period of development. While some theorists take the viewpoint that it does, others argue that adolescence may be a developmental stage in some cultural settings but not in others (Whiting, Burbank, & Ratner, 1986).

Among those specifically interested in studying adolescence from the ecological perspective are Garbarino (1985, 2000) and Muuss (1988; Muuss & Porton, 1998). In the words of Muuss (1988), a strong adherent of this approach: "An ecological model goes far beyond what is presently known, opening up new perspectives and generating new hypotheses that are bound to move developmental research from the clearly defined, easily controllable research laboratory into the ecological field" (p. 300).

The Ecological Systems Approach and Adolescence

From an ecological systems perspective, we will look at the structures that influence the development of adolescents, irrespective of the cultures in which they live. First, various microsystems are involved, including the primary one of the family (parents, siblings, extended family members); the system involving friends, peers, and school; and perhaps other systems made up of neighbors and other social groups. As we learned in earlier chapters, microsystems are continually undergoing change, as are the individuals who move in and out of them. As Muuss (1996) points out, a healthy microsystem is one based on reciprocity, especially in the relationships between parents and adolescents: "If a microsystem is rich in information, it enhances learning and development by providing opportunities in which questions are asked and answered, exploration and experimentation encouraged, and guidance provided [and it] . . . will foster opportunities for success in later life" (p. 324).

Next, there is the mesosystem, which links the adolescent's various microsystems (e.g., family, school, and peers). In many cultures, conflicts exist between the parents' values and peer group values. This lack of agreement can result in family conflict, regardless of culture. White (1993) provides the following quote from a Japanese adolescent (which could just as easily have been made by a North American, European, or Latin American young woman): "When I'm with my best friend I feel safe. Talking to her gives me peace. She never gets angry, or tries to get me to change. And she never embarrasses me in public the way my mother does" (p. 144).

While an adolescent may not actively participate in the next ecological level, the exosystem, much of what goes on there (e.g., at local government meetings, in parents' workplaces, or in the mass media) may indirectly affect her (Muuss, 1996). For example, the school board in Salto, Uruguay, may determine that school enrollment will be down next year and be unable to hire fourteen-year-old Manuel Sacco's mother, Graciela, to teach for them. This will lower the family income and mean that Manuel and his brother and sister will have fewer new clothes and less food and may have to transfer to other schools.

Finally, there is the adolescent's macrosystem. Although of considerable importance, this is probably the least studied of all ecological systems; except for anthropological research, it almost never receives systematic investigation. As Muuss (1996) points out, "Although the macrosystem does not impinge directly on the life of the individual adolescent . . . it contains an overarching societal ground plan for the ecology of human development. [This includes] . . . a core of general cultural, political, social, legal, religious, economic, and educational values and, most important, public policy. As such, a macrosystem may be thought of as a societal blueprint" (p. 330).

These macrosystem values frequently find expression in social customs and what the culture considers fashionable at various times. For example, the macrosystem determines standards of physical attractiveness and what is appropriate and inappropriate behavior for each sex (Muuss, 1996). Physical attractiveness appears to be important to adolescents throughout the world, yet one culture's definition of physically attractive may differ from another's. As we will see in Chapter 10, in many Western countries, especially the United States, the media (television, movies, magazines) portray thinness as the female ideal. In certain African cultures, scarring of the face is considered physically attractive. In China, at one point in its history, binding a woman's feet to keep them small and dainty was a sign of beauty.

Cross-Cultural Differences in Adolescent Peer Relationships

The role of **peers**—*individuals of similar age and sometimes the same gender*—is very important in the microsystems and exosystems as well as in the social settings component of the developmental niche of some adolescents. There are significant social and cultural differences in the specific influences peers and friends have on adolescents. For example, Muuss (1988) suggests that peer groups play a much greater role in Western societies, where extended education is the norm, than in more traditional societies, where schooling ends in the early adolescent years. In the latter, he points out, orientation becomes vertical in relation of one's elders, rather than horizontal in relation to one's peers. As evidence, he cites an early study by Hsu, Watrous, and Lord (1961) in which second-, third-, and fourth-generation adolescents of Chinese background in Hawaii were compared to a matched group of Chicago adolescents. Findings revealed that the Hawaiian group was more family oriented, less rebellious, and less troubled by adolescence than the Chicago group, which tended to be more oriented toward peers. More recent research suggests that the influence of peers versus parents and family undergoes a significant transformation during the middle to late adolescent years (Grotevant & Cooper, 1985).

Along similar lines, Bronfenbrenner (1967) looked at the role of peer groups in the Soviet Union, his native country, and the United States, his adopted country. He noted that in the United States, a country whose macrosystem consists of pluralistic political and social structures, the distance between peer group and adult values is greater than it is in the Soviet Union, where the values of these two groups tend to cluster around a politically endorsed nucleus. The result, he suggests, is that adolescents in the United States (and in cultures with similar ecological structures) will be more likely to be influenced by peer group pressures. On the other hand, in a now classic comparison of human development in the United States and the Soviet Union, Bronfenbrenner (1970) expresses his concern that the Russians "have gone too far in subjecting the child and his peer group to conformity to a single set of values imposed by the adult society" (p. 165). With the breakup of the Soviet Union and the infusion of democratic ideals into Russian society, it would be interesting to revisit this issue and consider any changes that may have resulted from these events.

Schlegal and Barry (1991), in a well-designed and pioneering interdisciplinary study, looked at a wide range of cultural groups and the role played by the cultural context in adolescent development, particularly the influence of group similarities and differences. This work provides a model for future research on cross-cultural human development. Using data from 186 cultures and 340 variables representing a broad range of adolescent issues, Schlegal and Barry offer detailed comparisons and contrasts on parent–adolescent relationships, adolescent sexuality, social markers defining transitions from childhood to adolescence and to adulthood, rites of passage, changes in social roles, and a variety of other topics. Throughout their investigation, they attempt to assess adolescent behavior as it occurs across cultures while carefully analyzing which behaviors appear to be culture-specific and which can be considered universal.

One final comment from White (1993) effectively illustrates how parental belief systems affect the way parents perceive the role of peers in the United States and in Japan: "Peer pressure in America is popularly seen as a negative force, rather than, as in Japan, a source of support and socialization for adult roles" (p. 37). With this said, we move to adulthood and aging.

◇ ADULTHOOD AND AGING

Early in this book, we noted that we would be looking at development from a lifespan orientation. There is a good reason for this, as illustrated by parent-child relationships in the years of adulthood and old age. As Zarit and Eggebeen (1995) make clear, "Parent–child relationships are a life-span issue. Rather than ceasing when children are launched from the family, these relationships endure with often complex patterns of interaction, support, and exchange that wax and wane around key transitions in the adult years" (p. 119). If couples have been successful in meeting the challenges of parenthood and have been able to get their own children grown up and on the way to parenthood themselves, they may look forward to the day when they achieve a new status in the life cycle—that of grandparents.

Grandparenthood

Smith (1991) has pointed out that when the first articles focusing on grandparents appeared during the 1930s and 1940s, they tended to portray grandparents in negative terms. During the next two decades, a more balanced view began to emerge (Staples, 1952). In a recent review, Adkins (1999) presents evidence showing that grandparents have a positive effect on children's affective and cognitive development, serve as a major support system during divorce and family breakdown, and when raising grandchildren on their own are as successful as are biological parents.

With a few notable exceptions, the majority of grandparent research has been conducted in the United States (Cherlin & Furstenberg, 1986; Kornhaber, 1996). However, more recent studies from European industrialized societies and African nonindustrialized cultures have become available (Smith, 1991; Sangree, 1992). Several studies comparing grandparent behaviors across cultures, notably China and the United States, and across generations have begun to appear in recent years (Strom & Strom, 2000; Strom, Strom, Wang, Shen, Griswold, Chan, & Yang, 1999). Nevertheless, it is clear that more comparative cross-cultural studies, using the ecological systems approach and other theories, are necessary if we are to describe, explain, and understand both the similarities and differences in grandparenting between and across cultures.

According to Smith (1995) the study of grandparenting is at the same time both easier and more difficult than the study of parenting. It is easier because objective analysis of grandparent–parent–grandchild relationships does not involve as intense emotions as those present in parent–child relationships. It is more difficult because "there are more varieties of grandparent than of parent, and one is studying three generations rather than two. . . . The study of grandparenthood is also challenging, in that the grandparent–parent–grandchild set of relationships confronts us squarely with the processes of socialization, intergenerational transmissions, and change over historical periods" (p. 89).

Due to the high divorce rate in the United States and the increase in single parents, who often have difficulty managing childrearing on their own, increasing numbers of grandparents are actively involved in raising their grandchildren. This adds a new layer of influence to the ecological system, as grandparents represent specific beliefs and values from a different historical period that may be contrary to the values of their children or even their own parents (Mills, 1999). Recalling the definition of culture (Chapter 1), just as individuals in Thailand or Mexico exhibit cultural differences, so do grandparents and parents represent two distinct cultures, each with their own shared set of values and beliefs.

In a pioneering longitudinal study of contemporary grandparenting, Kornhaber (1996) has noted that a body of research, based on a historical and cross-cultural perspective, is beginning to emerge and helping to clarify the meaning of grandparenthood and its function in various cultural settings. While pointing to the stable and important role grandparents play in modern societies, he also comments that "one of the dangers of 'modernization' most feared by leaders of emerging countries is the possible dismembering of the family and the inevitable loss of the grandparent's honored place in the family and society" (p. 22). Considering what we have said in earlier chapters about a culture's attitudes toward the aging process and the elderly, it should be apparent that these attitudes contribute to determining the status of grandparents. In cultures characterized by large extended families and a reverence for elders (e.g., China, Mexico, and many Asian and African societies), grandparents are likely to live with their families, be part of the social support system, and contribute to an intergenerational ecological setting (Benoit & Parker, 2000; Lubben & Becerra, 1987; Thomas, 1994). Let us now look at some of the interactions among these characteristics and the specific roles played by grandparents in several of the world's cultures.

Japan

Japan, a country continuing to experience modernization, is an interesting example of a culture dealing with the changing role of contemporary grandparents. Traditionally, Japanese grandparents have been respected, honored, and provided with ritualized status through a rite of passage that allows grandmothers to "wear the color red as a badge of her status" (Kornhaber, 1996, p. 22). This once-privileged role is undergoing dramatic change, causing increased concern among some social scientists (Strom et al., 1995; Strom & Strom, 1993). Before World War II, most Japanese lived in an extended family made up of three or more generations and governed by a rigid hierarchical system characterized by filial piety (respect) and strong parental authority. Following the democratization of the country at the end of the war, family life underwent significant changes (e.g., abolishment of the patriarchal family structure and granting of equal legal status to women; Fukada, 1991).

In an extensive three-generation study, Strom and colleagues (1995) found that Japanese grandparents believe their status in the family is eroding. While they want to continue to have an influence, social policy has yet to include education for their changing role in society. The authors analyzed responses to a questionnaire identifying strengths and needs of Japanese grandparents as perceived by 239 grandparents, 266 parents, and 274 school-age grandchildren from cities and small towns across Japan. Their findings reveal that grandparents report more satisfaction, greater success, and more

A Japanese grandfather enjoys an outing with his grandchild. (Bill Gillette/Liaison Agency, Inc.)

extensive involvement in teaching than was observed by parents and grand-children. In addition, grandparents said they felt greater difficulty, more frustration, and less informed to carry out their grandparenting role than was reported by parents and grandchildren. According to the authors, the factors most influencing responses related to grandparent performance were generation, grandchild's gender and age, generations living together, frequency of grandchild care by grandparent, and the amount of time they spent together. The authors have proposed the development of education programs to assist grandparents in adapting to their changing roles in Japan (Strom et al., 1995) as well as other cultures including China and the United States (Strom, 1999).

In a study of adolescents coming of age in Japan and the United States, White (1993) noted that grandparents often play a crucial role, particularly when they live near, although not with, the family and are able to provide support for the young person without creating dissension within the family. White quotes one working adolescent who delays going home by stopping at her grandmother's: "My mother asks too many questions. . . . So I go to my grandmother's house whenever I can, and I sometimes even call home to say I'm staying overnight there. She empties her refrigerator to cook wonderful meals for me. I am her favorite. And when I leave, she loads me down with fruit and food and sweets" (p. 68). Another adolescent, who takes care of a disabled grandmother, said, "I give her a massage every afternoon after school. I like to do it because she tells me stories about living in Nagano in the old days, and she really listens to me, and helps me with my problems" (p. 68).

Urbanization and technological advancements have contributed to a steady decrease in the number of Japanese extended families, from about 44 percent in 1955 to approximately 15 percent in 1985. The result is that the number of elderly (*rojin*) living on their own has risen sharply and will continue to rise in the future, presenting serious problems for a nation once known for its extended family structure. Still, according to Fukada (1991), Japan is finding creative ways to make use of its elderly and their skills. One such innovative concept is "silver banks." *Rojin* with superior abilities or knowledge in various fields are matched, through applications, with those needing their expertise and are paid for their services.

China

In the People's Republic of China (mainland China), grandparents have historically played a critical function in family life. According to Tien and Lee (1988), in the 1980s, about 40 percent of rural families and 24 percent of urban families were made up of three generations. Wolf (1978) notes that it was common for grandmothers to frequently intervene when they felt parents were punishing children too harshly. In commenting on the role of Chinese grandfathers, Wolf states that they are "a source of pennies for sweets, an occasional place for solace when the rest of the childhood world turns against them, and a good place for stories when nothing else is doing" (p. 142).

In an extensive investigation, similar to the one conducted among Japanese grandparents, Falbo (1991) surveyed almost 1,500 Chinese schoolchildren between the ages of six and ten to determine the impact of quality contact on children's behavior. Among her findings, she reports that contrary to the popular image of grandparents overindulging their grandchildren, there appears to have been no negative effect on personality or academic performance. In fact, "contact with educated grandparents was correlated with positive academic achievement. Contact with better educated grandfathers was correlated with . . . a more desirable personality as judged by both mothers and teachers" (p. 372). Her conclusion is that Chinese grandparents have a very positive influence on their grandchildren.

Stevenson, Chen, and Lee (1992) suggest that this influence, and the role grandparents play in families, largely depends on the sex of their own child as well as the sex of their grandchildren. For example, they state that "their son's children are considered to be their 'true' grandchildren . . . the ones for whose socialization they bear an important responsibility and for whom they assume a role as disciplinarian. . . . Grandparents feel no great need to be responsible for the children of their daughter, for their daughter's children are considered the children of their son-in-law. In fact, they are called 'outside' grandchildren, with whom it is permissible to establish a more playful relationship than with the 'true' grandchildren" (p. 23).

United States

According to Tinsley and Parke (1984), about 70 percent of American men and women will one day be grandparents. Women will typically become grandmothers around the age of fifty and men will be grandfathers about two years later. As Smith (1995) states, "Grandparenthood is thus an important part of the life cycle for most people, both as a personal experience and for its impact on others" (p. 90).

As mentioned earlier, most of the relatively limited research on grandparenting has been conducted in modern, urban, industrialized societies such as the United States and, to a lesser degree, some of the countries in Western Europe and, more recently, Asia. In one study of American grandparents and their satisfaction with their role, Brubaker (1985) reported that 80 percent were happy in their relationships and a majority found it easier and more enjoyable than parenting.

Harry and Ormsin Gardiner with their first grandchild—Macinnes Charoen Lamont. (Photo courtesy of the authors.)

Several researchers (Cherlin & Furstenberg, 1986; Peterson, 1989) hypothesize that the role grandparents play and their interactions within families will change significantly as family structures change and life expectancy increases. For example, four-generation families are becoming more common, with some grandparents becoming great-grandparents. In one study (Doka & Mertz, 1988), a sample of elderly great-grandparents reported that they found their role significant and emotionally fulfilling, providing them with a sense of personal and familial renewal, as well as a sign of longevity. With higher rates of divorce and remarriage, the issue of visitation rights for grandparents is also becoming an increasing concern for many (Stanton, 1998).

Another aspect of grandparenting in the United States that is different than that in other countries results from ethnic diversity. According to Lockery (1991), grandparents of Asian American, African American, Hispanic American, and Italian American backgrounds are more likely to play an active role in the lives of their grandchildren than are those of other ethnicities. In fact, as Barresi and Menon (1990) report, increasing numbers of older African Americans are becoming actively involved in caregiving among their grandchildren and great-grandchildren. According to Minkler and Roe (1991), approximately 13 percent of African American children, 3 percent of Hispanic American children, and 2 percent of European American children live with their grandparents.

Having active and vital grandparents can provide grandchildren with positive role models for old age, as illustrated by the following quote from a young girl named Patty, who said with great admiration about her grandmother, "She is a dynamo. A speedball. When my mom was in the hospital, she came over and cleaned the house and did the cooking. I helped her; we did it together. We dance, and I get tired before she does. She even chops wood. I hope I am like that. She says I am" (Kornhaber, 1996). (For more about grandparenting in the United States, we recommend the book by Kornhaber in the Further Readings section of this chapter.)

Caring for the Elderly

For generations, respect for those who have reached their later years has been higher in Japan, China, and many other countries than it has in the United States (Ikels, 1989; Jones, 1995; Yu, 1993). While this may still be true, in the case of the Japanese, the image may be overly idealized (Takada, 1993). As we pointed out earlier in this chapter, fewer elderly Japanese today are living with their children, and more are returning to low-paying jobs to support themselves.

Just as Japan is changing, so too is China, another of the world's oldest cultures. In China, the elderly were once revered, and the extended family was the primary unit of care for the elderly. While the family is still a central focus, it is facing problems and its role is changing. For example, with increased industrialization, many rural farmers are moving to the cities, leaving their aging relatives behind (Kosberg, 1992). Those families that remain in rural areas often develop a reciprocal arrangement in which a married son provides for his elderly parents and in return receives help from them with child care, housework, and even gardening (Olson, 1994). Those who are elderly and have no children may be eligible to move into one of the country's new homes for the elderly. To do so, one must meet four criteria: (1) have no living children nearby to provide care, (2) not be bedridden or require constant medical care, (3) be willing to enter the home, and (4) qualify for local welfare assistance (Olson, 1994). In addition to the difficulties already mentioned, elder abuse, inadequate housing, and insufficient retirement programs are becoming serious problems (Kosberg & Garcia, 1995).

In Germany, community-based services are also increasing but are unable to meet the growing numbers of elderly, 75 percent of whom need help with daily activities and 10 percent of whom are bedridden (Olson, 1994).

In the United States, and many other countries, as individuals live longer, it is becoming increasingly common that adult children in middle adulthood are required to provide care for aging relatives, particularly parents (Coward, Horne, & Dwyer, 1992) as well as for their own children. Finding themselves caught between the needs of two generations, these individuals are often referred to as the *sandwich generation*. As Olson (1994) has shown, up to 70 percent of this caregiving is currently provided by women, most often adult daughters, wives, and daughters-in-law. In the United States, families provide about 80 percent of all long-term care for the elderly (Kosberg, 1992).

In many countries—notably France, Sweden, Finland, and Israel—health care and social services are considered "rights," not privileges for those who can afford them. This is becoming a particularly difficult problem in France, where in the last couple of decades there has been a drop in the fertility rate accompanied by a corresponding increase in life expectancy. Currently, France has one of the longest life expectancies in the world, with approximately 3.8 million people over the age of seventy-five. This figure is expected to increase to 5.6 million by the year 2020 (Olson, 1994). The French microsystem is not working very well, as less than 10 percent of those sixty-five years or older live with family members and barely 5 percent live in institutions. This means the majority of elderly are living on their own. It is obvious that new ways of providing care are needed, and soon. For a view of how Koreans, Latinos, Africans, and Arabs treat their elderly, see Box 9.2 on pages 240–242.

While the elderly in most nonindustrialized traditional societies continue to receive respect from younger people and to play a role in their culture, this is not as true in faster-changing, modern, industrialized societies.

BOX 9.2

 CULTURAL VIEWS AND
TREATMENT OF THE ELDERLY

As individuals grow older, they experience changes in physical, cognitive, and social abilities. The following sections highlight some of the ways in which elderly are viewed and treated across cultures.

Korean Elderly

Historically, Korean society has been strongly influenced by Chinese culture and, in particular, Confucianism, which provides guidelines governing relationships between father and son, minister and ruler, husband and wife, elder and younger brothers, and friends. Broadly speaking, Korea is a collectivist or "relationship culture" in which the group is placed above the individual, resulting in pressure to conform to cultural norms and group demands.

The *Book of Rites* states that Koreans must respect parents, take good care of them, and bring no dishonor to them or family. Filial responsibility is the obligation of an adult child, and elderly parents typically live with their first married son who, with help from siblings, provides financial support and health care. The family remains of utmost importance in Korea today, although the proportion of elderly living apart from their children has been on the rise. Growing concern over rapid industrialization, urbanization, and changes in filial care by the younger generation has resulted in recent welfare laws and an increase in the provision of social and health services for the elderly (Sung, 1992).

Latino Elderly

While Latinos or Hispanics come from many different countries, they are united by a common language, and although differences exist across cultures, some generalizations are possible. For example, certain attitudes and values are common in Latino cultures. One of these is *familialism*, emphasizing sharing and cooperation, rather than competition. A sense of family pride and loyalty and extended family support is the norm. Families remain the traditional support system despite urbanization and modernization. Other cultural values include *simpatia*, with its stress on loyalty, dignity, friendliness, politeness, affection, and respect for others; *personalismo*, emphasizing the importance of personal goodness and getting along with others over individual ability and individual success; *respeto*, valuing and acknowledging hierarchies that define an individual's proper place in society on the basis of age, gender, race, and class (Levitt, Guacci-Franco, & Levitt, 1993). These values play a major role in beliefs about care of the elderly, as does the Catholic religion with its emphasis on charity as a virtue. The result is that

BOX 9.2 CONTINUED

Latinos often do not behave assertively and believe that problems or events are meant to be and cannot be altered (Wing Sue & Sue, 1990).

In Latino cultures, the elderly are believed to have an inner strength that can be a resource for the younger generation. They see themselves as important members of the family because they are links to the past, and do not feel useless or like a burden and are not ashamed to ask for help (Holmes & Holmes, 1995; Paz, 1993). They occupy a central role in the family and are treated with respect (*respecto*), status (*su lugar*), and authority (*su experiencia y sabiduria;* Paz, 1993).

Children, particularly daughters, play a major role in caring for the elderly and providing assistance, although not all elderly may necessarily live with their children. Interestingly, if daughters do not care for their mothers, complaints are more hostile than if they are neglected by their sons. Daughters are also expected to visit and phone more frequently than sons (Holmes & Holmes, 1995; Paz, 1993). When a parent's condition severely deteriorates, formal services may be used by the family, although institutionalization is rare (Holmes & Holmes, 1995).

African Elderly

Black African societies vary in their views and treatment of the elderly. At times, older individuals are held in esteem as vast storehouses of knowledge and power. At other times, their legitimacy to knowledge and power is questioned (Diop, 1989).

In a majority of African societies, old age is viewed as a sign of divine blessing. In fact, in several African languages the elder is the "big person" (Diop, 1989). Many African women who reach middle age experience the removal of restrictions in an often gender-typed society and their status and power is approximately the same as men (Brown, 1992; Udvardy & Cattell, 1992). However, not all views and treatment of the elderly are positive. In many societies, young people no longer fear the influence or ancestral powers of elders and, as poverty increases, there is less support for the elderly (Udvardy & Cattell, 1992).

In Nigeria, many older persons have little personal income and usually live with their children. Typically, first sons and all daughters care for their aged parents (Kalu & Kalu, 1993), although homes for the elderly have existed since the early 1900s for elders without family support (Ekpenyong, 1995). Most elderly would prefer to die where they were born and those physically able to make the journey often do so (Kalu & Kalu, 1993).

Among the Hausa, a Muslim society concentrated primarily in Northern Nigeria, elderly women have control over the respect and tolerance from male children and have a voice in the selection of a wife for their sons,

(continued)

BOX 9.2 CONTINUED

frequently for their grandsons, and in some cases a brother's child. Old Muslim Hausa women, but not young or middle-aged women, may pray in the mosque along with men (Holmes & Holmes, 1995).

Arab Elderly

Arabs have many traits in common, but generalizing about Arab culture is difficult because of major regional differences. Nevertheless, some generalizations help in understanding how elderly are treated in Arab cultures.

Muslim ideology, as presented in the *Koran,* provides a sociological and legal framework of life containing the doctrines that guide Muslims to "correct" behaviors. The word "Islam" means "submission to the will of God" and a Muslim is "one who submits" (Nydell, 1987). Thus, religion guides and affects an Arab's entire way of life and thinking.

The extended family has always been highly valued in Arab cultures. Typically, fathers provide for the family, discipline the children, and maintain the cohesiveness, order, honor, and social standing of the family while mothers are responsible for the care and nurturance of the children. An elderly person's status commands authority in an Arab Muslim household and increases with age. Honor and respect for the elderly is contained in the Koran and it is assumed that families will look after the elderly. Traditionally, elderly parents live with the oldest son (Luna, 1989).

Although a small number of nursing home facilities exist, they are still rare in the Middle East. The thought of "putting one's parents in a nursing home" is not acceptable to Arab Muslims. Arab families do not abandon their elderly or their sick no matter how impractical the demands and responsibilities for their care (Spector, 1991).

Interestingly, senility among older Arab Muslims is rare and might be related to the fact that, in the Middle East, elderly gain status and do not experience the loss of self-esteem or self-worth that often occurs in Western culture (Elkholy, 1981).

Source: Adapted from *Culture and Aging* by Vicki Ritts, 2000, unpublished manuscript, St. Louis Community College. Reprinted by permission.

Considering what has been covered in this section, the ecological systems approach seems to be alive and well and functioning effectively in more traditional cultures. Perhaps it is time to return to this model, consider its many positive characteristics, and possibly adapt and fine-tune it to the evolving cultures of today's contemporary world.

◇ THE CHANGING CONTEXT
OF FAMILIES

Before bringing this chapter to a close, it should be recognized that the eco-logical settings of families throughout the world have been changing over the last several decades. This is especially true in the United States. The stereotype of the "all-American family," consisting of two children (a girl and a boy) living in a single-family home in a middle-class neighborhood with the father working and the mother staying at home to provide child care, is no longer the norm—if it ever was.

According to Fuller (1992), only 7 percent of mothers in two-parent homes stay with children while their spouses go to work. Today's families are more likely to consist of single parents, parents who are not married but living together, or gay parents; blended families made up of stepparents and stepchildren; or families in which grandparents are responsible for raising minor-age children. As Fay (1993) has reported, families headed by a mar-ried couple declined from 40.3 percent in 1970 to 25.9 percent in 1991, while only 30 percent of adults in 1991 were married with children, down 9 percent from 1977.

In addition to these changing demographics, efforts to understand the ecology of families and the developmental niche of children within them are complicated by the fact that some children are born into an intact family, spend time in a single-parent family following a divorce, move into one of thirty-two different types of blended family environments when the custo-dial parent remarries, and may even be cared for by grandparents at some point (Fuller, 1992). While the challenges may be great, the need to under-stand how families throughout the world raise their children and the influ-ence culture has on this process is even greater.

◇ SUMMARY

This chapter opened with a description of the family life cycle and was fol-lowed by a discussion of mate selection and marriage rites in a variety of cul-tures throughout the world stressing the influence of one's ecological setting in determining the important influences on each of these events. In an ex-ploration of the birth process, the focus was on the ecology of birth and sim-ilarities and differences in cultural practices, most notably in Yucatan, Hol-land, Sweden, and the United States. With the transition to parenthood, cultural belief systems begin to play a major role in family decision making as illustrated in mothering and fathering behavior during the years of infancy and childhood. Next, adolescence was viewed from the ecological systems approach and the importance of peer relationships was discussed from a cross-cultural perspective. For many, the years of adulthood frequently consist of the raising of adolescent children (and even adult children) as well as caring for elderly parents. Finally, the transition to becoming a grandparent in Japan, China, and the United States received considerable attention as did the recognition that family ecology is undergoing dramatic change.

◇ FURTHER READINGS

Leonore Loeb Adler. (Ed.). (1991). *Women in Cross-Cultural Perspective.* Westport, CT: Praeger.

> A vivid presentation of traditional and evolving socialization of women and cultural perceptions of their contemporary roles. Seventeen chapters range across the globe from the Arctic to Latin America, Poland to Egypt and the Sudan, Thailand to Australia, India to Samoa. Each chapter contains short historical background sketches followed by chronologically organized information from infancy through school years, marriage, pregnancy and childbirth, adult activities, and aging.

Arthur Kornhaber. (1996). *Contemporary Grandparenting.* Thousand Oaks, CA: Sage.

> The first text of its kind, written by one of the key figures in the grandparenting activist movement. This book brings to life the diversity of today's grandparents in a lively and readable way. "A must read."

Robert Levine, Suguru Sato, Tsukasa Hashimoto, & Jyoti Verma. (1995). Love and marriage in eleven cultures. *Journal of Cross-Cultural Psychology, 26,* 554–571.

> What kinds of views do college students have on the topics of love and marriage? This study reports on students from India, Pakistan, Thailand, Mexico, Brazil, Japan, Hong Kong, the Philippines. Australia, England, and the United States.

CHAPTER TEN

CULTURE AND HEALTH

Hiroki Hashimoto is fourteen and lives with his family in the northern city of Akita on the island of Honshu. He attends a private school, where one of his British teachers, Alison Perrin, is concerned about Hiroki's obsessive neatness, extreme shyness, and apparent lack of many close friends. Based on her previous experiences with adolescents in her own country and during a teaching appointment in Canada, she feels he may have an obsessive-compulsive neurosis as well as very poorly developed interpersonal skills. She mentions to a Japanese colleague that she is about to recommend that his parents take him to see a child psychologist. Her colleague explains that Hiroki is more likely showing signs of a rather common disorder in Japan known as taijin kyofushu syndrome *(TKS) in which an individual is afraid of offending others while engaged in social situations. Loosely translated as "interpersonal anxiety" or simply "fear of people," TKS appears related to two salient behavior patterns in Japanese culture: an almost universal appearance of shyness or modesty and a great concern with cleanliness.*

The sun has just appeared over the small village near Huascaran, an extinct volcano and the highest peak in the Andes Mountains, in the Peruvian highlands, where Eric Summerville, an Australian physician, works among the runakuna *(native Quechua people). He has just been summoned to the thatched-roof home of a family whose young daughter appears to be suffering from* susto, *a disorder he has observed many times before among Indian tribes in Peru, Colombia, and Bolivia.* Susto *(Spanish for fright) is frequently the result of a frightening experience, and its symptoms may include excitability, severe anxiety, depression, rapid heartbeat, and often loss of weight. According to cultural beliefs, it can be caused by a variety of circumstances, including*

contact with strangers, supernatural spirits, or even "bad air" from cemeteries. The village healer has already made the traditional diagnosis by examining a guinea pig's intestines. Dr. Summerville now assists with the usual treatment of rubbing a variety of plants over the girl's skin while the healer performs an animal sacrifice to pacify the Earth, where it is believed the girl's soul is trapped.

As individuals, we differ from one another in numerous ways, but in one way we are all alike—our susceptibility to becoming ill. Each of the above vignettes illustrates a unique cultural orientation to the diagnosis and practice of medicine. In both cases, making an accurate diagnosis and planning effective treatment are of chief importance. However, the explanations for the behavior and the etiology (causes) of the symptoms differ. In the case of Hiroki, cultural beliefs about social behavior and expectations within his ecological setting play a major role in his symptoms. In Peru, native beliefs about a variety of frightening circumstances lead to a culturally unique diagnosis and treatment using indigenous methods that are an extension of the developmental niche.

◊ CULTURAL CONCEPTS OF HEALTH AND HEALING

Cultural traditions determine, in large part, how individuals look at their physical and mental health. What is considered healthy behavior in one society may be viewed as unhealthy in another. For example, there are many ways in which people deal with stress and tension (e.g., withdrawal, overt expressions of anger, overeating, or not eating at all). Which approach to dealing with problems would one consider healthy and which unhealthy? The answer varies depending on the culture, developmental niche, and interaction among unique ecocultural systems: the individual (microsystem), who lives and interacts with others in a particular village or neighborhood (mesosystem), and the specific cultural health beliefs and practices that help to shape what goes on within the wider exosystem and macrosystem.

Culture influences attitudes toward health in a variety of ways. A reciprocal process exists in which cultural beliefs, traditions, and progression of knowledge about health shape the views of a particular society, and the views of society, in turn, determine methods and treatments. Frequently, the signs and treatment of an illness are manifested in the beliefs themselves. For example, in remote parts of Sabah and Sarawak in East Malaysia, an individual who exhibits the symptoms of depression would seek the treatment of a village *bomoh* (medicine man) to remove the charms presumably evoked by jealous clans. In contrast, many North Americans view depression as a biological disorder explainable as a chemical imbalance in the brain and usually treated with antidepressants. You can imagine how the nature and treatment of depression in either culture might be perceived by the other.

This gives rise to an important concept in cross-cultural psychology discussed earlier—the distinction between emic and etic factors. As you may recall, **emic** refers to *culture-specific concepts,* whereas **etic** refers to *culture-general concepts* (Berry, Poortinga, Segall, & Dasen, 1992). In this regard, the symptoms characteristic of certain illness in one culture cannot be generalized across cultures. For example, Beardsley and Pedersen (1997) point out that while eating disorders are particularly unique to young women in Western countries, such disorders may not be as common in developing countries, where the food supply is scarce. Each culture's delicate balance of ecological systems and developmental niches make up the emic values to be considered when diagnosing and treating illness.

Culture-Bound Syndromes

Medical anthropologists and ethnopsychiatrists have known about seemingly unique forms of psychological illnesses for a long time. These researchers observed (1) symptoms of known illnesses that expressed themselves in unique ways in different cultures and (2) certain illnesses that occurred only among members of a specific cultural group. Because the unique patterns of symptoms did not fit any conventional classification system of disorders, these disorders were largely ignored by the medical community. Finally, in 1994, the fourth edition of the *Diagnostic and Statistical Manual of the American Psychiatric Society* (DSMV-IV) acknowledged the existence of these culture-bound syndromes. The DSM-IV defines **culture-bound syndrome** as: "recurrent, locality-specific patterns of aberrant and troubling experience that may or may not be linked to a particular DSM-IV diagnostic category. Many of these patterns are indigenously considered to be 'illnesses,' or at least afflictions, and most have local names" (p. 844). Box 10.1 on pages 248–250 presents examples of some of the better known syndromes. While the inclusion of culture-bound syndromes represents an improvement in the validity of Western diagnostic systems, current researchers suggest that this is just the foundation for the practice of culturally sensitive medicine. For instance, Azhar and Varma (2000) suggest that a new form of psychotherapy could be used to treat culture-bound syndromes (*koro, amok*) in Malaysia. This treatment is based on Western techniques of cognitive therapy but includes culture-specific religious beliefs and practices to reduce symptoms and achieve overall well-being.

BOX 10.1

CULTURE-BOUND SYNDROMES

How individuals view their mental and physical health is determined, in part, by cultural traditions, for example, what is considered healthy in one society may be seen as unhealthy in another. While psychological disorders can be found in all cultures, the ways in which they are formed and expressed appear to be highly influenced by cultural belief systems, and according to Draguns (1997), shaped by cultural factors.

One of the most widely used systems for classifying abnormal behavior into categories is the DSM-IV (*Diagnostic and Statistical Manual of Mental Disorders*). The latest edition (APA, 1994) includes cultural variations of specific disorders and discusses twenty-five culture-bound syndromes. These syndromes are thought to be exaggerated manifestations of superstitions and belief patterns within cultures that do not fit into existing Western diagnosis.

China

Koro, found primarily in China (as far back as 3000 B.C.) and some other South and East Asian countries, is associated with acute anxiety involving the fear that one's genitals (the penis in a man and the vulva and nipples in women) are shrinking and retracting into the body and may result in death. Chinese folk culture provides some insight into the syndrome's origins, which can be found in fears about nocturnal emissions and impotence. These fears originated in the traditional Chinese beliefs about the balance of *yin* (female) and *yang* (male) humors, which held that during masturbation or nocturnal emissions an unhealthy loss of *yang* was thought to occur and to place an individual in an unbalanced condition (Pfeiffer, 1982).

Koro has been identified primarily in younger men, twenty-one to forty years of age. It is believed that guilt and anxiety arise out of real or imagined sexual excesses. People with *koro* demonstrate typical anxiety symptoms such as sweating, breathlessness, and heart palpitations. Men with the disorder have been known to use mechanical devices, such as chopsticks, to try to prevent the penis from retracting into the body. Reassurance by medical professionals that the genitals are not retracting often puts an end to *koro* episodes, and the disorder passes with time (Pfeiffer, 1982). Most cases, however, are handled by traditional medical or folk healers outside of the established health care system (Lin, 1985).

Japan

Taijin-kyofu-sho (TKS) is characterized by an excessive fear and anxiety that a person will behave in ways that will embarrass or offend other people, for example, blushing, emitting odors, staring inappropriately, or presenting

BOX 10.1 CONTINUED

improper facial expressions, and results in social withdrawal and avoidance. Affecting primarily young Japanese men, the syndrome is believed to be related to an emphasis in Japanese culture on not embarrassing others as well as deep concerns about issues of shame (Kirmayer, 1991; Pfeiffer, 1982; Russell, 1989; Takahashi, 1989). TKS is also found in Korea (Kim, 1995).

Upon examining the symptoms of TKS and using a Western diagnostic system, patients with TKS would typically be diagnosed as having anxiety reactions, obsessive-compulsive reactions, or social phobias. Traditional therapy for TKS occurs in the context of a ritual setting and includes physiological applications (sweating and massage), behavioral restrictions (diet), and social support (Kirmayer, 1991; Pfeiffer, 1982).

Korea

Shin-byung (a divine illness) is a possession syndrome often occurring in the course of a prolonged psychosomatic illness. People believe they are possessed by a dead ancestor and, through a dream or a hallucination, are persuaded to become a shaman, after which the patient becomes "cured" of the ailment. The occurrence of *shin-byung* is reported to be decreasing (Kim, 1995).

India

Dhat is a disorder affecting Indian males and involves intense fear or anxiety over the loss of semen through ejaculations or through nocturnal emissions. Some men also believe, incorrectly, that semen mixes with urine and is excreted by urinating. In Indian culture, semen is considered to be the elixir of life, on both the physical and mystical sense. There is a popular belief that loss of semen drains a man of his vital natural energy, while its preservation guarantees health and longevity. Loss of semen through masturbation, excessive sexual intercourse, or nocturnal emission is believed to lead to weakness (Chadda & Ahujan, 1990; Pfeiffer, 1982). The most common symptoms of *dhat* are fatigue, weakness, body aches, severe headaches, depression, anxiety, loss of appetite, and suicidal feelings. Indian males believe that this is caused by heated foods, a fiery constitution, sexual excesses, and the use of intoxicants. A "cooling diet," "cooling medications," and baths are recommended. A tonic may also be given to increase sperm production (Chadda & Ahujan, 1990; Pfeiffer, 1982).

Nigeria

"Missing genitals" is a syndrome that has been reported in Nigeria. The victim, typically a man, exchanges greetings by shaking hands with another man; this gesture is followed by fear that the genitals have disappeared. It is usually claimed that supernatural forces have been invoked to make the genitals

(continued)

BOX 10.1 CONTINUED

disappear. While objective examination of the genitals reveals that they are intact, pointing this out to the victim does not convince him (Sijuwola, 1995).

Latino Culture

Susto ("magical fright") is found in some Latino cultures, primarily among the Kechua-speaking Indians of the Andes. It is triggered by a frightening experience, in which the soul is thought to separate from the body and become trapped on earth, and the person falls to the ground. Symptoms include loss of appetite and weight, physical weakness, restless sleep, depression, introversion, and apathy. By looking at the intestines of a guinea pig, a healing expert makes the diagnosis and then attempts to appease the earth through sacrifices so that the soul will return to the body (Pfeiffer, 1982). *Amok,* a type of dissociative episode or a sudden change in consciousness or self-identity, is found in traditional Puerto Rican and Navajo cultures in the West. It is marked by a violent or aggressive outburst followed by a period of brooding, often precipitated by a perceived slight or insult. The person, who sometimes experiences amnesia, returns to his or her usual state of functioning following the episode. In the West, the expression "running amuck" refers to an episode of losing oneself and running around in a violent frenzy (Pfeiffer, 1982).

Native American Culture

Windigo, also known as witiko, is a rare, culture-bound disorder reported among some North American Indian tribes, including the Cree and Ojibwa. It is characterized by symptoms of melancholia and a delusion of transformation into a *witiko* or man-eating monster, who either has a heart of ice or vomits ice, and who will turn the victim into a homicidal cannibal. Cannibalism seldom, if ever, occurs. Suicidal ideation to avoid acting on the cannibalistic urges may take place (Trimble, Manson, Dinges, & Medicine, 1984).

Source: Adapted from *Infusing culture into parenting issues: A supplement for psychology instructors* by Vicki Ritts, 2000, unpublished manuscript, St. Louis Community College. Reprinted by permission.

Medical Diagnosis Across Cultures

The emic–etic distinction is germane to another important issue in culture and health—namely, the reliability and validity of diagnostic tests and measurement. Before making a diagnosis, physicians and other health professionals need to consider the medical criteria on which they base their treatment decisions. Often, doctors trained in Western societies use their familiar inventories and diagnostic criteria to evaluate medical conditions in patients from non-Western societies, with a resulting misdiagnosis. The emic or culture-specific values and beliefs that are part of a particular doctor's eco-cultural perspective cannot be readily applied in diagnosing and treating people raised in a culturally different developmental niche. Lonner and Ibrahim (1989) suggest that accurate assessment should take into consideration the beliefs, values, and perceptions of the patient and that doctors should employ culture-specific criteria when diagnosing illnesses.

In an interesting study focusing on illness beliefs, Cook (1994) asked 182 adult Chinese, Indian, and Anglo Celtic Canadians about their beliefs concerning chronic illness and how they should be treated. He found that each ethnic group viewed the causes and treatment differently, depending on geographical orientation, generation, and age. For example, older first- or second-generation Chinese emphasized a more traditional, spiritual dimension to help explain and treat physical illness, whereas younger Chinese tended to look to biomedical intervention. Once again, an individual's unique developmental niche and place in a specific ecological system help shape attitudes toward health. Failure to recognize this important link may result in misdiagnosis of medical conditions.

When individuals are misdiagnosed, their health generally deteriorates even more. There is little or no relief because treatment is completely ineffective. The chances of this occurring are greatest when physicians and health care professionals from one cultural orientation treat individuals from another. For example, in 1985, more than one hundred Cuban refugees were initially rejected from applying for U.S. citizenship because a medical review board composed entirely of American psychiatrists diagnosed them as having antisocial personality disorder. However, this diagnosis was overturned after an official appeal was made to a second medical board composed of physicians and psychiatrists from several different countries. Many of the psychiatrists serving on the initial screening board subsequently admitted not being aware of crucial ethnic and cultural differences when they made their original diagnosis (Boxer & Garvey, 1985).

Lisa Beardsley (1994) has outlined several reasons for misdiagnoses. A first reason is the use of clinical manuals (e.g., the *Diagnostic and Statistical Manual–Fourth Edition*, DSM-IV) in societies significantly different from the ones for which they were originally intended. For example, while Chinese and American psychiatrists largely agree on some clinical evaluations such as schizophrenia, they disagree on others, including depression and anxiety disorders.

A second reason for misidentifying a health problem frequently centers on the difference in definition between disease and illness behavior. According to Beardsley, **disease** is a *biological process*, whereas **illness behavior** is a *psychological experience and the social expression of disease* (p. 281). She goes on to point out that "cultural variables interact with biological processes, and as a result, there is overlap between culture-specific (emic) and culture-general (etic) features of a disease" (p. 281). A similar point has been made by Brislin (1993).

Finally, the use of culturally biased instruments and tests may contribute to misdiagnosis. For example, standardized intelligence tests, such as the Stanford-Binet and the Wechsler Intelligence Scale for Children (WISC), and personality inventories such as the Minnesota Multiphasic Personality Inventory (MMPI), were developed for use with specific American populations and even when carefully translated are not always appropriate for use in other cultures. Consequently, use of these instruments may result in a patient or client receiving ineffective treatment. For example, one of the authors (Gardiner) once had a Chinese student come to his office in tears because she had been given the results of her MMPI and the computerized analysis indicated she "demonstrates bizarre behavior and should be institutionalized and treated immediately." Knowing the cultural specificity of certain items on this test used to assess "psychopathological tendencies," he was able to calm her down by showing her how the answers she gave, while reasonable and healthy for her particular culture, were considered inappropriate and unhealthy when given by someone born and raised in the American culture. He strongly recommended that the personnel in the college counseling office, none of whom had had cross-cultural training, not use this instrument as a measure of anything with international students. As Brislin (1990) aptly states, "It is decidedly a creation of the 'Western' view of etiology and psychiatric classification (and is, therefore, culture-bound); its original normative samples came from small, rural parts of Minnesota (in the United States); and there is little or no 'theory' guiding its cross-cultural use" (p. 69). Nevertheless, the MMPI is available in more than one hundred languages and, since the incident mentioned above, has undergone revision and is seen by some as worthy of cross-cultural attention (Butcher, 1990, 1995; Butcher et al., 1990). However, we still agree with Brislin, who argues for caution if employing this instrument because "its misuse can lead to terrible errors and tragic consequences" (1990, p. 70).

The World Health Organization (WHO) has as its goal the promotion of health and prevention of misdiagnoses as well as the provision of medical services to countries throughout the world. One of WHO's major efforts is the Mental Health Program, which is aimed at protecting and promoting mental health. According to Sartorius (1994), this program consists of four parts: "(1) Mental Health programme formulation and evaluation, (2) psychosocial and behavioural factors affecting health and development, (3) organization of services for the prevention and treatment of mental and neurological illnesses, and (4) biomedical research on mental functioning in health

BOX 10.2

 TRAINING HEALTH CARE PROFESSIONALS
TO BE CULTURALLY SENSITIVE

In the United States, emergency rooms are treating increasing numbers of individuals from ethnically and culturally diverse backgrounds. For example, in 1992, more than a million legal immigrants and refugees entered the United States, many speaking little or no English. In an article in *U.S. News and World Report* (February 1993), Goode speaks to the importance of physicians becoming more sensitive to cultural diversity. Today, hospital staff are taking steps to ensure greater awareness and better understanding of cultural differences. Failure to do this will only increase the possibility of misdiagnosis, as in the case of a Mexican peasant woman who invented her symptoms because she was too embarrassed to describe her real problem (rectal fistula). Needless to say, such misunderstanding not only jeopardizes patients' health but also opens up the possibility of a lawsuit. Thus, many physicians are taking courses in multiculturalism and are enlisting the help of relatives or friends of patients when making daily rounds. In New York, a Chinatown outreach team from St. Vincent's Hospital is learning about the use of herbal remedies to treat ailments of the elderly. Also, folk healers are recruited at University Hospital in Minneapolis to help serve the large community of Laotian Hmong refugees.

and disease" (p. 262). Developing guidelines for improving mental health care and training mental health professionals are also integral parts of this program. As a result of these and other efforts, health care professionals are becoming more culturally sensitive (see Box 10.2).

Success in these efforts requires an understanding of human development from a cross-cultural perspective. The focus of this chapter, therefore, is to investigate how health is mediated by cultural factors across the lifespan.

◇ INFANCY AND CHILDHOOD

Professionals in today's health care delivery systems see infant care as one of their major challenges. Technological advances allow premature and extremely low-birth-weight babies that would not have survived a decade ago to live and grow into healthy children and adults. But the process is not always easy, and success or failure frequently depends on cultural factors.

Sudden Infant Death Syndrome (SIDS)

In addition to the problem of premature and low-birth-weight babies, **sudden infant death syndrome (SIDS)** is another public health concern. In the United States, SIDS is the second leading cause of infant mortality, after complications from birth defects (USDHHS, 1992). In SIDS, for reasons still not clearly understood, *newborns who test normal on post-delivery neurological and respiratory tests and appear healthy for much of the first year of life, suddenly stop breathing and die.* While several medical explanations have been offered, data from an international investigation of SIDS cases in the United States, Australia, the Netherlands, and New Zealand suggest that SIDS may be a result of infants sleeping on their stomachs (AAP Task Force, 1991). Pediatric authorities now recommend that infants sleep on their backs ("Back to Sleep").

The fear of suffocating infants is not new and has existed for centuries. In the Middle Ages, infants were sometimes asphyxiated when their mothers, sleeping in the same bed, rolled over on them in the middle of the night. This happened so frequently that local church authorities wrote a decree for-

Breast-feeding young infants is commonly practiced throughout the world. (Jim Whitmer/Stock Boston)

bidding parents to sleep next to their newborns (Nakajima & Mayor, 1996). Since then, health officials in many Western countries have attempted to discourage the practice of mothers and infants sleeping in the same bed because it is believed to increase the chances of the infant dying from SIDS. However, cross-cultural research conducted in Japan, where cosleeping is common, has shown this not to be the case. In fact, fewer babies die from SIDS in Japan and Sweden each year than almost anywhere in the world (Hoffman & Hillman, 1992). Nakajima and Mayor (1996) report research carried out in sleep laboratories in California that shows that infants who slept with their mothers, rather than in separate bedrooms, doubled their chance of being breast-fed, which provides nutrition and promotes healthy attachment (see Chapter 3). In addition, infants who slept with their mothers showed less distress and cried less often during the day.

This raises an important question: "How is the parent–infant relationship affected by the health of the infant?" Generalizations about parents' reactions to a premature baby are difficult to make. However, for most parents it is a time of intense confusion. On the one hand, they are happy with the birth of their newborn, but at the same time, they are worried and concerned about the possibility their infant might die from a variety of complications. In the next section, we consider the role culture plays in caring for premature babies or children with health problems.

Parental Beliefs About Caring for Infants and Children

Most parents are interested in knowing the long-term consequences of their child's medical condition. Findings from a landmark longitudinal study conducted by Werner and her colleagues (1989) provide important information on this topic. Beginning in the 1950s, more than 650 infants born on the Hawaiian island of Kauai were monitored for cognitive and emotional development throughout childhood and adulthood. While most were born without complications and were raised in supportive homes, a substantial number experienced a variety of difficulties, including some perinatal stress and prematurity. The researchers reported that infants raised in supportive and nurturing homes showed more competence than those who were not reared in such environments. Not surprisingly, they also found that premature and low-birth-weight infants developed significantly more slowly when their prenatal problems were combined with impoverished living conditions, dysfunctional family situations, and inadequate parenting. The premature infants who made the greatest progress tended to grow up in families with a great deal of physical stimulation, interaction with other family members, and supportive caregiving.

Beckwith, Rodning, and Cohen (1992) lent additional support to the importance of providing premature infants with warm and caring home environments. They reported that children born premature but raised in responsive environments had several advantages over those not raised in some homes, including improved self-esteem, higher measures of intelligence, and fewer behavioral problems.

The health of children is one of the world's most important concerns, since the survival of any society rests to some extent on the health of its children. How healthy are the world's children? In a United Nations report on the state of children's health, Grant (1993) estimated that the largest proportion of child deaths are caused by pneumonia, diarrhea, tetanus, and tuberculosis. Most of these illnesses occur in countries with the fewest resources to deal with them and could be prevented if antibiotics and vaccines were available.

On a more positive note, over the past one hundred years, we have witnessed a significant reduction in such often fatal communicable childhood illnesses as measles, smallpox, and scarlet fever. Many international health organizations dedicated to developing and maintaining programs that promote children's health, such as UNESCO and WHO, have been successful in increasing the awareness of children's health issues, including those of street children (see Box 10.3).

◇ ADOLESCENCE

Writing about the hurried child, Elkind (1984, 1988) characterizes American youth as growing up too fast too soon and states that "like Superman, Superkid has spectacular powers and precocious competence even as an infant. This allows us to think that we can hurry the little powerhouse with impunity" (p. xii).

The pressure to grow up affects most children at some point, but each culture has its own beliefs about when this is supposed to occur. In some societies, the process is gradual, whereas in others it is abrupt. No matter how smooth the transition might be, it brings with it challenges, possibilities, and health concerns.

Adolescence, *the time between childhood and adulthood,* was initially called a period of "storm and stress" by the "father" of modern adolescent psychology, G. Stanley Hall (1904), who described the frequent mood swings and conflict thought to characterize the period. Many of these early ideas have been refuted by more recent researchers (Feldman & Elliott, 1990; Medicus, 1992). Today, most lifespan psychologists view adolescence as a continuous process rather than a fixed stage in the life cycle (Muuss, 1996).

Adolescence is nevertheless a complex concept and is shaped by sociocultural beliefs and historical events. For example, just before the start of the twentieth century in the United States, the concept of adolescence did not

BOX 10.3

STREET CHILDREN
AND ISSUES OF HEALTH

With advances in satellite communication, we are able to witness firsthand the devastating effects of war and poverty on the lives of children in many of the world's countries. Aptekar (1994) and others (Cosgrove, 1990; Lusk, 1992; Visano, 1990) have spent more than a decade investigating street children in the developing world. Often, being victims of physical or sexual abuse and neglect, children in many cultures take to the streets in hopes of finding safety. In fact, for some children, life on the street is healthier than life at home (Connolloy, 1990). Aptekar (1988) believes that in some cases, street children have better physical and mental health than siblings living at home. It is estimated that there are between forty and fifty million street children in Latin America alone (Aptekar, 1994; Ortiz & Poertner, 1992). For some children, life on the street is the only life they have ever known, since they were born on the streets from parents who were street children themselves (Aptekar, 1994). However, street children are more often victims of extraordinary poverty and rely on begging for a living (Ojanuga, 1990). Out of sheer desperation, many of these children resort to child pornography and prostitution to support themselves. Gang violence, theft and robbery, alcohol and drug abuse, and extortion and racketeering are common experiences for many of these children. As the number of street children rises throughout the world, health authorities have become increasingly involved in efforts to reduce the growing incidence of runaway children and the health risks to which they are exposed.

In a review of the literature on street children, Aptekar (1994) cites a comparative study carried out by Veale (1992) involving street children in Ireland during the mid-nineteenth century and those currently living on the streets in Sudan. In both countries, civil unrest was the reason children chose life on the street. Violence from warring factions and political instability were responsible for the large number of street children in South Africa (Swart, 1988). Aptekar points out that other countries, such as Tanzania, have not experienced civil unrest, and consequently have fewer street children. What becomes of these children is still a subject of much debate. Aptekar believes that further cross-cultural research is needed to build a model to predict which combination of physical, economic, sociocultural, and psychological factors will most likely lead to a child choosing life on the street and what potential health risks are involved for themselves and others. For more information about the world's street children, their health, and related issues, see Van Acker and colleagues, 1999, and Aptekar and Ciano-Federoff, 1999 (Kenya); West, 1999 (Britain and Bangladesh); Matchinda, 1999 (Cameroon); Lalor, 1999 (Ethiopia and Latin America); D'Abreu and colleagues, 1999 (Brazil); Verma, 1999 (India); and le Roux and Smith, 1998 (South Africa).

Latin American street children help each other survive the challenges of everyday life. (Timothy Ross, The Image Works)

exist. Young persons were simply expected to take on adult responsibilities and contribute to the welfare of the family as soon as they were physically able to do so. Over time, however, this idea changed, and societies (especially those in the West) became more accepting of adolescence as a distinct stage in adult preparation. In recent years, the period of adolescence has shown signs of expanding so that children enter it earlier and stay in it longer, in some cases well into their early to mid-twenties. For many, biological changes during the adolescent years can be enormously stressful. (For a review of adolescent physical development, see Chapter 4.) For example, hormonal changes associated with puberty are frequently accompanied by fluctuations in social and emotional development. For many adolescents, these changes produce only minimal health risks although, for others, they can contribute to serious health problems, including eating disorders or alcohol and drug addiction.

Eating Disorders

Over the years, the topic of adolescent health has taken on new dimensions in cross-cultural human development. Because of the impact childhood illnesses can have on adult development (e.g., obesity and diabetes), international health organizations and relief agencies have devoted increasing attention to the identification of physical and mental illnesses among the world's adolescents. Today, a growing health concern among many professionals is the dramatic rise in the incidence of eating disorders, especially in highly in-dustrialized societies.

While in some societies stoutness is associated with good health and prosperity, in others it is not. For example, in parts of Southeast Asia, a plump waistline suggests abundance, wealth, and good fortune. It has been reported that young women of the nomadic Moors of Mauritania or the An-nang of Nigeria are force fed because large women are considered the most desirable (Brink, 1989; Cassidy, 1991). On the other hand, in North America, being slim and fit is important, whereas being overweight can be embarrass-ing. An obsession with being thin appears to be especially common among young women (Jackson, 1992).

A particularly interesting example of the desire for thinness in Ameri-can society was the celebration of the one-hundredth birthday of the Statue of Liberty. A new coin was issued with a likeness designed to resemble the original, with one exception: Lady Liberty's figure on the new coin had been "slimmed down" to more closely represent the culturally popular Western ideal of feminine thinness (Nichter & Nichter, 1991).

Research, as well as everyday experience, has demonstrated that ado-lescent girls are more likely to be dissatisfied with their physical appearance, particularly their weight, than are adolescent boys and are therefore more likely to go on diets (Pipher, 1995). While dieting alone does not produce a health risk, excessive dieting can lead to a number of serious disorders, in-cluding anorexia nervosa and bulimia.

Cultural Variations in Anorexia and Bulimia

Anorexia nervosa is *an eating disorder,* found primarily among young ado-lescent girls, *characterized by loss of appetite and extreme loss of weight.* In severe cases, hospitalization becomes necessary, menstruation may stop, and an in-dividual may lose 15 to 25 percent or more total body weight (Slaby & Dwenger, 1993; Thompson, 1992). It is estimated that between 5 and 15 per-cent of anorexic girls die of this disorder each year. By contrast, adolescents suffering from **bulimia,** again typically young women, *eat extremely large amounts of food, then purge it all by means of self-induced vomiting.* The aim is not to lose or gain weight but to maintain a specific weight. This practice dates back to the Roman Empire, when guests of the emperor were invited to the coliseum to celebrate an auspicious occasion by stuffing themselves with food and wine, followed by a trip to the "vomitorium" where they would ceremonially throw it all up. This was thought to relieve gas and stuffiness as well as cleanse the body from the inside out.

Both of these eating disorders can have serious adverse effects on one's personal health. But just how common are these disorders in countries throughout the world? Among the small number of cross-cultural studies looking at this problem, findings reveal fewer eating disorders and less dissatisfaction with body image among samples in Japan (Iwawaki & Kerner, 1974), Australia (Tiggemann & Rothblum, 1988), and Spain (Raich et al., 1992). There also is evidence showing a relationship between acculturation into some Western societies (e.g., the United States and Great Britain) and increases in negative body image as well as a preference for a thin figure (Furnham & Alibhai, 1983; Mumford, Whitehouse, & Choudry, 1992; Nasser, 1986). Unfortunately, the number of studies focusing on these disorders in developing countries remains small. Future research might well look at this and its possible relationship to ecological settings and the concept of the developmental niche.

In one cross-cultural study, Mukai and McCloskey (1996) investigated attitudes toward eating among 108 Japanese and American schoolgirls between eight and eleven years of age. Administering a children's version of an eating disorder test (ChEAT-26) and a revised form of the Demographic and Dieting Questionnaire, the authors report that nearly half of the girls in both Japan and the United States wished they were thinner and about a third indicated they had attempted to lose weight. In both countries, the dieting practices of friends had a significant influence on eating attitudes.

In another study (Furnham & Alibhai, 1983), comparisons were made among three groups of subjects: Caucasian women residing in Great Britain, Asian women living in Kenya, and Asian women living in Great Britain who had once resided in Kenya. In all cases, subjects rated drawings of women depicting body types ranging from anorexic to obese. Findings showed that the drawings of thin women were rated more positively and drawings of heavier women more negatively by the Asian immigrants and Caucasian women than they were by those Asian women who lived in Kenya. Our interpretation of these results suggests that these women were responding to these drawings on the basis of their developmental niche and the cultural beliefs that helped to define it.

Indran (1995) administered the EAT questionnaire to 140 Form Five women students (equivalent to approximately grade eleven or twelve in the United States) at a secondary school in the suburbs surrounding Kuala Lumpur, Malaysia. The findings, once again, support the interaction of our recurring themes, ecological systems theory and developmental niche, revealing that culture and family attitudes play a pivotal role in the Malaysian girls' eating habits. Interestingly, Malaysian girls paid less attention to being thin (than did Western girls) and paid greater attention to working hard to please their parents through academic success.

Finally, Cogan, Bhalla, Sefa-Dedeh, and Rothblum (1996) conducted a study of perceptions of obesity and thinness using 349 Ghanaian undergraduate students at the University of Ghana and 219 American undergraduates at the University of Vermont. All subjects completed a questionnaire containing demographic information and six measures of perceptions of obesity and thinness, including an eating disorders inventory. As hypothesized, compared to U.S. students, Ghanaian men and women rated a larger body size as the ideal. In addition, more Ghanaian than American students tended to select from a wider range of body sizes as "acceptable figures." For example, American subjects tended to have a narrower definition of the ideal figure and also tended to identify with figures smaller than they were and, in some cases, two sizes smaller than Ghanaian students, reflecting a thinner ideal. This was more true for females than for males. When weight preference was considered, both Ghanaian men and women agreed that heavier was best and idealized heavier-set body builds. For the U.S. sample, men tended to prefer somewhat heavier models than did women. Furthermore, Americans associated thinness with such positive attributes as extroversion, attractiveness, self-discipline, and self-confidence. Many American women also associated thinness with happiness. This was not the case for any of the Ghanaian students. Finally, American women reported more incidents of eating disorders than did American men or Ghanaian men or women.

Many young women suffer from anorexia nervosa.
(Kansas City Star/Liaison Agency, Inc.)

These findings, along with others already mentioned, reflect a cultural orientation in which young American women place a higher value on being thin and have a higher occurrence of eating disorders than young women in developing countries. Tiggemann and Rothblum (1988) provide further evidence in a comparison of Australian and American students' perceptions of thinness and obesity. They found that while students in both countries were concerned about weight, the U.S. sample reported significantly more concern. For example, dieting was more common among American students, who also reported being more self-conscious about their bodies than were Australian students.

A final example is a study by Banks (1992) that looks at anorexia nervosa and its possible relationship to religious and cultural contexts. Banks cites the cases of two anorectic women as evidence that for some, self-starvation may be interwoven with religious idioms and symbols about the body, food, and self. In an exhaustive review of the literature, she notes an interesting link between anorexia nervosa and **asceticism,** or the *practice of self-denial,* and hypothesizes that asceticism may be subjectively expressed through religious concepts about the body and food. She encourages further cross-cultural research examining the relationship between religion and other rituals of fasting and vomiting.

Taken as a group, these studies are important because they indicate that negative perceptions of body image and incidences of eating disorders tend to occur more often in Western societies in which thinness is viewed as a cultural ideal that young women feel they need to achieve.

Culture and Sexually Transmitted Diseases (STDs)

As adolescents become sexually active, they are more likely to acquire sexually transmitted diseases (STDs) than any other age group (Quadrel, Fishoff, & Davis, 1993). One sexually transmitted disease in particular, acquired immunodeficiency syndrome (AIDS), which is caused by the human immunodeficiency virus (HIV), has become a critically important international health issue. Since 1981, when AIDS was first diagnosed in Los Angeles, people with HIV have been found in more than 169 countries (Cotran, Kumar, & Robbins, 1994). **AIDS** is *a disease that attacks the body's immune system,* leaving an individual weak and susceptible to infections that generally prove fatal. With an increasing number of adolescents becoming sexually active at younger ages and large numbers engaging in unsafe practices, there is serious concern that many have become infected with the HIV virus and will die of AIDS when they reach the third decade of their lives (Centers for Disease Control, 1992; Harvard Mental Health Letter, 1999).

Discussion of HIV and the AIDS epidemic should be made within the context of culture and how it influences the interpretation, diagnosis, and treatment of the disease. In an unusually persuasive article on the relationship between culture and the media's influence on HIV and AIDS in Asia, Wolffers (1997) stresses that culture is not a passive entity but rather a dynamic process within which members of a society are continuously acting on their needs and interpreting what they see and experience. One of the major sources of cultural influence throughout the world is the media. In Southeast Asia, the media has devoted considerable time and energy to informing and educating the public about the causes and transmission of HIV. However, as Wolffers points out, many local newspapers have a policy of not printing information about HIV and its relationship to sexual behavior, because this sometimes conflicts with religious and cultural beliefs. Instead, in an effort to combat the illegal use and trafficking of drugs, emphasis is often placed on the occurrence of HIV and AIDS among drug users and their use of dirty needles. The concern, as Wolffers points out, is that under these circumstances many people, particularly those who are young, uneducated, and living at the poverty level, will not be adequately informed about the potential sources of contracting the virus and that this ignorance will substantially contribute to the increasingly large number of AIDS cases throughout the world.

Culture and Adolescent Drug Use

Misuse of drugs and alcohol has also become a global health concern. In North America, young people are experimenting with alcohol and drugs at increasingly younger ages (Arnett, 1999). One national survey reported that nine out of ten high school seniors had consumed alcohol on occasion and many had experimented with illegal drugs at least once (Johnston et al., 1992). Drugs most often abused are alcohol, tobacco, and marijuana (Centers for Disease Control and Prevention, 1998; U.S. Bureau of the Census, 1992). Health problems associated with such abuse include chemical dependency, diabetes, cirrhosis of the liver, kidney failure, cardiac and lung complications, fetal anomalies, injuries from accidents, and homicide. In addition, adolescents who use drugs and alcohol regularly are likely to engage in unprotected sex, thereby increasing the chance of contracting HIV (Jemmot & Jemmot, 1993).

In a longitudinal study involving male adolescents who consumed alcohol regularly in France, Weill and Le Bourhis (1994) identified several psychological correlates predictive of future drinking. They found the heaviest drinkers were those who possessed negative, self-defeating attitudes, whereas those who were positive and enthusiastic and exhibited more religiosity consumed less alcohol and were more aware of the health dangers associated with drinking.

Adolescents experiment with smoking and other drugs at increasingly younger ages. (Photo News/Liaison Agency, Inc.)

In the United States, drug use is highest among minority populations living in the inner city or on Indian reservations (Beauvais, Oetting, Wolf, & Edwards, 1989; Swaim et al., 1993). However, according to some authorities, the strongest factor in predicting drug use among adolescents is the type of friends they associate with (Oetting & Beauvais, 1986, 1987).

Swaim and colleagues (1993) investigated the nature and extent of drug use among eleven- and twelve-year-olds on American Indian reservations using the peer cluster theory—dyads of best friends who support and encourage each other in the use of alcohol and drugs. Over four hundred northern Plains and Southwest American Indians from two reservations were given a survey consisting of several different scales, including a Religious Identification and Peer Drug Association Scale. Data were compared to findings reported in an earlier study by Oetting and Beauvais (1987) among Anglo adolescents. With rare exception, most variables correlated higher among Anglos than among American Indians. For example, there were more peer clusters formed among Anglo adolescents than among American Indian adolescents. Swaim and colleagues (1993) conclude, "Association with drug-using peers does not appear to play as central a role in the substance use of

Indian youths as it does among Anglos" (p. 640). According to the authors, the extended family system common in American Indian culture may account for the difference in the use of peer clusters. On the reservation, young people live together, often in crowded facilities, with same-age siblings, aunts, uncles, and cousins that may be regarded as "peers" or "friends" and perform the same role as peer clusters in Anglo adolescents. These and other health concerns not only directly affect the lives of adolescents but also have relevance for the health of adults.

◇ EARLY AND MIDDLE ADULTHOOD

The transition from adolescence to adulthood is more gradual than that from childhood to adolescence. Exactly when an individual becomes an adult is not always clear and there is likely to be just as much variation within cultures as there is among cultures.

Transition to Maturity

The manner in which individuals move from adolescence into adulthood is determined largely by their culture—its ecological setting and developmental niche. Each culture has its own way of recognizing this change in status, and its unique rituals can encourage an easy, healthy transition or can cause stress that may produce unhealthy changes or responses.

In a cross-cultural study involving New Zealand–born Chinese high school students, New Zealand–born Maori young adults, and Filipino university students, Siegert and Chung (1995) noted the frequency of four illness clusters: general illnesses, sleep disturbance, anxiety and dysphoria, and severe depression. While the primary goal was to further validate the cross-cultural use of the General Health Questionnaire (Goldberg, 1972), findings indicated that students in all three groups reported experiencing all clusters of illness to about the same extent. At times, these illnesses produced significant emotional distress, frequently affecting scholastic achievement and the quality of relationships with others and thereby adversely affecting students' overall general health.

In another study, Essau and Trommsdorff (1996) administered the Ways of Coping Checklist (WOCC), a problem-focused scale, and an emotion-focused scale to determine how university students coped with emotional problems, some of which were caused by stress, and how these problems contributed to overall feelings of being healthy or unhealthy. Subjects surveyed were from Malaysia, Germany, Canada, and the United States. The researchers hypothesized that Malaysian students, living in a collective culture, would score higher on emotion-focused coping and lower on problem-focused coping than North American and German students from highly individual cultures. Results showed that Malaysian students coped with emotional problems by keeping to themselves, fearing to bother family members or friends with their problems. In this culture, it is more important to put group members ahead of individual concerns. In this culture there is a strong devotion to Islam, a religion that stresses the importance of submitting all matters to God. On the other hand, North American and German students tended to focus on the problems and seek help from friends as a way of reducing stress.

In a comparative study of 300 Italian and 250 Dutch university students, Zammuner and Fischer (1996) presented subjects with several vignettes that provoked stress and severe emotional reactions. While both groups exhibited some signs of physical distress, there were differences in the expression of emotion. For example, Dutch students tended to display more anxiety and surprise than Italian students, who were more annoyed and angered by situations perceived as flirtatious. Women in both groups were more open in expressing their emotions, particularly when responding to vignettes about personal relationships.

Mental Health Issues

In addition to the effects of stress, other mental health issues concern adults. Among these are depression and schizophrenia. While it is not our intention to provide a comprehensive analysis of psychopathology in adulthood, we examine some of the different approaches to viewing these illnesses from a cross-cultural perspective.

Depression

As already noted, every culture has its own beliefs regarding the causes and treatment of illness and stress. This is true for depression as well, and once again, there is often more variation in interpretation within cultures than among cultures. For example, in the United States, individuals react in many different ways when hearing that someone is experiencing depression. Responses may range from "There's nothing to worry about, he's just a little moody these days, He'll soon be fine" to "She's had a long history of serious depression, just like her mother and father, It seems to run in the family." Because the term tends to be used so freely in everyday conversation and in the media, it is sometimes difficult to recognize the symptoms of depression.

Depression is *a serious psychological disorder* involving periods of sadness and other negative feelings, such as hopelessness, despair, sleep disturbance, and loss of energy. Cultural variations in beliefs about depression and other illnesses have important implications for the health status of individuals worldwide. Health authorities have become increasingly alarmed by the growing number of reported cases of depression among adults. It is estimated that at least one hundred million people around the world experience the symptoms of depression each year (Douki & Tabbane, 1996). This figure is expected to rise as people live longer and more people are exposed to chronic stress. It is also feared that the sudden exodus of families migrating to new countries and abandoning native customs and traditions, as well as the breakup of the extended family, will result in increased incidences of depression in younger people. Some experts worry that this will lead to greater consumption of alcohol and the abuse of drugs, which will only intensify the depression (Sartorius, 1993). Obviously, the magnitude of this problem presents enormous public health concerns.

Since depression has varying emotional, physical, and behavioral symptoms, it is common for many cases to go undetected. For this and other reasons, diagnosing and treating depression among young adults continue to be major problems for health care professionals in many cultures. In Western countries, depression is described in terms of being sad, disconnected, and withdrawn. Sometimes, these are accompanied by somatic complaints, such as headaches, stomach cramps, or nausea. However, in parts of India and South Africa, depression is described in quasi-spiritual or metaphysical terms—"suffering of the spirit" (Douki & Tabbane, 1996). Recent findings suggest that depression in some developing countries is gradually beginning to mimic depressive symptoms seen in the West. For example, an epidemiological study done among adults in Tunisia revealed that out of the five thousand patients sampled, most registered the same complaints concerning depression as their Western counterparts. Rapid socioeconomic development and mass urbanization were two of the reasons given to explain the depressive symptoms of young Tunisians (Douki & Tabbane, 1996). Thus, it appears that while there are certain culture-specific characteristics associated with depression, there also are several universal features.

In 1983, the World Health Organization (WHO) conducted a cross-national study of patients in Canada, Japan, Switzerland, and the Islamic Republic of Iran. Findings revealed a cluster of core depressive symptoms, including long periods of sadness, lack of energy and affect, inability to concentrate, feelings of inadequacy, and loss of self-esteem. As Douki and Tabbane (1996) indicate, while the frequency and extent of reported depressive cases may vary among cultures, depression is a major universal problem that usually requires treatment.

In China, depressive episodes and stress-related disorders among adults are often accompanied by somatization (Kleinman, 1982). This has also been reported in parts of Latin America, Asia, and Africa (Tseng & Hsu, 1980).

Many young people seek counseling for their depression. (Will Hart)

Somatization refers to *physical ailments resulting from stress or emotional distress.* One explanation may be that in many collectivistic societies individuals are discouraged from voicing their psychological complaints in the company of friends or extended family members. Furthermore, depression is viewed as a minor, transient illness not requiring immediate family intervention. Consequently, an individual who experiences a depressive episode is often forced to use somatization to signal distress and thereby gain attention. As Draguns (1990) states, in the case of depression, "somatization serves as a culturally sanctioned cry for help" (p. 311). Thus, the nature and treatment of depression, like many other illnesses, reflects the interaction among eco-cultural systems, historical and sociocultural factors, and developmental niche.

Today, depression is often referred to as the "common cold" of psychological disorders, and Prozac (used to treat depression) is one of the most widely prescribed drugs in the world. It is customary to think of depression as occurring primarily in developed countries, often as a result of living and working in a highly industrialized and hurried society. However, as Draguns (1994) points out, "Depression is not the exclusive property of Judeo-Christian cultures" (p. 168). In fact, depression is probably experienced to some degree in most, if not all, of the world's cultures. Even so, health care professionals have yet to agree on a set of depression symptoms that can be universally applied, and it is unlikely that they ever will because of the role played by cultural variables. Draguns (1994) affirms this: "The cross-cultural study of depression has not yet progressed to the point of being able to pinpoint the worldwide invariant manifestations of depression" (p. 168).

Schizophrenia

During the last two hundred years, schizophrenia has been one of the most frequently studied psychopathic disorders. **Schizophrenia** refers to *a group of severe psychological disorders characterized by disturbances in thought, perception, and affect or emotion.* In recent years, increasing attention has been given to the study of cultural variations in schizophrenia. For example, in 1973, the World Health Organization began conducting a series of studies in China, Taiwan, Colombia, Czechoslovakia, Denmark, India, Nigeria, the former Soviet Union, the United Kingdom, and the United States. The goal of these investigations has been to determine the extent of schizophrenia and the sociocultural and historical factors surrounding it. Findings have pointed to the identification of several core symptoms, including restricted affect, thinking aloud, lack of insight, poor rapport, incoherent speech, and widespread bizarre delusions (Draguns, 1994). In addition, three symptoms were identified that, although exotic or unusual, would not be considered symptoms of schizophrenia: waking early, depressed facial features, and expressions of extreme elation (Draguns, 1990). Subsequent research conducted by WHO (1979) and Sartorius, Jablensky, Korten, and Ernberg (1986) reports a greater likelihood of these symptoms occurring in Colombia, India, and Nigeria than in the other industrialized countries mentioned earlier. One explanation may lie in the finding that schizophrenia is inversely proportionate to educational and occupational level (Dohrenwend & Dohrenwend, 1969). In fact, according to Draguns (1994), poorer and less educated patients in developing countries (e.g., India and Nigeria) recovered most quickly from this illness.

In the last ten years, WHO has continued to conduct cross-cultural research on more than three thousand schizophrenic patients in over twenty countries. Results indicate that schizophrenia occurs in nearly all cultures and that the prognosis is better in developing countries than it is in highly industrialized developed countries. Apparently, the support and encouragement provided by extended family members help reduce some of the symptoms associated with schizophrenia (Jablensky et al., 1992; Lin & Kleinman, 1988).

Day and his colleagues (1987) investigated the nature and prevalence of schizophrenia in nine countries in Asia, Europe, and South and North America. Contrary to the medical model often used to explain schizophrenia in the West, most of these schizophrenias were associated with stressful events not initiated by the patients themselves but caused by external forces (e.g., charms or evil spirits).

Schizophrenia has been studied in India, where Katz and his colleagues (1988) found the symptoms to be similar to those reported by schizophrenics in Western countries and to include hallucinations, delusions, and withdrawal. The separation of the schizophrenic from others and the disruption of the cohesive family system is the most mysterious aspect of this illness to the normal population. It is not the disease itself that is puzzling but rather the inclination toward self-indulgence and egocentrism. The nature of the disease threatens collectivist values and clashes with ecological orientation and developmental niche.

◇ LATER ADULTHOOD

When we think of aging, we frequently have mixed reactions. On the one hand, we think of a group of elderly people enjoying their "golden years" by visiting grandchildren, traveling, and perhaps volunteering. On the other hand, we sometimes perceive the elderly as frail, weak, dependent, and in need of extensive medical care. Certainly, among many North Americans, this can be a disturbing and confusing time.

Disease and Premature Aging

Senescence, or *the process of biological aging,* and the health issues surrounding it have been the topic of much research and debate. Elderly persons experiencing the normal signs of aging often complain of reduced energy, vision and hearing loss, dried and wrinkled skin, brittle bones, slower reaction time, diminished motor skills, and sometimes a loss of memory. These complaints, some subtle and others less so, are common in most cultures and are often legitimate. But what about those who age before their time?

Following research conducted on a rare and cruel disease known as Werner's syndrome, scientists at the University of Washington put forth some ideas regarding the aging process. People suffering from this disorder experience all the signs of normal aging, but they do so beginning in their mid-twenties and usually die before they reach their fiftieth birthday. They gray prematurely and develop wrinkled skin, first on the face, then on their hands, legs, and feet. They catch frequent colds, which often lead to pneumonia, and develop cancer, kidney and heart trouble, and osteoporosis. In addition, they show some of the same symptoms seen in Alzheimer's patients (e.g., problems in concentration, remembering, and decision making). In April 1996, scientists released findings that could be a major breakthrough in explaining why we age. They identified the Werner's gene, the first gene known to cause human aging. Although optimistically cautious, scientists at the National Institute on Aging called this discovery remarkable.

With more accurate identification and treatment of illnesses, as well as rapid advancements in technology, many cultures are experiencing lower mortality rates and longer life expectancies. However, the longer people live, the greater the chance of encountering a major physical or psychological problem. Throughout the world, many elderly die each year from heart disease, cancer, or stroke, and arthritis, osteoporosis, and injuries resulting from falls and other accidents require extended hospitalization or nursing home and hospice care for elderly sufferers.

Cultural Views on Dementia and Alzheimer's Disease

What is the relationship between age and psychological decline? How do a culture's ecocultural system and an individual's developmental niche contribute to the aging process? As just noted, in many industrialized nations people are living longer but at a cost to society. As the average lifespan has expanded, we have seen dramatic increases in cases of **dementia,** especially Alzheimer's disease (Davies, 1988; Qualls, 1999). In the United States persons diagnosed with Alzheimer's represent about 10 percent of the population over the age of sixty-five and as much as 50 percent of those eighty-five and older (Skoog, Nilsson, Palmertz, Andreasson, & Svanborg, 1993).

In the early stages, Alzheimer's disease resembles normal aging, with periodic memory loss, frequent agitation, problems speaking, and difficulty concentrating for long periods of time. However, as the disease worsens, the signs become more apparent. In the later stages, individuals forget how to perform the most basic tasks, such as changing clothes, eating, and going to the bathroom. They become completely dependent, require twenty-four-hour supervision, and are unable to recognize family members and medical personnel.

One factor that compounds the tragedy of Alzheimer's disease is our lack of understanding regarding its causes and diagnosis. Currently, the only reliable way of determining whether a person has Alzheimer's is after death when an autopsy is performed. Analyses from some autopsies have shown a cluster of plaques and neuron tangles located near the hippocampus; these have been associated with rapid destruction of healthy brain tissue (Cai, Golde, & Younkin, 1993). This is a crippling disease that touches many people, including Ronald Reagan, former president of the United States.

How do caregivers in different cultures respond to an elderly person suffering from Alzheimer's or similar diseases of aging? How do cultural beliefs about family values and relationships influence the course of these diseases?

Regardless of where it strikes, the devastating effects of Alzheimer's disease affect many people. For example, caring for a loved one with Alzheimer's can be very stressful. This is evident in Strong's (1984) study of caregiver support for Alzheimer's disease patients in which she compared

American Indian and Caucasian caregivers and found that both groups felt equally frustrated, angry, guilty, anxious, and helpless. The gradual deterioration of the patient left caregivers in both groups searching for answers. American Indian caregivers were much more communal and interdependent and employed more supportive, although passive, strategies in coping with the stress. For instance, common comments were "We just have to get used to this. There's nothing you can do about it but try and make them comfortable." Caucasian caregivers, on the other hand, initially tried to handle the situation by themselves, rarely turning to others for help and support.

The difference in the way the two groups responded to the stress of caregiving reflects their culture's ecocultural system and their own developmental niche. Strong (1984) reports the perspective of an American Indian caregiver: "The white man . . . is torn between two ideals; on the one hand he believes in freedom, in minding his own business, and in the right of people to make up their own minds; but on the other hand, he believes that he should be his brother's keeper" (p. 29). In Indian society, taking care of family members is the chief responsibility of each person, and nobody is exempt.

In another study, Cox (1993) conducted personal interviews with eighty-six Hispanic caregivers in New York to examine the ways in which cultural values and norms influence behavior. Her findings concur with those of Strong's (1984), suggesting that family cohesiveness plays a significant role in caregivers' behavior. As with American Indian caregivers, Hispanics appeared to passively accept the stresses of caregiving and believe it is part of their heritage to take care of the afflicted member. At no point did caregivers in either study consider admitting their relative to a nursing home or hospice.

In 1991, Meng conducted a survey in China and reported that 96 percent of elderly persons reside with family members and are cared for until they die. Strong family interdependence and cohesiveness were shown to have a positive impact on the physical and mental health of weak and frail elderly parents living at home. At no point in caring for their aging parents did caregivers consider the possibility of sending them to a medical facility or nursing home. To do so would have brought immediate disapproval and shame from the community. These findings are consistent with those obtained by Frazier and Glascock (1994) in their work with the frail elderly living in a kibbutz community in Israel. Kalu and Kalu (1993) found that frail elderly parents in Nigeria responded somewhat differently. Those who were plagued by physical and mental infirmities retrieved their umbilical cords, buried at birth in their native village. This act is believed to help slow down the aging process. The event is a festive, colorful celebration attended by family members and friends, who surround their loved one with love and support.

As we learn more about the genetic and environmental foundations of Alzheimer's and other diseases common among the elderly, along with methods of treatment from different parts of the world, we can anticipate that cures will be found in the future. In the meantime, efforts to discover why a person's brain at some point in the lifespan begins to self-destruct continue.

◇ SUMMARY

When we think about health and related issues, we usually don't consider the many ways these might be affected by culture. How do cultural beliefs influence one's well-being and ill health? This chapter explores cultural differences in health care and beliefs that influence development across the lifespan. We began with an overview of how standardized tests and diagnostic techniques often are incapable of detecting medical problems in cultures other than those for which they were originally designed.

Health problems, at birth and shortly afterward (e.g., preterm and low-birth-weight infants), can cause considerable concern for parents in many cultures. Variations in parental cultural beliefs, discussed extensively in previous chapters, play a major role in the way cultures care for problem birth infants.

Health issues during adolescence focus on the adolescent's search for the perfect body and physical appearance. Cultural variations in the occurrence and treatment of eating disorders such as anorexia and bulimia were examined in depth. Sexually transmitted diseases (STDs), including AIDS, also were discussed.

In early adulthood, pressures to achieve and to form interpersonal relationships with one's peers are frequently accompanied by the stress of adaptation and acculturation; these stressors produce a variety of medical problems. The ability to maintain a healthy lifestyle grows increasingly difficult for families that migrate to different countries. Similar difficulties exist for students who pursue formal education in other countries. Several cross-cultural studies involving the resettlement of young adults were examined.

Middle adulthood is sometimes referred to as the "sandwich generation" during which parents attempt to balance their own needs with the physical and emotional needs of their aging parents and growing children. This period can present unique challenges and also produce medical problems, including depression and schizophrenia. Cross-cultural research indicates that each culture approaches and treats these illnesses differently, depending on the ecocultural system and developmental niche.

The last stage in the lifespan, later adulthood, is often viewed as the "golden years," with opportunities for retirement and travel. However, this stage is also characterized by health problems. In the closing section, a cross-cultural comparison of the status of the elderly was addressed, along with cultural practices for nurturing those afflicted with dementia and Alzheimer's disease.

◇ FURTHER READINGS

Boston Women's Health Book Collective. (1992). *The New Our Bodies, Ourselves.* New York: Simon & Schuster.

This highly enjoyable and easy-to-read paperback addresses a wide range of women's health concerns. Topics covered include STDs and AIDS, chronic fatigue syndrome, sexual myths, menopause, breast reconstruction after mastectomy, and depression. A great book for either casual reading or for sparking open classroom discussion.

Ronald C. Simons and Charles C. Hughes. (Eds.). (1985). *The Culture-Bound Syndrome: Folk Illnesses of Psychiatric and Anthropological Interest.* Dodrecht, Netherlands: D. Reidel Publishing Company.

One of the best available compilations on culture-bound syndromes from many areas of the globe.

David B. Morris. (1998). *Illness and Culture in the Postmodern Age.* Berkeley: University of California Press.

In a narrative account, the author follows the concept of health and illness through modern history into the late twentieth century, providing a context for talk about health and illness, medicine and suffering. Anyone who wants to understand why people get sick differently in different cultures and what's making us sick here and now will enjoy this book.

CHAPTER ELEVEN

LOOKING TO
THE FUTURE

Phyllidia Ramirez is eleven and lives with her mother, Nina, in a village high in the mountains in the middle of Nicaragua's Central Highlands. Like many Nicaraguan women, Nina has lived a large part of her life as a single mother. Her husband, Luis, was a migrant laborer who left home each year for several months to harvest cotton in the lowlands of the Pacific region. The long absences caused serious disruptions, and he abandoned the family when Phyllidia was five years old. Nina and Phyllidia both work part time harvesting coffee. Although schools in the area are underfunded and inadequate, family and kinship are important and through compadrazgo—*a system of "coparenthood" that links parents, children, and godparents—Phyllidia is learning Spanish and weaving skills from her godmother, Maria.*

Montreal, the largest city in the province of Quebec, differs greatly from the rest of Canada due to the prominence of its French culture and language as well as the fact that most of its inhabitants belong to the Roman Catholic Church. Michel Lamoureux, thirteen years old, lives here with his mother Sylvie, father Jacques, brother Pierre, and sister Lise. His parents are well-to-do and are able to send their children to private Catholic schools and provide private lessons in foreign language, golf, and tennis. They set high standards for their children and, because their careers frequently keep them away from home, give Michel, the oldest child, a great deal of responsibility for the care of his younger brother and sister.

Our exploration of lives across cultures is nearly over. Before our journey comes to an end, we would like to briefly revisit our major themes, reconsider some of the theories we have discussed, and offer suggestions for modifying these to meet the needs of a rapidly changing world. A few simple revisions in specific theoretical positions might help make these theories more useful and appropriate for the study of lives across cultures. Finally, as we come to the end of our journey, we would like to gaze into our crystal ball and speculate as to where the young field of cross-cultural human development might be heading and make some recommendations for future research as we enter the first decade of the twenty-first century.

◇ LOOKING BACK: A REVIEW OF MAJOR THEMES AND THEORIES

We begin with a review of the major theories introduced in Chapter 2 and addressed throughout subsequent chapters. These include the ecological systems approach and developmental niche along with the work of Piaget, Vygotsky, Erikson, and Kohlberg.

Our purpose in doing this is to take one last look at the ideas we have scattered throughout chapters and pull them together into a final statement stressing the importance of viewing human development from a cross-cultural perspective and within a cultural context.

Ecological Systems Approach

As you will recall, the ecological systems approach of Bronfenbrenner (1989, 1993) focuses on the reciprocal relationships between and among children, their parents, and other family members and their connection with larger social and cultural traditions as well as the interaction among biological, sociocultural, and psychological factors in human development. Throughout the pages of this book, we have seen, through the use of opening vignettes, how the lives of individuals are deeply embedded in distinctly different ecocultural systems reflecting long-held and well-established patterns of thought and behavior governed by the interaction of micro-, meso-, exo-, and macrosystems (see Figure 2.1 in Chapter 2).

In terms of the microsystem (the cultural setting in which adult–child interactions take place at home or at school), we can see that the young lives of Phyllidia in Nicaragua and Michel in Canada, at the opening of this chapter, have been influenced in a variety of ways by their cultural surroundings.

At the same time, parts of each of their microsystems have been in contact with a second, larger circle of influence, the mesosystem, consisting of a number of overlapping social settings that have also helped to shape the individual development of Phyllidia and Michel. For example, Michel's private tutorial sessions are a routine activity among the upper-middle-class families in the educational community in Montreal.

Beyond this is the exosystem, consisting of community institutions that individuals experience indirectly. In Michel's case, his private school curriculum reflects the content and skill areas believed to be important in attaining competency, even though he was not directly involved in setting curricula.

Then, there is the macrosystem made up of the prominent cultural values and attitudes that influence a person's maturation. In Michel's case, beliefs about God and religion provide the foundation for worship and daily living. In Phyllidia's single-parent household, her part-time job and close contact with extended family reflect the values of the macrosystem found in most Nicaraguan villages.

The work of harvesting coffee is regularly performed by Nicaraguan women and girls. (Larry Luxner/ D. Donne Bryant)

As we saw in earlier chapters, sometimes several macrosystems operate within a single culture. In Malaysia and Singapore, for example, one macro-system consists of a rapidly emerging group of young middle-class wage earners who are moving out of their parents' homes in an effort to achieve personal success and financial independence. Another represents the more traditional extended family system in which parents and grandparents serve as principal caregivers for children, even those well into their adult years.

Since one of the major goals of cross-cultural research is to be aware of the varying influences of culture on behavior, by looking at how children interact within their culture's unique ecological system and gradually carve out a developmental niche, we hopefully have laid the foundation for a better understanding of how these forces shape and change development across the cultures we have considered as well as those the reader may encounter in the future.

Developmental Niche

The concept of a developmental niche emerged from cross-cultural research conducted in Kenya (Super & Harkness, 1994) and has contributed greatly to our understanding of the ways in which different components of a culture work together as a system and how parents and children behave within normal everyday settings.

The term *niche* originally was used in biological ecology and refers to the manner in which an animal or species adapts to its physical surroundings (e.g., our example of the pigeon and robin in the city park in Chapter 2). Super and Harkness (1994, 1999) set forth three components that they propose make up a specific child's developmental niche. These consist of one's everyday physical and social settings, child-care and childrearing customs, and the unique psychology of one's caretakers. Of particular interest to cross-cultural researchers is the influence a developmental niche may have on the development of a variety of lifelong behaviors. For example, as we have seen in earlier chapters, there is a significant body of findings that lend support to the notion that the cultural experience of childhood plays a critically important role in continuing to shape the thoughts, feelings, and behavior of individuals throughout their lives.

Applying the concept of a developmental niche to the vignettes at the opening of this chapter, we can see how Nina's experience as a single mother affects her daughter Phyllidia's views of work and family relationships. Similarly, Michel's parents' expectations regarding his responsibilities toward caring for his younger brother and sister help shape Michel's values and attitudes. Each of these vignettes presents the child's unique developmental niche and how it operates within the larger ecological system (see Figure 2.2 in Chapter 2). Over the lifespan, Phyllidia and Michel will each continue to react and respond to thousands of cultural messages that will eventually become internalized and help them understand their world and themselves.

Taken together, the ecological systems approach and the developmental niche provide a method for examining the social context of any group of people and explaining the similarities and differences in behavior from a cross-cultural and developmental perspective.

Vygotsky's Sociocultural Theory

As we discussed in Chapter 2, Vygotsky offers a contextualist's approach to the study of cognitive development. While most mainstream Western developmental theories have traditionally viewed individuals as separate from their physical and social environments, Vygotsky proposed a socio-cultural-historical theory. He believed that human development occurs over time within the context of culture. His influential mentor and friend, Alexandria Luria (1981), captured the essence of Vygotsky's theory best when he stated, "In order to explain the highly complex forms of human consciousness one must go beyond the human organism. One must seek the origins of conscious activity . . . in the external processes of social life, in the social and historical forms of human existence" (p. 25). Notice the contrast between the strong individualistic assumptions found in much of the psychological research conducted in Western societies and the historical and sociocultural contextualist approach employed by Vygotsky.

As Kagitcibasi (1996) has cogently observed, "This important body of thinking and research has brought in a corrective to traditional work in mainstream developmental psychology that was oblivious of culture. It has also helped to create a recognition of the 'indigenous' cognitive competence of people (children and adults alike) who were too readily labeled as lacking in competence because they did not perform well on standard psychometric tests . . . or school-related activities. Finally, it has contributed to a better understanding of the interactive nature of the learning process" (pp. 39–40).

You may recall from our discussion in Chapter 2 that Vygotsky theorized a zone of proximal development, or the distance between a child's present level of functioning and her or his overall potential when guided by an adult or capable peer (e.g., the amount of assistance an individual needs from others in contrast to how much he can do without help). Vygotsky viewed the zone of proximal development as a dyadic process involving an adult and a child in which the adult nurtures the cultivation of a child's mental abilities by adjusting behavior (or providing guided participation) to fit the child's cognitive level as he moves successfully through the zone. From the perspective of Vygotsky, learning ultimately occurs when a child and a more competent adult arrive at a shared understanding on how to attain mutual goals.

According to Vygotsky, individuals develop as a result of their participation in collaborative activities with more skilled individuals. Social interaction and cultural context provide the foundation for the development of mental abilities. Since development is a product of social interaction, Vygotsky reasoned that by changing the nature and the conditions of social interaction, one can bring about change that allows children to increasingly adjust to new and different social contexts so that they eventually require less assistance from adults.

If we apply Vygotsky's zone of proximal development to this chapter's opening vignettes, we see that the guided instruction provided by Phyllidia's godmother in the teaching and learning of weaving reflects both the family's ecological surroundings as well as her developmental niche. As Maria, the godmother, mentors Phyllidia's apprenticeship, she will move through the zone and increase her weaving skills. Her contributions to the family's collection of woven blankets and other objects strengthen her creativity while promoting family cohesiveness, cultural identification, and interdependency.

In the case of Michel, he is being carefully trained by his golf coach to develop good putting skills. In the early stages, Michel needed lots of advice to master the basics of good form and practice drills. As Michel has improved and moved through the zone, demonstrating increased competency, his coach gradually removes the amount of assistance offered until Michel can proceed without further help. In both of these situations, it is likely that elements of the ecological context—such as climate, types of terrain, urban or rural setting, population density, health care, and other factors—will be intertwined within a variety of social contexts. In short, culture is, to a large extent, a group's response to its physical ecology, ancestral heritage, and developmental niche.

Vygotsky's theory does have its problems, however, especially in its inability to transfer learning from one task to another unless, as Berry and his colleagues (1992) point out, similarities exist in the specifics. On the other hand, several researchers (Carraher, Schliemann, & Carraher, 1988; Nunes, Schliemann, & Carraher, 1993) report successful transfer of everyday mathematical skills and formal reasoning practices.

We believe that Vygotsky's theory is certain to receive increased attention from cross-cultural developmental researchers in the early years of the new century. This has surely been the case during the latter part of the last century with the theorist we look at next—Jean Piaget.

Piaget's Cognitive Developmental Theory

At the core of Piaget's theory of cognitive development are schemes—the building blocks of cognition, consisting of patterns of thought used to organize ideas and objects in the environment. Common to infants' experience are schemes for sucking their mothers' breast, grasping and holding objects, listening, and babbling. With growth and maturation, children become more experienced at manipulating objects, and increasingly more complex schemes develop to assist them in adapting to their environments. Continually confronted with new ideas and information, children strive to achieve a balance between assimilation (fitting new information into existing schemes) and accommodation (adjusting existing schemes to fit new information).

According to Piaget, cognitive development passes through four stages, each building on its predecessor. These stages (described in detail in Chapter 2) begin with the sensorimotor stage (birth to two years), when a child's behavior moves from a reliance on reflexes to increased use of sensory and motor abilities and an understanding of object permanence (recognition that objects continue to exist even when they cannot be seen). This is followed by the preoperational stage (two to seven years), when preschool children demonstrate their increasingly sophisticated ability to think and use language in symbolic ways, although their reasoning tends to be mainly subjective and intuitive.

With movement into the concrete operational stage (seven to eleven years), school-age children begin to think more like adults, even though their understanding of the world around them tends to be simplistic or concrete. During this period, children generally achieve conservation (the ability to recognize that properties of objects—such as number or amount—remain the same in spite of rearrangement or superficial modification in their appearance). For example, a child realizes that an older sister does not have more food because her sandwich is cut into quarters (four pieces) and his is cut into halves (two pieces).

In the fourth and final stage of formal operations (eleven years and older), adolescents and adults develop the ability to deal with hypothetical problems and abstract thinking.

When initially presenting his theory, Piaget stated that cognitive changes occurring during each of these stages were universal. However, cross-cultural findings suggested this might not be completely accurate—that is, although the same sequence of stages may occur in nearly all cultures, the age at which they are achieved may vary considerably across cultures. Piaget, to his credit, revised his position on the universality of his theory, especially with regard to the concrete and formal operational stages (Rogoff & Chavajay, 1995).

Applying Piaget's theory to our opening vignettes, it is clear that eleven-year-old Phyllidia's ability to recreate her godmother's weaving skills requires that she has the ability to distinguish between types and amounts of materials used, to be able to use symbols creatively, and to infer cause-and-effect relationships—all characteristics of concrete operational thinking. On the other hand, Michel's ability to hold the golf club properly and to speculate what will happen if the ball is driven three hundred yards or more requires that he be able to make use of hypotheses and form abstractions regarding golf skills. When he is able to do this, he displays some of the characteristics associated with formal operational thinking.

While each of these vignettes describes life in different cultures, the unique ecological settings, specific developmental niche, and distinctive social interactions experienced by Michel and Phyllidia strongly influence the nature and timing of the development of their cognitive abilities.

Kohlberg's Theory of Moral Development and Gilligan's Critique

According to Kohlberg (1981), morality is based on a belief in general principles of justice. He proposes that moral development consists of six levels ranging from an immature obedience and punishment orientation to an advanced application of universal ethical principles (see Chapter 2 for a detailed description).

The original research was based on responses to a number of hypothetical moral dilemmas by undergraduate males at Harvard University. These moral dilemmas (stories involving conflicts between an individual's desires or needs and the rules of society) focused on moral issues Kohlberg viewed as universal (e.g., stealing, keeping promises, breaking rules, and so on).

Gilligan (1982) severely criticized Kohlberg for his definition of mature morality as an orientation toward abstract norms of justice. Her own research showed that women reason about the same moral dilemmas "in a different voice." She suggested that moral reasoning among women is more likely defined by a caring attitude and the maintenance of a network of relationships rather than by rules and abstract principles of justice. However, Gilligan did not take the next logical step and formulate an alternative developmental model that would integrate both orientations (caring and justice) into an understanding of moral development.

From a cross-cultural perspective, Kohlberg's model is clearly limited in its research application. Based on Gilligan's critique that the justice orientation is not the only way of viewing morality, we wonder how many other moral orientations may be present in other cultures. For example, in Japan an individual frequently makes moral decisions based on a strict code of honor in which behavior is seen as right because it is the honorable thing to do. A common example involves the resignation of a company's president when someone in the organization behaves badly or commits an immoral act (e.g., overbilling), even though the president had no direct knowledge of, or connection to, the misbehavior. Moral reasoning such as this fits neither the justice nor the caring orientation and suggests that there are significant opportunities for more research in the area of moral development.

In this regard, a rarely cited model of moral development has been put forth by Haan, Aerts, and Cooper (1985). She and her colleagues propose that development of moral reasoning is not determined by general orientations such as caring or justice but is the result of understanding the interdependence of self and others that occurs in social interactions. In her model, the most mature moral reasoner attempts to make a moral decision that balances her needs, desires, strengths, and weaknesses with those of others affected by a particular moral issue. In this view, moral reasoning would take on different forms in different cultures simply because of wide variations in what is considered a need, desire, strength, or weakness.

The potential usefulness of Haan and others' model for the study of moral development across cultures as well as its relevance to the major themes expressed throughout this book permit us to study moral reasoning within the context of culture-specific interactions and culture-specific moral issues, resulting in an emic approach to moral development. For example, in a highly individualistic culture such as the United States, most individuals accept as fair the notion that those of greater ability receive higher pay. However, in a collective setting, like the one found in a kibbutz, it may be equally fair that individuals get paid according to their needs, not what they actually earn by their own work. While both concepts of what is fair or right are valid in each culture, they can only be reasonably evaluated within the appropriate context.

Applying these concepts of moral development to our opening vignettes suggests that Michel's view of what is right or wrong is strongly influenced by the religious values taught as part of his Roman Catholic faith, a centerpiece of the Quebec culture in which he lives. Although the majority of Nicaraguans during the early 1990s were nominally Roman Catholic, according to Merrill (1994), the church "touches the lives of most Nicaraguans only sporadically at best" (p. 84). Like most living in rural villages far from an organized church, Phyllidia has likely been taught the basics of moral behavior as defined by her parents and community—for example, being nice to others, saying only good things, not stealing, and "having a strong belief in divine power over human affairs . . . reflected in the use of phrases such as 'God willing' or 'if it is God's desire' in discussions of future events" (Merrill, 1994, p. 85).

Erikson's Theory of Psychosocial Development

We can think of Erikson's theory as analogous to a book with eight chapters. Like chapters in a "Book of Life," Erikson's developmental stages follow one another. Sometimes an issue introduced in one chapter is carried over into the next and may not be fully resolved until much later in the book. In order to understand the story completely and make sense of the plot, the reader must read the eight chapters in chronological order. As infants and children pass through the first four stages of Erikson's theory, they are confronted by a series of psychosocial crises (turning points with two possible resolutions, one positive and one negative) requiring successful resolution if healthy development is to take place at a later stage. These crises center on trust versus mistrust, autonomy versus shame and doubt, initiative versus guilt, and industry versus inferiority. The adolescent and young adult encounter the issue of identity versus role confusion, or identity diffusion. The mature adult first faces the challenge of intimacy versus isolation, followed by generativity versus stagnation or self-absorption. Finally, the older adult needs to resolve issues related to integrity versus despair. Erikson views these crises as a natural development common to everyone, regardless of their culture, through which we come to understand ourselves and our relationships with others. However, as with other stage theories, Erikson's approach is subject to the criticism that stages may vary from one culture to another in the time of occurrence, duration, and content.

Considering what we know about the subjects in our opening vignettes, we might hypothesize that Phyllidia and Michel have both been raised in warm and caring family environments in which they developed the trust that allowed them to explore their surroundings and establish positive social relationships with family members. With supportive parents, they gradually developed control over their behavior, realizing that their intentions could be acted out through imitation of those around them. Michel, guided by his teachers in school, influenced by his golfing instructor in private lessons, and encouraged by his parents to take responsibility for his younger siblings, has developed a strong sense of industry and is on the verge of establishing a strong personal identity. Phyllidia, working part time alongside her mother harvesting coffee as well as learning her culture's weaving skills from her godmother, feels an equally strong sense of industry and, in the life of her village, is on the verge of womanhood and preparing to assume an adult identity.

While Erikson's theory works well as a general framework within which some specific lifespan changes can be described and interpreted, it is less useful as a model for cross-cultural experimentation. An approach that may be more useful in accounting for the cultural context of lifespan development has been offered by Cantor and her associates (Cantor & Kihlstrom, 1985; Cantor, Norem, Niedenthal, Langston, & Brower, 1987).

Using the concept of "life-tasks" (the underlying goals that guide an individual's life or everyday behavior at a given time), Cantor and others (1987) studied a group of undergraduate students in the United States by having them keep records detailing their daily activities. While recording their activities, they also answered questions about the people they were with and their feelings about the activities. Findings revealed that students shared several "life-tasks," the two most important being "making friends" and "getting good grades." One advantage of using an approach like Cantor's in cross-cultural research is that it relies on self-generated "themes" based on people's culture-specific experience. This makes for a more emic approach than imposing a set of preformulated "themes" on individuals, as is the case with universalist theories such as Erikson's.

We are encouraged by the development of new approaches like this and encourage others to consider using them in formulating their cross-cultural human development research efforts.

◇ INTERPRETING THEORY IN AND OUT OF CULTURAL CONTEXT

As our earlier discussion has made clear, attempts to employ theoretical concepts or interpretations developed in one cultural setting to situations found in another may not always be appropriate and can lead to much misunderstanding of cultural behavior.

As an extended example, let us consider what might happen if we applied Erikson's theory of psychosocial development. As we noted earlier, infants as young as one year old begin to express their autonomy through the use of a few simple words or by exploring their environment (and frequently hiding in boxes or closets, getting too close to the monkey cage at the zoo, or deliberately jumping in a mud puddle). During early childhood, they struggle to achieve a sense of competence and industriousness by expanding their social development within peer and play settings and by learning to handle the tools of their society. At this age, the "tool world" consists of paper, paste, crayons, paints, and scissors (Gander & Gardiner, 1981). Independence becomes a prerequisite for establishing identity in adolescence, and the identity crisis has to be resolved before a young adult can enjoy true intimacy.

According to Erikson's perspective, a healthy individual is one who becomes increasingly independent. In North America, personnel managers often seek "self-starters" who exercise large degrees of autonomy and independence developed and nurtured over years of individual practice and private self-reflection. However, this is not the practice in many Pacific Rim cultures, such as Malaysia, which tend to promote strong collectivistic values. For example, in Malaysia, privacy, as many understand and practice it in Western societies, is nearly nonexistent. Children are raised to be reliant on parents, grandparents, and older siblings. In this society, intimacy needs to occur before one can be successful in achieving an identity. Anyone who attempts to compare and contrast the development of children and adolescents in Malaysia with any Western country, according to Erikson's theory, needs to be aware of these differences before interpreting findings, or the results will be totally inaccurate.

Misinterpretation of theories outside cultural context relates to the emic–etic distinction mentioned earlier in this book. As Poortinga (1997) aptly states, "Behavior is *emic,* or culture-specific, to the extent it can only be understood within the cultural context within which it occurs; it is *etic,* or universal, in as much as it is common to human beings independent of their culture" (p. 352). It follows that when a researcher or observer of behavior assumes that his own emic–etic distinction is true for all cultures, he is operating from an ethnocentric point of view and that cultural misunderstanding will result. For example, in the case of Erikson's theory, the development of autonomy and independence (the emic) "fits" well with Western cultural values. However, when we assume that independence is the goal of all (or even many) cultures, we are dealing with an "imposed etic" (Berry, 1994; Berry et al., 1992). The approach we have taken throughout this book— namely, viewing human development within cultural context by using the ecological systems approach and the concept of the developmental niche— keeps one aware of the need to avoid ethnocentric thinking and to be alert to and accepting of the richness of cultural variation.

The study of cross-cultural human development will be more effective and of greater practical value in the decades ahead if we refine and modify existing theories, discover new ways to apply them, and begin to utilize some of the more contemporary but underused theories we have just reviewed.

At this point in the book, you have probably come to the same conclusion we have: that many of the traditional theories of development devised within a specific cultural context and useful for interpreting behavior within that context no longer adequately describe, explain, or predict behavior beyond that limited setting. So much of our experience in this global society is centered around culture (in all its various meanings) that theories that explicitly attempt to account for cultural factors and influences are certainly far more valuable.

Encounters between people of different cultural backgrounds (within one culture or across cultures) and their social and psychological consequences are a very real part of many young people's daily lives, whether in an educational setting (anywhere from kindergarten to graduate school), the workplace (where more companies are becoming multinational or hiring increasing numbers of minority workers), during travel (within one's own country or abroad), or perhaps in a foreign study program (an increasingly popular option for students in many countries).

◇ WHERE DO WE GO FROM HERE? SOME FINAL THOUGHTS

Traditionally, the literature in mainstream developmental psychology has emphasized a Western European and North American orientation. For too long there has been what we might call a "psychological research ethnocentrism," that is, the assumption that research findings reported from studies conducted in one culture applied equally well to other cultures. Yet, Harkness and Keefer (2000) caution that "in our search for cross-cultural validity in comparative research, we must make sure to avoid a new kind of ethnocentrism based on non-Western constructs or measures. Such an approach would be as unrealistic as the former mistake of imposing Western measures on other contexts . . . [and we must avoid the] . . . problem of oversimplification of cultural variability—complete relativism, in which cross-cultural comparisons become impossible" (p. 105).

Although we have seen a steady increase in developmental studies in recent years, much of this research still focuses on childhood and adolescence within a Western context (Gardiner, 1994). By comparison, relatively few studies have addressed cultural variations in adulthood and old age, and even fewer have examined the end of the lifespan in non-Western societies.

By placing culture at the center of human development, we gain a better appreciation for the enormous influence culture has on our physical, cognitive, social, and emotional development. In the process, we may also find solutions for some of our most pressing global concerns. Two decades ago, Heron and Kroeger (1981) stated that "any serious and systematic attempt to study human behavior and experience must, in the very nature of things, be both developmental in depth and cross-cultural in breadth" (p. 1). Not long ago, a similar concern was expressed by Valsiner and Lawrence (1997), who make the point that "to understand how development occurs throughout life it is necessary to locate developing individuals within their specific cultures" (p. 71).

In the early years of the new century, we predict an increasing interest in viewing human development within an ecological and cross-cultural developmental perspective. Several recent efforts are at the forefront of this movement. One is the previously mentioned work of Kagitcibasi (1996), which looks at family and human development from the perspective of what were once called "Third World countries" but that Kagitcibasi more accurately calls the "Majority World"—"countries that do not participate fully in the benefits and problems of the industrial and postindustrial West" (p. ix). Her perspective is similar to ours, in that she takes a contextual-developmental-functional approach to human development, with the added goal of applying her findings to social policy issues in her native Turkey, most notably in the "Turkish Early Enrichment Project." In doing this, she moves from a position of theory to one of application, focusing on the fields of early childhood care and education. These are areas of induced change in which cross-cultural findings on human development can be used to develop intervention strategies and policy positions relevant to children and families within varying cultural contexts.

Another example of the type of research we hope to see more of in the future is an extensive study by Mishra, Sinha, and Berry (1996) examining the psychological adaptation of tribal groups in India. Three groups (the Asur, Oraon, and Birhar), differing in settlement and occupation patterns, were compared in terms of cultural lifestyles, patterns of child socialization, cognitive behavior, and acculturation attitudes and experiences. Similar to Kagitcibasi, the authors focus on the application of their findings, this time to problems of acculturative stress. In the decades ahead, we predict there will be more studies that stress the practical application of findings to real-world problems. We only wish there were more such examples at the present time.

In a recent review of cultural influences on child development, Super and Harkness (1997) have presented theoretical principles and research evidence in support of three specific approaches that, while varying in focus, emphasize "the structured, dynamic and integrative nature of the environment." These approaches include their developmental niche concept (Harkness & Super, 1992; Super & Harkness, 1986), which we have referred to extensively throughout this book, Worthman's proposed theory of developmental microniche (1994, 1995; Worthman, Stallings, & Jenkins, 1993), and Weisner's work on the ecocultural niche (Gallimore, Goldenberg, & Weisner, 1993; Weisner, 1996; Weisner, Matheson, & Bernheimer, 1996).

Following a comprehensive review of contemporary evidence, they point to three recurring themes they believe "will continue to occupy a central place in the work that lies ahead: how best to conceptualize variability within and across cultural settings, to characterize activities of the child's mind, and to improve methodological rigor in research in culture and development" (Super & Harkness, 1977, p. 30).

In stressing the need for conducting more comparative studies and the benefits they can provide, Super and Harkness (1977) state, "Comparative studies remind us that even in our own cultures we too often assume we know—or we overlook entirely—what kinds of settings, customs, and ideas characterize our children's lives. In this sense we cannot understand the development of our own children until we can understand the children of others" (p. 31).

In a recent review of cross-cultural human development research, Gardiner (2000) raised several critical and challenging questions that need to be answered in the near future: What types of cross-cultural developmental studies will be conducted in the future? How similar or different should these be to current research? In what ways will these studies contribute to our understanding of human development and the ever-changing and increasingly complex world in which people live? What implications will future research findings have for the construction of new developmental theories and how will these new theories affect the design of even newer studies? It will be interesting to learn the answers to these difficult and challenging questions.

In concluding an earlier review of child development studies, Gardiner (1994) made the following comment, which also appeared at the end of the first edition of *Lives Across Cultures:* "Cross-cultural study of development frequently resembles a confused mosaic of often contradictory findings. Yet therein lies the promise and excitement of future endeavors. . . . Much more needs to be done, and as the cross-cultural perspective reveals, discovery of similarities and dissimilarities in human behavior will make our understanding both easier and more difficult" (p. 72). This was true then, and it is true now.

Ahead of us lie tremendous challenges and opportunities. Speculating about where our cross-cultural journey will take us next is difficult. Wherever we go, it is certain to be an interesting and exciting adventure. Perhaps some of you will be the pioneer theorists and researchers who take us to the next point on this journey. We eagerly look forward to that day.

◇ SUMMARY

In this final chapter, we looked back at the major theories introduced at the beginning of our journey into human development and commented on their usefulness for explaining cultural similarities and differences in behavior across the lifespan. These included the ecological systems approach and developmental niche as well as the work of Piaget, Vygotsky, Erikson, and Kohlberg. Following a discussion of the difficulties of interpreting theory in and out of cultural context, we concluded with our view of some of the future directions the field of cross-cultural human development will (or should) take in the early years of this new century.

✧ FURTHER READINGS

Roy D'Andrade. (2000). The sad story of anthropology 1950–1999. *Cross-Cultural Research, 34*, 219–232.

> The author discusses how changing political attitudes over the past fifty years have affected the field of anthropology and its effectiveness as a discipline and what directions it might take in the future.

Cigdem Kagitcibasi and Ype H. Poortinga. (2000). Cross-cultural psychology: Issues and overarching themes. *Journal of Cross-Cultural Psychology, 31*, 129–144.

> The authors consider the difficulties of defining behavior–culture relationships, how the notion of culture is used in empirical studies, possible future trends in cross-cultural psychology, and how findings might be applied to problems of economic and social inequality to contribute globally to human well-being.

Heidi Keller and Patricia M. Greenfield. (2000). History and future of development in cross-cultural psychology. *Journal of Cross-Cultural Psychology, 31*, 52–62.

> A view of the future of cross-cultural human development and how developmental issues and methods can be used to advance theory and research.

REFERENCES

Abbott, S. (1992). Holding on and pushing away: Comparative perspectives on an Eastern Kentucky child-rearing practice. *Ethos, 20,* 33–65.

Abbott, S. (1997). *"You give 'em lots of love and use the flat of your hand": Patterns of child rearing in the mountains.* Paper presented at the twenty-sixth annual meeting of the Society for Cross-Cultural Research, San Antonio, TX.

Abel, E., & Sokol, R. (1987). Incidence of fetal alcohol syndrome and economic impact of FAS-related anomalies. *Drug and Alcohol Dependency, 19,* 51–70.

Aboud, F. E. (1998). *Health psychology in global perspective.* Thousand Oaks, CA: Sage.

Adamolekun, K. (1995). In-laws behavior as a social factor in subsequent and temporary upsurges of grief in Western Nigeria. *Omega: The Journal of Death and Dying, 31,* 23–34.

Adamopoulos, J., Kashima, Y., & Lonner, W. J. (1999). *Social psychology and cultural context.* Thousand Oaks, CA: Sage.

Adelson, J. (1985). Observations on research in adolescence. *Genetic, Social, and General Psychology Monographs, 111,* 249–254.

Adelson, J. (Ed.). (1980). *Handbook of adolescent psychology.* New York: Wiley.

Adkins, V. K. (1999). Grandparents as a national asset: A brief note. *Activities, Adaptations, & Aging, 24,* 13–18.

Ahmed, R. A. (1991). Women in Egypt and the Sudan. In L. L. Adler (Ed.), *Women in cross-cultural perspective* (pp. 107–133). Westport, CT: Praeger.

Ahmed, R. A., & Gielen, U. P. (1998). (Eds.), *Psychology in Arab countries.* Egypt: Menoufia University Press.

Ahnert, L., Mischner, T., & Schmidt, A. (2000). Maternal sensitivity and attachment in East German and Russian family networks. In P. M. Crittenden & A. H. Claussen (Eds.), *The organization of attachment relationships: Maturation, culture, and context.* New York: Cambridge University Press.

Ainsworth, M. D. S. (1967). *Infancy in Uganda: Infant care and the growth of love.* Baltimore: Johns Hopkins University Press.

Ainsworth, M. D. S. (1982). Attachment: Retrospect and prospect. In C. M. Parks & J. Stevenson-Hinde (Eds.), *The place of attachment in human behavior* (pp. 3–30). New York: Basic Books.

Ainsworth, M. D. S., & Wittig, B. A. (1969). Attachment and exploratory behavior of one-year-olds in a strange situation. In B. M. Foss (Ed.), *Determinants of infant behavior IV* (pp. 111–136). London: Methuen.

Aldous, J., Mulligan, G. M., & Bjarnason, T. (1998). Fathering over time: What makes the difference? *Journal of Marriage & the Family, 60,* 809–820.

American Academy of Pediatrics (AAP) Task Force on Infant Positioning and SIDS. (1992). Positioning and SIDS. *Pediatrics, 89*(6), 1120–1126.

American Psychiatric Association (APA). (1994). *Diagnostic and statistical manual of mental disorders* (4th ed.). Washington, DC: American Psychiatric Press.

Anderson, J. A. (1999). Hot flashes or power surges? A contextual analysis of menopause and its meaning. *Dissertation Abstracts International: Section B: The Sciences and Engineering, 60* (6-B), 2979.

Anderson, J. L., Crawford, C. B., Nadeau, J., & Lindberg, T. (1989). Was the Duchess of Windsor right? A cross-cultural review of the socioecology of ideals of female body shape. *Ethology and Sociobiology, 13,* 197–227.

Annett, M. (1985). *Left, right, hand, and brain: The right shift theory.* Hillsdale, NJ: Erlbaum.

Antonucci, T. C. (1990). Social Supports and Social Relationships. In R. H. Binstock and K. George (Eds.), *Handbook of Aging and the Social Sciences* (3rd ed., pp. 205–226). New York: Academic Press.

Aptekar, L. (1988). Colombian street children: Their mental health and how they can be served. *International Journal of Mental Health, 17,* 81–104.

Aptekar, L. (1989). Colombian street children: *Gamines* and *chupagruesos. Adolescence, 24,* 783–794.

Aptekar, L. (1994). Street children in the developing world: A review of their condition. *Cross-Cultural Research, 28*(3), 195–224.

Aptekar, L., & Ciano-Federoff, L. M. (1999). Street children in Nairobi: Gender differences in mental health. In M. Raffaelli (Ed.), *Homeless and working youth around the world: Exploring developmental issues.* San Francisco, CA: Jossey-Bass.

Archetti, E. P. (1999). *Masculinities: Football, polo, and the tango in Argentina.* Oxford, UK: Berg Publishers.

Armstrong, S. (1991, February). Female circumcision: Fighting a cruel tradition. *New Scientist,* 42–47.

Arnett, J. (1992a). Reckless behavior in adolescence: A developmental perspective. *Developmental Review, 12,* 339–373.

Arnett, J. (1992b). Socialization and adolescent reckless behavior: A reply to Jessor. *Developmental Review, 12,* 391–409.

Arnett, J. J. (1999). Adolescent storm and stress. *American Psychologist, 54,* 317–326.

Ashmore, R. D. (1990). Sex, gender, and the individual. In L. Pervin (Ed.), *Handbook of personality: Theory and research* (pp. 486–526). New York: Guilford Press.

Atkinson, D., Morten, G., & Sue, D. (1983). *Counseling American minorities.* Dubuque, IA: Brown.

Austin, J. K., Champion, V. L., & Tzeng, O. C. S. (1989). Cross-cultural relationships between self-concept and body image in high-school-age boys. *Archives of Psychiatric Nursing, 3,* 234–240.

Avedon, E. M., & Sutton-Smith, B. (1971). *The study of games.* New York: Wiley.

Azhar, M. Z., & Varma, S. L. (2000). Mental illness and its treatment in Malaysia. In I. Al-Issa (Ed.), *Al-Junun: Mental illness in the Islamic world.* Madison, WI: International Universities Press.

Baca Zinn, M., & Eitzen, D. S. (1993). *Diversity in families* (3rd ed.). New York: HarperCollins.

Baltes, P. B. (1987). Theoretical propositions of life-span developmental psychology: On the dynamics between growth and decline. *Developmental Psychology, 23,* 611–626.

Baltes, P. B. (1993). The aging mind: Potential and limits. *Gerontologist, 33,* 580–594.

Banks, C. G. (1992). "Culture" in culture-bound syndromes: The case of anorexia nervosa. *Social Science & Medicine, 34*(8), 867–884.

Barker, D. J. P. (1995). The Wellcome Foundation Lecture, 1994. The fetal origins of adult disease. *Proceedings of the Royal Society of London. Series B: Biological Sciences, 262,* 37–43.

Barnard, K. E., & Martell, L. K. (1995). Mothering. In M. H. Bornstein (Ed.), *Handbook of parenting* (Vol. 3, pp. 3–26). Mahwah, NJ: Erlbaum.

Barresi, C. M., & Menon, G. (1990). Diversity in black family caregiving. In Z. Harel, E. A. McKinney, & M. Williams (Eds.), *Black aged: Understanding diversity and service needs.* Newbury Park, CA: Sage.

Barrett, D. E., Radke-Yarrow, M., & Klein, R. E. (1982). Chronic malnutrition and child behavior: Effects of early caloric supplementation on social and emotional functioning at school age. *Developmental Psychology, 18,* 541–556.

Barry, H. III, & Paxson, L. M. (1971). Infancy and early childhood: Cross-cultural codes. *Ethnology, 10,* 466–508.

Basseches, M. (1984). *Dialectical thinking and adult development.* Norwood, NJ: Ablex.

Basseches, M. (1989). Dialectical thinking as an organized whole: Comments on Irwin and Kramer. In M. L. Commons, J. D. Sinnott, F. A. Richards, & C. Armon (Eds.), *Adult development: Vol. 1. Comparisons and applications of developmental models.* New York: Praeger.

Bates, E. (1976). *Language and context: The acquisition of pragmatics.* New York: Academic Press.

Beardsley, L. M. (1994). Medical diagnosis and treatment across cultures. In W. J. Lonner & R. Malpass (Eds.), *Psychology and culture.* Boston: Allyn & Bacon.

Beatty, S.E., Jeon, J.O., Albaum, G., & Murphy, B. (1994) A cross-national study of leisure activities. *Journal of Cross–Cultural Psychology, 25*(3), 409–422.

Beauvais, F., Oetting, E. R., Wolf, W., Edwards, R. W. (1989). American Indian youth and drugs,1976–1987: a continuing problem. *American Journal of Public Health, 79*(5), 634–636.

Beck, A. T. (1976). *Cognitive therapy and the emotional disorders.* New York: New American Library.

Beck, C. J. (1995). *Now Zen.* San Francisco: HarperCollins.

Beckwith, L., Rodning, C., & Cohen, S. (1992). Preterm children at early adolescence, and continuity and discontinuity in maternal responsiveness from infancy. *Child Development, 63,* 1198–1208.

Behrman, R. E. (1985). Preventing low birth weight: A pediatric perspective. *Journal of Pediatrics, 107*(6), 842–854.

Beidelman, T. O. (1971). *The Kagura: A matrilineal people of East Africa.* New York: Holt, Rinehart & Winston.

Beilin, H. (1994). Jean Piaget's enduring contribution to developmental psychology. In R. D. Parke, P. A. Ornstein, J. J. Rieser, & C. Zahn-Waxler (Eds.), *A Century of Developmental Psychology*. Washington, DC: American Psychological Association.

Bellamy, C. (1999). *The state of the world's children, 1999*. New York: UNICEF/United Nations Publications.

Belsky, J. (1985). Exploring individual differences in marital change across the transition to parenthood: The role of violated expectations. *Journal of Marriage and the Family, 47*, 1037–1044.

Bennett, D. A., & Knopman, D. S. (1994). Alzheimer's disease: A comprehensive approach to patient management. *Geriatrics, 49*(8), 20–26.

Benoit, D., & Parker, K. C. H. (2000). Stability and transmission of attachment across three generations. In D. Muir & A. Slater (Eds.), *Infant development: The essential readings*. Malden, MA: Blackwell.

Berk, L. E. (1992). Children's private speech: An overview of theory and the status of research. In R. M. Diaz & L. E. Berk (Eds.), *Private speech: From social interaction to self-regulation* (pp. 17–53). Hillsdale, NJ: Erlbaum.

Berk, L. E. (1994). *Child development* (3rd ed.). Boston: Allyn & Bacon.

Berman, A. L., & Jobes, D. A. (1991). *Adolescent suicide: Assessment and intervention*. Washington, DC: American Psychological Association.

Bernstein, B. (1971). *Class, codes and control* (Vol. 1). London: Routledge & Kegan Paul.

Berry, J. W. (1969). On cross-cultural comparability. *International Journal of Psychology, 4*, 119–128.

Berry, J. W. (1976). *Human ecology and cognitive style*. Beverly Hills, CA: Sage.

Berry, J. W. (1979). A cultural ecology of social behavior. In L. Berkowitz (Ed.), *Advances in experimental social psychology* (Vol. 12, pp. 177–207). New York: Academic Press.

Berry, J. W. (1983). The sociogenesis of social sciences: An analysis of the cultural relativity of social psychology. In B. Bain (Ed.), *The sociogenesis of language and human conduct*. New York: Plenum.

Berry, J. W. (1992). *On the unity of the field: Variations and communalities in understanding human behavior in cultural context*. Paper presented at the twenty-third congress of the International Association of Applied Psychology, Madrid.

Berry, J. W., & Dasen, P. (Eds.). (1974). *Culture and cognition*. London: Methuen.

Berry, J. W., Dasen, P. R., & Saraswathi, T. S. (Eds.). (1997). *Handbook of cross-cultural psychology: Vol. 2. Basic processes and human development* (2nd ed.). Boston: Allyn & Bacon.

Berry, J. W., Poortinga, Y. H., & Pandey, J. (Eds.). (1997). *Handbook of cross-cultural psychology: Vol. 1. Theory and method* (2nd ed.). Boston: Allyn & Bacon.

Berry, J. W., Poortinga, Y. H., Segall, M. H., & Dasen, P. R. (1992). *Cross-cultural psychology*. Cambridge, England: Cambridge University Press.

Berry, J. W., Segall, M. H., & Kagitcibasi, C. (Eds.). (1997). *Handbook of cross-cultural psychology: Vol. 3. Social behavior and applications* (2nd ed.). Boston: Allyn & Bacon.

Bersoff, D. M., & Miller, J. (1993). Culture, context, and the development of moral accountability judgments. *Developmental Psychology, 29*, 669–676.

Bertrand, J. T., Ward, V., & Pauc, F. (1992). Sexual practices among the Quiche-speaking Mayan population of Guatemala. *International Quarterly of Community Health Education, 12,* 265–282.

Best, D. L., House, A. S., Barnard, A. E., & Spicker, B. S. (1994). Parent–child interactions in France, Germany, and Italy: The effects of gender and culture. *Journal of Cross-Cultural Psychology, 25,* 181–193.

Best, D. L., & Ruther, N. M. (1994). Cross-cultural themes in developmental psychology: An examination of texts, handbooks, and reviews. *Journal of Cross-Cultural Psychology, 25*(1), 54–77.

Bhogle, S. (1999). Gender roles: The construct in the Indian context. In T. S. Saraswathi (Ed.), *Culture, socialization and human development: Theories, research, and applications in India.* Thousand Oaks, CA: Sage.

Biller, H. B. (1993). *Fathers and families.* Westport, CT: Auburn House.

Birren, J. E., & Schaie, K. W. (Eds.). (1995). *Handbook of psychology and aging.* San Diego, CA: Academic Press.

Bjorkqvist, K., & Niemela, P. (1992). *Of mice and women: Aspects of female aggression.* San Diego, CA: Academic Press.

Blau, F. D., & Ferber, M. A. (1986). *The economics of women, men, and work.* Englewood Cliffs, NJ: Prentice Hall.

Blieszner, R. (1988). Individual development and intimate relationships in middle and late adulthood. In R. M. Milardo (Ed.), *Families and social networks* (pp. 147–167). Newbury Park, CA: Sage.

Block, J. (1983). Differential premises arising from differential socialization of the sexes: Some conjectures. *Child Development, 54,* 1335–1354.

Bochner, S. (1994). Cross-cultural differences in the self-concept. A test of Hofstede's individualism/collectivism distinction. *Journal of Cross-Cultural Psychology, 25,* 273–283.

Bogg, R. A., & Hughes, J. (1973). Correlates of marijuana usage at a Canadian technological institute. *International Journal of the Addictions, 8,* 489–504.

Bolton, R. (1994). Sex, science, and social responsibility: Cross-cultural research on same-sex eroticism and sexual intolerance. *Cross-Cultural Research, 28,* 134–190.

Bond, T. G. (1998). Fifty years of formal operational research: The empirical evidence. *Archives de Psychologie, 66,* 221–238.

Bongaarts, J. (1994, March). Can the growing human population feed itself? *Scientific American,* 36–42.

Borgatti, S. P. (1992). ANTHROPAC 4.0: *Methods guide.* Columbia, SC: Analytic Technologies.

Bornstein, M. H. (1992). Perceptual development in infancy, childhood, and old age. In M. H. Bornstein & M. E. Lamb (Eds.), *Developmental psychology: An advanced textbook* (3rd ed.). Hillsdale, NJ: Erlbaum.

Bornstein, M. H. (1995). Parenting infants. In M. H. Bornstein (Ed.), *Handbook of parenting* (Vol. 1, pp. 3–39). Mahwah, NJ: Erlbaum.

Bornstein, M. H. (2000). Infant to conversant: Language and non-language processes in developing early communication. In N. Budwig, I. C. Uzgiris, and J. V. Wertsch (Eds.), *Communication: An arena of development.* Stamford, CT: Ablex Publishing.

Bornstein, M. H., Tal, J., Rahn, C., Galperin, C. Z., Pecheux, M.-G, Lamour, M., Azuma, H., Toda, S., Ogino, M., & Tamis-LeMonda, C. S. (1992). Functional analysis of the contents of maternal speech to infants of five and thirteen months in four cultures: Argentina, France, Japan, and the United States. *Developmental Psychology, 28,* 593–603.

Bornstein, M. H., Tal, J., & Tamis-LeMonda, C. S. (1991). Parenting in cross-cultural perspective: The United States, France, and Japan. In M. H. Bornstein (Ed.), *Cultural approaches to parenting* (pp. 69–90). Hillsdale, NJ: Erlbaum.

Bornstein, M. H., & Tamis-LeMonda, C. S. (1989). Maternal responsiveness and cognitive development in children. In M. H. Bornstein (Ed.), *Maternal responsiveness: Characteristics and consequences* (pp. 49–61). San Francisco: Jossey-Bass.

Bornstein, M. H., Toda, S., Azuma, H., Tamis-LeMonda, C. S., & Ogino, M. (1990). Mother and infant activity and interaction in Japan and the United States: II. A comparative microanalysis of naturalistic exchanges focused on the organization of infant attention. *International Journal of Behavioral Development, 13,* 289–308.

Bouchard, T. J., Lykken, D. T., McGue, M., Segal, N. L., & Tellegen, A. (1990). Sources of human psychological differences: The Minnesota study of twins reared apart. *Science, 250,* 223–228.

Bourguignon, E. (1979). *Psychological anthropology: An introduction to human nature and cultural differences.* New York: Holt, Rinehart & Winston.

Bower, B. (2000). Cultures of reason: Thinking styles may take Eastern and Western routes. *Science News, 157,* 56–58.

Bowlby, J. (1989). *Secure and insecure attachment.* New York: Basic Books.

Boxer, P. A., & Garvey, J. T. (1985). Psychiatric diagnoses of Cuban refugees in the United States: Findings of medical review boards. *American Journal of Psychiatry, 1421,* 86–89.

Bradley, R. H. (1995). Environment and parenting. In M. Bornstein (Ed.), *Handbook of parenting* (Vol. 2, pp. 235–261). Hillsdale, NJ: Erlbaum.

Brink, P. J. (1989). The fattening room among the Annang of Nigeria. *Medical Anthropology, 12,* 131–143.

Brislin, R. (1993). *Understanding culture's influence on behavior.* New York: Harcourt Brace Jovanovich.

Brislin, R. (Ed.). (1990). *Applied cross-cultural psychology.* Newbury Park, CA: Sage.

Brislin, R., & Yoshida, T. (Eds.). (1994). *Improving intercultural interactions: Modules for cross-cultural training programs.* Thousand Oaks, CA: Sage.

Bronfenbrenner, U. (1967). Response to pressure from peers versus adults among Soviet and American school children. *International Journal of Psychology, 2,* 199–207.

Bronfenbrenner, U. (1970). *Two Worlds of Childhood: U.S. and U.S.S.R.* New York: Russell Sage Foundation.

Bronfenbrenner, U. (1975). Reality and research in the ecology of human development. *Proceedings of the American Philosophical Society, 119,* 439–469.

Bronfenbrenner, U. (1977). Toward an experimental ecology of human development. *American Psychologist, 32,* 513–531.

Bronfenbrenner, U. (1979). *The ecology of human development: Experiments by nature and design*. Cambridge, MA: Harvard University Press.

Bronfenbrenner, U. (1986a). Ecological systems theory. In R. Vasta (Ed.), *Annals of Child Development* (Vol. 6, pp. 187–251). Greenwich, CT: JAI Press.

Bronfenbrenner, U. (1986b). Ecology of the family as a context for human development: Research perspectives. *Developmental Psychology, 22,* 723–742.

Bronfenbrenner, U. (1989). Ecological systems theory. In R. Vasta (Ed.), *Six theories of child development* (Vol. 6, pp. 187–250). Greenwich, CT: JAI Press.

Bronfenbrenner, U. (1990). Who cares for children? *Research and Clinical Center for Child Development, 12,* 27–40.

Bronfenbrenner, U. (1993). The ecology of cognitive development: Research models and fugitive findings. In R. H. Wozniak & K. W. Fischer (Eds.), *Development in context: Acting and thinking in specific environments* (pp. 3–44). Hillsdale, NJ: Erlbaum.

Bronfenbrenner, U. (1995). Developmental ecology through space and time: A future perspective. In P. Moen, G. H. Elder, Jr., & K. Luscher (Eds.), *Examining lives in context: Perspectives on the ecology of human development* (pp. 619–647). Washington, DC: American Psychological Association.

Bronfenbrenner, U. (1999). Environments in developmental perspective: Theoretical and operational models. In S. L. Friedman & T. D. Wachs (Eds.), *Measuring environment across the life span*. Washington, DC: American Psychological Association.

Bronfenbrenner, U., & Evans, G. W. (2000). Developmental science in the 21st century: Emerging questions, theoretical models, research designs and empirical findings. *Social Development, 9,* 115–125.

Bronfenbrenner, U., & Morris, P. (1998). The ecology of developmental processes. In R. M. Lerner (Ed.), *Handbook of child psychology, Vol. 1: Theoretical models of human development* (5th ed.). New York: Wiley.

Brook, J. S., Lukoff, I. F., & Whiteman, M. (1977). Correlates of marijuana use as related to age, sex, and ethnicity. *Yale Journal of Biological Medicine, 50,* 383–390.

Brooks, P. J., Jia, X., Braine, M. D. S., & DaGraca Dias, M. (1998). A cross-linguistic study of children's comprehension of universal quantifiers: A comparison of Mandarin Chinese, Portuguese, and English. *First Language, 18,* 33–79.

Brown, J. K. (1992). Lives of middle-aged women. In V. Kerns & J. K. Brown (Eds.) *In her prime: A new view of middle-aged women*. Chicago: University of Illinois Press.

Brown, B. B., Lohr, M. J., & Trujillo, C. (1990). Multiple crowds and multiple lifestyles: Adolescents' perceptions of peer-group stereotypes. In R. E. Muuss (Ed.), *Adolescent behavior and society* (4th ed.). New York: McGraw-Hill.

Brown, S. S. (1985). Can low birth weight be prevented? *Family Planning Perspectives, 17*(3), 112–118.

Brubaker, T. H. (1985). *Later life families*. Newbury Park, CA: Sage.

Budwig, N., Wertsch, J. V., & Uzgiris, I. C. (2000). Introduction: Communication, meaning, and development: Interdisciplinary perspectives. In N. Budwig, I. C. Uzgiris, and J. V. Wertsch (Eds.), *Communication: An arena of development*. Stamford CT: Ablex Publishing.

Burbank, V. K. (1988). *Aboriginal adolescence: Maidenhood in an Australian community.* New Brunswick, NJ: Rutgers University Press.

Buss, A. H., & Plomin, R. (1984). *Temperament: Early developing personality traits.* Hillsdale, NJ: Erlbaum.

Buss, D. M. (1988). The evolution of human intrasexual competition: Tactics of mate attraction. *Journal of Personality and Social Psychology, 54,* 616–628.

Buss, D. M. (1994a). *The evolution of desire: Strategies of human mating.* New York: Basic Books.

Buss, D. M. (1994b). Mate preferences in 37 cultures. In W. J. Lonner & R. Malpass (Eds.), *Psychology and culture* (pp. 197–201). Boston: Allyn & Bacon.

Butcher, J. N. (1990). *MMPI-2 in psychological treatment.* New York: Oxford University Press.

Butcher, J. N. (Ed.). (1995). *Clinical personality assessment: Practical approaches.* New York: Oxford University Press.

Butcher, J. N., et al. (Eds.). (1990). *Development and use of the MMPI-2 content scales.* Minneapolis: University of Minnesota Press.

Byrnes, J. P. (1988). Formal operations: A systematic reformulation. *Developmental Review, 8,* 66–87.

Cabaj, R. P., & Purcell, D. W. (Eds.) (1998). *On the road to same-sex marriage: A supportive guide to psychological, political, and legal issues.* San Francisco, CA: Jossey-Bass.

Caffrey, R. A. (1992). Caregiving to the elderly in Northeast Thailand. *Journal of Cross-Cultural Gerontology, 7*(2), 117–134.

Cai, X., Golde, T. E., & Younkin, S. C. (1993). Release of excess amyloid B protein from a mutant amyloid B protein precursor. *Science, 259,* 514–516.

Calabrese, R. L., & Noboa, J. (1995). The choice for gang membership by Mexican-American adolescents. *High School Journal, 78,* 226–235.

Calhoun, D. W. (1987). *Sport, culture, and personality* (2nd ed). Champaign, IL: Human Kinetics Publishers.

Campos, J. J., & Stenberg, C. R. (1981). Perception, appraisal, and emotion: The onset of social referencing. In M. E. Lamb & L. R. Sherrod (Eds.), *Infant social cognition: Empirical and social considerations.* Hillsdale, NJ: Erlbaum.

Camras, L. A., & Sachs, V. B. (1991). Social referencing and caretaker expressive behavior in a day care setting. *Infant Behavior and Development, 14,* 27–36.

Cantor, N., & Kihlstrom J. F. (1985). Social intelligence: The cognitive basis of personality. In P. Shaver (Ed.), *Self, situations, and social behavior* (pp. 15–34). Beverly Hills, CA: Sage.

Cantor, N., Norem, J. K., Niedenthal, P. M., Langston, C. A., & Brower, A. M. (1987). Life tasks, self-concept ideals, and cognitive strategies in a life transition. *Journal of Personality and Social Psychology, 53,* 1178–1191.

Capaldi, E. J., & Proctor, R. W. (1999). *Contextualization in psychological research? A critical review.* Thousand Oaks, CA: Sage.

Carnegie Council on Adolescent Development. (1995). *Great transitions: Preparing adolescents for a new century.* New York: Carnegie Corporation.

Carpo, R. H. (1995). Factors in the cross-cultural patterning of male homosexuality: A reappraisal of the literature. *Cross-Cultural Research, 29,* 178–202.

Carraher, T. N., Schliemann, A. D., & Carraher, D. W. (1988). Mathematical concepts in everyday life. In G. B. Saxe & M. Gearhart (Eds.), *Children's mathematics: New directions in child development* (pp. 71–87). San Francisco: Jossey-Bass.

Caselli, C., Casadio, P., & Bates, E. (1999). A comparison from first words to grammar in English and Italian. *Journal of Child Language, 26,* 69–111.

Casey, M. B. (1996). Understanding individual differences in spatial ability within females: A nature/nurture interactionist framework. *Developmental Review, 16,* 241–260.

Cassidy, C. M. (1991). The good body: When big is better. *Medical Anthropology, 13,* 181–213.

Catell, R. B. (1963). Theory of fluid and crystallized intelligence: A critical experiment. *Journal of Educational Psychology, 54,* 1–22.

Cattell, M.G. (1997). African widows, culture and social change: Case studies from Kenya. In J. Sokolovsky (Ed.), *The cultural context of aging: World wide perspectives* (pp. 71–98). Westport, CT: Bergin & Garvey.

Caudill, W., & Plath, D. (1966). Who sleeps by whom? Parent–child involvement in urban Japanese families. *Psychiatry, 29,* 344–366.

Caudill, W., & Weinstein, H. (1969). Maternal care and infant behavior in Japan and America. *Psychiatry, 32,* 12–43.

Centers for Disease Control. (1992). Selected behaviors that increase the risk for HIV infection among high school students—U.S. 1990. *Morbidity and Mortality Weekly, 41,* 231–240.

Centers for Disease Control and Prevention (1998). *CDC Surveillance Summaries.* Atlanta, GA: U.S. Department of Health and Human Services.

Central Intelligence Agency. (2000). *The World Fact Book, 2000.* Washington, DC: U.S. Government Printing Office.

Chadda, R. K., & Ahuja, N. (1990). Dhat Syndrome. *British Journal of Psychiatry, 156,* 577–579.

Chagnon, N. A. (1983). *Yanomamo: The fierce people* (3rd ed.). New York: CBS College Publishing.

Chamberlain, P., & Patterson, G. R. (1995). Discipline and child compliance in parenting. In M. Bornstein (Ed.), *Handbook of parenting* (Vol. 4, pp. 205–225). Hillsdale, NJ: Erlbaum.

Chao, R. K. (1994). Beyond parental control and authoritarian parenting style: Understanding Chinese parenting through the cultural notion of training. *Child Development, 65,* 1111–1119.

Chao, R. K. (1996). Chinese and European American mothers' beliefs about the role of parenting in children's school success. *Journal of Cross-Cultural Psychology, 27*(4), 403–423.

Charles, M., & Hopflinger, F. (1992). Gender, culture and the division of household labor: A replication of U.S. studies for the case of Switzerland. *Journal of Comparative Family Studies, 23,* 375–387.

Chase-Lansdale, P. L., Gordon, R. A., Coley, R. L., Wakschlag, L. S., & Brooks-Gunn, J. (1999). Young African American multigenerational families in poverty: The contexts, exchanges, and processes of their lives. In E. M. Hetherington (Ed.), *Coping with divorce, single parenting, and remarriage: A risk and resiliency perspective.* Mahwah, NJ: Erlbaum.

Cheek, J. M. (1989). *Conquering shyness.* New York: Putnam.

Chen, C., & Uttal, D. H. (1988). Cultural values, parents' beliefs, and children's achievement in the United States and China. *Human Development, 31,* 351–358.

Cherlin, A. J., & Furstenberg, F. F., Jr. (1986). *The new American grandparent: A place in the family, a life apart.* New York: Basic Books.

Chodorow, N. (1978). *The reproduction of mothering.* Berkeley: University of California Press.

Cicchetti, D., Toth, S. L., & Maughm, A. (2000). An ecological-transactional model of child maltreatment. In A. Sameroff, M. Lewis, & J. Miller (Eds.), *Handbook of developmental psychology* (2nd ed.). New York: Plenum.

Clark, K. B., & Clark, M. P. (1947). *Racial identification and preference in Negro children.* New York: Holt.

Clausen, J. A. (1986). *The life course.* Englewood Cliffs, NJ: Prentice Hall.

Clausen, J. A. (1993). *American lives: Looking back at the children of the great depression.* New York: Free Press.

Cogan, J. C., Bhalla, S. K., Sefa-Dedeh, A., & Rothblum, E. D. (1996). A comparison study of United States and African students on perceptions of obesity and thinness. *Journal of Cross-Cultural Psychology, 27*(1), 98–113.

Cole, M. (1990). Cognitive development and formal schooling: The evidence from cross-cultural research. In L. C. Moll (Ed.), *Vygotsky and education* (pp. 89–110). Cambridge, England: Cambridge University Press.

Cole, M. (1992a). Culture and cognitive development: From cross-cultural comparisons to model systems of cultural mediation. In A. F. Healy, S. M. Kosslyn, & R. M. Shiffrin (Eds.), *Essays in honor of William K. Estes* (pp. 279–305). Hillsdale, NJ: Erlbaum.

Cole, M. (1992b). Culture in development. In M. H. Bornstein & M. E. Lamb (Eds.), *Developmental psychology: An advanced textbook* (3rd ed., pp. 731–789). Hillsdale, NJ: Erlbaum.

Cole, M. (1995). Culture and cognitive development: From cross-cultural research to creating systems of cultural mediation. *Culture and psychology, 1,* 25–52.

Cole, M., & Cole, S. R. (1989). *The development of children.* New York: Freeman.

Cole, M., & Cole, S. R. (1993). *The development of children* (2nd ed.). New York: Freeman.

Cole, M., & Cole, S. R. (1996). *The development of children* (3rd ed.). New York: Freeman.

Cole, M., & Cole, S. R. (2001). *The development of children* (4th ed.). New York: Worth Publishers.

Cole, M., Super, C. M., Harkness, S., & Cole, S. (In preparation). *Human development across the lifespan.* New York: Freeman.

Colin, V. L. (1996). *Human attachment.* New York: McGraw-Hill.

Collins, W. A. (1990). Parent–child relationships in the transition to adolescence: Continuity and change in interaction, affect, and cognition. In R. Montemayor, G. Adams, & T. Gullotta (Eds.), *Advances in adolescent development: From childhood to adolescence: A transitional period?* (Vol. 2, pp. 85–106). Beverly Hills, CA: Sage.

Collins, W. A., & Russell, G. (1991). Mother–child and father–child relationships in middle childhood and adolescence: A developmental analysis. *Developmental Review, 11,* 91–136.

Coltrane, S. (1996). *Family man: Fatherhood, housework, and gender equity.* New York: Oxford University Press.

Condon, J. C. (1984). *With respect to the Japanese.* Yarmouth, ME: Intercultural Press.

Connolly, M. (1990). Adrift in the city: A comparative study of street children in Bogota, Colombia and Guatemala City. In N. Boxhill (Ed.), *Homeless children: The watchers and the waiters* (pp. 129–149). New York: Haworth Press.

Cook, P. (1994). Chronic illness beliefs and the role of social networks among Chinese, Indian, and Angloceltic Canadians. *Journal of Cross-Cultural Psychology, 25,* 452–465.

Cooley, C. H. (1902). *Human nature and the social order.* New York: Scribner's.

Coren, S. (1992). *The left-hander syndrome.* New York: Free Press.

Coren, S., & Halpern, D. F. (1991). Left-handedness: A marker for decreased survival fitness. *Psychological Bulletin, 109,* 90–106.

Corman, H. H., & Escalona, S. K. (1969). Stages in sensori-motor development: A replication study. *Merrill-Palmer Quarterly, 15*(4), 351–361.

Corsaro, W. A. (1988). Routines in the peer culture of American and Italian nursery school children. *Social Education, 61,* 1–14.

Corsaro, W. A., & Eder, D. (1990). Children's peer cultures. *Annual Review in Sociology, 16,* 197–220.

Cosgrove, J. (1990). Towards a working definition of street children. *International Social Work, 33,* 185–192.

Cosminsky, S. A., Mhlovi, M., & Ewbank, D. (1993). Child feeding practices in a rural area of Zimbabwe. *Social Science and Medicine, 36,* 937–947.

Cotran, R. S., Kumar, V., & Robbins, S. L. (1994). *Robbins' pathologic basis of disease* (5th ed.). Philadelphia: Saunders.

Coupland, N., Coupland, J., & Giles, H. (1991). *Language, society, and the elderly.* Oxford, UK: Blackwell.

Cousins, S. D. (1989). Culture and self-perception in Japan and the United States. *Journal of Personality and Social Psychology, 56,* 124–131.

Coverman, S. (1985). Explaining husband's participation in domestic labor. *Sociological Quarterly, 26,* 81–97.

Coward, R. T., Horne, C., & Dwyer, J. W. (1992). Demographic perspectives on gender and family caregiving. In J. W. Dwyer & R. T. Coward (Eds.), *Gender, families and elder care.* Newbury Park, CA: Sage.

Cox, C. (1993). Hispanic culture and family care of Alzheimer's patients. *Health and Social Work, 18*(2), 92–101.

Crittenden, K. S. (1991). Asian self-effacement or feminine modesty? Attributional patterns of women university students in Taiwan. *Gender and Society, 5,* 98–117.

Cross, W. (1978). The Thomas and Cross models of psychological nigrescence: A literature review. *Journal of Black Psychology, 4,* 13–31.

Cummings, L. L. (1994). Fighting by the rules: Women street-fighting in Chihuahua, Mexico. *Sex Roles, 30,* 189–198.

Cunningham, F. G., MacDonald, P. C., Gant, N. F., Leveno, K. J., Gilstrap, L. C., Hankins, C. D., & Clark, S. L. (1997). *Williams Obstetrics* (20th ed.). Stamford, CT: Appleton & Lange.

Cushner, K. (1990). Cross-cultural psychology and the formal classroom. In R. W. Brislin (Ed.), *Applied cross-cultural psychology* (pp. 98–120). Newbury Park, CA: Sage.

D'Abreu, R. C., Mullis, A. K., & Cook, L. A. (1999). The resiliency of street children in Brazil. *Adolescence, 34*(136), 745–751.

Damon, W. (1973). Early conceptions of positive justice as related to the development of logical operations. *Child Development, 46,* 301–312.

D'Andrade, R. (1990). Some propositions about the relations between culture and human cognition. In J. W. Stigler, R. A. Shweder, & G. Herdt (Eds.), *Cultural psychology* (pp. 65–129). New York: Cambridge University Press.

D'Andrade, R. G., & Strauss, C. (Eds.). (1992). *Human motives and cultural models.* New York: Cambridge University Press.

Dasen, P. R. (1972a). Cross-cultural Piagetian research: A summary. *Journal of Cross-Cultural Psychology, 7,* 75–85.

Dasen, P. R. (1972b). The development of conservation in Aboriginal children. A replication study. *International Journal of Psychology, 7,* 75–85.

Dasen, P. R. (1975). Concrete operational development in three cultures. *Journal of Cross-Cultural Psychology, 6,* 156–172.

Dasen, P. R. (Ed.). (1977). *Piagetian psychology: Cross-cultural contributions.* New York: Gardner Press.

Dasen, P. R., & Heron, A. (1981). Cross-cultural tests of Piaget's theory. In H. C. Triandis & A. Heron (Eds.), *Handbook of cross-cultural psychology* (Vol. 4). Boston: Allyn & Bacon.

Dasen, P. R., Inhelder, B., Lavellee, M., & Retschitzki, J. (1978). *Naissance de l'intelligence chez l'enfant Baoule de Côte d'Ivoire.* Berne: Hans Huber.

Datan, N., Antonovsky, A., & Moaz, B. (1984). Love, war, and the life cycle of the family. In K. A. McCluskey & H. W. Reese (Eds.), *Life-span developmental psychology: Historical and generational effects* (pp. 143–159). New York: Academic Press.

Davenport, D. S., & Yurich, J. M. (1991). Multicultural gender issues. *Journal of Counseling and Development, 70,* 64–71.

Davies, H., Priddy, J. M., & Tinkleberg, J. R. (1988). Support groups for male caregivers of Alzheimer's patients. *Clinical Gerontology, 5,* 385–395.

Dawes, A. (1990). The effects of political violence on children. A consideration of South African and other studies. *International Journal of Psychology, 25,* 13–31.

Day, R., Nielsen, J., Korten, A., Ernberg, M., et al. (1987). Stressful life events preceding the onset of schizophrenia: A cross-cultural study from the World Health Organization. *Culture, Medicine, and Psychiatry, 11,* 123–205.

Declercq, E. R. (1993). Where babies are born and who attends their births: Findings from the revised 1989 United States standard certificate of live births. *Obstetrics and Gynecology, 81,* 997–1004.

Delaney, C. H. (1995). Rites of passage in adolescence. *Adolescence, 30,* 891–897.

Dennis, W., & Dennis, M. G. (1940). The effect of cradling practices upon the onset of walking in Hopi children. *Journal of Genetic Psychology, 56,* 77–86.

Dentan, R. K. (1968). *The Semai: A nonviolent people of Malaya*. New York: Holt, Rinehart & Winston.

Desmond, M., Price, J. H., Gray, N., & O'Connell, J. K. (1986). The etiology of adolescents' perceptions of their weight. *Journal of Youth and Adolescence, 15*, 461–474.

Dettwyler, K. A. (1989). Style of infant feeding: Parental/caretaker control of food consumption in young children. *American Anthropologist, 91*, 696–703.

DeVries, M. W. (1994). Kids in context: Temperament in cross-cultural perspective. In W. B. Carey & S. C. Devitt (Eds.), *Prevention and early intervention: Individual differences as risk factors for the mental health of children*. New York: Brunner/Mazel.

DeVries, M. W., & Sameroff, A. J. (1984). Culture and temperament: Influences on temperament in three East African societies. *American Journal of Orthopsychiatry, 54*, 83–96.

Dexter, C. R. (1985). Women and the exercise of power in organizations: From ascribed to achieved status. *Women and Work, 1*, 239–258.

Dhawan, N., & Roseman, I. J. (1988). *Self-concept across two cultures: India and the United States*. Paper presented at the ninth conference of the International Association for Cross-Cultural Psychology, Newcastle, Australia.

DiLalla, L. F., & Jones, S. (2000). Genetic and environmental influences on temperament in preschoolers. In V. J. Molfese & D. Molfese (Eds.), *Temperament and personality development across the life span*. Mahwah, NJ: Erlbaum.

Dion, K. L., & Dion, K. K. (1993). Gender and ethnocultural comparisons in styles of love. *Psychology of Women Quarterly, 17*, 463–473.

Diop, A. M. (1989). The place of the elderly in African society. *Impact of Science on Society, 153*, 93–98.

Dohrenwend, B. P., & Dohrenwend, B. S. (1969). *Social status and psychological disorder*. New York: Wiley.

Doka, K. J., & Mertz, M. E. (1998). The meaning and significance of great-grandparenthood. *Gerontologist, 28*, 192–197.

Domino, G. (1992). Cooperation and competition in Chinese and American children. *Journal of Cross-Cultural Psychology, 23*(4), 456–467.

Douki, S., & Tabbane, K. (1996). Culture and depression. *World Health Magazine, 49*(2), 22–26.

Draguns, J. (1990a). Applications of cross-cultural psychology in the field of mental health. In R. Brislin (Ed.), *Applied cross-cultural psychology* (pp. 302–324). Newbury Park, CA: Sage.

Draguns, J. G. (1990b). Normal and abnormal behavior in cross-cultural perspective: Toward specifying the nature of their relationship. In J. J. Berman (Ed.), *Nebraska symposium on motivation 1989* (pp. 236–277). Lincoln: University of Nebraska Press.

Draguns, J. G. (1994). Pathological and clinical aspects. In L. L. Adler & U. P. Gielen (Eds.), *Cross-cultural topics in psychology*. Westport, CT: Praeger.

Draguns, J. R. (1997). Abnormal behavior patterns across cultures: Implications for counseling and psychotherapy. *International Journal of Intercultural Relations, 2*, 213–248.

Draper, P., & Cashdan, E. (1988). Technological change and child behavior among the !Kung. *Ethnology, 27,* 348.

Duda, J. L., & Allison, M. T. (1990). Cross-cultural analysis in exercise and sport psychology: A void in the field. *Journal of Sport and Exercise Psychology, 12,* 14–131.

Dybdahl, R. (1996, August). The child in context: Exploring childhood in Somalia. Paper presented at the Twenty-sixth International Congress of Psychology, Montreal.

Dybdahl, R., & Hundeide, K. (1998). Childhood in the Somali context: Mothers' and children's ideas about childhood and parenthood. *Psychology and Developing Societies, 10,* 131–145.

Eckensberger, L. H. (1994). Moral development and its measurement across cultures. In W. J. Lonner and R. S. Malpass (Eds.), *Psychology and culture* (pp. 71–78). Boston: Allyn & Bacon.

Edwards, C. P. (1989). The transition from infancy to early childhood: A difficult transition, and a difficult theory. In V. R. Bricker & G. H. Gossen (Eds.), *Ethnographic encounters in Southern Mesoamerica: Essays in honor of Evon Z. Vogt, Jr.* (pp. 167–175). Austin: University of Texas.

Edwards, C. P. (1996). Parenting toddlers. In M. H. Bornstein (Ed.), *Handbook of parenting* (Vol. 1, pp. 41–63). Hillsdale, NJ: Erlbaum.

Edwards, M. (1994). Pollution in the former U.S.S.R.: Lethal legacy. *National Geographic Magazine, 186*(2), 70–99.

Eisenberg, N., Boehnke, K., Schuhler, P., & Silbereisen, R. K. (1985). The development of prosocial behavior and cognition in German children. *Journal of Cross-Cultural Psychology, 16,* 69–82.

Ekpenyong, S. (1995). The structural adjustment programme and the elderly in Nigeria. *International Journal of Aging and Human Development, 41,* 266–280.

Ekvall, S. W. (1993). Nutritional assessment and early intervention. In S. W. Ekvall (Ed.), *Pediatric nutrition in chronic diseases and developmental disorders: Prevention, assessment, and treatment.* New York: Oxford University Press.

Elder, G. H., Jr. (1974). *Children of the great depression.* Chicago: University of Chicago Press.

Elder, G. H., Jr. (1998a). Life course and development. In R. M. Lerner (Ed.), *Handbook of child psychology Vol. 1: Theoretical models of human development* (5th ed.). New York: Wiley.

Elder, G. H., Jr. (1998b). *Children of the great depression (25th anniversary edition).* Boulder, CO: Westview Press.

Elder, G. H., Modell, J., & Parke, R. D. (Eds.). (1993). *Children in time and place.* New York: Cambridge University Press.

Eldering, L. (in press). *Child rearing in bicultural settings: A cultural ecological approach.* Psychology and developing societies: A journal. New York: Garland.

Elgin, S. H. (2000). *The language imperative.* Cambridge, MA: Perseus Books.

Elkholy, A. (1981). The Arab American family. In C. Mindel & P. Habenstein (Eds.), *Ethnic families in America: Patterns and variations* (pp. 145–162). New York: Elsevier.

Elkin, F., & Handel, G. (1989). *The child and society: The process of socialization* (5th ed.). New York: Random House.

Elkind, D. (1984). *All grown up and no place to go*. Reading, MA: Addison-Wesley.

Elkind, D. (1988). *The hurried child: Growing up too fast too soon*. Reading, MA: Addison-Wesley.

Ellis, A. (1962). *Reason and emotion in psychotherapy*. New York: Carol Publishing Group.

Ember, C. R., & Ember, M. (1993). *Cultural anthropology* (7th ed.). Englewood Cliffs, NJ: Prentice Hall.

Ember, C. R., & Ember, M. (2000). *Cross-cultural research methods*. Walnut Creek: AltaMira Press.

Ember, C. R., & Levinson, D. (1991). The substantive contributions of worldwide cross-cultural studies using secondary data. *Behavior Science Research, 25*, 79–140.

Engels, J. (1993). *Pocket guide to pediatric assessment* (2nd ed.). St. Louis: Mosby.

England, P., Hermsen, J. L., & Cotter, D. (2000). The devaluation of women's work: A comment on Tam. *American Journal of Sociology, 105*, 1741–1751.

Engle, P. L., Zeitlin, M., Medrano, Y., & Garcia, L. M. (1996). Growth consequences of low-income Nicaraguan mothers' theories about feeding 1-year-olds. In S. Harkness & C. M. Super (Eds.), *Parents' cultural belief systems* (pp. 428–446). New York: Guilford Press.

Enright, R. D., Bjerstedt, A., Enright, W. F., Levy, V. M., Buss, R. R., Harwell, M., & Zindler, M. (1984). Distributive justice development: Cross-cultural, contextual, and longitudinal evaluations. *Child Development, 55*, 1737–1751.

Enright, R. D., Franklin, C. C., & Manheim, L. A. (1980). Children's distributive justice reasoning: A standardized and objective scale. *Developmental Psychology, 16*, 193–202.

Epstein, L. H. (1985). Family-based treatment for pre-adolescent obesity. In M. Wolraich & D. K. Routh (Eds.), *Advances in developmental and behavioral pediatrics* (Vol. 6). Greenwich, CT: JAI Press.

Epstein, L. H. (1992). Exercise and obesity in children. *Journal of Applied Sport Psychology, 4*, 120–133.

Epstein, J. L. (1983). Longitudinal effects of family–school–person interactions on student outcomes. *Research in Sociology of Education and Socialization, 4*, 101–107.

Erikson, E. H. (1963). *Childhood and society* (2nd ed.). New York: Norton.

Erikson, E. H. (1969). *Gandhi's truth*. New York: Norton.

Erikson, E. H. (1982). *The life cycle completed*. New York: Norton.

Erikson, E. H., Erikson, J. M., & Kivnick, H. G. (1986). *Vital involvement in old age*. New York: Norton.

Espinosa, M. P., Sigman, M. D., Newmann, C. G., Bwibo, N. O., & McDonald, M. A. (1992). Playground behaviors of school-age children in relation to nutrition, schooling, and family characteristics. *Developmental Psychology, 28*, 1188–1195.

Essau, C. A., & Trommsdorff, G. (1996). Coping with university-related problems: A cross-cultural comparison. *Journal of Cross-Cultural Psychology, 27*(3), 315–328.

Evans, G. W., Lepore, S. J., Shejwal, B. R., & Palsane, M. N. (1998). Chronic residential crowding and children's well being: An ecological perspective. *Child Development, 69*, 1514–1523.

Evans, G. W., & Saegert, S. (2000). Residential crowding in the context of inner city poverty. In S. Wapner, J. Demick, T. Yamamoto, & H. Minami (Eds.), *Theoretical perspectives in environment-behavior research*. NY: Kluwer Academic/Plenum Publishers.

Fagot, B. I., & Leinbach, M. D. (1989). The young child's gender schema: Environmental input, internal organization. *Child Development, 60,* 663–672.

Falbo, T. (1991). The impact of grandparents on children's outcomes in China. *Marriage & Family Review, 16*(3–4), 369–376.

Farver, J. A. M., & Howes, C. (1988). Cross-cultural differences in social interaction: A comparison of American and Indonesian children. *Journal of Cross-Cultural Psychology, 19,* 203–215.

Farver, J. A. M., & Wimbarti, S. (1995). Indonesian children's play with their mothers and older siblings. *Child Development, 66,* 1493–1503.

Farver, J. M. (1993). Cultural differences in scaffolding pretend play: A comparison of American and Mexican mother–child and sibling–child pairs. In K. MacDonald (Ed.), *Parent–child play* (pp. 349–366). Albany: State University of New York Press.

Farver, J. M., Kim, Y. K., & Lee-Shin, Y. (2000). Within cultural differences: Examining individual differences in Korean American and European American preschoolers' social pretend play. *Journal of Cross-Cultural Psychology, 31,* 583–602.

Fay, W. B. (1993). Families in the 1990s. *Marketing Research, 5*(1), 47.

Feldman, S. S., & Elliott, G. R. (Eds.). (1990). *At the threshold: The developing adolescent.* Cambridge, MA: Harvard University Press.

Ferrante, J. (1992). *Sociology: A global perspective.* Belmont, CA: Wadsworth.

Figler, S. K., & Whitaker, G. (1995). *Sport and play in American life.* Dubuque, IA: Brown & Benchmark.

Fischer, K. (1987). Relations between brain and cognitive development. *Child Development, 58,* 623–632.

Fishbein, H. D. (1984). *The psychology of infancy and childhood: Evolutionary and cross-cultural perspectives.* Hillsdale, NJ: Erlbaum.

Fishman, J. A. (1971). *Advances in the sociology of language* (Vol. 1). The Hague: Mouton.

Fitzgerald, M. H. (1990). The interplay of culture and symptoms: Menstrual symptoms among Samoans. *Medical Anthropology, 12,* 145–167.

Flanagan, C. A., & Eccles, J. S. (1993). Changes in parents' work status and adolescents' adjustment to school. *Child Development, 64,* 246–258.

Fleming, J., Watson, C., McDonald, D., & Alexander, K. (1991). Drug use patterns in Northern Territory Aboriginal communities, 1986–1987. *Drug and Alcohol Review, 10,* 367–380.

Flieller, A. (1999). Comparison of the development of formal thought in adolescent cohorts aged 10 to 15 years (1967–1996 and 1972–1993). *Developmental Psychology, 35,* 1048–1058.

Floderus-Myrhed, B., Pedersen, N., & Rasmuson, I. (1980). Assessment of heritability for personality, based on a short form of the Eysenck Personality Inventory: A study of 12,898 twin pairs. *Behavior Genetics, 10,* 153–162.

Ford, D. L., & Lerner, R. M. (1992). *Developmental systems theory: An integrative approach.* Newbury Park, CA: Sage.

Forman, G. E., & Sigel, I. E. (1979). *Cognitive development: A life-span view.* Monterey, CA: Brooks/Cole.

Forman, S. G. (1993). *Coping skills interventions for children and adolescents.* San Francisco: Jossey-Bass.

Francis-Connolly, E. (2000). Toward an understanding of mothering: A comparison of two motherhood stages. *American Journal of Occupational Therapy, 54,* 281–289.

Frazier, C. L., & Glascock, A. P. (1994). Aging and old age in cross-cultural perspective. In L. L. Adler & U. P. Gielen (Eds.), *Cross–cultural topics in psychology* (pp. 103–111). Westport, CT: Praeger.

Freedman, D. G. (1974). *Human infancy: An evolutionary perspective.* Hillsdale, NJ: Erlbaum.

Freeman, D. (1983). *Margaret Mead and Samoa.* Cambridge, MA: Harvard University Press.

Freund, C. S. (1990). Maternal regulation of children's problem-solving behavior and its impact on children's performance. *Child Development, 61,* 113–126.

Friedman, A., Todd, J., & Kariuki, P. W. (1995). Cooperative and competitive behavior of urban and rural children in Kenya. *Journal of Cross-Cultural Psychology, 26*(4), 374–383.

Friedman, S. L., & Wachs, T. D. (Eds.) *Conceptualization and assessment of environment across the lifespan.* Washington DC: American Psychological Association.

Fukada, N. (1991). Women in Japan. In L. L. Adler (Ed.), *Women in cross-cultural perspective* (pp. 204–219). New York: Praeger.

Fuller, M. L. (1992). Today's demographics don't leave it to Beaver. *Education Digest, 58*(6), 54–57.

Furnham, A., & Alibhai, N. (1983). Cross-cultural differences in the perception of female body shapes. *Psychological Medicine, 13,* 829–837.

Furnham, A., Kirkcaldy, B. D., & Lynn, R. (1994). National attitudes to competitiveness, money, and work among young people: First, second, and third world differences. *Human Relations, 47*(1), 119–132.

Gabrenya, W. K., Jr. (1999). Psychological anthropology and the "levels of analysis" problem: We married the wrong cousin. In J.-c Lasry, J. Adair, & K. Dion (Eds.), *Latest contributions to cross-cultural psychology.* Lissa, The Netherlands: Swets & Zeitlinger.

Gallimore, R., Goldenberg, C. N., & Weisner, T. S. (1993). The social construction and subjective reality of activity settings: Implications for community psychology. *American Journal of Community Psychology, 21,* 537–559.

Gallimore, R., Weisner, T. S., Kaufman, S. Z., & Bernheimer, L. P. (1989). The social construction of ecocultural niches: Family accommodation of developmentally delayed children. *American Journal on Mental Retardation, 94,* 216–230.

Gander, M. J., & Gardiner, H. W. (1981). *Child and adolescent development.* Boston: Little, Brown.

Gannon, L., & Stevens, J. (1998). Portraits of menopause in the mass media. *Women & Health, 27,* 1–15.

Garbarino, J. (1985). *Adolescent development: An ecological perspective.* Columbus, OH: Merrill.

Garbarino, J. (2000). The soul of fatherhood. *Marriage and Family Review, 29,* 11–21.

Gardiner, A. J., Gardiner, H. W., & Gardiner, O. S. (1994). Support groups in higher education: The Asian-American experience. In A. White-Parks, D. D. Buffton, U. Chiu, C. M. Currier, C. G. Manrique, & M. M. Piehl (Eds.), *A gathering of voices on the Asian-American Experience* (pp. 145–150). Fort Atkinson, WI: Highsmith Press.

Gardiner, H. W. (2001). Child and adolescent development. In L. L. Adler and U. P. Gielen (Eds.), *Cross-cultural topics in psychology* (2nd ed.). Westport, CT: Greenwood.

Gardiner, H. W. (2001). Development. In D. Matsumoto (Ed.), *Handbook of culture and psychology.* New York: Oxford University Press.

Gardiner, H. W. (1994). Child Development. In L. L. Adler & U. P. Gielen (Eds.), *Cross-cultural topics in psychology* (pp. 61–72). New York: Praeger.

Gardiner, H. W. (1995, March/April). The life of a Buddhist monk. *Calliope: World history for young people.* Peterborough, NH: Cobblestone Publishing.

Gardiner, H. W. (1996). *Cross-cultural content in contemporary developmental textbooks.* Paper presented at the thirteenth congress of the International Association for Cross-Cultural Psychology, Montreal, Canada.

Gardiner, H. W., & Gardiner, O. S. (1991). Women in Thailand. In L. L. Adler (Ed.), *Women in cross-cultural perspective* (pp. 174–187). New York: Praeger.

Gardiner, H., & Mutter, J. D. (1992a). *Developing multicultural awareness: A model for integrating learning and culture.* Paper presented at the eleventh international congress of the International Association for Cross-Cultural Psychology and the Association for Intercultural Research, Liege, Belgium.

Gardiner, H. W., & Mutter, J. D. (1992b). *Positive attitudes and cross-cultural experiences.* Paper presented at the twenty-first annual meeting of the Society for Cross-Cultural Research, Santa Fe, NM.

Gardiner, H. W., & Mutter, J. D. (1993). *An approach to integrating teaching and formal learning in a multicultural context.* Paper presented at the twenty-second annual meeting of the Society for Cross-Cultural Research, Santa Fe, NM.

Gardiner, H. W., & Mutter, J. D. (1994). *Measuring multicultural awareness and identity: A model.* Paper presented at the twenty-third annual meeting of the Society for Cross-Cultural Research, Santa Fe, NM.

Gardiner, H. W., Mutter, J. D., & Kosmitzki, C. (1997). *A model for understanding cultural identity.* Unpublished manuscript.

Gardner, H. (1983). *Frames of mind: The theory of multiple intelligences.* New York: Basic Books.

Garvey, C. (1990). *Play.* Cambridge, MA: Harvard University Press.

Geertz, C. (1973). *The interpretation of cultures.* New York: Basic Books.

Gelman, S. A., Tardif, T. (1998). Acquisition of nouns and verbs in Mandarin and English. In Eve Clark (Ed.), *The proceedings of the twenty-ninth annual child language research forum* (pp. 27–36). Stanford, CA: Center for Study of Language and Information.

Gergen, K. J. (1994). *Realities and relationships: Soundings in social construction.* Cambridge, MA: Harvard University Press.

Gergen, K. J., Gulerce, A., Lock, A., & Misra, G. (1996). Psychological science in cultural context. *American Psychologist, 51,* 496–503.

Geschwind, N. (1984). The biology of cerebral dominance: Implications for cognition. *Cognition, 17,* 193–208.

Gibbons, J. L., Stiles, D. A., Perez-Prada, E., Shkodriani, G. M., & Medina, M. (1996, February). Adolescents' beliefs about women's and men's roles in Iceland, Mexico, Spain, and the United States. Paper presented at the 25th annual meeting of the Society for Cross-Cultural Research, Pittsburgh, PA.

Gibbons, J. L., Stiles, D. A., & Shkodriani, G. M. (1991). Adolescents' attitudes toward family and gender roles: An international comparison. *Sex Roles, 25,* 625–643.

Gibson, J. T., Westwood, M. J., Ishiyama, F. I., Borgen, W. A., et al. (1991). Youth and culture: A seventeen nation study of perceived problems and coping strategies. *International Journal for the Advancement of Counselling, 14,* 203–216.

Gielen, U. P. (1994). American mainstream psychology and its relationship to international and cross-cultural psychology. In A. L. Comunian & U. P. Gielen (Eds.), *Advancing psychology and its applications: International perspectives* (pp. 26–40). Milan, Italy: FrancoAngeli.

Gilligan, C. (1982). *In a different voice: Psychological theory and women's development.* Cambridge, MA: Harvard University Press.

Ginsberg, H. P., Choi, Y. E., Lopez, L. S., Netley, R., & Chao-Yuan, C. (2000). Happy birthday to you: Early mathematical thinking of Asian, South American, and U.S. children. In T. Nunes & P. Bryant (Eds.), *Learning and teaching mathematics: An international perspective.* New York: Psychology Press.

Gladwin, T., & Sarason, S. B. (1953). *Truk: Man in paradise.* (Viking Fund Publications in Anthropology No. 20). New York: Wenner-Gren Foundation for Anthropological Research.

Goldberg, D. P. (1972). *The detection of psychiatric illness by questionnaire.* Windsor: NFER.

Goldberg, S. (1972). Infant care and growth in urban Zambia. *Human Development, 15,* 77–89.

Goldman, D. (1995). *Emotional intelligence.* New York: Bantam Books.

Gonzales, G. F., & Villena, A. (1996). Body mass index and age at menarche in Peruvian children living at high altitudes and at sea level. *Human Biology, 68*(2), 265–276.

Goode, E. E. (1993). The cultures of illness: Health care professionals learn to appreciate immigrants' beliefs. *U.S. News and World Report, 114*(6), 74–77.

Goodnow, J. J. (1962). A test of milieu effects with some of Piaget's tasks. *Psychological Monographs, 76*(36, Whole Issue No. 555).

Goodnow, J. J. (1988). Parents' ideas, actions, and feelings: Models and methods from developmental and social psychology. *Child Development, 59,* 289–320.

Goodnow, J. J. (1990). The socialization of cognition. In J. W. Stigler, R. A. Shweder, & G. Herdt (Eds.), *Cultural psychology: Essays on comparative human development.* Cambridge, England: Cambridge University Press.

Goodnow, J. J., & Bethon, G. (1966). Piaget's tasks: The effects of schooling on intelligence. *Child Development, 37,* 573–582.

Goodnow, J. J., & Collins, W. A. (1990). *Development according to parents: The nature, sources, and consequences of parents' ideas.* Hillsdale, NJ: Erlbaum.

Gopal-McNicol, S. (1995). A cross-cultural examination of racial identity and racial preference of preschool children in the West Indies. *Journal of Cross-Cultural Psychology, 26,* 141–152.

Gormly, A. V., & Brodzinsky, D. M. (1993). *Lifespan Human Development* (5th ed.). Orlando, FL: Harcourt Brace Jovanovich.

Gotowiec, A., & Beiser, M. (1993). Aboriginal children's mental health: Unique challenges. *Canada's Mental Health, 41,* 7–11.

Grant, J. P. (1994). *The state of the world's children.* New York: UNICEF and Oxford University Press.

Green, J. A., Irwin, J. R., & Gustafson, G. E. (2000). Acoustic cry analysis, neonatal status and long-term developmental outcomes. In R. G. Barr, B. Hopkins, & J. A. Green (Eds.), *Crying as a sign, a symptom, & a signal.* New York: Cambridge University Press.

Greenfield, P. M., Brazelton, T. B., & Childs, C. P. (1989). From birth to maturity in Zinacantan: Ontogenesis in cultural context. In V. R. Bricker & G. H. Gossen (Eds.), *Ethnographic encounters in Southern Mesoamerica: Essays in honor of Evon Z. Vogt, Jr.* (pp. 177–216). Austin: University of Texas.

Greenfield, P. M., & Cocking, R. R. (1994). *Cross-cultural roots of minority child development.* Hillsdale, NJ: Erlbaum.

Grossman, B., Wirt, R., & Davids, A. (1985). Self-esteem, ethnic identity, and behavioral adjustment among Anglo and Chicano adolescents in West Texas. *Journal of Adolescence, 8,* 57–68.

Grossmann, K., Grossmann, K. E., Huber, F., & Wartner, U. (1981). German children's behavior towards their mothers at 12 months and their fathers at 18 months in Ainsworth's strange situation. *International Journal of Behavioral Development, 7,* 157–181.

Grotevant, H., & Cooper, C. (1985). Patterns of interaction in family relationships and the development of identity exploration in adolescence. *Developmental Psychology, 56,* 415–428.

Grotevant, H. D., & Cooper, C. R. (1998). Individuality and connectedness in adolescent development: Review and prospects for research on identity, relationships, and context. In E. E. A. Skoe & A. L. von der Lippe (Eds.), *Personality development in adolescence: A cross national and life span perspective.* New York: Routledge.

Grusec, J. E., & Goodnow, J. J. (1994). Impact of parental discipline methods on the child's internalization of values: A reconceptualization of current points of view. *Developmental Psychology, 30,* 4–19.

Gustafson, G. E., Green, J. A., & Kalinowski, L. L. (1993). *The development of communicative skills: Infants' cries and vocalizations in social context.* Paper presented at the biennial meeting of the Society for Research in Child Development, New Orleans, LA.

Gustafson, G. E., & Harris, K. L. (1990). Women's responses to young infants' cries. *Developmental Psychology, 26,* 144–152.

Haan, N., Aerts, E., & Cooper, B. B. (1985). *On moral grounds: The search for a practical morality.* New York: New York University Press.

Haight, W. L., Wang, X., Fung, H., Williams, K., & Mintz, J. (1999). Universal, developmental, and variable aspects of young children's play: A cross-cultural comparison of pretending at home. *Child Development, 70,* 1477–1488.

Hakansson, N.T. (1994). The detachability of women: Gender and kinship in processes of socioeconomic change among the Gusii of Kenya. *American Ethnologist, 21,* 516–538.

Haley, A. (1974). *Roots.* New York: Dell.

Hall, G. S. (1904). *Adolescence.* New York: Appleton-Century-Crofts.

Hall, G. S. (1922). *Senescence: The last half of life.* New York: Appleton-Century-Crofts.

Hall, M. (1997). *The big book of sumo: History, practice, ritual, fight.* Berkeley, CA: Stone Bridge Press.

Halpern, D. F. (1996). Sex, brain, hands, and spatial cognition. *Developmental Review, 16,* 261–270.

Halverson, C. F., Kohnstamm, G. A., & Martin, R. P. (Eds.). (1994). *Development of the structure of temperament and personality from infancy to adulthood.* Hillsdale, NJ: Erlbaum.

Hamilton, C. E. (2000). Continuity and discontinuity of attachment from infancy through adolescence. *Child Development, 71,* 690–694.

Hardy, J. A., & Higgins, G. A. (1992). Alzheimer's disease: The amyloid cascade hypothesis. *Science, 256,* 184–185.

Harkness, S. (1992). Cross-cultural research in child development: A sample of the state of the art. *Developmental Psychology, 28,* 622–625.

Harkness, S., Raeff, C., & Super, C. M. (2000). Variability in the social construction of the child. *New directions for child and adolescent development #87.* San Francisco: Jossey-Bass.

Harkness, S., & Super, C. M. (1985). The cultural context of gender segregation in children's peer groups. *Child Development, 56,* 219–224.

Harkness, S., & Super, C. M. (1992a). The cultural foundations of fathers' roles: Evidence from Kenya and the U.S. In B. S. Hewlett (Ed.), *The father–child relationship: Anthropological perspectives* (pp. 191–212). New York: Aldine.

Harkness, S., & Super, C. M. (1992b). The developmental niche: A theoretical framework for analyzing the household production of health. *Social Science and Medicine, 38,* 217–226.

Harkness, S., & Super, C. M. (1995). Culture and parenting. In M. Bornstein (Ed.), *Handbook of parenting* (Vol. 2, pp. 211–234). Hillsdale, NJ: Erlbaum.

Harkness, S., & Super, C. M. (Eds.). (1996). *Parents' cultural belief systems: Their origins, expressions, and consequences.* New York: Guilford Press.

Harlow, H. F., & Harlow, M. K. (1962). Social deprivation in monkeys. *Scientific American, 207,* 136–146.

Harlow, H. F., & Zimmermann, R. R. (1959). Affectional responses in the infant monkey. *Science, 130,* 421–432.

Harris, M. G. (1994). *Cholas,* Mexican-American girls, and gangs. *Sex Roles, 30,* 289–301.

Harter, S. (1982). The perceived competence scale for children. *Child Development, 53,* 87–97.

Harvard Mental Health Letter (March, 1999). AIDS and mental health, Part 1. *The Harvard Mental Health Letter, 15,* 1–4.

Harwood, R. L., Miller, J. G., & Irizarry, N. L. (1997). *Culture and attachment: Perceptions of the child in context.* New York: Guilford Press.

Hatfield, E., & Rapson, R. L. (1996). *Love & sex: Cross-cultural perspectives.* Boston: Allyn & Bacon.

Hatfield, E., & Sprecher, S. (1995). Men's and women's mate preferences in marital partners in the United States, Russia, and Japan. *Journal of Cross-Cultural Psychology, 26,* 728–750.

Hauser, S. T., & Kasendorf, E. (1983). *Black and white identity formation* (2nd ed.). Malabar, FL: Krieger.

Heinicke, C. M. (1995). Determinants of the transition to parenting. In M. H. Bornstein (Ed.), *Handbook of parenting* (Vol, 3, pp. 277–303). Mahwah, NJ: Erlbaum.

Helson, R., Mitchell, V., & Moane, G. (1984). Personality patterns of adherence and nonadherence to the social clock. *Journal of Personality and Social Psychology, 46,* 1079–1096.

Hendrick, J. B. (1990). Early childhood. In R. M. Thomas (Ed.), *The encyclopedia of human development and education: Theory, research, and studies.* Oxford: Pergamon.

Hendry, J. (1986). *Becoming Japanese.* Honolulu: University of Hawaii Press.

Hendry, J. (1993). Becoming Japanese: The arenas and agents of socialization. In R. H. Wozniak (Ed.), *Worlds of childhood reader.* New York: HarperCollins.

Herdt, G. (1986). Aspects of socialization for aggression in Sambia ritual and warfare. *Anthropology Quarterly, 59,* 160–164.

Heron, A., & Kroeger, E. (1981). Introduction to developmental psychology. In H. C. Triandis, & A. Heron (Eds.), *Handbook of cross-cultural psychology,* (1st ed., Vol. 4). Boston: Allyn & Bacon.

Herskovits, M. J. (1948). *Man and his works: The science of cultural anthropology.* New York: Knopf.

Hewlett, B. (Ed.). (1992). *Father–child relations: Cultural and biosocial contexts.* Hawthorne, NY: Aldine De Gruyter.

Hindley, C. B., Filliozat, A. M., Klackenberg, G., Nicolet-Neister, D., & Sand, E. A. (1966). Differences in age of walking for five European longitudinal samples. *Human Biology, 38,* 364–379.

Hitchcock, D. I. (1994). *Asian values and the United States: How much conflict?* Washington, DC: Center for Strategic and International Studies.

Hoffman, H. J., & Hillman, L. S. (1992). Epidemiology of the sudden infant death syndrome: Maternal, neonatal, and postneonatal risk factors. *Clinics in Perinatology, 19*(4), 717–737.

Hofstede, G. (1997a). *Cultural organizations: Software of the mind.* New York: McGraw-Hill.

Hofstede, G. (1997b). *Uncommon sense about organizations: Cases, studies, and field observations.* Thousand Oaks, CA: Sage.

Holland, D. C., & Valsiner, J. (1988). Cognition, symbols, and Vygotsky's developmental psychology. *Ethos, 16,* 247–272.

Hollos, M., & Leis, P. E. (1989). *Becoming Nigerian in Ibo society.* New Brunswick, NJ: Rutgers University Press.

Hollos, M., & Richards, F. A. (1993). Gender-associated development of formal operations in Nigerian adolescents. *Ethos, 21,* 24–52.

Holmbeck, G. N., Paikoff, R. L., & Brooks-Gunn, J. (1995). Parenting adolescents. In M. H. Bornstein (Ed.), *Handbook of parenting* (Vol. 1, pp. 91–118). Mahwah, NJ: Erlbaum.

Holmes, E. R., & Holmes, L. D. (1995). *Other cultures, elder years.* Thousand Oaks, CA: Sage.

Hong, L. K. (1987). Potential effect of the one-child policy on gender equality in the People's Republic of China. *Gender and Society, 1,* 317–326.

Hopkins, B. (1991). Facilitating early motor development: An intracultural study of West Indian mothers and their infants living in Britain. In J. K. Nugent, B. M. Lester, & T. B. Brazelton (Eds.), *The cultural context of infancy* (Vol. 2). Norwood, NJ: Ablex.

Hopkins, B., & Westra, T. (1988). Maternal handling and motor development: An intracultural study. *Genetic, Social and General Psychology Monographs, 14,* 377–420.

Hopkins, B., & Westra, T. (1990). Motor development, maternal expectations and the role of handling. *Infant Behavior and Development, 13,* 117–122.

Horn, J. L., & Cattell, R. B. (1967). Age differences in fluid and crystalized intelligence. *Acta Psychologica, 26,* 107–129.

Horn, J. L., & Donaldson, G. (1980). Cognitive development: II. Adulthood development of human abilities. In O. G. Brim & J. Kagan (Eds.), *Constancy and change in human development.* Cambridge, MA: Harvard University Press.

Horn, J. L., & Hofer, S. M. (1992). Major abilities and development in the adult period. In R. J. Sternberg and C. A. Berg (Eds.), *Intellectual development.* Cambridge, England: Cambridge University Press.

Houston, L. (1984). Black consciousness and self-esteem. *Journal of Black Psychology, 11,* 1–7.

Hsu, F. L. K. (1985). The self in cross-cultural perspective. In A. J. Marsella, G. DeVos, & F. L. K. Hsu (Eds.), *Culture and self: Asian and Western perspectives* (pp. 24–55). New York: Tavistock.

Hsu, F. L. K., Watrous, B. G., & Lord, E. M. (1961). Culture pattern and adolescent behaviour. *International Journal of Social Psychiatry, 7,* 33–53.

Hu, Y.-H. (1995). Elderly suicide risk in family context: A critique of the Asian family care model. *Journal of Cross Cultural Psychology, 10,* 199–217.

Hudgins, J. E., & Williams-Snyder, V. (1995). *African wedding guide.* Netscape: New Perspectives Technologies Company. (http://www.melanet.com/wedding/wed.html)

Huebner, A. M., & Garrod, A. C. (1993). Moral reasoning among Tibetan monks. A study of Buddhist adolescents and young adults in Nepal. *Journal of Cross-Cultural Psychology, 24,* 167–185.

Human Development Report, 2000. Oxford: Oxford University Press.

Huntsinger, C. S., Jose, P. E., Liaw, F-R., Ching, W-D. (1997). Cultural differences in early mathematics learning: A comparison of Euro-American, Chinese-American, and Taiwan-Chinese families. *International Journal of Behavioral Development, 21,* 371–388.

Hutchinson, J. (1991, Spring). What crack does to babies. *American Educator: The Quarterly Journal of the American Federation of Teachers,* 31–32.

Hymes, D. (1974). *Foundations in sociolinguistics: An ethnographic approach.* Philadelphia: University of Pennsylvania Press.

Hymes, D. (1996). *Ethnography, linguistics, narrative inequality: Toward an understanding of voice.* London: Taylor & Francis.

Hymes, D. (Ed.). (1999). *Reinventing anthropology.* Ann Arbor: University of Michigan Press.

Ikels, C. (1989). Becoming a human being in theory and practice: Chinese views of human development. In D. I. Kertzer & K. W. Schaie (Eds.), *Age structuring in comparative perspective* (pp. 109–141). Hillsdale, NJ: Erlbaum.

Indran, S. K. (1995). Brief report: Eating attitudes among adolescent girls in Malaysian secondary school using the EAT questionnaire. *International Journal of Social Psychiatry, 41*(4), 299–303.

Ingram, D. D., Makuc, D., & Kleinman, J. C. (1986). National and state trends in use of prenatal care, 1970–1983. *American Journal of Public Health, 76*(4), 415–423.

Inhelder, B., & Piaget, J. (1958). *The growth of logical thinking from childhood to adolescence.* New York: Basic Books.

Inhelder, B., & Piaget, J. (1959). *The early growth of logic in the child: Classification and seriation.* New York: Harper & Row.

Isralowitz, R. E., & Hong, O. T. (1990). Singapore youth: The impact of social status on perceptions of adolescent problems. *Adolescence, 98,* 357–362.

Iwawaiki, S., & Kerner, R. M. (1974). Cross-cultural analysis of body build stereotypes of Japanese and American males and females. *Psychologia, 17,* 75–81.

Jablensky, A., Sartorius, N., Ernberg, G., Anker, M., Korten, A., Cooper, J. E., Day, R., & Bertelsen, A. (1992). Schizophrenia: Manifestations, incidence and course in different cultures: A World Health Organization ten-country study. *Psychological Medicine (Monograph Suppl. No. 20).*

Jackson, L. A. (1992). *Physical appearance and gender: Sociobiological and sociocultural perspectives.* Albany, NY: SUNY Press.

Jackson, S. (1987). Great Britain. In M. E. Lamb (Ed.), *The father's role: Cross-cultural perspectives* (pp. 29–57). Hillsdale, NJ: Erlbaum.

Jacobson, J. L., Jacobson, S. W., & Humphrey, H. E. B. (1992). Effects of in utero exposure to polychlorinated biphenyls and related contaminants on cognitive functioning in young children. *Journal of Pediatrics, 116,* 36–45.

Jacobson, S., Fein, G., Jacobson, J., Schwartz, P., & Dowler, J. (1984). Neonatal correlates of prenatal exposure to smoking, caffeine, and alcohol. *Infant Behavior and Development, 7,* 253–265.

Jahoda, G. (1986). A cross-cultural perspective on developmental psychology. *International Journal of Behavioral Development, 9,* 417–437.

Jahoda, G., & Krewer, B. (1997). History of cross-cultural and cultural psychology. In J. W. Berry, Y. H. Poortinga, & J. Pandey (Eds.), *Handbook of cross-cultural psychology: Theory and method* (Vol. 1, pp. 1–42). Boston: Allyn & Bacon.

Janssen, J. P. (2000). Foundations of a functional theory of human handedness. *Theory & Psychology, 10,* 375–398.

Jeffreys, M. D. W. (1952). Samsonic suicide or suicide of revenge among African Americans. *African Studies, 11,* 118–122.

Jegede, R., & Bamgboye, E. (1981). Self-concept in young Nigerian adolescents. *Psychological Reports, 49,* 451–454.

Jemmott, J. B., III, & Jemmott, L. S. (1993). Alcohol and drug use during sexual activity. Predicting the HIV-risk-related behavior of inner-city black male adolescents. *Journal of Adolescent Research, 8,* 41–57.

Johnson, C. L. (1988). Relationships among family members and friends in later life. In R. M. Milardo (Ed.), *Families and social networks* (pp. 168–189). Newbury Park, CA: Sage.

Johnson, M. M. (1988). *Strong mothers, weak wives.* Berkeley: University of California Press.

Johnston, L. D., O'Malley, P. M., & Bachman, J. G. (1992). *Smoking, drinking, and illicit drug use among American secondary school students, college students and young adults, 1975–1991.* Rockville, MD: National Institute on Drug Abuse.

Jones, P. S. (1995). Paying respect: Care of elderly parents by Chinese and Filipino American women. *Health Care for Women International, 16,* 385–398.

Jones, R. E. (1997). *Human reproductive biology.* San Diego, CA: Academic Press.

Jones, R. L., & Kurz Jones, S. (1976). *The Himalaja woman.* Palo Alto, CA: Mayfield.

Jordan, B. (1978). *Birth in four cultures: A crosscultural investigation of childbirth in Yucatan, Holland, Sweden and the United States.* St. Albans, VT: Eden Women's Publications.

Jordan, B. (1993). *Birth in four cultures: A crosscultural investigation of childbirth in Yucatan, Holland, Sweden and the United States* (4th ed.). Prospect Heights, IL: Waveland Press.

Jourard, S., & Secord, P. (1955). Body cathexis and personality. *British Journal of Psychology, 46,* 130–138.

Kaffman, M. (1993). Kibbutz youth: Recent past and present. *Journal of Youth and Adolescence, 22,* 573–604.

Kagan, J. (1994). Yesterday's premises, tomorrow's promises. In R. D. Parke, P. A. Ornstein, J. J. Rieser, & C. Zahn-Waxler (Eds.), *A century of developmental psychology.* Washington, DC: American Psychological Association.

Kagan, J., Kearsley, R. B., & Zealazo, P. (1978). *Infancy: Its place in human development.* Cambridge, MA: Harvard University Press.

Kagan, J., & Klein, R. E. (1973). Cross-cultural perspectives on early development. *American Psychologist, 28,* 947–961.

Kagan, J., Snidman, N., & Arcus, D. (1993). On the temperamental categories of inhibited and uninhibited children. In K. H. Rubin & J. B. Asendorpf (Eds.), *Social withdrawal, inhibition, and shyness in childhood.* Hillsdale, NJ: Erlbaum.

Kagitcibasi, C. (1990). *A critical appraisal of individualism and collectivism: Towards a new formulation.* Paper presented at the International Conference on Individualism and Collectivism: Psychological Perspectives from East and West, Seoul, Korea.

Kagitcibasi, C. (1995). Is psychology relevant to global developmental issues? Experience from Turkey. *American Psychologist, 50,* 293–300.

Kagitcibasi, C. (1996). *Family and human development across cultures.* Mahwah, NJ: Erlbaum.

Kagitcibasi, C., & Poortinga, Y. H. (2000). Cross-cultural psychology: Issues and overarching themes. *Journal of Cross-Cultural Psychology, 31,* 33–51.

Kalu, W., & Kalu, O. (1993). Nigeria. In L. L. Adler (Ed.), *International handbook on gender roles* (Chap. 17). Westport, CT: Greenwood Press.

Kamara, A. I. (1971). *Cognitive development among school-age Themne children of Sierra Leone.* Unpublished doctoral dissertation, University of Illinois.

Kamara, A. I., & Easley, J. A., Jr. (1977). Is the rate of cognitive development uniform across cultures? A methodological critique with new evidence from Themne children. In P. R. Dasen (Ed.), *Piagetian psychology: Cross-cultural contributions* (pp. 26–63). New York: Gardner/Wiley.

Katz, D., & Braly, K. W. (1933). Racial stereotypes of 100 college students. *Journal of Abnormal and Social Psychology, 28,* 280–290.

Keller, H., & Greenfield, P. M. (2000). History and future of development in cross-cultural psychology. *Journal of Cross-Cultural Psychology, 31,* 52–62.

Kelly, M. (1977). Papua New Guinea and Piaget—An eight-year study. In P. R. Dasen (Ed.), *Piagetian psychology: Cross-cultural contributions* (pp. 169–202). New York: Gardner Press.

Kelso, B. J. (1994, September/October). Movement to combat female mutilation. *African Report, 60*–61.

Kemper, S. (1992). Language and aging. In F. I. M. Craik & T. A. Salthouse (Eds.), *The handbook of aging and cognition.* Hillsdale, NJ: Erlbaum.

Kenkel, W. F. (1985). *The family in perspective* (5th ed.). Houston, TX: Cap and Gown Press.

Kerig, P. K., Alyoshina, Y. Y., & Volovich, A. (1993). Gender-role socialization in contemporary Russia: Implications for cross-cultural research. *Psychology of Women Quarterly, 17,* 389–408.

Kett, J. (1977). Rites of passage: *Adolescence in America, 1790 to the present.* New York: Basic Books.

Khan, A., & Cataio, J. (1984). *Men and women in biological perspective.* New York: Praeger.

Killen, M., & Wainryb, C. (2000). Independence and interdependence in diverse cultural contexts. In S. Harkness, C. Raef, & C. Super (Eds.), *Variability in the social construction of the child. New directions for child and adolescent development, No. 87.* San Francisco: Jossey-Bass.

Kim, K. (1995). Culture and mental illness in South Korea. In I. Al-Issa (Ed.), *Handbook of culture and mental illness.* Madison, WI: International Universities Press.

Kim, U., & Berry, J. W. (1993). *Indigenous psychologies: Experience and research in cultural context.* Newbury Park, CA: Sage.

Kim, U., Park, Y-S., & Park, D. (2000). The challenge of cross-cultural psychology: The role of the indigenous psychologies. *Journal of Cross-Cultural Psychology, 31,* 63–75.

Kim, U., Triandis, H. C., Kagitcibasi, C., Choi, S., & Yoon, G. (1994). *Individualism and collectivism: Theory, method, and applications.* Thousand Oaks, CA: Sage.

Kim-Bae, L. S. (2000). Cultural identity as a mediator of acculturative stress and psychological adjustment in Vietnamese-American adolescents. *Dissertation Abstracts International: Section B: The Sciences & Engineering, 60* (7-B), 3570.

Kirkby, R. J., Kolt, G. S., & Hable, K. (1998). Cultural factors in exercise participation of older adults. *Perceptual and Motor Skills, 87,* 890.

Kirmayer, L.J. (1991). The place of culture in psychiatric nosology: Taijinkyofusho and the DSM-III-R. *Journal of Nervous and Mental Disease, 179,* 19–28.

Kleinman, A. (1982). Neurasthenia and depression: A study of somatization and culture in China. *Culture, Medicine, and Psychiatry, 6,* 117–190.

Koff, E., Rierdan, J., & Stubbs, M. L. (1990). Gender, body image, and self-concept in early adolescence. *Journal of Early Adolescence, 10,* 56–68.

Koffka, K. (1935). *Principles of gestalt psychology.* New York: Harcourt Brace.

Kohlberg, L. (1976). Moral stages and moralization: The cognitive-developmental approach. In T. Lickona (Ed.), *Moral development and behavior.* New York: Holt, Rinehart and Winston.

Kohlberg, L. (1981). *Essays on moral development* (Vol. 1). New York: Harper & Row.

Kohlberg, L., & Gilligan, C. (1971). The adolescent as philosopher: The discovery of self in a post-conventional world. *Daedalus, 100,* 1051–1086.

Kohler, K. (1938). *The place of value in a world of facts.* New York: Liveright.

Konner, M. J. (1976). Maternal care, infant behavior and development among the !Kung. In R. B. Lee & I. DeVore (Eds.), *Kalahari hunter-gatherers: Studies of the !Kung San and their neighbors.* Cambridge, MA: Harvard University Press.

Kopp, C. B., & Kaslow, J. B. (1982). *The Child.* Reading, MA: Addison-Wesley.

Korn, S., & Gannon, S. (1983). Temperament, culture variation, and behavior disorders in preschool children. *Child Psychiatry and Human Development, 13,* 203–212.

Kornhaber, A. (1996). *Contemporary grandparenting.* Thousand Oaks, CA: Sage.

Kosberg, J. I. (Ed.). (1992). *Family care for the elderly: Social and cultural changes.* Thousand Oaks, CA: Sage.

Kosberg, J. I., & Garcia, J. L. (Eds.) (1995). *Elder abuse: International and cross-cultural perspectives.* New York: Haworth Press.

Kosik, K. S. (1992). Alzheimer's disease: A cell biological perspective. *Science, 256,* 780–783.

Kostelny, K., & Garbarino, J. (1994). Coping with the consequences of living in danger: The case of Palestinian children and youth. *International Journal of Behavioral Development, 17,* 595–611.

Kozulin, A. (1990). *Vygotsky's psychology: A biography of ideas.* New York: Harvester Wheatsheaf.

Krishnan, L. (1997). Socialization antecedents of allocation rule preference in India. *Psychology and Developing Societies, 9,* 133–148.

Krishnan, L. (1999). Socialization and cognitive–moral influences on justice rule preferences: The case of Indian culture. In T. S. Saraswathi (Ed.), *Culture, socialization and human development: Theory, research, and applications in India*. Thousand Oaks, CA: Sage Publications.

Kroeber, A. L., and Kluckhohn, C. (1952). *Culture, Part III*. Papers of the Peabody Museum of Harvard University.

Kuhn, M. H., & McPartland, R. (1954). An empirical investigation of self-attitudes. *American Sociological Review, 19*, 68–76.

Kulin, H. E. (1991a). Hypothalamic-pituitary changes of puberty. In R. M. Lerner, A. C. Petersen, & J. Brooks-Gunn (Eds.), *Encyclopedia of adolescence*. New York: Garland.

Kulin, H. E. (1991b). Spermarche. In R. M. Lerner, A. C. Petersen, & J. Brooks-Gunn (Eds.), *Encyclopedia of adolescence*. New York: Garland.

Kumari, R. (1988). *Female sexuality in Hinduism*. Delhi: Joint Women's Programme by ISPCK.

Labouvie-Vief, G. (1986). *Mind and self in life-span development*. Symposium on developmental dimensions of adult adaptation: Perspectives in mind, self, and emotion. Presented at the 1986 meeting of the Gerontological Association of America, Chicago, IL.

Lalor, K. J. (1999). Street children: A comparative perspective. *Child Abuse & Neglect, 23*, 759–770.

Lamb, D. R. (1984). *Physiology of exercise: Response and adaption* (2nd ed.). New York: Macmillan.

Lamb, M. E. (Ed.). (1987). *The role of the father: Cross-cultural perspectives*. Hillsdale, NJ: Erlbaum.

Lamb, M. E., Frodi, A. M., Hwang, C. P., Frodi, M., & Steinberg, J. (1982). Effects of gender and caretaking role on parent-infant interaction. In R. M. Emde & R. J. Harmon (Eds.), *Attachment and affiliative systems*. New York: Plenum.

Lamb, M. E., Hwang, C. P., Frodi, M., & Frodi, M. (1982). Security of mother– and father–infant attachment and its relation to sociability with strangers in traditional and non-traditional Swedish families. *Infant Behavior and Development, 5*, 355–367.

Lamb, M. E., Pleck, J., Charnov, E. L., & Levine, J. A. (1987). A biosocial perspective on paternal behavior and involvement. In J. B. Lancaster, J. Altmann, A. Rossi, & L. R. Sherrod (Eds.), *Parenting across the life span: Biosocial perspectives* (pp. 111–142). Chicago, IL: Aldine.

Lamb, M. E., Sternberg, K. L., Hwang, C.-P., & Broberg, A. C. (Eds.). (1992). *Child care in context: Cross-cultural perspectives*. Hillsdale, NJ: Erlbaum.

Lambert, W. W. (1971). Cross–cultural backgrounds to personality development and the socialization of aggression: Findings from the six culture study. In W. Lambert and R. Weisbrod (Eds.), *Comparative perspectives on social psychology* (pp. 49–61). Boston: Little, Brown.

Lancy, D. (1980). Work and play: The Kpelle children during rapid cultural change. In D. F. Lancy & B. A. Tindall (Eds.), *The anthropological study of play: Problems and prospects*. West Point, NY: Leisure Press.

Larson, R. (1991). Egocentrism theory and the "new look" at the imaginary audience and personal fable in adolescence. In R. M. Lerner, A. C. Petersen, & J. Brooks-Gunn (Eds.), *Encyclopedia of adolescence*. New York: Garland.

Launer, L. J. (1993). The work patterns of lactating women in Madura. *Social Science & Medicine, 37*(4), 555–563.

Laurendeau-Bendavid, M. (1977). Culture, schooling, and cognitive development: A comparative study of children in French Canada and Rwanda. In P. R. Dasen (Ed.), *Piagetian psychology: Cross-cultural contributions* (pp. 123–168). New York: Gardner Press.

Lave, J. (1977). Tailor-made experiments and evaluating the intellectual consequences of apprenticeship training. *Quarterly Newsletter of the Institute for Comparative Human Development, 1*, 1–3.

Lave, J. (1988). *Cognition in practice: Mind, mathematics and culture in everyday life*. Cambridge, England: Cambridge University Press.

Lave, J., & Wenger, E. (1991). *Situated learning: Legitimate peripheral participation*. Cambridge, England: Cambridge University Press.

Leadbeater, B. (1986). The resolution of relativism in adult thinking: Subjective, objective, or conceptual. *Human Development, 29*, 291–300.

Leaper, C. (Ed.). (1994). *Childhood gender segregation: Causes and consequences. New Directions for child development, No. 65*. San Francisco: Jossey-Bass.

Lebra, T. (1999). *Feminism from a Japanese perspective: The experience of Japanese professional women*. Paper presented at the Feminists Doing Psychological Anthropology Year 2000 Conference, Stockholm, Sweden.

Lecours, A. R. (1982). Correlates of developmental behavior in brain maturation. In T. Bever (Ed.), *Regressions in mental development*. Hillsdale, NJ: Erlbaum.

Lee, R., & Daly, R. (1987). Man's domination and woman's oppression: The question of origins. In M. Kaufman (Ed.), *Beyond patriarchy: Essays by men on pleasure, power, and change* (pp. 30–44). New York: Oxford University Press.

Lefrancois, G. R. (1996). *The lifespan* (5th ed.). Belmont, CA: Wadsworth.

Legault, F., & Strayer, F. F. (1990). The emergence of sex-segregation in preschool peer groups. In F. F. Strayer (Ed.), *Social interaction and behavioral development during early childhood*. Montreal: La Maison D'Ethologie de Montreal.

Lennartsson, C (1999). Social ties and health among the very old in Sweden. *Research on Aging, 21*, 657–681.

Lerner, R. M. (1990). Plasticity, person-context relations, and cognitive training in the aged years: A developmental contextual perspective. *Developmental Psychology, 26*, 911–915.

Lerner, R. M. (1991). Changing organism-context relations as the basic process of development: A developmental contextual perspective. *Developmental Psychology, 27*, 27–32.

le Roux, J., & Smith, C. S. (1998). Psychological characteristics of South African street children. *Adolescence, 33*, 891–899.

Lester, B. M., Boukydis, C. F. Z., Garcia-Coll, C. T., Hole, W., & Peucker, M. (1992). Infantile colic: Acoustic cry characteristics, maternal perception of cry, and temperament. *Infant Behavior and Development, 15*, 15–26.

Levine, N. E. (1980a). Asian and African systems of polyandry. *Journal of Comparative Family Studies, 11,* 385–410.

Levine, N. E. (1980b). Nyinba polyandry and the allocation of paternity. *Journal of Comparative Family Studies, 11,* 283–298.

LeVine, R. A. (1988). Human parental care: Universal goals, cultural strategies, individual behavior. In R. A. LeVine, P. M. Miller, & M. M. West (Eds.), *Parental behavior in diverse societies. New directions for child development* (No. 40). San Francisco: Jossey-Bass.

LeVine, R. A., & Miller, P. (1990). Commentary. *Human Development, 33,* 73–80.

LeVine, R. A., Miller, P., & West, M. (Eds.). (1988). *Parental behavior in diverse societies. New Directions for Child Development* (No. 40). San Francisco: Jossey-Bass.

Levitt, M.J., Guacci-Franco, N., & Levitt, J.L. (1993). Convoys of social support in childhood and early adolescence: Structure and function. *Developmental Psychology, 29,* 811–818.

Levy, B. S., Wilkinson, F. S., & Marine, W. M. (1971). Reducing neonatal mortality rate with nurse midwives. *American Journal of Obstetrics and Gynecology, 109,* 50–58.

Levy, R. (1996). Essential contrasts: Differences in parental ideas about learners and teaching in Tahiti and Nepal. In S. Harkness & C. M. Super (Eds.), *Parents' cultural belief systems: Their origins, expressions, and consequences.* New York: Guilford.

Lewin, K. (1935). *A dynamic theory of personality.* New York: McGraw-Hill.

Lewis, M., Feiring, C., & Rosenthal, S. (2000) Attachment over time. *Child Development, 71,* 707–720.

Liddell, C., Kvalsvig, J., Qotyana, P., & Shabalala, A. (1994). Community violence and young South African children's involvement in aggression. *International Journal of Behavioral Development, 17,* 613–628.

Lin, K. M., & Kleinman, A. M. (1988). Psychopathology and clinical course of schizophrenia: A cross-cultural perspective. *Schizophrenia Bulletin, 14,* 555–567.

Lin, T. S. (1985). Mental disorders and psychiatry in Chinese culture: Characteristic features and major issues. In W. S. Tseng & D. Y. H. Wu (Eds.), *Chinese culture and mental health.* Orlando: Academic Press.

Lindisfarne, N. (1998). Gender, shame, and culture: An anthropological perspective. In P. Gilbert & B. Andrews (Eds.), *Shame: Interpersonal behavior, psychopathology, and culture.* New York: Oxford University Press.

Lock, M. (1991). Contested meanings of the menopause. *Lancet, 337,* 1270–1272.

Lockery, S. (1991). Caregiving among racial and ethnic minority elders. *Generations, 15*(4), 58–62.

Logan, D. D. (1980). The menarche experience in twenty-three foreign countries. *Adolescence, 58,* 247–256.

Long, G. M., & Crambert, R. F. (1990). The nature and basis of age-related change in dynamic visual acuity. *Psychology and Aging, 5,* 138–143.

Lonner, W. J., & Ibrahim, F. A. (1989). Assessment in cross-cultural counseling. In P. Pedersen, J. Draguns, W. Lonner, & J. Trimble (Eds.), *Counseling across cultures* (3rd ed., pp. 229–334). Honolulu: University of Hawaii Press.

Lonner, W. J., & Malpass, R. (Eds.). (1994). *Psychology and culture.* Boston: Allyn & Bacon.

Loscocco, K., & Kalleberg, A. (1988). Age and the meaning of work in the United States and Japan. *Social Forces, 67,* 337–357.

Low, B. S. (1989). Cross-cultural patterns in the training of children: An evolutionary perspective. *Journal of Comparative Psychology, 103,* 311–319.

Lozoff, B. (1989). Nutrition and behavior. *American Psychologist, 44,* 231–236.

Lubben, J. E., & Becerra, R. M. (1987). Social support among black, Mexican and Chinese elderly. In D. E. Gelfand & C. M. Barresi (Eds.), *Ethnic dimensions of aging* (pp. 130–144). New York: Springer.

Luna, L.J. (1989). Transcultural nursing care of Arab Muslims. *Journal of Transcultural Nursing, 1,* 22–26.

Luria, A. R. (1981). *Language and cognition* (J. V. Wertsch, Ed.). New York: Wiley Intersciences.

Lusk, M. (1992). Street children of Rio de Janeiro. *International Social Work, 35,* 293–305.

Luster, T., & Okagaki, L. (Eds.). (1993). *Parenting: An ecological perspective.* Hillsdale, NJ: Erlbaum.

Lykken, D. T. (2000). Reconstructing fathers. *American Psychologist, 55,* 681–682.

Ma, H. K. (1989). Moral orientation and moral judgment in adolescents in Hong Kong, Mainland China, and England. *Journal of Cross-Cultural Psychology, 20,* 152–177.

MacClancy, J. (1996). *Sport, identity, and ethnicity.* Oxford, UK: Berg Publishers.

Maccoby, E. E. (1980). *Social development: Psychological growth and the parent–child relationship.* New York: Harcourt Brace Jovanovich.

Maccoby, E. E. (1990). Gender and relationships. A developmental account. *American Psychologist, 45,* 513–520.

Maccoby, E. E. (1992). The role of parents in the socialization of children: An historical overview. *Developmental Psychology, 28,* 1006–1017.

Maccoby, E. E. (1998). *The two sexes.* Cambridge, MA: Harvard University Press.

Mackey, W. C. (1985). *Fathering behaviors: The dynamics of the man–child bond.* New York: Plenum Press.

MacKinnon, C. A. (1987). *Feminism unmodified: Discourses in life and law.* Cambridge, MA: Harvard University Press.

MacLeod, R. B. (1947). The phenomenological approach to social psychology. *Psychological Review, 54,* 193–210.

MacNeilage, P. F., & Davis, B. L. (2000). On the origin of internal structure of word forms. *Science, 288,* 527–531.

Madsen, M. C. (1971). Developmental and cross-cultural differences in the cooperative and competitive behavior of young children. *Journal of Cross-Cultural Psychology, 2,* 365–371.

Mahler, M., & Pine, F. (1975). *The psychological birth of the infant.* New York: Basic Books.

Main, M., & Solomon, J. (1990). Procedures for identifying infants as disorganized/disoriented during the Ainsworth strange situation. In M. Greenberg, D. Cicchetti, & E, M. Cummings (Eds.), *Attachment in the preschool years: Theories, research, and intervention.* Chicago, IL: University of Chicago Press.

Marano, L. (1985). Windigo psychosis: the anatomy of an emic–etic confusion. In Ronald C. Simons & Charles C. Hughes (Eds.). (1985). *The culture-bound syndrome: Folk illnesses of psychiatric and anthropological interest.* Dodrecht, Netherlands: D. Reidel Publishing Company.

Marcia, J. E. (1980). Identity in adolescence. In J. Adelson (Ed.), *Handbook of adolescent psychology* (pp. 150–187). New York: Wiley.

Marcia, J. E. (1999). Representational thought in ego identity, psychotherapy, and psychosocial developmental theory. In I. E. Sigel (Ed.), *Development of mental representation: Theories and applications.* Mahwah, NJ: Erlbaum.

Markus, H., & Kitayama, S. (1991). Culture and the self: Implications for cognition, emotion, and motivation. *Psychological Review, 98,* 224–253.

Markus, H. R., & Kitayama, S. (1998). The cultural psychology of personality. *Journal of Cross-Cultural Psychology, 29,* 63–87.

Markus, H., & Wurf, E. (1987). The dynamic self-concept. A social psychological perspective. *Annual Review of Psychology, 38,* 199–337.

Marshall, L. (1976). *The !Kung of Nyae Nyae.* Cambridge, MA: Harvard University Press.

Marsiglio, W., & Cohan, M. (2000). Contextualizing father involvement and paternal influence: Sociological and qualitative themes. *Marriage & Family Review, 29,* 75–95.

Matchinda, B. (1999). The impact of home background on the decision of children to run away: The case of Yaounde city street children in Cameroon. *Child Abuse & Neglect, 23,* 245–255.

Marton, F., Dall'Alba, G., & Tse, L. K. (1993). *The paradox of the Chinese learner.* Paper presented at the European Association for Research on Learning and Instruction, Aix-en-Provence, France.

Matsumoto, D. (2000). *Culture and psychology: People and the world* (2nd ed.). Belmont, CA: Wadsworth.

Matthews, K. A. (1992). Myths and realities of menopause. *Psychosomatic Medicine, 54,* 1–9.

Maynard, A. E. (1999). *Cultural teaching: The social organization and development of teaching in Zinacantec Maya sibling interactions.* Unpublished doctoral dissertation. University of California—Los Angeles.

Maxwell, E., & Maxwell, R. (1980). Contempt for the elderly: A cross-cultural analysis. *Current Anthropology, 21,* 569–570.

McAdams, D. P., & de St. Aubin, E. (Eds.) (1998). *Generativity and adult development: How and why we care for the next generation.* Washington, DC: American Psychological Association.

McCrae, R. R., & Costa, P. C., Jr. (1984). *Emerging lives, enduring dispositions.* Boston: Little, Brown.

McCrae, R. R., & Costa, P. T. Jr. (1990). *Personality in adulthood.* New York: Guilford Press.

McCrae, R. R., Costa, P. T., Jr., Pedroso de Lima, M., Simoes, A., Ostendorf, F., Angleitner, A., Marusic, I., Bratco, D., Caprara, G. V., Bararanell, C., Chae, J-H., & Piedmont, R. L. (1999). Age differences in personality across the adult life span: Parallels in five cultures. *Developmental Psychology, 35,* 466–477.

McKenna, J. J. (1993). Rethinking "Healthy" Infant Sleep. *Breastfeeding Abstracts,* February 1993.

McManus, Sik, Cole, Mellon, Wong, & Kloss (1988). The development of handedness in children. *British Journal of Developmental Psychology, 6*(3), 257–273.

Mead, G. H. (1934). *Mind, self, and society.* Chicago: University of Chicago Press.

Mead, M. (1973). *Coming of age in Samoa: A psychological study of primitive youth.* New York: American Museum of Natural History. (Original work published 1928.)

Medicus, G. (1992). The inapplicability of the biogenetic rule to behavioral development. *Human Development, 35,* 1–7.

Meijer, L., Super, C. M., & Harkness, S. (1997). *Culture, temperament, and parents' perceptions of children's "difficult" behavior in the Netherlands and the U.S.* Paper presented at the twenty-sixth annual meeting of the Society for Cross-Cultural Research, San Antonio, TX.

Meldrum, B. (1984). Traditional child-rearing practices of the Oje market women of Ibadan. In H. Curran (Ed.), *Nigerian children: Developmental perspectives* (pp. 174–196). London: Routledge & Kegan Paul.

Meng, J. M. (1991). The pattern of family and quality of life. *Journal of Gerontology, 3,* 135–140.

Meredith, H. V. (1978). Research between 1960 and 1970 on the standing height of young children in different parts of the world. In H. W. Reece & L. P. Lipsitt (Eds.), *Advances in Child Development and Behavior* (Vol. 12). New York: Academic Press.

Meredith, H. V. (1987). Variations in body stockiness among and within ethnic groups at ages from birth to adulthood. In H. W. Reese (Ed.), *Advances in child development and behavior* (Vol. 20). New York: Academic Press.

Merrill, T. (Ed.). (1994). *Nicaragua: A country study.* Library of Congress (3rd ed.). Washington, DC: U.S. Government Printing Office.

Meyers, S. A. (1993). Adapting parent education programs to meet the needs of fathers: An ecological perspective. *Family Relations, 42*(4), 447–453.

Michel, G. F. (1981). Right-handedness. *Science, 212,* 685–687.

Milardo, R. M. (Ed.). (1988). *Families and social networks.* Newbury Park, CA: Sage.

Miller, C. A. (1987). Infant mortality in the U.S. *Scientific American, 253,* 31–37.

Miller, E. (1975). Self-evaluation among Jamaican high school girls. *Social and Economic Studies, 22,* 407–426.

Miller, J., & Bersoff, D. M. (1994). Cultural influences on the moral status of reciprocity and the discounting of endogenous motivation. *Personality and Social Psychology Bulletin, 20,* 592–602.

Miller, J. G. (1984). Culture and the development of everyday social explanation. *Journal of Personality and Social Psychology, 46,* 961–978.

Miller, J. G. (1997). Theoretical issues in cultural psychology. In J. W. Berry & Y. H. Poortinga (Eds.), *Handbook of cross-cultural psychology: Theory and method* (Vol. 1.). Boston: Allyn & Bacon.

Miller, P. H. (1993). *Theories of developmental psychology* (3rd ed.). New York: Freeman.

Mills, T. L. (1999). When grandparents grow up: Role transition and family solidarity among baby boomer grandchildren and their grandparents. *Journal of Aging Studies, 13,* 219–239.

Minkler, M., & Roe, K. (1991). *Preliminary findings from the grandmother caregiver study of Oakland, California.* Berkeley: University of California Press.

Mishra, R. C., Sinha, D., & Berry, J. W. (1996). *Ecology, acculturation and psychological adaptation.* Thousand Oaks, CA: Sage.

Miyake, K., Chen, S. J., & Campos, J. J. (1985). Infant temperament, mother's mode of interaction, and attachment in Japan: An interim report. In I. Bretherton & E. Waters (Eds.), Growing points of attachment theory and research. *Monographs of the Society for Research in Child Development, 50,* 276–297.

Modgil, S., & Modgil, C. (1976). The growth of logical concrete and formal operations. In *Piagetian Research* (Vol. 3.). Atlantic Highlands, NY: Humanities Press.

Moeller, S., & Schoenweiler, R. (1999). Analysis of infant cries for the early detection of hearing impairment. *Speech Communication, 28,* 175–193.

Moghaddam, F. M., Taylor, D., & Wright, S. C. (1993). *Social psychology in cross-cultural perspective.* New York: Freeman.

Molfese, D. L., & Molfese, V. J. (2000). *Temperament and personality development across the life span.* Mahwah, NJ: Erlbaum.

Molitor, A. E., & Eckerman, C. O. (1992). *Behavioral cues of distress/avoidance in preterm infants.* Paper presented at the International Conference on Infant Studies, Miami, FL.

Morelli, G. A., Rogoff, B., Oppenheim, D., & Goldsmith, D. (1992). Cultural variation in infants' sleeping arrangements: Questions of independence. *Developmental Psychology, 28,* 604–613.

Morinaga, Y., Frieze, I. H., & Ferligoj, A. (1993). Career plans and gender-role attitudes of college students in the United States, Japan, and Slovenia. *Sex Roles, 29,* 317–334.

Mukai, T., & McCloskey, A. A. (1996). Eating attitudes among Japanese and American elementary schoolgirls. *Journal of Cross-Cultural Psychology, 27*(4), 424–435.

Mumford, D. B., Whitehouse, A. M., & Choudry, I. Y. (1992). Survey of eating disorders in English-medium schools in Lahore, Pakistan. *International Journal of Eating Disorders, 11,* 173–184.

Mundy-Castle, A. C. (1974). Social and technological intelligence in Western and non-Western cultures. *Universita* (University of Ghana), *4,* 46–52.

Mundy-Castle, A. C. (1976). *Psychology and the search for meaning.* Unpublished manuscript, University of Lagos.

Mundy-Castle, A. C., & Okonji, M. D. (1976). *Mother–infant interaction in Nigeria.* Unpublished manuscript, University of Lagos.

Murdock, G. P. (1967). *Ethnographic atlas.* Pittsburgh, PA: Pittsburgh University Press.

Muuss, R. E. (1988). *Theories of adolescence* (5th ed.). New York: Random House.

Muuss, R. E. (1996). *Theories of adolescence* (6th ed.). New York: McGraw-Hill.

Muuss, R. E., & Portion, H. D. (1998). *Adolescent behavior and society: A book of readings* (5th ed.). New York: McGraw-Hill.

Mwamwenda, T. S. (1992). Cognitive development in African children. *Genetic, Social, and General Psychology Monographs, 118*(1), 7–72.

Naisbitt, J. (1996). *Megatrends Asia.* New York: Simon & Schuster.

Naito, T. (1994). A survey of research on moral development in Japan. *Cross-Cultural Research, 28,* 40–57.

Nakajima, H., & Mayor, F. (1996). Culture and health. *World Health, 49*(2), 13–15.

Nasser, M. (1986). Comparative study of the prevalence of abnormal eating attitudes among Arab female students of both London and Cairo Universities. *Psychological Medicine, 16,* 621–625.

National Center for Health Statistics. (1994). *Births, marriages, divorces, and deaths for 1993* (Monthly Vital Statistics Rep. Vol. 42, No. 12). Hyattsville, MD: Public Health Service.

National Institute on Drug Abuse. (1994). *Monitoring the future of drug abuse survey.* Washington, DC: U.S. Government Printing Office.

Natsopoulos, D., Kiosseoglou, G., & Xeromeritou, A. (1992). Handedness and spatial ability in children: Further support for Geschwind's hypothesis of "pathology of superiority" and for Annett's theory of intelligence. *Genetic, Social, and General Psychology Monographs, 118*(1) 103–126.

Nelson, L. W. (1992). Cultural context and cultural code in the oral life narratives of African-American women: An ethnography of speaking. *Dissertation Abstracts International, 53* (2A), 544.

Nelson, M. B. (1994). *The stronger women get, the more men love football: Sexism and the American culture of sport.* New York: Harcourt Brace.

Neugarten, B. L. (1979). Time, age, and the life cycle. *American Journal of Psychiatry, 136,* 887–894.

Nichter, M., & Nichter, M. (1991). Hype and weight. *Medical Anthropology, 13,* 249–284.

Nicolopoulou, A. (1993). Play, cognitive development, and the social world: Piaget, Vygotsky, and beyond. *Human Development, 36,* 1–23.

Niedbala, B., and Tsang, R. (1993). The small for gestational age infant. In S. W. Ekvall (Ed.), *Prediatric nutrition in chronic diseases and developmental disorders: Prevention, assessment and treatment.* New York: Oxford University Press.

Niethammer, C. (1977). *Daughters of the earth: The lives and legends of American Indian women.* New York: Macmillan.

Nkanginieme, K., & Eke, N. (1999). Female genital mutilation: A global bug that should not cross the millennium bridge. *World Journal of Surgery, 23,* 1082–1087.

Nsamenang, A. B. (1992). *Human development in cultural context: A third world perspective.* Newbury Park, CA: Sage.

Nunes, T., Schliemann, A. D., & Carraher, D. W. (1993). *Street mathematics and school mathematics.* Cambridge, England: Cambridge University Press.

Nurmi, J. E. (1991). How do adolescents see their future? A review of development of future orientation and planning. *Developmental Review, 11,* 1–59.

Nydell, M.K. (1987). *Understanding Arabs.* Yarmouth, ME: Intercultural Press.

Nyiti, R. M. (1982). The validity of "cultural differences explanations" for cross-cultural variation in the rate of Piagetian cognitive development. In D. A. Wagner & H. W. Stevenson (Eds.), *Cultural perspectives on child development.* San Francisco: Freeman.

Obermeyer, C. M. (1999). Female genital surgeries: The known, the unknown, and the unknowable. *Medical Anthropology Quarterly, 13,* 79–106.

O'Boyle, M. W., & Benbow, C. P. (1990). Handedness and its relationship to ability and talent. In S. Coren (Ed.), *Left-handedness: Behavior implications and anomalies.* Amsterdam: North-Holland.

Ochs, E. (1988). *Culture and language development.* Cambridge, UK: Cambridge University Press.

Ochse, R., & Plug, C. (1986). Cross-cultural investigation of the validity of Erikson's theory of personality development. *Journal of Personality and Social Psychology, 50*(6), 1240–1252.

Oetting, E. R., & Beauvais, F. (1986). Peer cluster theory: Drugs and the adolescent. *Journal of Counseling and Development, 65*(1), 17–22.

Oetting, E. R., & Beauvais, F. (1987a). Common elements in youth drug abuse: Peer clusters and other psychosocial factors. *Journal of Drug Issues, 17*(1–2), 133–151.

Oetting, E. R., & Beauvais, F. (1987b). Peer cluster theory, socialization characteristics and adolescent drug use: A path analysis. *Journal of Counseling Psychology, 34*(2), 205–213.

Offer, D., Ostrov, E., Howard, K. I., & Atkinson, R. (1988). *The teenage world: Adolescents' self-image in ten countries.* New York: Plenum.

Ojanuga, D. (1990). Kaduma beggar children: A study of child abuse and neglect in northern Nigeria. *Child Welfare, 69,* 371–380.

Okafor, N. A. O. (1991). Some traditional aspects of Nigerian women. In L. L. Adler (Ed.), *Women in cross-cultural perspective* (pp. 134–141). Westport, CT: Praeger.

Olowu, A. A. (1983). A cross-cultural study of adolescent self-concept. *Journal of Adolescence, 6,* 263–274.

Olowu, A. A. (1990). The self-concept in cross-cultural perspective. In A. A. Olowu (Ed.), *Contemporary issues in self-concept studies.* Ibadan, Kenya: Shaneson C.I. Ltd.

Olson, L. K. (Ed.). (1994). *The graying of the world: Who will care for the frail elderly?* Binghamton, NY: Haworth Press.

Ortiz, S., & Poertner, J. (1992). Latin American street children: Problem, programmes and critique. *International Social Work, 35,* 413–415.

Page, R. C., & Berkow, D. N. (1991). Concepts of the self: Western and Eastern perspectives. *Journal of Multicultural Counseling and Development, 19,* 83–93.

Paikoff, R. L., & Brooks-Gunn, J. (1991). Do parent–child relationships change during puberty? *Psychological Bulletin, 110,* 47–66.

Pareek, U. (1990). Culture-relevant and culture-modifying action research for development. *Journal of Social Issues, 46*(3), 119–131.

Paris, S. G., & Cross, D. R. (1988). The zone of proximal development: Virtues and pitfalls of a metaphorical representation of children's learning. *Genetic Epistemologist, 26,* 27–37.

Parke, R. D. (1995). Fathers and families. In M. H. Bornstein (Ed.), *Handbook of parenting* (Vol. 3, pp. 27–63). Mahwah, NJ: Erlbaum.

Parke, R. D. (2000). Father involvement: A developmental psychological perspective. *Marriage and Family Review, 29,* 43–58.

Parke, R. D., Ornstein, P. A., Rieser, J. J., & Zahn-Waxler, C. (Eds.). (1994). *A Century of Developmental Psychology.* Washington, DC: American Psychological Association.

Parke, R. D., & Stearns, P. N. (1993). Fathers and child rearing. In G. H. Elder, J. Modell, & R. D. Parke (Eds.), *Children in time and space* (pp. 147–170). New York: Cambridge University Press.

Patterson, G. R., Reid, J. B., & Dishion, T. J. (1998). Antisocial boys. In J. M. Jenkins, K. Oatley, & N. L. Stein (Eds.), *Human emotions: A reader.* Malden, MA: Blackwell Publishers.

Paul, M., & Fisher, J. (1980). Correlates of self-concept among black early adolescents. *Journal of Youth and Adolescence, 9,* 163–173.

Paxton, S. J., Wertheim, E. H., Gibbons, K., Szmukler, G. I., Hillier, L., & Petrovich, J. L. (1991). Body image satisfaction, dieting beliefs, and weight loss behaviors in adolescent girls and boys. *Journal of Youth and Adolescence, 20,* 361–377.

Paz, J. J. (1993). Support of Hispanic elderly. In H. McAdoo (Ed.), *Family ethnicity* (pp. 177–190). Newbury Park, CA: Sage.

Peabody, D. (1985). *National characteristics.* New York: Wiley.

Perlman, D. (1988). Loneliness: A life-span, family perspective. In R. M. Milardo (Ed.), *Families and social networks* (pp. 190–220). Newbury Park, CA: Sage.

Peterson, E. T. (1989). Grandparenting. In S. J. Bahr & E. T. Peterson (Eds.), *Aging and the family.* Lexington, MA: Lexington Books.

Pfeiffer, W. M. (1982). Culture-bound syndromes. In I. Al-Issa (Ed.), *Culture and psychopathology.* Baltimore: University Park Press.

Philip, H., & Kelly, M. (1974). Product and process in cognitive development: Some comparative data on the performance of school age children in different cultures. *British Journal of Educational Psychology, 44,* 248–265.

Phillips, A. S. (1973). *Adolescence in Jamaica.* Kingston: Jamaica Publishing House.

Phinney, J. S. (1990). Ethnic identity in adolescents and adults: Review of research. *Psychological Bulletin, 108,* 499–514.

Phinney, J. S., Lochner, B., & Murphy, R. (1990). Ethnic identity development and psychological adjustment in adolescents. In A. Stiffman & L. Davis (Eds.), *Ethnic issues in adolescent mental health.* Newbury Park, CA: Sage.

Piaget, J. (1954). *The construction of reality in the child.* New York: Basic Books.

Piaget, J. (1972). Intellectual evolution from adolescence to adulthood. *Human Development, 15,* 1–12.

Pipher, M. (1995). *Reviving Ophelia: Saving the selves of adolescent girls.* New York: Ballantine Books.

Pitskhelauri, G. Z. (1982). *The long-living of Soviet Georgia* (Trans. Gari Lesnoff-Caravaglia). New York: Human Science Press.

Plomin, R., DeFries, J. C., & McClearn, G. E. (1980). *Behavioral genetics: A primer.* San Francisco: Freeman.

Pollitt, E., Gorman, K. S., Engle, P., Martorell, R., & Rivera, J. (1993). Early supplemental feeding and cognition: Effects over two decades. *Monographs of the Society for Research in Child Development, 235*(58), No. 7.

Poortinga, Y. (1997). Towards convergence? In J. W. Berry, Y. H. Poortinga, & J. Pandey (Eds.), *Handbook of cross-cultural psychology* (2nd ed., Vol. 1, pp. 347–387). Boston: Allyn & Bacon.

Pratt, M. W., Hunsberger, B., Pancer, S. M., Roth, D., & Santolupo, L. (1993). Thinking about parenting: Reasoning about developmental issues across the lifespan. *Developmental Psychology, 29,* 585–595.

Pratt, M. W., Kerig, P., Cowan, P. A., & Cowan, C. P. (1988). Mothers and fathers teaching 3-year-olds: Authoritative parenting and adult scaffolding of young children's learning. *Developmental Psychology, 24*(6), 832–839.

Price-Williams, D. R., Gordon, W., & Ramirez, M., III. (1969). Skills and conservation: A study of pottery-making children. *Developmental Psychology, 1,* 769.

Proos, L. A., Hofvander, Y., & Tuvemo, T. (1991a). Menarcheal age and growth pattern of Indian girls adopted in Sweden I. Menarcheal Age. *Acta Pediatrica Scandinavia, 80,* 852–858.

Proos, L. A., Hofvander, Y., & Tuvemo, T. (1991b). Menarcheal age and growth pattern of Indian girls adopted in Sweden II. Catch-up growth and final height. *Indian Journal of Pediatrics, 58,* 105–114.

Punyahotra, S., & Dennerstein, L. (1997). Menopausal experience of Thai women: Part 2. The cultural context. *Maturitas, 26,* 9–14.

Purdie, N., Douglas, G., & Hattie, J. (1996). Student conceptions of learning and their use of self-regulated learning strategies: A cross-cultural comparison. *Journal of Educational Psychology, 88*(1), 87–100.

Quadrel, M. J., Fishoff, B., & Davis, W. (1993). Adolescent (in)vulnerability. *American Psychologist, 48,* 102–116.

Qualls, S. H. (1999). Mental health and mental disorders in older adults. In J. C. Cavanaugh & S. K. Whitbourne (Eds.), *Gerontology: An interdisciplinary perspective.* New York: Oxford University Press.

Queen, S. A., Habenstein, R. W., & Quadagno, J. S. (1985). *The family in various cultures* (5th ed.). New York: Harper & Row.

Radin, N. (1993). Primary caregiving fathers in intact families. In A. Gottfried & A. Gottfried (Eds.), *Redefining families* (pp. 11–54). New York: Plenum.

Rahula, W. (1959). *What the Buddha taught.* New York: Grove Press.

Raich, R. M., Rosen, J. C., Deus, J., Perez, O., Requene, A., & Gross, J. (1992). Eating disorders symptoms among adolescents in the United States and Spain: A comparative study. *International Journal of Eating Disorders, 11,* 63–72.

Rakowski, W., & Mor, V. (1992). The association of physical activity with mortality among older adults in the longitudinal study of aging. *Journal of Gerontology, 47*(4), 122–129.

Randhawa, B. S., & Gupta, A. (2000). Cross-national differences in mathematics achievement, attitude, and self-efficacy within a common intrinsic structure. *Canadian Journal of School Psychology, 15,* 51–66.

Raphael, D., & Davis, F. (1985). *Only mothers know: Patterns of infant feeding in traditional cultures.* Westport, CT: Greenwood Press.

Recio Adrados, J. L. (1995). The influence of family, school, and peers on adolescent drug misuse. *International Journal of the Addictions, 30,* 1407–1423.

Reid, I. R., Ames, R. W., Evans, M. G., Gamble, G. D., & Sharpe, S. J. (1993). Effect of calcium supplementation on bone loss in postmenopausal women. *New England Journal of Medicine, 328*(7), 460–464.

Reilly, R. (1988, August). Here no one is spared. *Sports Illustrated,* 70–77.

Reisberg, B. F., Steven, D. L., Mony, J., & Crook, T. (1985). Age-associated cognitive decline and Alzheimer's disease: Implications for assessment and treatment. In M. Bergener, M. Ermini, & H. B. Stahelin (Eds.), *Thresholds in aging.* London: Academic Press.

Repetti, R. L. (1993). Short-term and long-term processes linking job stressors to father-child interaction. *Social Development, 3,* 1–15.

Reskin, B. F. (1988). Bringing the men back in: Sex differentiation in the devaluation of women's work. *Gender and Society, 2,* 58–81.

Retschitzki, J. (1989). Evidence of formal thinking in Baule airele players. In D. M. Keats, D. Munro, & L. Mann (Eds.), *Heterogeneity in cross-cultural psychology.* Amsterdam: Swets & Zeitlinger.

Reynolds, P. (1989). *Children in cross-roads.* Grand Rapids, MI: Eerdmans.

Rhode, D. L. (Ed.). (1990). *Theoretical perspectives on sex differences.* New Haven, CT: Yale University Press.

Rice, F. P. (1992). *Intimate relationships, marriages, and families.* Mountain View, CA: Mayfield.

Richman, A. L., LeVine, R. A., New, R. S., Howrigan, G. A., Welles-Nystrom, B., & LeVine, S. (1988). Maternal behavior to infants in five cultures. In R. A. LeVine, P. M. Miller, & M. M. West (Eds.), *Parental behavior in diverse societies: New directions for child development* (No. 40). San Francisco: Jossey-Bass.

Richman, A. L., Miller, P. M. & LeVine, R. A. (1992). Cultural and educational variations in maternal responsiveness. *Developmental Psychology, 28,* 614–621.

Riegel, K. F. (1975). Toward a dialectical theory of development. *Human Development, 18,* 50–64.

Ritts, V. (2000). *Culture and aging.* St. Louis Community College: Unpublished manuscript.

Ritts, V. (2000). *Infusing culture into parenting issues: A supplement for psychology instructors.* St. Louis Community College: Unpublished manuscript.

Robarchek, C. A., & Robarchek, C. J. (1998). Reciprocities and realities: World views, peacefulness, and violence among Semai and Waorani. *Aggressive Behavior, 24,* 123–133.

Rogoff, B. (1981). Schooling and the development of cognitive skills. In H. C. Triandis & A. Heron (Eds.), *Handbook of cross-cultural psychology* (Vol. 4, pp. 233–294). Boston: Allyn & Bacon.

Rogoff, B. (1990). *Apprenticeship in thinking: Cognitive development in social context.* New York: Oxford University Press.

Rogoff, B., & Chavajah, P. (1995). What's become of research on the cultural basis of cognitive development? *American Psychologist, 50,* 859–873.

Rogoff, B., & Morelli, G. (1989). Perspectives on children's development from cultural psychology. *American Psychologist, 44,* 343–348.

Rohner, R. P. (1986). *The warmth dimension: Foundations of parental acceptance-rejection theory.* Newbury Park, CA: Sage. (Reprinted by UConn Coop, U-19, Storrs, CT, 1991.)

Rohner, R. P. (1994). Patterns of parenting: The warmth dimension in worldwide perspective. In W. J. Lonner & R. Malpass (Eds.), *Psychology and culture* (pp. 113–120). Boston: Allyn & Bacon.

Rohner, R. P. (2000). Enculturative continuity and adolescent stress. *American Psychologist, 55,* 278.

Roopnarine, J. L., & Carter, D. B. (1992a). The cultural context of socialization: A much ignored issue! In J. L. Roopnarine & D. B. Carter (Eds.), *Parent–child socialization in diverse cultures.* Norwood, NJ: Ablex.

Roopnarine, J. L., & Carter, D. B. (Eds.). (1992b). *Parent-child socialization in diverse cultures.* Norwood, NJ: Ablex.

Rosenblith, J. F. (1992). *In the beginning* (2nd ed.). Newbury Park, CA: Sage.

Rosenthal, D. A., Moore, S. M., & Taylor, M. J. (1983). A study of the self-image of Anglo-, Greek, and Italian-Austrian working class adolescents. *Journal of Youth and Adolescence, 12*(2), 117–135.

Rossiter, J. C. (1994). The effect of a culture-specific education program to promote breastfeeding among Vietnamese women in Sydney. *International Journal of Nursing Studies, 31,* 369–379.

Rossner, S. (1998). Childhood obesity and adulthood consequences. *Acta Paediatrica, 87,* 1–5.

Roth, M. W., Claude, M., Evans, N., & Mountjoy, C. (1985). Convergence and cohesion of recent neurobiological findings in relation to Alzheimer's disease and their bearing on its etiological basis. In M. Bergener, M. Ermini, & H. B. Stahelin (Eds.), *Thresholds in aging.* London: Academic Press.

Rozee, P. D. (1993). Forbidden or forgiven? Rape in cross-cultural perspective. *Psychology of Women Quarterly, 17,* 499–514.

Ruan, F. F. (1991). *Sex in China: Studies in sexology in Chinese culture.* New York: Plenum Press.

Rubin, K. H., Fein, G. G., & Vandenberg, B. (1983). Play. In Paul H. Mussen (Ed.), *Handbook of child psychology: Vol. 4. Socialization, personality and social development.* New York: Wiley.

Rushton, J. P., Fulker, D. W., Neale, M. C., Nias, D. K., & Eysenck, H. J. (1986). Altruism and aggression: The heritability of individual differences. *Journal of Personality and Social Psychology, 50,* 1192–1198.

Russell, G., & Russell, A. (1987). Mother–child and father–child relationships in middle childhood. *Child Development, 58,* 1573–1585.

Russell, J. G. (1989). Anxiety disorders in Japan: A review of the Japanese literature on shinkeishitsu and taijinkyofuso. *Culture, Medicine, and Psychiatry, 13,* 391–403.

Rutter, M. & the ERA Study team (1998). Developmental catch-up and deficit, following adoption and after severe global early privation. *Journal of Child Psychology and Psychiatry and Allied Disciplines, 39,* 465–476.

Ryan, A. S., Rush, D., Krieger, F. W., & Lewandowski, G. E. (1991). Recent declines in breast-feeding in the United States, 1984 through 1989. *Pediatrics, 88,* 719–727.

Ryan, E. B., Giles, H., Bartolucci, G., & Henwood, K. (1986). Psycholinguisitc and social psychological components of communication by and with the elderly. *Language and Communication, 6,* 1–24.

Sagi, A. (1990). Attachment theory and research in cross-cultural perspective. *Human Development, 33,* 10–22.

Sagi, A., Lamb, M. E., Lewkowicz, K. S., Shoham, R., Dvir, R., & Estes, D. (1985). Security of infant–mother, –father, and –metaplot attachments among kibbutz-related Israeli children. In I. Bretherton & E. Waters (Eds.), Growing points of attachment theory and research. *Monographs of the Society for Research in Child Development, 50,* 257–275.

Sahin, N., & Sahin, N. H. (1995). Dimensions of concerns: The case of Turkish adolescents. *Journal of Adolescence, 18,* 49–69.

Salamone, F. A. (1983). Children's games as mechanisms for easing ethnic interaction in ethnically heterogeneous communities: A Nigerian case. In J. C. Harris and R. J. Park (Eds.), *Play, games, and sports in cultural contexts* (pp. 461–472). Champaign, IL: Human Kinetics.

Salthouse, T. A. (1987). The role of experience in cognitive aging. In K. W. Schaie & K. Eisdorfer (Eds.), *Annual Review of Gerontology and Geriatrics* (Vol. 7). New York: Springer.

Salthouse, T. A., & Coon, V. E. (1993). Influence of task-specific processing speed on age differences in memory. *Journal of Gerontology, 48,* 245–255.

Sanchez, L. (1993). Women's power and the gendered division of labor in the third world. *Gender and Society, 7,* 434–459.

Sangree, W. H. (1992). Grandparenthood and modernization: The changing status of male and female elders in Tiriki, Kenya, and Irigwe, Nigeria. *Journal of Cross-Cultural Gerontology, 7,* 331–361.

Sapir, E. (1951). The status of linguistics as a science. In D. Mendelbaum (Ed.), *Selected writings* (No. 5, pp. 207–214). Berkeley: University of California Press. (Original work published 1929.)

Sartorius, N. R. (1993). A WHO method for the assessment of health-related quality of life (WHOQOL). In S. R. Walker & R. M. Rosser (Eds.), *Quality of life assessment: Key issues in the 1990s* (pp. 201–207). London: Kluwer Academic Publishers.

Sartorius, N. R. (1994). Description of WHO's Mental Health Programme. In W. J. Lonner & R. Malpass (Eds.), *Psychology and culture.* Boston: Allyn & Bacon.

Sartorius, N. R., Jablensky, A., Korten, A., Ernberg, G., Anker, M., Cooper, J. E., & Day, R. (1986). Early manifestations and first contact incidence of schizophrenia in different cultures: A preliminary report on the initial evaluation phase of the WHO Collaborative Study on Determinants of Outcome of Severe Mental Disorders. *Psychological Medicine, 16,* 909–928.

Schaie, K. W. (1977–1978). Toward a stage theory of adult cognitive development. *Journal of Aging and Human Development, 8,* 129–138.

Schaie, K. W. (1984). The Seattle Longitudinal Study: A 21–year exploration of psychometric intelligence in adulthood. In K. W. Schaie (Ed.), *Longitudinal studies of adult psychological development*. New York: Guilford.

Schaie, K. W. (1989). Individual differences in rate of cognitive change in adulthood. In V. L. Bengston & K. W. Schaie (Eds.), *The course of later life*. New York: Springer.

Schaie, K. W., & Willis, S. L. (1993). Age differences in patterns of psychometric intelligence in adulthood: Generalizability within and across ability domains. *Psychology and Aging, 8,* 44–55.

Scheper-Hughes, N. (1990). Mother love and child death in northeast Brazil. In J. W. Stigler, R. A. Shweder, & G. Herdt (Eds.), *Cultural psychology: Essays on comparative human development* (pp. 542–565). Cambridge, England: Cambridge University Press.

Schlegal, A., & Barry, H. (1991). *Adolescence: An anthropological inquiry*. New York: Free Press.

Schliemann, A., Carraher, D., & Ceci, S. J. (1997). Everyday cognition. In J. W. Berry, P. R. Dasen, & T. S. Saraswathi (Eds.), *Handbook of cross-cultural psychology* (Vol. 2, 2nd ed., pp. 177–216). Boston: Allyn & Bacon.

Schwartz, T. (1981). The acquisition of culture. *Ethos, 9,* 4–17.

Schwartzman, H. B. (1983). Socializing play: Functional analysis. In J. C. Harris & R. J. Park (Eds.), *Play, games, and sports in cultural contexts*. Champaign IL: Human Kinetics.

Scott, J. P. (1992). Aggression: Functions and control in social systems. *Aggressive Behavior, 18,* 1–20.

Searleman, A., Porac, C., & Coran, S. (1989). Relationship between birth order, birth stress, and lateral preferences: A critical review. *Psychological Bulletin, 105,* 397–408.

Searle-White, J. (1996). Personal boundaries among Russians and Americans: A Vygotskian approach. *Cross-Cultural Research, 30*(2), 184–208.

Segall, M. H. (1979). *Cross-Cultural Psychology*. Belmont, CA: Wadsworth.

Segall, M. H., Dasen, P. R., Berry, J. W., & Poortinga, Y. H. (1990). *Human behavior in global perspective*. New York: Pergamon Press.

Segall, M. H., Dasen, P. R., Berry, J. W., & Poortinga, Y. H. (1999). *Human behavior in global perspective* (2nd ed.). Boston: Allyn & Bacon.

Segall, M. H., Lonner, W. J., & Berry, J. W. (1998). Cross-cultural psychology as a scholarly discipline: On the flowering of culture in behavioral research. *American Psychologist, 53,* 1101–1110.

Seligman, M. E. P. (1989). Research in clinical psychology: Why is there so much depression today? In I. Cohen (Ed.), *The G. Stanley Hall Lecture Series* (Vol. 9). Washington, DC: American Psychological Association.

Seligman, M. E. P. (1990). *Learned optimism*. New York: Pocket Books.

Serpell, R. (1993). *The significance of schooling: Life-journeys in an African society*. New York: Cambridge University Press.

Sharabany, R., & Wiseman, H. (1993). Close relationships in adolescence: The case of the kibbutz. *Journal of Youth and Adolescence, 22,* 671–695.

Sharma, N., & Sharma, B. (1999). Children in difficult circumstances: Familial correlates of advantage while at risk. In T .S. Saraswathi (Ed.), *Culture, socialization and human development: Theory, research and applications in India* (pp. 398–418). Thousand Oaks, CA: Sage Publications.

Shavelson, R. J., & Bolus, R. (1982). Self-concept: The interplay of theory and method. *Journal of Educational Psychology, 74,* 1–17.

Shea, J. D. (1985). Studies of cognitive development in Papua New Guinea. *International Journal of Psychology, 20,* 33–61.

Sheriff, M., & Cantril, H. (1947). *The psychology of ego involvement.* New York: Wiley.

Shields, D. L. L., & Bredemeier, B. J. L. (1995). *Character development and physical activity.* Champaign, IL: Human Kinetics.

Shostak, M. (1981). Nissa: The life and words of a !Kung woman. Cambridge, MA: Harvard University Press.

Shucard, J. L., & Shucard, D. W. (1990). Auditory evoked potentials and hand preference in 6-month-old infants: Possible gender-related differences in cerebral organization. *Developmental Psychology, 26,* 923–930.

Shwalb, D. W., & Shwalb, B. (Eds.). (1996). *Japanese childrearing: Two generations of scholarship.* NY: Guilford.

Shweder, R. A., Jensen, L. A., & Goldstein, W. M. (1995). Who sleeps with whom revisited: A method for extracting the moral goods implicit in practice. *New Directions for Child Development, 67,* 21–39.

Shweder, R. A., Goodnow, J., Hatano, G., LeVine, R. A., Markus, H., & Miller, P. (1998). The cultural psychology of development: One mind, many mentalities. In R. M. Lerner (Ed.), *Handbook of Child Psychology* (5th ed.) *Vol 1: Theoretical models of human development.* New York: Wiley.

Shweder, R., Mahapatra, M., & Miller, J. G. (1987). Culture and moral development. In J. Kagan & S. Lamb (Eds.), *The emergence of morality in young children* (pp. 1–82). Chicago: University of Chicago Press.

Siegert, R. J., & Chung, R. C. (1995). Dimensions of distress: A cross-cultural factor replication. *Journal of Cross-Cultural Psychology, 26*(2), 169–175.

Sigel, I. E. (Ed.). (1985). *Parental belief systems: The psychological consequences for children.* Hillsdale, NJ: Erlbaum.

Sigel, I. E., McGillicuddy-DeLisi, A. V., & Goodnow, J. J. (Eds.). (1992). *Parental belief systems: The psychological consequences for children* (2nd ed.). Hillsdale, NJ: Erlbaum.

Sigelman, C. K., & Shaffer, D. R. (1995). *Life-Span Human Development.* Pacific Grove, CA: Brooks/Cole.

Sigman, M., McDonald, M. A., Newmann, C., & Bwibo, N. O. (1991). Prediction of cognitive competence in Kenyan children from toddler nutrition, family characteristics and abilities. *Journal of Child Psychology and Psychiatry, 32,* 307–320.

Sigman, M., & Sena, R. (1993). Pretend play in high-risk and developmentally delayed children. In M. H. Bornstein & A. W. O'Reilly (Eds.), *The role of play in the development of thought: New directions for human development* (No. 59). San Francisco: Jossey-Bass.

Sijuwola, O. A. (1995). Culture, religion, and mental illness in Nigeria. In I. Al-Issa (Ed.), *Handbook of culture and mental illness* (pp. 65–72). Madison, WI: International Universities Press.

Singh, S., Forrest, J. D., & Torres, A. (1989). *Prenatal care in the United States: A state and county inventory.* New York: Alan Guttmacher Institute.

Sinha, J. B. P. (1984). Toward partnership for relevant research to the third world. *Indian Journal of Psychology, 19,* 169–178.

Sinha, J. B. P. (1993). The bulk and the front of psychology in India. *Psychology and Developing Societies, 5,* 135–150.

Skoog, L., Nilsson, L., Palmertz, B., Andreasson, L., & Svanborg, A. (1993). A population-based study for dementia in 85-year-olds. *New England Journal of Medicine, 328,* 153–158.

Slaby, A. E., & Dwenger, R. (1993). History of anorexia nervosa. In A. J. Giannini and A. E. Slaby (Eds.), *The eating disorders.* New York: Springer-Verlag.

Slobin, D. I. (1990). The development from child speaker to native speaker. In J. W. Stilger, R. A. Shweder, & G. Herdt (Eds.), *Cultural Psychology.* Cambridge, UK: Cambridge University Press.

Slonim, M. B. (1991). *Children, culture, and ethnicity.* New York: Garland.

Smith, D. E., & Blinn Pike, L. (1994). Relationship between Jamaican adolescents' drinking patterns and self-image: A cross-cultural perspective. *Adolescence, 29,* 429–437.

Smith, D. E., & Cogswell, C. (1994). A cross-cultural perspective on adolescent girls' body perception. *Perceptual and Motor Skills, 78,* 744–746.

Smith, D. E., & Reynolds, T. E. (1992). Adolescents' self-image: A cross-cultural perspective. *Child Study Journal, 22,* 303–315.

Smith, J., & Baltes, P. B. (1990). Wisdom-related knowledge: Age/cohort differences in response to life-planning problems. *Developmental Psychology, 26*(3), 494–505.

Smith, J. S. (1992). Women in charge: Politeness and directiveness in the speech of Japanese women. *Language in Society, 21,* 59–82.

Smith, M. G. (1965). The Hausa of northern Nigeria. In J. L. Gibbs, Jr. (Ed.), *Peoples of Africa* (pp. 119–155). New York: Holt, Rinehart & Winston.

Smith, P. K. (1991). Introduction: The study of grandparenthood. In P. K. Smith (Ed.), *The psychology of grandparenthood: An international perspective* (pp. 1–16). London: Routledge & Keagan Paul.

Smith, P. K. (1995). Grandparenthood. In M. H. Bornstein (Ed.), *Handbook of parenting* (Vol. 3, pp. 89–112). Mahwah, NJ: Erlbaum.

Snarey, J. R. (1985). Cross-cultural universality of socio-moral development. A critical review of Kohlbergian research. *Psychological Bulletin, 97,* 202–232.

Solomon, G. B. (1997). Fair play in the gymnasium: Improving social skills among elementary school children. *Journal of Physical Education, Recreation, and Dance, 68,* 22–25.

Song, M., Smetana, J. G., & Kim, S. Y. (1987). Korean children's conceptions of moral and conventional transgressions. *Developmental Psychology, 23,* 577–582.

Sonko, S. (1994). Fertility and culture in sub-Saharan Africa. *International Social Science Journal, 46,* 397–411.

Sparkes, K. K. (1991). Cooperative and competitive behavior in dyadic game-playing: A comparison of Anglo-American and Chinese children. *Early Child Development and Care, 68,* 37–47.

Spector, R. E. (1991). *Cultural diversity in health and illness.* Norwalk, CT: Appleton & Lange.

Spence, A. P. (1989). *Biology of human aging.* Englewood Cliffs, NJ: Prentice-Hall.

Spirduso, W. W., & MacRae, P. G. (1990). Motor performance and aging. In J. E. Birren & K. W. Schaie (Eds.), *Handbook of the psychology of aging* (3rd ed., pp. 184–200). San Diego, CA: Academic Press.

Spiro, M. E. (1993). Is the Western conception of the self "peculiar" within the contexts of world cultures? *Ethos, 21,* 107–153.

Spock, B., & Rothenberg, M. B. (1992). *Dr. Spock's baby and child care.* New York: Pocket Books.

Stack, C. B. (1974). *All our kin: Strategies for survival in a black community.* New York: Harper & Row.

Stanton, A. M. (1998). Grandparents' visitation rights and custody. Child & *Adolescent Psychiatric Clinics of North America, 7,* 409–422.

Staples, R. (1952). Appreciations and dislikes regarding grandmothers as expressed by granddaughters. *Journal of Home Economics, 44,* 340–343.

Stein, R. C. (1986). *South Africa.* Chicago: Childrens Press.

Steinberg, L. (1990). Interdependence in the family: Autonomy, conflict, and harmony in the parent-adolescent relationship. In S. S. Feldman & G. L. Elliott (Eds.), *At the threshold: The developing adolescent* (pp. 255–276). Cambridge, MA: Harvard University Press.

Steinberg, L., & Brown, B. B. (1989). *Beyond the classroom: Parent and peer influences on high school achievement.* Invited paper presented to the Families as Educators Special Interest Group at the annual meetings of the American Educational Research Association, San Francisco.

Steinberg, L., Darling, N. E., & Fletcher, A. C. (1995). Authoritative parenting and adolescent adjustment: An ecological journey. In P. Moen, G. H. Elder, Jr., & K. Luscher (Eds.), *Examining lives in context: Perspectives on the ecology of human development* (pp. 423–466). Washington, DC: American Psychological Association.

Sternberg, L. (1987). Impact of puberty on family relations: Effects of pubertal status and pubertal timing. *Developmental Psychology, 23,* 451–460.

Sternberg, L. (1988). Reciprocal relation between parent–child distance and pubertal maturation. *Developmental Psychology, 24,* 122–128.

Sternberg, L. (1989). Pubertal maturation and adolescent distance: An evolutionary perspective. In G. R. Adams, R. Montemayor, & T. P. Gullotta (Eds.), *Biology of adolescent behavior and development.* Newbury Park, CA: Sage.

Sternberg, R. J. (1985). *Beyond IQ: A triarchic theory of human intelligence.* Cambridge, England: Cambridge University Press.

Sternberg, R. J., & McGrane, P. A. (1993). *Intellectual development across the life span.* Unpublished manuscript, Yale University, New Haven, CT.

Stevenson, H. W., Chen, C., & Lee, S. (1991). Chinese families. In J. L. Roopnarine & D. B. Carter (Eds.), *Parent–child socialization in diverse cultures* (pp. 17–33). Norwood, NJ: Ablex.

Stevenson, H. W., & Stigler, J. W. (1992). *The learning gap: Why our schools are failing and what we can learn from Japanese and Chinese education.* New York: Simon & Schuster.

Steward, E. P. (1994). *Beginning writers in the zone of proximal development.* Hillsdale, NJ: Erlbaum.

Stiles, D., De Silva, S. S., Gibbons, J. (1996). Girls' relational self in Sri Lanka and the United States. *Journal of Genetic Psychology, 157,* 191–203.

Stiles, D. A., & Gibbons, J. L. (1995). *Gender role expectations of Norwegian adolescents.* Paper presented at the twenty-fourth annual meeting of the Society for Cross-Cultural Research, Savannah, GA.

Stiles, D., Gibbons, J., & de la Garza-Schnellman, J. (1990). Opposite sex ideal in the U.S.A. and Mexico as perceived by young adolescents. *Journal of Cross-Cultural Psychology, 21,* 180–199.

Stokols, D. (1999). Human development in the age of the internet: Conceptual and methodological horizons. In S. L. Friedman & T. D. Wachs (Eds.), *Measuring environment across the life span.* Washington, DC: American Psychological Association.

Storz, N., & Greene, W. H. (1983). Body weight, body image, and perception of fad diets in adolescent girls. *Journal of Nutrition Education, 15,* 15–18.

Stratton, P. (1988). Parents' conceptualization of children as the organizer of culturally structured environments. In J. Valsiner (Ed.), *Child development within culturally structured environments: Vol. 1. Parental cognition and adult–child interaction* (pp. 5–29). Norwood, NJ: Ablex.

Strauss, R. (1999). Childhood obesity. *Current Problems in Pediatrics, 29,* 1–29.

Strom, R. D. (1999). Lifelong learning for grandparents: Cultural considerations in Taiwan and the United States. *Journal of Family Studies, 5,* 157–179.

Strom, R. D. & Strom, S. K. (2000). Intergenerational learning and family harmony. *Educational Gerontology, 26,* 261–283.

Strom, R. D., & Strom, S. K. (1993). Grandparents raising grandchildren: Goals and support groups. *Educational Gerontology, 19,* 705–715.

Strom, R. D., Strom, S., Collinsworth, P., Sato, S., Makino, K., Sasaki, Y., Sasaki, H., & Nishio, N. (1995). Grandparents in Japan: A three-generational study. *International Journal of Aging and Human Development, 40*(3), 209–227.

Strom, R. D., Strom, S. K., Wang, C., Shen, Y., Griswold, D., Chan, H., & Yang, C. (1999). Grandparents in the United States and the Republic of China: A comparison of generations and cultures. *International Journal of Aging and Human Development, 49,* 279–317.

Strong, C. (1984). Stress and caring for elderly relatives: Interpretations and coping strategies in an American Indian and White sample. *Gerontologist, 24*(3), 251–256.

Sue, D. W., & Sue, D. (1990). Counseling American Indians. In D. W. Sue & D. Sue (Eds.), *Counseling the culturally different: Theory and practice* (pp. 175–188). New York: Wiley.

Sung, K. T. (1992). Motivations for parent care: The case of filial children in Korea. *International Journal of Aging and Human Development, 34,* 109–124.

Super, C. M. (1976). Environmental effects on motor development: The case of "African infant precocity." *Developmental Medicine and Child Neurology, 18,* 561–567.

Super, C. M. (1979). *A cultural perspective on theories of cognitive development.* Paper presented at the meeting of the Society for Research in Child Development, San Francisco.

Super, C. M. (1981). Cross-cultural research on infancy. In H. C. Triandis and A. Heron (Eds.), *Handbook of cross-cultural psychology: Vol. 4. Developmental Psychology.* Boston: Allyn & Bacon.

Super, C. M., & Harkness, S. (1982). The infants' niche in rural Kenya and metropolitan America. In L. L. Adler (Ed.), *Cross-cultural research at issue* (pp. 47–55). New York: Academic Press.

Super, C. M., & Harkness, S. (1986). The developmental niche: A conceptualization of the interface of child and culture. *International Journal of Behavioral Development, 9,* 545–570.

Super, C. M., & Harkness, S. (1994a). The developmental niche. In W. J. Lonner & R. Malpass (Eds.), *Psychology and culture* (pp. 95–99). Boston: Allyn & Bacon.

Super, C. M., & Harkness, S. (1994b). Temperament and the developmental niche. In W. B. Carey & S. C. Devitt (Eds.), *Prevention and early intervention: Individual differences as risk factors for the mental health of children.* New York: Brunner/Mazel.

Super, C. M., & Harkness, S. (1997). The cultural structuring of child development. In J. W. Berry, P. R. Dasen, & T. S. Saraswathi (Eds.), *Handbook of cross-cultural psychology* (Vol. 2, 2nd ed., pp. 1–39). Boston: Allyn & Bacon.

Super, C. M., & Harkness, S. (in preparation). *The developmental niche: Culture and expressions of human growth.* New York: Guilford Press.

Super, C. M., & Harkness, S. (1999). The environment as culture in developmental research. In S. L. Friedman & T. D. Wachs (Eds.), *Measuring environment across the life span.* Washington, DC: American Psychological Association.

Super, C. M., Harkness, S., & Blom, M. (1997). *Cultural differences in Dutch and American infants' sleep patterns: How do they get that way?* Paper presented at the twenty-sixth annual meeting of the Society for Cross-Cultural Research, San Antonio, TX.

Super, C. M., Herrena, M. G., & Mora, J. O. (1990). Long-term effects of food supplementation and psychosocial intervention on the physical growth of Colombian infants at risk of malnutrition. *Child Development, 61,* 29–49.

Susman, E. J., & Dorn, L. D. (1991). Hormones and behavior in adolescence. In R. M. Lerner, A. C. Petersen, & J. Brooks-Gunn (Eds.), *Encyclopedia of adolescence.* New York: Garland.

Suzuki, T. (1998). Children's comprehension of Japanese passives: A different perspective. In Eve Clark (Ed.), *The proceedings of the twenty-ninth annual child language research forum* (pp. 91–100). Stanford, CA: Center for Study of Language and Information.

Swaim, R. C., Oetting, E. R., Thurman, P. J., Beauvais, F., & Edwards, R. W. (1993). American Indian adolescent drug use and socialization characteristics: A cross-cultural comparison. *Journal of Cross-Cultural Psychology, 24*(1), 53–70.

Swart, J. (1988). *An anthropological study of street children in Hillsbrow, Johannesburg, with special reference to their moral values.* Unpublished master's thesis, University of South Africa, Pretoria.

Tajfel, H. (1981). *Human groups and social categories.* Cambridge, England: Cambridge University Press.

Takada, K. (1993). Aging workers in Japan: From reverence to redundance. *Aging International, 20,* 17–20.

Takahashi, K. (1990). Are the key assumptions of the "strange situation" procedure universal? A view from Japanese research. *Human Development, 33,* 23–30.

Takahashi, T. (1989). Social phobia syndrome in Japan. *Comprehensive Psychiatry, 30,* 45–50.

Tamis-LeMonda, C. S., Bornstein, M. H., Cyphers, L., Toda, S., & Ogino, M. (1992). Language and play at one year: A comparison of toddlers and mothers in the United States and Japan. *International Journal of Behavioral Development, 15,* 19–42.

Tanaka-Matsumi, J. & Draguns, J. G. (1996). Culture and psychopathology. In J. W. Berry, P. R. Dasen, & T. S. Saraswathi (Eds.), *Handbook of cross-cultural psychology,* Vol. 2. Boston: Allyn & Bacon.

Tang, T. L-P., Furnham, A., & Davis, G. M-T. (2000). A cross-cultural comparison of pay differentials as a function of rater's sex and money ethic endorsement: The Matthew Effect revisted. *Personality & Individual Differences, 29,* 685–697.

Tanner, J. M. (1989). *Fetus into man: Physical growth from conception to maturity.* Cambridge, MA: Harvard University Press.

Tape, G. (1987). *Milieu africain et developpement cognitif: Une etude du raisonnement experimental chez l'adolescent ivoirien.* [The African environment and cognitive development: A study of experimental reasoning in adolescents from Cote d'Ivoire.] Unpublished doctoral dissertation, Universite de Caen, France.

Thomas, A., & Chess, S. (1977). *Temperament and development.* New York: Brunner/Mazel.

Thomas, R. M. (1999). *Human development theories: Windows on culture.* Thousand Oaks, CA: Sage.

Thomas, W. I., & Znaniecki, F. (1927). *The Polish peasant in Europe and America.* New York: Knopf.

Thompson, B. W. (1992). "A way outa no way." Eating problems among African-American, Latina, and White women. *Gender and Society, 6,* 546–561.

Thompson, R. A., & Lamb, M. E. (1983). Security of attachment and stranger sociability in infancy. *Developmental Psychology, 19,* 184–191.

Tien, H. Y., & Lee, C. F. (1988). New demographics and old designs: The Chinese family and induced population transition. *Social Science Quarterly, 69,* 605–628.

Tiggemann, M., & Rothblum, E. D. (1988). Gender differences in social consequences of perceived overweight in the United States and Australia. *Sex Roles, 18,* 75–86.

Ting-Toomey, S. (1991). Intimacy expressions in three cultures: France, Japan, and the United States. *International Journal of Intercultural Relations, 15,* 29–46.

Tinsley, B. J., & Parke, R. D. (1984). Grandparents as support and socialization agents. In M. Lewis (Ed.), *Beyond the dyad* (pp. 161–194). New York: Plenum.

Tirosh, E., Stein, M., Harel, J., Scher, A. (1999). Hand preference as related to development and behavior in infancy. *Perceptual & Motor Skills, 89,* 371–380.

Tremblay, H. (1988). *Families of the world.* New York: Farrar, Straus & Giroux.

Triandis, H. C. (1989). The self and social behavior in differing cultural contexts. *Psychological Bulletin, 96,* 506–520.

Triandis, H. C., Brislin, R., & Hui, C. H. (1988). Cross-cultural training across the individualism-collectivism divide. *International Journal of Intercultural Relations, 12,* 269–289.

Trimble, J. E., Manson, S. M., Dinges, N. G., & Medicine, B. (1984). American Indian concepts of mental health: Reflections and directions. In P. B. Pedersen, N. Sartorius, & A. J. Marsella (Eds.), *Mental health services: The cross-cultural context.* Beverly Hills: Sage.

Tronick, E. Z., Morelli, G. A., & Ivey, P. K. (1992). The Efe forager infant and toddler's pattern of social relationships: Multiple and simultaneous. *Developmental Psychology, 28,* 568–577.

Tronick, E. Z., Thomas, R. B., & Daltabuit, G. (1994). The manta pouch: A regulatory system for Peruvian infants at high altitude. *Children's Environments, 11*(2), 142–146.

Tse, S., & Bailey, D. M. (1992). Tai chi and postural control in the well elderly. *American Journal of Occupational Therapy, 46*(4), 295–300.

Tseng, W., & Hsu, J. (1980). Minor psychological disturbances of everyday life. In H. C. Triandis & J. Draguns (Eds.), *Handbook of cross-cultural psychology* (Vol. 6, pp. 61–97). Boston: Allyn & Bacon.

Tu, W. (1978). The Confucian Perception of Adulthood. In E. Erikson (Ed.), *Adulthood* (pp. 113–127). New York: Norton.

Tu, W. (1985). *Confucian thought: Selfhood as creative transformation.* Albany: State University of New York Press.

Tylor, E. B. (1871). *Primitive culture* (2 vols.). London: Murray.

Tzuriel, D. (1992). The development of ego identity at adolescence among Israeli Jews and Arabs. *Journal of Youth and Adolescence, 21,* 551–571.

Udvardy, M., & Cattell, M. (1992). Gender, aging, and power in Sub Saharan Africa: Challenges and puzzles. *Journal of Cross-Cultural Gerontology, 7,* 275–288.

United Nations. (1990). *Human Development Report, 1990.* New York: United Nations Development Program.

UNICEF. (1993). *Child malnutrition: Progress toward the world summit for children goal.* New York: Statistics and Monitoring Section, United Nations International Children's Emergency Fund.

United Nations Children's Fund/UNICEF (2000). *The state of the world's children, 2000.* New York: United Nations Publications.

U.S. Bureau of the Census. (1992). *Statistical abstract of the United States: 1992* (112th ed.). Washington, DC: U.S. Government Printing Office.

U.S. Bureau of the Census. (1993). *Statistical abstract of the United States: 1993* (113th ed.). Washington, DC: U.S. Government Printing Office.

U.S. Department of Health and Human Services (USDHHS). (1992). *Health United States 1991, and Prevention Profile.* (DHHS Pub. No. PHS 92–1232). Washington, DC: U.S. Government Printing Office.

Uzgiris, I. C., & Raeff, C. (1995). Play in parent-child interactions. In M. H. Bornstein, *Handbook of parenting* (Vol. 4). Mahwah, NJ: Erlbaum.

Valsiner, J. (1987). *Culture and the development of children's action.* Chichester: Wiley.

Valsiner, J. (1988). Organization of children's social development in polygamic families. In J. Valsiner (Ed.), *Child development in cultural context* (pp. 67–86). Toronto: Hogrefe & Huber.

Valsiner, J. (1989a). *Child development in cultural context.* Toronto: Hogrefe & Huber.

Valsiner, J. (1989b). *Human development and culture.* Lexington, MA: Heath.

Valsiner, J. (2000). *Culture and human development.* Thousand Oaks, CA: Sage.

Valsiner, J., & Benigni, L. (1986). Naturalistic research and ecological thinking in the study of child development. *Developmental Review, 6,* 203–223.

Valsiner, J., & Lawrence, J. (1997). Human development in culture across the life span. In J. W. Berry, P. R. Dasen, & T. S. Saraswathi (Eds.), *Handbook of cross-cultural psychology* (Vol. 2, 2nd ed., pp. 69–106). Boston: Allyn & Bacon.

Van Acker, J., Oostrom, B., Rath, B., & de Kemp, R. (1999). Street children in Nairobi: Hakuna Matata? *Journal of Community Psychology, 27,* 393–404.

Van den Heuvel, H., Tellegen, G., & Koomen, W. (1992). Cultural differences in the use of psychological and social characteristics in children's self-understanding. *European Journal of Social Psychology, 22,* 353–362.

van de Vijer, F. J. R., & Leung, K. (2000). Methodological issues in psychological research on culture. *Journal of Cross-Cultural Psychology, 31,* 33–51.

Van Esterik, P. (1989). *Beyond the breast-bottle controversy.* New Brunswick, NJ: Rutgers University Press.

Van Ijzendoorn, M. H., & Kroonenberg, P. M. (1988). Cross-cultural patterns of attachment: A meta-analysis of the strange situation. *Child Development, 59,* 147–156.

Van Reek, J., Adriaanze, H., & Knibbe, R. (1994). Alcohol consumption and correlates among children in the European Community. *International Journal of the Addictions, 29,* 15–21.

Varma, V.K., & Chakrabarti, S. (1995). Social correlates and cultural dynamics of mental illness in traditional society: India. In I. Al-Issa (Ed.), *Handbook of culture and mental illness* (pp. 115–127). Madison, WI: International Universities Press.

Veale, A. (1992). Towards a conceptualization of street children: The case from Sudan and Ireland. *Troaire Developmental Review* (Dublin), 107–128.

Verma, S. (1999). Socialization for survival: Developmental issues among working street children in India. In M. Raffaelli (Ed.), *Homeless and working youth around the world: Exploring developmental issues.* San Francisco: Jossey-Bass.

Visano, L. (1990). The socialization of street children: The development and transformation of identities. *Sociological Studies of Child Development, 3,* 139–161.

Vondra, J., & Belsky, J. (1993). Developmental origins of parenting: Personality and relationship factors. In T. Luster & L. Okagaki (Eds.), *Parenting: An ecological perspective* (pp. 1–33). Hillsdale, NJ: Erlbaum.

Vygotsky, L. S. (1978). *Mind in society: The development of higher psychological processes.* Cambridge, MA: Harvard University Press.

Vygotsky, L. S. (1986). *Thought and language* (Trans./rev. by A. Kozulin). Cambridge, MA: MIT Press. (Original work published 1934.)

Wachs, T. D. (1987). *Comparative salience of physical and social environmental differences.* Paper presented at the biennial meeting of the Society for Research in Child Development, Baltimore, MD.

Wachs, T. D. (1999). Celebrating complexity: Conceptualization and assessment of the environment. In S. L. Friedman & T. D. Wachs (Eds.), *Measuring environment across the life span.* Washington, DC: American Psychological Association.

Wachs, T. (2000). Linking nutrition and temperament. In V. J. Molfese & D. Molfese (Eds.), *Temperament and personality development across the life span.* Mahwah, NJ: Erlbaum.

Wallace, A. F. C. (1961). Mental illness, biology, and culture. In F. Hsu (Ed.), *Psychological anthropology.* Cambridge, MA: Schenkman.

Wardlaw, G. M., & Insel, P. M. (1993). *Perspectives in nutrition* (2nd ed.). St. Louis: Mosby.

Watanabe, Y. (1986). Distributive justice development. *Japanese Journal of Educational Psychology, 34,* 84–90.

Waters, E., Hamilton, C. E., & Weinfield, N. S. (2000). The stability of attachment security from infancy to adolescence and early childhood: General introduction. *Child Development, 71,* 678–683.

Waters, E., Merrick, S., Treboux, D., Crowell, J., & Albersheim, L. (2000). Attachment security in infancy and early adulthood: A twenty-year longitudinal study. *Child Development, 71,* 684–689.

Waters, E., & Valenzuela, M. (1999). Explaining disorganized attachment: Clues from research on mild-to-moderately undernourished children in Chile. In J. Solomon & C. George (Eds.), *Attachment Disorganization.* New York: The Guilford Press.

Waterson, E. J., & Murray-Lyon, I. M. (1990). Preventing alcohol related birth damage: A review. *Social Science and Medicine, 30,* 349–364.

Watkins, D., & Dhawan, N. (1989). Do we need to distinguish the constructs of self-concept and self-esteem? *Journal of Social Behavior and Personality, 4,* 555–562.

Watkins, D., Mortazavi, S., & Trofimova, I. (2000). Independent and interdependent conceptions of self: An investigation of age, gender, and culture differences in importance and satisfaction ratings. *Cross-Cultural Research, 34,* 113–134.

Weill, J., & Le Bourhis, B. (1994). Factors predictive of alcohol consumption in a representative sample of French male teenagers: A five-year prospective study. *Drug & Alcohol Dependence, 35,* 45–50.

Weinfield, N., Sroufe, L. A, & Egeland, B. (2000). Attachment from infancy to early adulthood in a high-risk sample: Continuity, discontinuity, and their correlates. *Child Development, 71*, 695–702.

Weisfeld, C., Weisfeld, G., & Callaghan, J. (1982). Female inhibition in mixed-sex competition among young adolescents. *Ethology and Sociobiology, 3*, 29–42.

Weisfeld, G. (1997). Puberty rites as clues to the nature of human adolescence. *Cross-Cultural Research, 31*(1), 27–54.

Weisner, T. S. (1996). The 5-to-7 transition as an ecocultural project. In A. J. Sameroff & M. M. Haith (Eds.), *The five to seven year shift: The age of reason.* Chicago: University of Chicago Press.

Weisner, T. S., Matheson, C. C., & Bernheimer, L. P. (1996). American cultural models of early influence and parent recognition of developmental delays: Is earlier always better than later? In S. Harkness & C. M. Super (Eds.), *Parents' cultural belief systems: Their origins, expressions, and consequences* (pp. 496–531). New York: Guilford.

Wellman, H. M., & Gelman, S. A. (1992). Cognitive development: Foundational theories of core domains. *Annual Review of Psychology, 43*, 337–375.

Werner, E. E. (1979). *Cross-cultural child development.* Belmont, CA: Wadsworth.

Werner, E. E. (1989). Children of the garden island. *Scientific American, 260*, 101–111.

Wertsch, J. V., & Tulviste, P. (1994). Lev Semyonovich Vygotsky and contemporary developmental psychology. In R. D. Parke, P. A. Ornstein, J. J. Rieser, & C. Zahn-Waxler (Eds.), *A Century of Developmental Psychology.* Washington, DC: American Psychological Association.

Wertz, R. W., & Wertz, D. C. (1979). *Lying-in: A history of childbirth in America.* New York: Schocken.

West, A. (1999). Children's own research: Street children and care in Britain and Bangladesh. *Childhood: A Global Journal of Child Research, 6*, 145–155.

West, C., & Zimmerman, D. H. (1987). Doing gender. *Gender and Society, 1*, 125–151.

Westermeyer, J., & Peake, E. (1983). A ten-year follow up of alcoholic Native Americans in Minnesota. *American Journal of Psychiatry, 140*, 189–194.

Whitall, J. (1991). The developmental effect of concurrent cognitive and locomotor skills: Time-sharing from a dynamical perspective. *Journal of Experimental Child Psychology, 51*, 245–266.

White, C., & Burke, P. (1987). Ethnic role identity among black and white college students: An interactionist approach. *Sociological Perspectives, 30*, 310–331.

White, M. (1987). *The Japanese educational challenge: A commitment to children.* New York: Free Press.

White, M. (1993). *The material child: Coming of age in Japan and America.* New York: Free Press.

Whiting, B. B. (1963). *Six cultures: Studies of child rearing.* Cambridge, MA: Harvard University Press.

Whiting, B. B., & Edwards, C. P. (1988). *Children of different worlds: The formation of social behavior.* Cambridge, MA: Harvard University Press.

Whiting, B. B., & Whiting, J. W. M. (1975). *Children of six cultures: A psycho-cultural analysis.* Cambridge, MA: Harvard University Press.

Whiting, J. W. M., Burbank, V. K., & Ratner, M. S. (1986). The duration of maidenhood. In J. B. Lancaster & B. A. Hamburg (Eds.), *School age pregnancy and parenthood*. Hawthorne, NY: Aldine de Gruyter.

Williams, J., & Best, D. (1990). *Sex and psyche: Gender and self viewed cross-culturally.* Newbury Park, CA: Sage.

Wilson, J. O., & Herrnstein, R. J. (1985). *Crime and human nature.* New York: Simon & Schuster.

Wilson-Oyelaran, E. B. (1988). Toward contextual sensitivity in developmental psychology: A Nigerian perspective. In J. Valsiner (Ed.), *Child development in cultural context* (pp. 51–66). Toronto: Hogrefe & Huber.

Winegar, L. T., & Valsiner, J. (Eds.). (1992a). *Children's development within social context: Vol 1. Parental cognition and adult–child interaction.* Hillsdale, NJ: Erlbaum.

Winegar, L. T., & Valsiner, J. (Eds.). (1992b). *Children's development within social context: Vol 2. Research and methodology.* Hillsdale, NJ: Erlbaum.

Wiseman, H., & Lieblich, A. (1992). Individuation in a collective community. *Adolescent Psychiatry, 18,* 156–179.

Wisniewski, L., & Marcus, M. (1998). Childhood obesity. In V. B. Van Hasselt & M. Hersen (Eds.), *Handbook of psychological treatment protocols for children and adolescents.* Mahwah, NJ: Erlbaum.

Wolf, A. M., Gortmaker, S. L., Cheung, L., & Gray, H. M. (1993). Activity, inactivity, and obesity: Racial, ethnic, and age differences among schoolgirls. *American Journal of Public Health, 83,* 1625–1627.

Wolf, A. P. (1964). *Marriage and adoption in a Hokkien village.* Unpublished doctoral dissertation, Department of Anthropology, Cornell University.

Wolf, A. P. (1978). *Studies in Chinese society.* Stanford, CA: Stanford University Press.

Wolf, A. W., Lozoff, B., Latz, S., & Pauladetto, R. (1996). Parental theories in the management of sleep routines in Japan, Italy and the United States. In S. Harkness & C. M. Super (Eds.), *Parents' cultural belief systems.* New York: Guilford Press.

Wolf, M. (1972). *Women and the family in rural Taiwan.* Stanford, CA: Stanford University Press.

Wolfe, W. S., Campbell, C. C., Frongillo, E. A., Haas, J. D., & Melnik, T. A. (1994). Overweight schoolchildren in New York state: Prevalence and characteristics. *American Journal of Public Health, 84,* 807–813.

Wolffers, I. (1997). Culture, media, and HIV/AIDS in Asia. *Lancet, 349* (9044), 52–59.

Wong, L-K. (1999). Young lives in Australia: Stress and coping of Hong Kong Chinese adolescent immigrants. *Dissertation Abstracts International: Section A: Humanities & Social Sciences, 59* (8-A), 3214.

Wood, D. J. (1989). Social interaction as tutoring. In M. H. Bornstein, & J. S. Bruner (Eds.), *Interaction in human development.* Hillsdale, NJ: Erlbaum.

Wood, D. J., & Middleton, D. (1975). A study of assisted problem solving. *British Journal of Psychology, 66,* 181–191.

Worchel, F. F., & Allen, M. (1997). Mother's ability to discriminate cry types in low-birthweight premature and full-term infants. *Children's Health Care, 26,* 183–195.

World Health Organization. (1979). *Schizophrenia: An international follow-up study.* New York: Wiley.

Worthman, C. M. (1994). Developmental microniche: A concept for modeling relationships of biology, behavior, and culture in development. *American Journal of Physical Anthropology Supplement, 18,* 210.

Worthman, C. M. (1995). Biocultural bases of human variation. *ISSBD Newsletter, 27*(1), 10–13.

Worthman, C. M., Stallings, J. F., & Jenkins, C. L. (1993). Developmental effects of sex-differentiated parental care among Hagahai foragers. *American Journal of Physical Anthropology Supplement, 16,* 212.

Wylie, L. (1974). *Village in the Vaucluse* (3rd ed.). Cambridge, MA: Harvard University Press.

Yang, J-A. (1999). An exploratory study of Korean fathering of adolescent children. *Journal of Genetic Psychology, 160,* 55–68.

Yi, S. H. (1993). Transformation of child socialization in Korean culture. *Early Childhood Development, 85,* 17–24.

Yu, L. C. (1993). Intergenerational transfer of resources within policy and cultural contexts. In S. H. Zarit, L. I. Pearlin, & K. W. Schaie (Eds.), *Caregiving systems.* Hillsdale, NJ: Erlbaum

Zammuner, V. L., & Fischer, A. H. (1995). The social regulation of emotions in jealousy situations: A comparison between Italy and the Netherlands. *Journal of Cross-Cultural Psychology, 26*(2), 189–208.

Zarit, S. H., & Eggebeen, D. J. (1995). Parent–child relationships in adulthood and old age. In M. H. Bornstein (Ed.), *Handbook of parenting* (Vol. 1, pp. 119–140). Hillsdale, NJ: Erlbaum.

Zeskind, P. S., Klein, L., & Marshall, T. (1992). Adults' perceptions of experiential modifications of durations of pauses and expiratory sounds in infant crying. *Developmental Psychology, 28,* 1153–1162.

Zeskind, P. S., Platzman, K., Coles, C. D., & Schuetze, P. A. (1996). Cry analysis detects subclinical effects of prenatal alcohol exposure in newborn infants. *Infant Behavior & Development, 19,* 497–500.

Zeskind, P. S., Sale, J., Maio, M. C., Huntington, L., & Weiseman, J. R. (1985). Adult perceptions of pain and hunger cries: A synchrony of arousal. *Child Development, 56,* 549–554.

Zevalkink, J., Riksen-Walraven, J. M., Van Lieshout, C. F. M. (1999). Attachment in the Indonesian Caregiving Context. *Social Development, 8,* 21–40.

Zhang, Y., Proenca, R., Maffel, M., Barone, M., et al. (1994). Positional cloning of the mouse obese gene and its human homologue. *Nature, 372,* 425–442.

Zimmerman, B. J. (1990). Self-regulated learning and academic achievement: An overview. *Educational Psychologist, 25,* 3–17.

AUTHOR INDEX

Abbott, S., 188
Abel, E., 83
Adkins,V.K., 233
Adler, L.L., 244
Adriaanze, H., 200
Aerts, E., 283
Ahmed, R.A., 227
Ahnert, L., 182
Ahujan, N., 249
Ainsworth, M.D.S., 181, 182
Albersheim, L., 182, 188
Aldous, J., 227
Alexander, K., 201
Alibhai, N., 260
Allison, M.T., 191
Alyoshina, Y.Y., 163, 171
American Academy of Pediatrics Task Force on Infant Positioning and SIDS, 254
American Psychiatric Association, 248
Amstrong, S., 73
Anderson, J.A., 98
Anderson, J.L., 145
Andreasson, L., 271
Annett, M., 92
Antonovsky, A., 99
Antonucci, T.C., 207
Aptekar, L., 70, 257
Archetti, E.P., 206
Arnett, J.J., 200, 263
Ashmore, R.D., 152
Atkinson, D., 198
Atkinson, R, 144
Austin, J.K., 146
Avedon, E.M., 191
Azhar, M.Z., 247
Azuma, H., 109

Baca Zinn, M., 54
Bailey, D.M., 100
Baltes, P.B., 119, 121
Bamgboye, E., 140
Banks, C.G., 262
Barnard, K.E., 225, 226
Barresi, C.M., 238
Barrett, D.E., 87, 111
Barry, D., 16
Barry, H., 71, 232
Barry & Paxson, 59
Bartolucci, G., 122
Basseches, M., 118
Bates, E., 109, 181
Beardsley, L.M., 247, 251
Beatty, S.E., 204
Beatty, Jeon, Albaum, & Murphy, 203
Beauvais, Oetting, Wolf & Edwards, 264
Becerra, R.M., 234
Beck, A.T., 135
Beckwith, L., 256
Behrman, R.E., 85
Beidelman, T.O., 72, 96
Beiser, M., 200–201
Belsky, J., 221
Benoit, D., 234
Bentsen, C., 208
Berkow, D.N., 134
Bernheimer, L.P., 223, 288
Berry, J.W., 3, 5, 7, 8, 37, 39, 42, 66, 107, 112, 247, 280, 286, 288
Bersoff, D.M., 37, 194, 195
Bertrand, J.T., 168, 169
Best, D., 7, 160
Bethon, G., 116
Bhalla, S.K., 260

Bhogle, S., 174
Birren, J.E., 74
Bjarnason, T., 227
Bjorqvist, K., 153, 156
Blau, F.D., 172
Block, J., 153
Blom, M., 57
Bochner, S, 138
Boehnke, K., 195
Bolton, R., 214
Borgatti, S.P., 45
Bornstein, M.H., 57, 109, 110, 222
Boston Women's Health Book Collective, 274
Bouchard. T.J., 127
Bourguignon, E., 65
Bowlby, J., 62
Boxer, P.A., 251
Braine, M.D.S., 114
Brazelton, T.B., 51
Bredemeier, B.J.L., 193
Brink, P.J., 259
Brislin, R., 51, 84, 252
Bronfenbrenner, 46
Bronfenbrenner, U., 11, 20–24, 47, 52, 107, 223, 227, 231, 276–278
Brooks, P.J., 114
Brooks-Gunn, J., 229
Brower, A.M., 285
Brown, B.B., 23, 46
Brown, J.K., 241
Brown, S.S., 85
Brubaker, T.H., 237
Budwig, N., 105
Burbank, V.K., 70, 229
Burke, P., 199
Buss, D.M., 126, 156, 157, 211–212
Byrnes, J.P., 116

345

SUBJECT INDEX

Psychosocial development, Erikson's
    theory of, 33–35, 284–285
  on adulthood, 201–202
  formal *vs.* informal learning in, 69
  infancy in, 58
  late adulthood in, 77–79
  middle adulthood in, 76–77
  religious vocation in, 76
  transition to adulthood in, 74
Puberty, 96–98. *See also* Adolescence
Public policy, 173–175
Pygmy culture, 224–225

Quest, vision, 73
Questioning, structured, 44, 45
Questionnaire, EAT, 260
Quick-mindedness, value of, 120
Quotient, heritability, 127

Rape, 165
Reading, 114–116
Rebirth, concept of, 136–137
Reciprocity, 195
Rehydration therapy, oral, 86
Reintegrative stage, 118
Relationship
  father-child, 228–229
  homosexual, 214
  intimate, 74–75
  long-term, 210–216
  marriage, 212–213
  mother-child, 225–227
  peer culture and, 190–193
Reliability of research, 38
Religion, gender relations and, 173–175
Religious vocation, 76
Replicable research, 38
Reproduction
  evolutionary perspective on, 156–157
  gender socialization and, 162–163
Research
  hologeistic, 40
  strengths and weaknesses of, 42
Resources, fair distribution of, 195
Responsible stage, 118
Right-handedness
  for feeding *vs.* hygiene, 51–52
  motor skill development and, 92–93
Rite of passage, 71–74
Role, gender, 170–175
Role confusion, 74

Russian culture
  adolescent peer groups in Soviet Union,
    231–232
  gender socialization in, 163–164
  terminal-limb deficiency in, 84
  women in work force and, 171

Same-sex peer, 166–168
Same-sex relationship, 214
Samoan culture
  female social clock in, 148–149
  language in, 106
  menstruation in, 97
Sandwich generation, 239
Sati, 175
Scaffolding, 106
Scale, distributive justice, 195–198
Scheme in Piaget's cognitive development
    theory, 30, 31
Schizophrenia, 269–270
School, Japanese, 68–69
Securely attached child, 182
Segregation, occupational, 171–172
Self-concept, 125–150
  in adolescence, 141–144
  in adulthood, 144–149
  body image and, 145
  in Buddhism, 134–137
  content and context of, 137–141
  culture-specific aspects of, 133–134
  emergence of, 131
  individualism *vs.* collectivism and,
    131–132
  personhood and, 132–133
  temperament and, 126–130
Self-denial, 262
Self-esteem, 139–141
  ethnic identity and, 198–199
Semai culture, 66
Senescence, 270–271
Sensorimotor intelligence, 107–108
Sensorimotor period of development, 29
Sensorimotor stage, 281
Setting, for birth, 217–220
Sex, 152. *See also* Gender issues
Sexual maturity, 168
Sexuality
  in adolescence, 168–170
  chastity and, 168–169, 174, 210–211
Sexually transmitted disease, 262–263
Sharing by child, 191